Handbook
of
French
Popular Culture

HANDBOOK
OF
FRENCH
POPULAR CULTURE

Edited by
PIERRE L. HORN

GREENWOOD PRESS
New York • Westport, Connecticut • London

Library of Congress Cataloging-in-Publication Data

Handbook of French popular culture / edited by Pierre L. Horn.
     p. cm.
   Includes bibliographical references and index.
   ISBN 0–313–26121–0 (alk. paper)
     1.   France—Popular culture—History—20th century.   I. Horn,
   Pierre L.
   DC33.7.H29   1991
   306.4'0944—dc20   90–23170

British Library Cataloguing in Publication Data is available.

Library of Congress Catalog Card Number: 90–23170
ISBN: 0–313–26121–0

First published in 1991

Greenwood Press, 88 Post Road West, Westport, CT 06881
An imprint of Greenwood Publishing Group, Inc.

Printed in the United States of America

The paper used in this book complies with the
Permanent Paper Standard issued by the National
Information Standards Organization (Z39.48–1984).

10 9 8 7 6 5 4 3 2 1

To Mary Beth

Contents

Preface

Even before there was a recognized French language, let alone an official nation, mass popular culture flourished and continued flourishing, right alongside eventually world-renowned literature, music, and fine arts. From images on the walls of the Lascaux caves to juggling and clowning at medieval fairs to modern comics and television, the general public has always preferred popular activities, in and by which it sees itself reflected, entertained, and informed. Popular culture practitioners have responded to this demand with unparalleled success, and their audiences (either active or passive) have greatly benefited from an abundance of popular manifestations, as the following chapters clearly demonstrate.

That a dichotomy existed—and to some extent still exists—between so-called "high" and "low" culture is an accepted fact. From "nos ancêtres les Gaulois" to the good burghers of Louis XIV to the *cadres* of the Fifth Republic (not to mention the working classes), it quickly came to light, however, that only a very small elite partook of high culture. Not only was the majority functionally illiterate until the 1880s, when Jules Ferry's reforms were passed making elementary schooling free and mandatory, but those who had received an education read popular—and popularizing—books, not the Classics, and attended low-brow stage entertainment, not the opera or the tragedies of Racine. The top best sellers, for instance, all belong to popular literature: the fairy tales of Charles Perrault, the science fiction of Jules Verne, and the Maigret novels of Georges Simenon.

Thanks to the approach taken by the *Annales* school of historians, led by the late Fernand Braudel (whose Volume One of his last magnum opus [1979] is titled *Les Structures du quotidien*), a renewed interest in daily life developed as the contemporary French sought to know and understand how their predecessors actually lived. Various sociohistorical book series covering, albeit superficially, a certain class at a certain time in a certain environment, such as *La Vie quotidienne* . . . (Hachette) or *La Vie* . . . ("Que sais-je?," Presses Universitaires de France) are extremely successful. Cultural myths and snobbery aside, intellectuals in France and abroad (whether they are named Roland Barthes, Umberto Eco, Michel Serres, Tzvetan Todorov, or Georges Perec, who, in a 1979 interview published in *L'Arc*, was not afraid to indicate that his "models" included Hergé, Pierre Dac, Gotlib, Jules Verne) increasingly acknowledge and appreciate the merits and artistic value of French popular culture. If, as Jack Lang, the French Culture Minister, declared, "culture is a battle for the right to live freely," then the varied creativity of all is equally valid and equally worthy.

Since the end of World War II especially, both within academe and without, there has been an explosion of books and articles, mostly in French, on French popular culture. This handbook represents an attempt in English to fill a gap by bringing together in one place thirteen scholarly essays dealing with its various facets. It also serves to introduce nonspecialists to the history and bibliography of the most important aspects of French popular culture. In addition, it explains why French popular culture has acquired a high worldwide reputation (Maxim's in China!), and nowhere less so than in the United States. At the same time, despite a rearguard action to the contrary, a seminal American influence on French popular culture, sometimes decried by M. Lang, continues to be very strong. Television, pop music, movies, not to mention the language itself, are just a few examples of such interchanges.

In setting about to realize this project, however, I almost immediately encountered a problem concerning which aspects of popular culture to consider and which to omit. After much discussion with American and French colleagues in the field, and using the *Handbook of American Popular Culture* (M. T. Inge) and the *Handbook of Latin American Popular Culture* (H. E. Hinds and C. M. Tatum) as models, I elaborated a table of contents that would fit within space limitations and be as representative as possible. Readers may well question the inclusion of certain topics to the detriment of others. There probably ought to have been studies of children's popular culture, fashion, stage entertainment, romance and popular fiction. . . . These and perhaps others may be treated in a second edition or a discrete handbook of French popular literature now in the planning stage. Yet, in the end, any collection reflects the point of view of its editor. I only hope that my choices have not been too subjective or idiosyncratic.

The authors included here cover a wide array of subjects and employ different approaches, but all offer a very useful and erudite panorama of how the French live, learn, and play. Most also provide information concerning research centers that are often eager to welcome and assist foreign scholars. They suggest as well possibilities for further inquiry ranging from specialized bibliographies and reference books to in-depth examinations of specific areas and endeavors. Particularly needed are publications in English. Finally, given the great interest that certainly exists in this area, our general consensus must be that French popular culture remains an inexhaustible and worthwhile subject of study.

Acknowledgments

No project of this sort can succeed without the assistance of many people. It is with pleasure, therefore, that I wish to express my gratitude to the scholars who have contributed their expertise, sometimes under difficult constraints. My thanks go also to Marilyn Brownstein of Greenwood Press for her confidence; to Professor Anni Whissen for her constant encouragement; to the Wright State University College of Liberal Arts for their financial support; to Leslie Knecht for secretarial services beyond the call of duty. A final note of gratitude goes to my wife for the editorial help she has so cheerfully given.

1

Advertising

CLAUDIA DOBKIN

France is in the process of establishing a new advertising ethic. Yesterday's *affiches, réclames*, and *publicité* are being replaced by *la communication globale*. The social reality of pan-European advertising is changing the nature of the art much as typographic and economic realities did for previous eras. Having more affinities with the *affiche illustrée* of the nineteenth century than with the con-sumeristic pleas of the 1970s, French advertising of the 1980s will not be con-sidered just another evolutionary phase. Without a doubt, this is the decade of the *exploit publicitaire*.

The most characteristic trait of modern French advertising is the conspicuous use of the medium and the institution. There is a marked tendency to create films and posters that can be consumed for themselves as if this were a prerequisite for selling products. Agencies sign their advertisements and, in one case, a billboard posting company, alias Myriam, physically revealed its identity after a four-day striptease for the French billboard public! Just two years ago the city of Paris received an advertising facelift and turned many of its streets, parks, and museums into an arena for self-indulgence, celebrating *Le mois de l'affiche*. By any measure, this event was a large-scale restatement of advertising's many models: the advertisement as pleasure in itself.

A significant sign of the importance that advertising has acquired in recent years is the growth of the Musée de l'Affiche, which, in 1983, changed its name to Musée de la Publicité. Celebrations of advertising also have continuity and recognition. In addition to the world-famous film festival, Cannes hosts an annual advertising festival. Film advertising from the entire world is compared and ranked. Another, less orthodox celebration is the annual *Nuit des publivores*, an all-night marathon show of France's best television and cinema commercials. This annual celebration draws people, young and old, from all over France.

Together they join in a celebration of the art which resembles the cult following of the *Rocky Horror Picture Show* in this country.

The attention awarded to advertising in France may seem surprising to foreign observers, unaccustomed as they may be to even thinking about advertising. Understanding the content of some of the billboards and films is an even greater task, since advertising messages in France very often hinge on references to other messages or the medium itself. The challenge and reward that await those who set out on this journey is uncovering the source of such enthusiasm.

HISTORICAL OUTLINE

Advertising has existed since antiquity, when shopkeepers in Athens would compete with each other with posters, signs, cries, and graffiti. But in France, it is perhaps Montaigne who can claim to be its founding father. In his short essay entitled "D'un défaut de nos polices," he suggests promoting both commerce and social security through use of *offices publiques* and *petites annonces* (classified ads). *Les Pères fondateurs*, by Gérard Lagneau, presents a good historical summary of developments in the French advertising industry. Montaigne's idea was to be adopted by Théophraste Renaudot in 1631 with his *Gazette*, which was to become the prototype of all advertising agencies under the Old Regime. The real precursor of French advertising is Émile de Girardin, who, in 1836, reintroduced advertising into his daily *La Presse* by combining news and *annonces*.

During the nineteenth century, the development of advertising in France follows or explains that of the press. Charles-Louis Havas created the first French advertising agency and built a quasi-monopoly which was to last a hundred years. Following in his footsteps, Bleustein-Blanchet created radio advertising in 1930. It was essentially after World War II, however, that advertising as we understand it got into full swing.

The relatively recent and sudden expansion of the advertising industry in France is due in large part to several factors: the standardization of products, the modernization of businesses, heightened competition, the increase in purchasing power, and the economic growth of society. Because of its increased role, the status of the industry in recent years has received considerable attention in the media and in society at large. In *La Publicité à travers les âges*, Galliot provides a good overview of the evolution of the industry and its creative mechanisms, as well as some background on the sociology of advertising in France. Although published in 1955, this is still a reliable source of background information.

In later years, advertising people in France came to be seen as acrobats of wit and as agents of "evil capitalism." Although still present today, this type of criticism no longer carries the same weight it did in the 1960s and 1970s. In those days, *capitaliste* and *bourgeois* were common insults. Today the same terms are flourishing in advertising language charged with positive connotations, clearly reflecting a change in attitude. If you are poor, no matter: "Embourgeoisez-vous pour moins de cent sacs" (Become a bourgeois for under one hundred francs), says the mattress manufacturer Duvivier-Durer. If you are rich, it's all right, but you can do better with the Renault 18 American 2; the advertisement for the Renault photographed in front of the White House is captioned "Devenez capitaliste pour 58.200F" (Become a capitalist for 58,200 francs). These examples of consumerism are not unusual. What is unusual is the lack of attention given in the literature to this evolution in language and themes.

Bookstores, libraries, and research centers have traditionally classified *la publicité* as marketing. However, recent years have seen the rediscovery of France's long and rich tradition of advertising art. The real star and precursor of modern French advertising is the *affiche illustrée* (illustrated poster). The *affiche* enjoyed its golden age during the second part of the nineteenth century. Artists such as Chéret, Daumier, Manet, Bonnard and, of course, Toulouse-Lautrec essentially revolutionized graphic arts in the West while promoting institutions such as the Folies-Bergère and the Moulin Rouge and publications such as *Les Chats*.

The most revealing works of this period are the collections of posters themselves. *La Belle Époque* and *Les Maîtres de l'Affiche* are good sources for a historical perspective as well as for the themes and effects utilized. Between 1914 and 1918, most advertising work is devoted to the war effort, although institutional advertising also sees its birth in campaigns for the Bon Marché department store and Les Ballets Russes. Sports, leisure, and travel are also big consumers of *affiches*. René Vincent's posters for Peugeot and Bugatti are masterpiece examples. It is also through ads like Roger Broders' *Côte d'Azur* and *Sainte-Maxime* that we discover the wonders of the French Riviera. Artists, like Don, give us a glimpse of the fashionable resorts like Biarritz and the *Palm Beach* in Cannes. Cinema advertising begins to flourish in the early 1920s although the artistic accomplishments are generally regarded as mediocre. *L'Affiche miroir de l'histoire*, by Max Gallo, captures the causes and effects of technological innovations, as well as the themes and style of advertising work in the 1920s.

The most prominent figures of the 1930s period are Cassandre, creator of such famous posters as *Le Normandie*; Colin, creator of *La revue Nègre*; Jean Carlu, of Monsavon fame; and Charles Loupot. In *Le Livre de l'Affiche*, Réjane Bargiel-Harry and Christophe Zagrodzki offer an overview of the historical evolution of the *affiche* with good biographical and bibliographical references as well as a wealth of examples. A number of images from this period can be seen metamorphosed in modern advertisements. There is a graphic and cultural tradition which is kept very much alive through advertising.

Much like technological progress today, nineteenth-century innovations in graphic art were not the sole impetus for the future development of the medium. The success of the *affiche* at the end of the nineteenth century was fed by a powerful movement away from the classification of art as high or low. Its spokesmen dreamed of seeing art penetrate all spheres of human activity, placing applied art on an equal footing with painting and sculpture. Designing advertising posters was no longer to be regarded as a degrading activity. Today we can say that the success enjoyed by the advertising phenomenon owes much to Jacques Séguéla and his contribution to elevating the industry's image.

In 1974, Jacques Séguéla simultaneously developed poster campaigns for all three presidential candidates: François Mitterrand, Jacques Chirac, and Valéry Giscard d'Estaing. Then, in 1981, Séguéla went on to create winning campaigns for the Parti Socialiste, "La Force Tranquille," and in 1988, "La France Unie." The fact that the art of advertising was used to promote political figures provoked as much controversy and interest as the policies it presented. Since at least 1981, advertising in France has gained new status.

An additional link to the past can be observed in the enthusiasm that generally accompanies any discussion of advertising in France. In their historical overviews, John Barnicoat and Alain Weill both pay special attention to the early twentieth-century concern with the modern. They see *le Modern Style* (art nouveau) or *Style Rétro* (twenties style), *l'affichomanie* (billboard mania), and the influence of the cinema in graphic art techniques as keys to understanding the nature of the art. It would appear that enthusiasm with the modern and the power of industrialization seems to be finding an echo today in video clips and in technology that makes it all possible.

By its very nature, advertising has always reflected in some way the most modern phenomena for any given era. Modernity and "inness" as themes, however, seem to be characteristic of the French, particularly for early as well as recent advertising. In today's version, science fiction, comic strips, detective-style narratives, and the *branché* (1980s version of hip) are often incorporated structurally or thematically. The underlying trend seems to be an all-out recruitment of readers, a sort of burden of proof that is presented. Perhaps the most characteristic description of modern French advertising was given by Philippe Gavi in an interview with Radio Télévision Luxembourg (RTL). Summarizing the evolution of the relationship between the French public and the advertising industry, he said from "Dites-nous combien cette voiture est chouette" (Tell us how neat this car is) the French have gone, in just a few years, to "Dites-nous comment vous savez dire combien elle est chouette" (Tell us how well you can tell us how neat this car is).

GUIDE TO THE LITERATURE

Background Works

The critical literature is, for the most part, quite dated. With few exceptions, most nontrade literature devoted to French advertising deals with the social and rhetorical dimensions. The late 1960s brought American marketing techniques to France—scientific studies of memory, impact, and recognition of advertising messages, multimedia campaigns, different modes of production and distribution. All this efficiency and calculation left little room for artistic creativity and much room for speculation about the effects of advertising on innocent eyes and ears.

A number of influential works appeared during this period. The most significant is *La Publicité*. In their work, Cadet and Cathelat offer one of the most comprehensive analyses of the role of advertising in modern France. Their focus is primarily on the economic nature of the phenomenon and how it is incorporated in society. They make a strong case for advertising as a point of convergence and a mode of production of patterns, myths, symbols, and stereotypes shared by a social group. Jean Baudrillard echoed a number of issues in *Le Système des objets*, not the least of which is the pervasive nature of consumerism. In addition, Baudrillard has produced numerous works on the sociological implications of objects and possessions. Today, this perspective almost rings trite. Yet in 1968, at the time of their publication, these works not only gave proof that advertising was a significant force to be considered in French society, but also provided the necessary intellectual framework for understanding it.

Bernard Cathelat has since become one of the leading sociologists in France and now heads one of the most prominent market research centers. In his 1977 publication, *Les Styles de vie des Français*, he offers a fascinating study of French consumers, which attempts to describe in a formal manner what makes French men and women "tick." Cathelat has defined three *microcultures* for France: a utilitarian France, a centrist France, and an adventurous France. Each of these is comprised of a *sociotype* which can be described as a typical profile of beliefs, attitudes, thoughts, language, and habits that give some depth to the sociostructure. This work contains a wealth of data which, in addition to allowing better targeting of advertising messages, help to identify and personalize the objects of the infamous *matraquage publicitaire* (advertising bombardment).

Another seminal thinker in France is Georges Péninou. One of his better-known works is *L'Intelligence de la publicité*. Péninou exposes the psychological element and the utilitarian efficacy of the advertising medium. Along the same lines, but much less convincingly, works by Durand and Jeudy also focus on these presumed effects.

A few English-language works stand out, for they provide a good foundation in several theoretical approaches. No study of advertising can begin without several readings of Marshall McLuhan's *Culture Is Our Business*. It is in this work that we discover the context and support for the well-known phrase "the medium is the message." Nowhere is this statement more evident than in contemporary French advertisements, which make such conspicuous use of their medium. A fascinating look at the advertising industry which has directly impacted most modern advertising is *Ogilvy on Advertising*. The master of modern American advertising gives his views on the industry in general and explains the effects of some of the world's most creative campaigns.

Another important aspect of the cultural appropriation of advertising messages is the cognitive dimension. Markin's *Consumer Behavior: A Cognitive Orientation* offers an excellent description of the cognitive processes at work in the reception and processing of advertising messages. This is invaluable information for developing a true understanding of the motivational dimension which is often subsumed in studies of rhetorical devices or impact. In a similar vein, Ries's *Positioning: The Battle for Your Mind* offers the advertising industry's view of their craft. Although very few examples of non-American advertising are given, this is nevertheless a rich source of devices and examples and a fascinating look at the intelligence behind advertising campaigns.

THEORETICAL AND GENERAL APPROACHES TO THE STUDY OF ADVERTISING

There seems to be a tacit agreement that advertising merits study for the cultural information it harbors. Still, there are relatively few studies that substantiate the nature and manifestations of this information. More than ever, advertising in France is deserving of a sound theoretical framework for study. For lack of a structured approach, there are certain fundamental elements that can help attain a better understanding of the advertising phenomenon in France. Before acknowledging the phenomenon and focusing on some of its technical dimensions, it is useful to define the substance of the themes and objects that find their way to a billboard or a film.

In an article entitled ''American Advertising Explained as Popular Art,'' Leo Spitzer provides the methodology for treating advertising as a genre of applied art and takes a cue from the French. In his close reading of a 1940s advertisement for Tropicana orange juice, Spitzer cites the French as being able to recognize even in the most trivial detail the expression of an implicit national faith. Any study of French advertising must begin here. The single most distinguishing feature of most French advertisements is the recruitment of the reader to decipher references to the fabric of his society. Spitzer's close reading provides a brilliant example of the capacity for seeing the relationship between an everyday detail and a cultural entity which, although not unknown, is separately conceived. It is in this way, he claims, that our capacity for feeling at home in this civilization and of enjoying it will be increased.

It is often the most banal of items and events that find a place in modern advertising. As such, it is essential to understand their role in our complex world. Barthes's seminal work *Mythologies* offers a reading of the implications of certain events and items in French society. It is often difficult to preserve the integrity of ''myths'' when the analysis adopts a sociological or thematic approach. The myths of the American West and hamburgers or fast-food chains, for example, have developed their very own French character, and modern advertising reflects this evolution in structure and form. It is no longer sufficient to invoke the American ethos or simply utilize an American style to convey the goodness of a product. Consequently, we could expect themes, myths, and objects to be demystified in any analysis. *Mythologies* offers a framework of reference as well as a holistic approach for contextualizing events and objects.

Pascal Bruckner and Alain Finkielkraut adopt a more philosophical view of everyday French life in their work, *Au coin de la rue, l'aventure*. In this series of essays, the reader will find a formidable wealth of information about the stereotypes, commonplaces, and small realities of modern French society. Although this work offers a traditional categorization of themes such as vacation, cars, and the urban space, it is a creative and philosophical interpretation of why certain components of French society function as they do. For example, a thematic analysis of the French campaign for Club Méditerranée would probably yield nothing more than cultural and academic stereotypes of nudity and exoticism. Yet this information would hardly suffice to capture the impact of the campaign. To understand the wealth of meaning in the simplicity of verbs such as *manger, dormir, boire*, it is necessary to delve into French vacation habits, elitist tendencies, and the role of the billboard in the urban setting. Bruckner and Finkielkraut's analysis of the Club Med institution provides just this type of information. Other aspects which find attention in their work include the role of daily newspapers, the home, and of course, love and relationships.

An essential part of capturing the essence of French advertising is assessing the critical differences between the media utilized. Unfortunately, there is a clear lack of definition of the different advertising genres emerging in modern France. No catalogue, analysis, or critique has focused on film or television advertising. Consequently, most publications present a restricted view of the advertising space in France. The most creative, innovative, and sometimes pervasive ads are in film or video formats. The difficulty of obtaining examples has unfortunately prevented study from extending into these areas. On the other hand, examples of billboard and press advertising are readily available. This is in fact the corpus that has served most analyses, which, not surprisingly, focus on the rhetorical, often linguistic dimension of the ad.

The utilization of language in French ads and cinema commercials is relatively restricted. A great number of ads in France do not inform the public about price, features, or quality; rather, they seek to foster an awareness and create an image for a product. Consequently, the topics encountered in most studies are derived from the very structure and communicative function of the ad, which offers subtle combinations of visual, linguistic, cultural, and cognitive elements. One example of the subtle use of a word and its figuration is the ad for Dubonnet, where, from image to image, we see *Dubo, Dubon, Dubonnet* progressively fuller in color and meaning. Another proverbial example is Perrier's campaign "Perrier c'est fou" (Perrier is crazy), which surrealistically juxtaposed images and exalting music and eventually manifested its ultimate madness through the inverted "Ferrier c'est pou." The structural complexity of this type of advertising is generally subsumed in studies of the rhetorical dimension.

The rhetorical elements discussed in the literature really encompass two aspects of the communication process: the perception and reception of advertising messages. A number of studies deal with perception of ads and focus on the structural variables, which are those contained within the physical "stimuli," such as the frequency of a message or the number of words. Studies of political propaganda and rhetorical systems generally focus on this aspect.

Henri-Claude Lafitte, in his study "Contribution respective du visuel, du scriptural et de leur communication du sens dans l'annonce publicitaire," provides some validation for the importance of text in the perception of advertising. Although the impact of a poster may be greater (more easily remembered) with a photograph, Lafitte offers convincing evidence that information about a brand or a product is received mostly through the text. Muzet provides a list of linguistic devices utilized in the magazine *L'Express* (*"L'Express*: un style publicitaire") and offers a methodology for classification. In "La Transaction et les formes dans la rhétorique publicitaire," Bya makes some cogent remarks about the types of text and rhetorical devices used by different advertisements. A more detailed analysis of the functions of billboard advertisements and how language is maximized is given in an interesting analysis by Françoise Enel in *L'Affiche: Fonctions, langage, rhétorique.*

Two works stand out in this category, since they really go beyond explaining the rhetorical value that language takes on in the space of an ad. Richaudeau and Fischer both explain why the simplicity encountered in French ads is so effective and powerful.

"Baranne est une crème" is the slogan of a well-known campaign for shoe cream and the title of Sophie Fischer's close reading. Fischer performs an excellent exercise in decorticating the levels and complexity of a simple active affirmative declarative sentence. She discusses the subtle interplay, for example, of text and image (just a tube) and of the novelty of the product and its description. She proves that it is the strength of simplicity (as well as a hint of paronomasia) that persuades the reader of the ad. This is the type of analysis that helps us understand a prize-winning campaign for Johnnie Walker Red and Black Labels ("Sans le rouge rien ne va plus" and "Colère noire," "Roman noir"). It is certainly true that these slogans and their images integrate linguistic, literary, and popular culture themes and much humor. A more essential observation is that the strength of this campaign is derived from the virtually inseparable combination of color, words, and image. Although it may not be inherently true that no occasion is feasible without Johnnie Walker Red or as powerfully mysterious as Johnnie Walker Black, we are one step closer to believing this under the impact of the advertisements.

Richaudeau explains the structure of ads, and billboards in particular, with a more clinical perspective in *Le Langage efficace.* The most interesting part of his analysis is the claim that readers rarely perceive the exact form of messages. Richaudeau states that only categories such as noun, verb, adjective or syntactic strings such as subject-verb-adjective or interrogative forms are in fact perceived. He also discusses the feed-forward effect of anticipation and conclusion of messages. These are important considerations for the analysis of billboard ads with limited use of text, such as Vichy's "Maigrir. Vite Vichy." If the punctuation is not perceived, the readings can vary; the message, however, remains: "For quick weight loss, there is Vichy."

The other approach to the study of the rhetorical dimension of French advertising has to do with degree of receptivity of messages, often determined by function variables, which are those within the perceiver, such as needs, moods, past experiences, and so on. Studies of motivation, themes, or cultural elements generally fall in this category.

Although it is claimed that advertising is very culture-specific, Castagnotto, in *Semantica della pubblicità*, discusses the effects and the collective impact of advertising from a European perspective. The most insightful work in this area is Joannis' *De l'étude de la motivation à la création publicitaire et à la promotion des ventes*. Joannis discusses some of the factors that influence the reception of a message, such as status, value, and brand names. He also offers information on trends and characteristics of the French buying public. He states, for example, that brand sensitivity is strong for champagne in France, whereas there is relatively little sensitivity for table wines.

Indirectly, Joannis manages to summarize the distinctive character of French advertising as being quite different from the American tendency to search for the "bigger and better" idea. Effective advertising, he states, is where the concept is by all appearances quite distant from the satisfaction it seeks to promote in the reader. The important element is seducing readers and having their active participation in the "decoding" of the ad. Joannis also provides well-constructed examples of the types of ads that fit the existing patterns of understanding, attitudes, values, and goals of the French people. In the process of describing strategies for promoting *biscottes* (rusks) in the French context, Joannis offers one of the most detailed and revealing descriptions of the functional value of the *baguette* (thin loaf of bread) in a French context.

Political propaganda and the role of rhetoric and motivation are often alluded to in studies of advertising. In "Les Langages de la publicité et de la propagande," Carvalho deals primarily with the similarities among linguistic forms and styles utilized in political and advertising communications. In *La Politique et ses images*, Gourévitch discusses political campaigns as if they were product campaigns. He focuses on the significant differences between the *marque* (brand) of a political candidate and his *image de marque* (public image). However, Gourévitch does describe the components that keep political communications distinct from product advertising and religious communications, both of which clearly seek to motivate readers. Gourévitch also describes the significance and effects of acronyms and offers a good collection of representative campaigns from France and abroad. Beyond providing a thorough analysis of the role of the image in political posters, this work is a solid foundation on the semiotic codes invoked by communication.

Jean-Marie Dru noted in *Le Saut créatif* that the essential difference between American and French advertising is one of philosophy. Americans are in the

"business of ideation" while the French are busy creating "l'art de la diffé-
rentiation" (the art of differentiating). This difference in perspective may very
well lead to the adoption of a different analytical framework from what is
commonly observed in the literature. Although highly complex, Georges Roque's
Ceci n'est pas un Magritte offers a model alternative.

Roque's semiotic analysis of Magritte's art and his influence on advertising
is a most impressive interpretation of the creative mechanism, the mythology,
and the effects on the individual and society. The first part of the study offers
an exhaustive discussion of Magritte's accomplishments, both as a painter and
graphic designer. The central thesis is that Magritte's use of images challenges
the very analogy between the image and the object it is supposed to represent.
The image represents nothing other than itself and the world created by the image
and its reader. As for the effects on the individual, in Magritte's world (and in
the world of advertising) the power of images is derived exclusively from the
associations made by the reader; consequently all associations are possible.

Roque views the representation of products as a *mise-en-scène* (staging). This
is a persuasive argument for the power of art to create a world within which an
object, albeit a consumer product, is situated. This is quite opposed to the
common view that advertisements present a justification for the product or its
purchase. Roque claims that the basic opposition between the individual and
society fades into a state of symbiosis between reader and image. The powerful
adhesion of two elements, such as consumers and merchandise, is mediated by
the mythology of that combination itself. A manifestation of this concept can
be seen in a thirty-second film for Nescafé instant coffee which received much
critical acclaim in the press. The film shows a man in his study savoring a cup
of Nescafé. The aroma and taste evoke a series of images of Colombia bathing
the viewer in a bacchanalian atmosphere as they file through the screen. The
program music is a popular South American tune, as exotic and poetic as the
scenes themselves. Through the music and images, the cinema commercial becomes to the product Nescafé what aroma and taste are to the Colombia imagined
by the coffee drinker. Consequently, drinking instant coffee is not perceived as
being the furthest removed from the authentic, but rather as the quickest way
of experiencing it. It is through this power of adhesion and this type of myth-
making that Roque demonstrates how and why Magritte's opus is frequently
appropriated and easily utilized by advertisers.

CREATION, PRODUCTION, AND COLLECTION

Whereas the *annonce* and the *réclame* of previous years informed the public
about features, quality, and at times price, *la publicité* of the 1980s creates
personalities. Séguéla is the leader of this advertising genre. His "star system"
has abandoned traditional copy strategy for the all-out pursuit of brand personality. The tenets of this philosophy are set out in his inspirational text *Hollywood
lave plus blanc* (Hollywood Washes Whiter). In it, he exhorts his followers to

"leave without shame or regret the deathly Styx of publicity and approach the living banks of communication." Most advertisers seem to be following suit, since there are many examples of this creative approach. Jean-Marie Dru, in *Le Saut créatif*, provides a good source of campaign history and agency styles.

The quality achieved by the new style of advertising is greatly responsible for the high degree of awareness that exists in France today. The French are often capable of recognizing an agency style or individual producers. Every advertisement is signed by the agency that produces it; however, very little is documented about contemporary creators and artists. Moles, in *La Sociodynamique de la culture*, and Edgar Morin, in *Essai sur la culture de masse*, offer a novel perspective on the incorporation of advertising in society. In both works, advertising is viewed as an organic component of society and thus representative of social tendencies. Duvignaud, in *La Planète des jeunes*, and Schifres, in "La Look génération," offer good insight on the type of concerns of young people and the place of advertising in their world. *La pub* has become, at least in the last five years, the sine qua non of the *branchés*.

Newspapers have contributed as well to the visibility of advertising. Newspaper columns in France devote space to media developments and offer commentaries on unusual campaigns (unlike American journalists, who seem to be concerned exclusively with agency takeovers). The newspaper *Libération* runs a daily column. Other major newspapers offer weekly commentaries. There also exist major publications devoted to advertising. *Médias* and *Stratégies* focus on industry and trade issues. *Création* focuses on artistic and graphic accomplishments, and on the academic front, *Communications* often has articles on the language or rhetoric of advertising.

Obtaining the primary sources, however, is often difficult. Company archives are not easily accessible. The Musée de la Publicité houses the only library of advertising slides and films available, to this writer's knowledge. This is in addition to the permanent collection of *affiches* and the constant exhibits of billboard advertising. A commercially available source is Hachette's pedagogical series, which includes a videotape of television commercials. The largest private collection is *La Nuit des publivores*, which offers twelve hours of viewing. With the presence of six television channels in France, documentation and accessibility will, it is hoped, improve.

FUTURE RESEARCH

In 1985 a critical film on the *Bande Annonce* (film trailers, or previews) was shown as part of the exhibit *Affiches de Cinéma* organized by the Musée de la Publicité. Starting with examples from the 1950s and 1960s, the forty-minute film demonstrated how trailers attempt to convey an image of the film being promoted. The most significant aspect of this film is that it successfully defined a genre of advertising never before identified. There is a clear need to continue along these lines and uncover the characteristics of different advertising genres and distinctive authoring styles. The most immediate need, however, is to capture and make film advertising available for study and analysis.

Much more needs to be understood about the reference systems used or redefined by advertising. French ads very often do not actually denote, represent, or signify the product at all. Instead, language and images seem to function deictically, supporting the actual discourse. There is an entire intertextual dimension which remains unexplored. Magritte's images can still be found in advertisements, and the Métro based an entire campaign on the utilization of old posters as well as contemporary ones. This is a unique opportunity for studying the implications for theories of reference.

Finally, a new framework of analysis must also be developed, one that encompasses the concerns of this generation. We need to understand the incorporation of advertising as a cultural and artistic phenomenon, not an economic one. An historical dimension is desperately needed for our understanding of advertising's communication (not industry) as a reflection of the times. A close reading of numerous advertisements quickly reveals echoes, references, and utilization of past campaigns. There is also a striking continuity of certain figures, witness the proverbial presence of the little girl in the campaign for Chocolat Menier, la Mère Denis for Vedette washing machines, and Myriam for the Avenir billboard posting company. Studies of the evolution and metamorphosis of a product over time may very well be the best way of giving substance to a social memory or, at the very least, of providing artistic and cultural depth for a badly understood phenomenon.

BIBLIOGRAPHY

L'Affichomanie, Catalogue du Musée de l'Affiche. Paris 1979.

Andrén, Gunnar. "The Rhetoric of Advertising." *Journal of Communication* 30, No. 4 (1980):74–80.

Bargiel-Harry, Réjane, and Zagrodzki, Christophe. *Le Livre de l'Affiche*. Paris: Éditions Alternatives, 1985.

Barnicoat, John. *A Concise History of Posters*. New York: Oxford University Press, 1972.

Barthes, Roland. *Mythologies*. Paris: Seuil, 1957.

Baudrillard, Jean. *Le Système des objets*. Paris: Gallimard, 1968.

La Belle Époque. Catalogue du Musée des Arts Décoratifs. Paris, 1964.

Bretagne, Christian. "La Mère Denis: Personne ne m'avait jamais appelée Madame." *Elle*, October 18, 1976, n.p.

Bruckner, Pascal, and Finkielkraut, Alain. *Au coin de la rue, l'aventure*. Paris: Seuil, 1979.

Bya, J. "La Transaction et les formes dans la rhétorique publicitaire." *Degrés* 5 (1974): 1–15.

Cadet, André, and Cathelat, A. B. and B. *La Publicité*. Paris: Payot, 1968.

Carvalho, Véra. "Les Langages de la publicité et de la propagande." In *Linguistique*, Frédéric François, ed. Paris: Presses Universitaires de France, 1980, pp. 529–48.

Castagnotto, Ugo. *Semantica della pubblicità*. Rome: Silva, 1970.

Cathelat, Bernard. *Les Styles de vie des Français, 1978–1998*. Paris: Stanké, 1977.

Cohen, Maurice. *Vers un nouveau style de publicité*. Paris: Dunod, 1973.

Dru, Jean-Marie. *Le Saut créatif*. Paris: Lattès, 1985.

Durand, Jacques. "Rhétorique et image publicitaire." *Communications* 15 (1970): 70–95.

Duvignaud, Jacques. *La Planète des jeunes*. Paris: Stock, 1975.

Enel, Françoise. *L'Affiche: Fonctions, langage, rhétorique*. Paris: Mame, 1973.

Fischer, Sophie. "Baranne est une crème." *Communications* 20 (1973): 160–181.

Galliot, Marcel. *La Publicité à travers les âges*. Paris: Éditions Hommes et techniques, 1955.

Gallo, Max. *L'Affiche miroir de l'histoire*. Paris: Laffont, 1973.

Gourévitch, Jean-Paul. *La Politique et ses images*. Paris: Édilig, 1986.

Jeudy, Henri-Pierre. *Variations des structures du langage publicitaire et transformations du système des contraintes sociales*. Paris: A.R.E.E., 1975.

Joannis, Henri. *De l'étude de la motivation à la création publicitaire et à la promotion des ventes*. Paris: Dunod, 1971.

———. *Le Processus de création publicitaire: stratégie, conception et réalisation des messages*. Paris: Dunod, 1978.

Lafitte, Henri-Claude. "Contribution respective du visuel, du scriptural et de leur communication du sens dans l'annonce publicitaire." Dissertation, C.E.L.S.A.-Sorbonne, 1977.

Lagneau, Gérard. *Les Pères fondateurs*. Paris: Presses Universitaires de France, 1982.

McLuhan, Marshall. *Culture Is Our Business*. New York: McGraw-Hill, 1970.

Maîtres de l'affiche. Paris: Chaix, 1900. Reprint. New York: Images Graphiques, 1977.

Markin, Rom J. *Consumer Behavior: A Cognitive Orientation*. New York: Macmillan, 1974.

Mazzoni, Paolo, and Sabrina Charvet. *Étude psychologique sur la communication publicitaire et la publicité*. Paris: Mazzoni, 1977.

Moles, Abraham. *L'Affiche dans la société urbaine*. Paris: Dunod, 1970.

———. *La Sociodynamique de la culture*. The Hague: Mouton, 1971.

Morin, Edgar. *L'Esprit du temps: Essai sur la culture de masse*. Paris: Grasset, 1962.

Muzet, Denis. "*L'Express*: un style publicitaire." *Communications*, 1978, pp. 157–72.

Ogilvy, David, *Ogilvy on Advertising*. New York: Vintage, 1985.

Péninou, Georges. *L'Intelligence de la publicité*. Paris: Laffont, 1972.

Reboul, Olivier. "Le Slogan et les fonctions du langage." *Le Français dans le Monde* 143 (1979): 21–26.

Richaudeau, François. *Le Langage efficace*. Paris: Denoël, 1973.

Ries, Al. *Positioning: The Battle for Your Mind*. New York: McGraw-Hill, 1981.

Roque, Georges. *Ceci n'est pas un Magritte. Essai sur Magritte et la publicité*. Paris: Flammarion, 1983.

Schifres, Alain. "La Look génération." *Le Nouvel Observateur*, February 1983, pp. 42–47.

Séguéla, Jacques. *Hollywood lave plus blanc*. Paris: Flammarion, 1982.

Silber, A. "Les Spots éclairés." *Le Nouvel Observateur*, October 1982.

Smith, Raoul and N. Smith. "Prolegomena to Linguistic Theory of Marketing Communication." *Centerpoint: A Journal of Interdisciplinary Studies* 4 (1980): 58–75.

Spitzer, Leo. "American Advertising Explained as Popular Art," in *A Method of Interpreting Literature*. Northampton, Mass.: Smith College, 1949.
Trois siècles d'affiches françaises. Catalogue du Musée de l'Affiche. Paris, 1979.
Weill, Alain. *L'Affiche française*. Paris: Presses Universitaires de France, 1982.

2

Comics

MAURICE HORN

While there may be places where the comics are even more avidly consumed, there is none where the comics are as much appreciated as they are in France. According to a survey published in the newspaper *Le Monde* of November 12, 1982, comics make up 7 percent of all reading matter enjoyed by the French and—unlike what takes place in most other countries—comics are more likely to be read by people of higher education and/or socioeconomic status: 15 percent of professionals and executives read comics regularly (and an additional 37 percent read them occasionally), while among farm workers the figures are less than 1 percent and 12 percent, respectively. Nor do the French take their comics lightly: even President de Gaulle had strong opinions about Tintin and Astérix, while his current successor in the Élysée Palace, François Mitterrand, is known to have strong sympathies for the medium.

This cultural interest has been translated into official policy, with the government subsidizing activities in favor of the comics, just as it does with other cultural and artistic activities judged worthwhile. There is a section on comics at the level of the Ministry of Culture and a comics commission at the Centre National des Lettres (roughly equivalent to the National Endowment for the Humanities in the United States). The Comics Salon, held each January in the city of Angoulême since 1973, has received visits from a number of cabinet ministers and in 1985 from President Mitterrand himself, while in 1983 the Ministry of Culture enacted a program aimed at promoting the French comics industry locally and abroad.

Despite their cultural chauvinism the French do acknowledge that American comics paved the way to the eventual flowering of the medium in France. As I stated in my study "American Comics in France: A Cultural Evaluation" (in Allen F. Davis, ed., *For Better or Worse: The American Influence in the World*):

"In the French view, the comics constitute an original and distinctive twentieth-century art form that can only be compared in importance to the cinema. The preponderant role played by American artists and editors in the pioneering and development of this form is to them testimony of the vitality, imagination and preeminence of the American culture in the modern world." At the same time the French have evolved their own very sophisticated brand of comics as deserving of study as any other of their many cultural achievements. In France, comics are called *bandes dessinées* (or BD for short); it is highly significant that this appellation has now become as widely recognized as the American name for the medium.

HISTORICAL OUTLINE

To give a complete panorama of the French-language comic strip in a few pages is clearly impossible. In historical importance, in artistic quality, and in sheer output it is second only to the American production. The Swiss Rodolphe Töpffer (with his *Histoires en Estampes* as early as 1846) and the French Christophe (who started *La Famille Fenouillard* in 1889) are among the acknowledged precursors of the modern comic strip. Louis Forton's *Les Pieds-Nickelés* (1908) is the oldest European strip in existence (and the second oldest in the world, after *The Katzenjammer Kids*).

All these series (and countless others), however, never used balloons (except for the *Pieds-Nickelés*) but printed instead a lengthy text under the pictures. In 1925 Alain Saint-Ogan, with *Zig et Puce*, was the first French cartoonist to make exclusive use of the balloon for his dialogues.

In France most of the illustrated stories appeared in newspapers for children, the weekly *journaux illustrés* (illustrated newspapers) which carried tales, stories, articles, pearls of wisdom as well as comics. But in the 1930s these weeklies were invaded and eventually replaced by translations of American comics, more colorful, more suspenseful, jazzier. Had it not been for the war and the German occupation, when American comics were banned, the French comics industry would most likely have gone under.

By necessity French (and Belgian) newspapers turned to local talent. Most of the new production was at first mediocre and heavily imitative of American comics, but it steadily increased in quality as well as in originality. A vigorous crop of new talents emerged not only in France but also in Belgium which, under the leadership of Hergé, became a major center of comics production.

After the war the situation was again touch-and-go, with the American comics making a massive comeback. But by then the French and Belgian cartoonists had become too well entrenched, and with the help of the lamentable French censorship law of 1949 (purposefully aimed against American comics) they firmly established themselves at the vanguard of the revived European comic strip.

Of all the French-language strips Hergé's *Tintin* is without a doubt the most universally known. Twenty-three adventures have appeared since *Tintin*'s inception in 1929 (they are issued in the United States by Atlantic-Little, Brown). Tintin is a young reporter engaged in every kind of adventure from detective work to treasure-hunting. He has roamed the whole planet (and even outer space, as in *Explorers on the Moon*) from Tibet (*Tintin in Tibet*) to Peru (*Prisoners of the Sun*) to the South Seas (*Red Rackham's Treasure*), but Tintin's favorite place remains the mythical kingdom of Syldavia (*King Ottokar's Scepter, The Calculus Affair,* etc.).

Of Hergé's draftmanship little should be said here. It is subordinate to the story and very skillful in its unobtrusiveness. The most remarkable facet of Hergé's talent resides in his creation of characters. Tintin's faithful fox terrier Milou (Snowy in the English version), who, long before Snoopy came along, was one dog who let no human put one over on him; Captain Haddock, the irascible rum-guzzling sailor; the dim-witted twin detectives Dupont and Dupond (Thomson and Thompson); Tournesol (Calculus), the absent-minded (and deaf to boot) professor; and countless others form an ever-changing gallery among whom our hero moves.

In the technical handling of his often complex plots, in the skillful rendering of mood and building of suspense, in his uncanny sense of timing Hergé comes very close to Alfred Hitchcock. Just as in Hitchcock's films, innocent objects take on dark meanings, unsuspecting characters wander in and out of the plot, unaware of the sinister goings-on, and, under the veneer of suspense, like a play within a play, a delightful comedy of manners unfolds. And while *Tintin* remains foremost a funny strip aimed at attracting and holding its child-followers, it is a fitting tribute to Hergé's talent, imagination, and integrity that adults can find equal enjoyment and meaning in it. Hergé died in 1983, but his creation lives on.

Tintin's success spawned its first rival in 1938 with *Spirou*, created by the French Rob Vel (Robert Velter). Spirou was a bellboy at the Moustic Hotel, and his adventures were not very remarkable at first. During the war Jijé took over the character and gave him an animal companion, a squirrel named Pip, and a human companion Fantasio whose whimsicality was a welcome counterpoint to Spirou's earnestness. *Spirou* was developed as a major feature by André Franquin, who succeeded Jijé in 1946. Franquin launched Spirou into his most unforgettable adventures and created a cast of secondary characters second only to Hergé's. One should mention Zantafio, Fantasio's megalomaniacal cousin, the more than somewhat eccentric inventor Count of Champignac, and, best of all, the marsupilami, the most likable, versatile, and fanciful animal ever to grace the comics page since Segar's jeep.

In addition to *Spirou* (which he was eventually to abandon in 1969) Franquin is also known for his creation of *Gaston Lagaffe*. Gaston is an aggravating, bumbling, and incompetent newspaper office-boy whose antics and flights of fancy have been delighting Franquin's readers since 1957.

Franquin's style, definitive in line and exact to the minutest detail, is also highly effective and always enchanting even to the most jaded eye.

In the forties the Belgian cartoonists came more and more to dominate the entire scene. Their specialty was the humorous adventure story, as exemplified by *Tintin* and *Spirou*. Following in their footsteps *Lucky Luke*, a Western parody by Morris (Maurice de Bevère), appeared in 1946. Lucky Luke quickly became famous, along with his horse Jolly Jumper and his slightly deprecating refrain: "I am a poor lonesome cowboy." The strip became more and more realistic with time and incorporated into its dramatis personae authentic figures from the history of the West: Judge Roy Bean, Calamity Jane (depicted as an ugly, toothless harridan), Billy the Kid, and others. To those should be added the four (imaginary) brothers Dalton, Lucky Luke's most persistent foes, and the cowboy's dog companion Ran-tan-plan (an obvious take-off on Rin-tin-tin), the most hapless canine on this or any side of the Mississippi.

In the fifties the overworked Morris, while continuing the drawing of *Lucky Luke*, entrusted the writing to René Goscinny. Goscinny is famous of course for his creation of *Astérix*, which he started in 1959 with Albert Uderzo and which was to top *Tintin* in popularity in the sixties. Astérix is a diminutive Gaul made invulnerable by drinking a magic potion; with the help of his loyal companion, the dim-witted but strong-as-an-ox Obélix, and his fellow villagers, Astérix is able to keep Julius Caesar's Roman legions at bay (the Romans are invariably depicted as dumb, cowardly, rapacious, and gullible). There are good things in *Astérix* (the clever use of balloons, a drawing which is clean and uncluttered, some genuinely funny situations) but the basic plot is tiresome. Goscinny's death in 1977 did not stop *Astérix*'s exploits, which are now continued by Uderzo alone.

Much more delightful and a lot wittier is Peyo's creation *Les Schtroumpfs*. The schtroumpfs (known as the smurfs in the United States) are a people of gentle, civilized, and utterly charming elves whose ingenuity triumphs over all the mishaps that often befall their sleepy village. Identical in appearance and costume, but each with his own personality, the schtroumpfs form a microcosm of society under the wise and enlightened guidance of the "Grand Schtroumpf." The strip is drenched in a poetic atmosphere directly derived from European folklore, and its landscapes are often reminiscent of *Little Nemo*'s fairy-tale scenery. Peyo's style, subdued and simple like his stories, is never too cute or mannered, despite the temptations of the genre. (The same unfortunately cannot be said of their American Saturday morning television series.)

French and Belgian cartoonists have traditionally been as fond of dogs as American artists have been of cats. In recent years no fewer than three canines (in addition to Milou/Snowy and Ran-tan-plan) have become the heroes of popular strips—and one of them, Pif, has even given his name to the publication in which he was appearing.

Pif le chien (Pif the Dog) is the creation of the Spaniard José Cabrero-Arnal (who signs Arnal). Neither the drawing style nor the weekly gags are outstanding; yet Pif, a good-natured, rather cheerful mutt, met with instant success (mostly due to younger readers). To Americans Pif's weekly encounters with animal and human cardboard caricatures would seem quite conventional and more than a bit cloying.

In another class is Marcel Gotlib's *Gai Luron*, which also appeared in the merged publications *Vaillant-Pif*. Gai Luron (his name, meaning "jolly fellow," is a misnomer) was a canine philosopher whose hang-dog face reflected all the vicissitudes of a world-weary life. Disabused and sarcastic, he comments on (in a uniform, slightly disparaging tone) and reacts to (with a visible reluctance of effort) the various indignities an uncaring world keeps throwing at him.

To round out (and round out is the right term!) this dog-gone trio, there is Dupa's *Cubitus*. An almost spherical ball of tuft, Cubitus lives in a dilapidated house in the company of a moth-eaten retired sailor named Sémaphore. Cubitus' life would be idyllic were it not for a number of nuisances like Sénéchal, the neighbor's cat, a bothersome (and sports-crazy) phantom, and the mysterious Isidore, whose elusive presence sometimes disturbs the canine's generally placid digestion. Dupa's humor, unpredictable, fast, and loony, coupled with an easy-going but accurate line, have made *Cubitus* into one of the best European gag strips of the decade.

Another popular animal strip is *Chlorophylle*, about a group of field mice involved in various allegorical adventures. The strip, created by Raymond Macherot, is now drawn by the aforementioned Dupa and written by Greg (the editor-in-chief of *Tintin* magazine and the scriptwriter for most of the strips appearing in it).

Greg's editorial achievements should not obscure his talents as a cartoonist. With *Achille Talon (Walter Melon* in the English translation) he has created the unforgettable portrait of a typical French *petit-bourgeois* in what is one of the most hilariously funny European comic strips.

While French and Belgian cartoonists have not yet been able to create a *Peanuts* or a *Pogo*, in the field of the action strip they have forged far ahead of their American counterparts. This is nowhere as striking as in the science-fiction genre, where they have produced a number of original creations, and at least one undisputed masterpiece: E. P. Jacobs' superb *Blake et Mortimer*.

Captain Francis Blake (from British Intelligence) and Professor Philip Mortimer join forces in a series of powerful adventures where mystery, suspense, and even archaeology are cleverly woven into the overall science-fiction scheme. In his strip Jacobs has dealt with some of the most important themes of post–World War II science fiction: survival after a nuclear holocaust and the dehumanization wrought by a technology-mad society ("The Diabolical Trap"), the horrors of mind-control ("The Yellow Mark"), the aliens among us ("The Enigma of Atlantis"), the blind unleashing of unknown cosmic forces ("S.O.S. Meteors"). Very often the enemies of the two heroes are the blind emissaries of a science gone mad (like Professor Septimus) or the willing agents of (totalitarian) darkness best personified in the demoniacal Colonel Olrik (a creation on a par with Ming the Merciless). In all of Jacobs' stories there appear the same currents of humanistic concern and passionate commitment to truth as in the works of Ray Bradbury, Arthur C. Clarke, and Richard Matheson. To the reader weaned on the slick (but meaningless) acrobatics of comic-book superheroes Jacobs' graphic style may seem static, but in epic sweep, in breadth and scope of imagination, in sheer imagery power, *Blake et Mortimer* often equals and sometimes surpasses *Buck Rogers, Brick Bradford*, and even *Flash Gordon*.

Compared to *Blake et Mortimer* Poïvet's *Les Pionniers de l'Espérance* (The Pioneers of the *Hope*) looks more conventional. The *Hope* is a spaceship, and her crew of men and women of different nationalities go through all the thrills and perils of the genre. The scenarios (written by Roger Lécureux) are very imaginative but never stray far from the tried-and-true formulas of classical science fiction. Raymond Poïvet has been compared by some to Alex Raymond, although his style is probably closer to that of Austin Briggs, Raymond's successor (no mean compliment either). His compositions are very effective and he makes the action move at a brisk pace. Where *Les Pionniers* is weakest is in the creation of memorable characters (even the protagonists blur after a while), but it is nonetheless an excellent comic strip whose popularity has remained constant for almost thirty years.

The ballyhoo generated by *Barbarella* should not obscure its merits. The first outstanding space heroine of the comics since Godwin's Connie, Barbarella has already been through a string of harrowing adventures, from her sexual encounters with assorted weirdos (including a robot) to her exploration of bizarre worlds, all of them told with tongue-in-cheek relish by J.-C. Forest. Forest's line is elegant, perhaps too elegant, and somewhat brittle, but he remains a master in the evocation of disquieting places (the city of Sogo, for instance) and of haunting faces (Barbarella herself; the Black Queen).

On the other hand, Philippe Druillet's *Lone Sloane* is probably the most overrated of all science-fiction strips. The images that Druillet creates are impressive and sometimes (though not often) awesome, but they simply never seem to fit together in any recognizable pattern: they just hang there like disjointed illustrations, never quite coming together to give birth to a genuine continuity strip. H. P. Lovecraft has had a lasting influence on Druillet, who tries accordingly to sound mysterious but mainly succeeds in sounding incoherent. What Druillet seems to need most is a good editor to straighten him out.

Lone Sloane appeared in *Pilote*, a comics magazine, as two other notable science-fiction and fantasy strips still do: J.-C. Mézières' *Valérian* and *Philémon* by Othon Aristides (who signs "Fred").

In 2720 A.D. the peoples of the earth have extended their power over the whole galaxy, and Valérian, a "spatio-temporal agent," and his pretty partner Laureline are crack troubleshooters for the Terran Empire. Pierre Christin (a professor of journalism at the University of Bordeaux who writes the strip under the pseudonym "Linus") keeps the action going at a crackling pace in the best space-opera tradition. Mézières' graphic style is without surprises, but full of solid craftsmanship and well suited to this craftsmanlike series.

With *Philémon*, on the other hand, we squarely step over the fine line between science fiction and fantasy. Philémon, Fred's stringy farm-boy hero, crosses accidentally into a parallel world, landing on one or another of the letters of the words "Atlantic Ocean" in the mythical Sea of Maps. Along with the old well-digger Barthélémy he runs into countless perils, which include sinking into a mirage while fighting a deadly grand piano. Fred's universe is full of weird creatures, magical landscapes, and surreal vistas reminiscent of *Krazy Kat*.

In spite of their rich past, the Europeans have had few historical strips of note. One of those is undisputably François Craenhals' *Chevalier Ardent* about a young knight at King Arthus' court and his lady fair, Arthus' own daughter Gwendoline. The plot sounds familiar, but Craenhals makes it all seem fresh, mainly through his well-plotted adventures. The drawing is vigorous and full of dash, and the depictions of tournaments, pageants, and fights are not unworthy of some of *Prince Valiant*'s scenes.

Paradoxically the European cartoonists have always seemed to be more fascinated with American history than with their own: while American cowboy strips have always been small in number, there are more European Westerns than can be counted. Only a few of those are deserving high praise, and chief among them are the French *Lieutenant Blueberry* and the Belgian *Comanche*.

Written by Jean-Michel Charlier and drawn by Gir (Jean Giraud), *Lieutenant Blueberry* was the most vigorous, exciting, and authentic Western to come along since the early *Red Ryder*. Lieutenant Mike S. Blueberry, of the U.S. Cavalry, is a somewhat disillusioned soldier, and the other characters are drawn with a sure hand by Gir. Gir's depiction of action is masterful, his delineation of background sharp and assertive, and his use of color is nothing short of inspired.

Comanche by Hermann and Greg is a more conventional tale about a ranch hand named Red Dust, his comic sidekick Ten Gallons, and Comanche, the young and pretty ranch owner he works for. Hermann's style is bold and powerful, his compositions visually striking, but he tends to clutter his pictures with too many details.

Hermann and Greg's more famous creation *Bernard Prince* is a straight adventure strip in the classic tradition. Bernard Prince is a former Interpol agent turned adventurer and soldier of fortune. Aboard his yacht *The Cormorant* and in company of his loyal crew, the hirsute and hard-drinking Barney Jordan and the teenaged Djinn, Bernard Prince embarks on adventures in the wilds of Amazonia, the deserts of Central Asia, and—most dangerous of all—the jungles of Manhattan. Another good adventure series is *Michel Tanguy*, an aviation strip excellently drawn by Uderzo (and later by Jijé). Charlier, the scriptwriter, is a former pilot and at least knows what he is talking about.

Probably the best of the current French-language adventure strips is being done by an Italian, Hugo Pratt. *Corto Maltese* is a spin-off from Pratt's earlier effort *Una ballata del Mare Salato* (A Ballad from the Salty Sea). Corto is a sea captain without a ship and, by all appearances, a man without a country. The action takes place around 1910, when there were still worlds to conquer, treasures to discover, and causes to fight for. The atmosphere hangs heavy in these tales full of sound and fury, where magic and witchcraft play a large part.

While strongly influenced in style by Milton Caniff, in his use of bold blacks, of violent chiaroscuros, of figures etched in a few decisive brush strokes, Pratt brought the techniques further than any of Caniff's followers (except at times Frank Robbins) and has made *Corto Maltese* into the most exciting adventure strip since Caniff's own *Terry*.

Numerous other strips of note should be cited here, but for lack of space, let us just mention *Cellulite*, Claire Bretécher's hilarious account of a homely, sex-hungry princess; Cezard's *Arthur le Fantôme* (Arthur the Ghost, less innocent but funnier than Casper); Jacques Martin's *Alix*, an exciting tale of adventures during the Roman Empire; the even more remote *Rahan* by Chéret, which takes place in prehistoric times; and, last but not least, the good science-fiction series *Luc Orient* by Paape and Greg.

Toward the close of the 1960s the French-language comics scene thus presented a serene, if somewhat predictable, panorama that was shattered, as so many other things French, in the wake of the student and worker rebellions of May 1968. The mood of confrontation and revolt led many creators to break away from their traditional publishers and go their own way. This ferment gave rise to a number of new monthly comics magazines, decidedly iconoclastic in tone and outlook, and much more radical in style and content; often experimental in their artistic policy, they were aimed at an adult public.

While the adult comics magazine had its birth in Italy (*Linus*, 1965), its most impressive flowering now took place in France. The first French publication of this kind was *Charlie*, which hit the newsstands in the late 1960s. At its inception it looked almost like a clone of *Linus*, with a similar magazine-size format, and almost the same line-up of comic features, *Peanuts* chief among them (indeed its title came from Charlie Brown). An emanation of the satirical weekly *Hara-Kiri*, *Charlie*'s greatest achievement was to bring, over the years, artists from other cartooning fields, including Georges Wolinski (sometimes called the French Jules Feiffer), Gébé (Georges Blondeau, whose dark parables contain a subtle message of hope), and Jean-Marc Reiser, who satirized the idiocies and absurdities of middle-class life with a savage pen.

As the 1970s rolled along, *Charlie* took on a more diversified look. Cabu came over from *Pilote* to weave the tales of the collegiate Duduche and the man-hungry Catherine within its pages, Alex Barbier made himself a depicter of the lower depths, the painter Jacques Rochberny contributed a number of vignettes filled with offbeat humor, while Dimitri (Guy Mouminoux) managed to milk laughter out of a grim Soviet "reeducation camp" in *Le Goulag*. Among foreign contributors to *Charlie* mention should be made of José Muñoz and Carlos Sampayo (the Argentinian creators of *Alack Sinner*) and Harvey Kurtzman.

Charlie's initial success brought on a number of imitators. First came *L'Écho des Savanes*, founded by several dissident cartoonists from *Pilote* in a revolt led by Nikita Mandryka, who had been infuriated at having one of his stories censored by *Pilote*'s editors. Humor (usually of the black variety) was *L'Écho*'s stock in trade. In addition to Mandryka's off-the-wall musings (which have included *Anodin et Inodore*, about two philosophically inclined losers), the magazine featured Yves Got's gallery of monstrous psychopaths; François Barbe's anti-social, antifeminist tirades; and Philippe Vuillemin's terrifying satires of every-day occurrences (riot-wracked soccer games, murderous Sunday outings, etc). Mandryka later departed to rejoin *Pilote*, but was advantageously replaced by Martin Veyron, who was able to mix traditional themes and unconventional humor in a novel way.

Modeled on *L'Écho*, *Fluide Glacial* was also launched by a former *Pilote* cartoonist, Marcel Gotlib. *Fluide* has been characterized by a frankly scatological outlook and by explicit displays of sexual activity. In addition to Gotlib's con-tributions (*Superdupont*, *Rhaa Lovely*, *Pervers Pépère*, etc.) the magazine could also boast of the work of Jean Solé, Max Cabannes, and especially Daniel Goosens, whose story depicting drug-addicted comic characters (Tintin, Mickey Mouse, Donald Duck) drew heavy fire. With its heavy emphasis on photographs and text pieces, *Fluide Glacial* probably came closer in format and content to *National Lampoon* than any other French publication.

The proliferation of these magazines and the acceptance they had encountered with both the general public and the media prompted the curious conversion of *Pilote* into an adult (or at least adolescent) monthly from the children's weekly it had been previously. Having coasted for years on *Astérix*'s fabulous success, it was now confronted with the loss of its most popular feature after a bitter and protracted court battle. It could still boast of a stable of brilliant artists, such as Jean Giraud (*Lieutenant Blueberry*), Fred (Othon Aristides), Alexis (Dominique Vallet), and others, but they felt constricted by the publication's heavy-handed editorial policies. As soon as opportunity arose, therefore, many of them deserted a magazine that, in their eyes, had grown stale in order to pursue more satisfying careers elsewhere. In desperation *Pilote* (whose readership had gone steadily downhill) changed its policies in the mid-1970s and veered its course toward a more adult public. As a result, by the end of the 1970s it was able to attract new talent (such as the Yugoslav-born Enki Bilal) and to bring back some of its dissidents (including Mandryka, who returned to the fold in 1979). Jean-Claude Mézières, Gérard Lauzier, Régis Franc, Caza (Philippe Cazamayou) are some of the authors who completed a very impressive lineup.

However, the decade came to be dominated by *Métal Hurlant*, founded in 1975 around the seminal presence of Jean Giraud ("Moebius") and Philippe Druillet. At first a quarterly, later a monthly, *Métal Hurlant* was for a long time almost exclusively devoted to science fiction and fantasy, making itself a power to be reckoned with in the field with exciting stories, dazzling visuals, and trailblazing themes. Moebius' most original creations (*Arzach*, *Major Fatal*, *The Airtight Garage*, etc.) first appeared there, as did Druillet's *Salammbô* (loosely based on Gustave Flaubert's novel), Bilal's *Exterminateur 17* (on a script by Jean-Pierre Dionnet, the magazine's publisher), and many others. The magazine was immediately successful, and its fame spread all over Europe and even to the United States, where an American version, *Heavy Metal*, was started in 1977.

With the French comic magazines in a state of constant flux in the 1970s, many writers and artists were reluctant to sign exclusive contracts; and this spawned a further growth of titles on the market. One of the most interesting of the newcomers to the field was (*À Suivre*) (To Be Continued), founded in 1978. As the title implies, (*À Suivre*) has been devoting most of its pages to serialized comics; broadly open to new talent (Benoît Sokal, Chantal Montellier, Thierry "Ted" Benoit), its reputation ultimately rested on the shoulders of two solidly established craftsmen: Jacques Tardi and Hugo Pratt. In stories like *Ici Même* (Right Here) Tardi created the kind of characters (determinedly crazy people under a bourgeois exterior) and the type of milieu (the opulent French society of the *Belle Époque*) that had made him previously noticed. With *Corto Maltese in Siberia*, Pratt put his famous soldier of fortune through one of his most exciting adventures, replete with colorful characters, a stolen gold train, and some very peculiar goings-on in the midst of the Bolshevik revolution. (*À Suivre*) at first only used black and white, but later cautiously experimented with color.

Also a relative newcomer, *Circus* began publication in 1975 though it came into its own only at the end of the decade. Because in its beginnings remuneration was low, it relied mainly on foreign artists and on young French talent. Among its early discoveries mention should be made of Annie Goetzinger, Alain Mounier, Pierre Wininger, and especially François Bourgeon, whose *Les Passagers du Vent* (The Passengers of the Wind) weaves a picturesque tapestry of skulduggery, derring-do, and high-seas adventure in the time of the tall ships.

The late 1970s and early 1980s saw the heyday of French comics: their popularity was unprecedented with the public, adult as well as juvenile, and they were given respectful treatment from intellectuals and media alike. New authors and new concepts were introduced at a dizzying pace in the many comics publications of the time, and if successful, they were later published in book form. This system allowed the publishers to use the magazines as testing grounds for fresh talent at little or no financial risk. The public, however, became tired of paying twice for the same stories, and in increasing numbers, readers stopped buying the magazines and waited for the publication of their favorite strips in album or book form; magazine sales fell sharply as a result, spelling disaster for many publishers and their authors.

At the beginning of the decade its founders sold *Charlie* to Dargaud (the publishers of *Pilote*); the publication continued for a while as an independent title, though with radically altered editorial policies. When its former readers started deserting in droves, it was merged with *Pilote* (which became *Pilote-Charlie* for a time), then dropped altogether. *Métal Hurlant*, the publication which in many respects had become the guiding light of French comics magazines, fared no better, with many of its charter artists leaving for other horizons;

Moebius, however, stayed loyal and even contributed to its pages one of the most interesting stories, *L'Incal*, on a script by noted filmmaker Alexandro Jodorowsky. Yet this was not enough to pull *Métal* out of its slump, with the rest of the publication increasingly given over (because of financial difficulties) to a host of newcomers with uncertain talent. As Umberto Eco remarked in 1980, many of the strips in *Métal Hurlant* had become "as hermetic, specious, and boring as the bad experimenters for the 'happy few' in previous decades could be" (*Travels in Hyperreality*, p. 147). After a number of bankruptcies and reorganizations, *Métal Hurlant* finally disappeared in the mid-1980s. (By that time Moebius had left not only the publication, but the country as well: he is now settled in southern California.)

Another drawback has been the generalization of the 48-page album formula: while it evidently satisfied the public of collectors eager for uniformity in size and format, it also produced a feeling of monotony and predictability in the general reading public, speeding its disaffection. Paradoxically this decline occurred at the time of greatest official recognition of the comics as an artform, when Jack Lang, himself an ardent supporter of the comics, was Minister of Culture.

Thus it is not surprising that the 1980s, unlike the preceding decades, did not produce a commercial success comparable to *Astérix*, or an artist of the same caliber as Moebius. Yet new talents came to the fore, and older hands confirmed their position in this period. F'Murr (Richard Peyzaret) honed his satirical skills with his caustic comments on the current scene; Frank Margerin continued his hilarious depictions of punk rockers and their groupies; Martin Veyron treated with acidity such contemporary themes as "Executive Woman"; while Theo van der Bogaard created the overbearing Léon la Terreur. Astride between humor and adventure, Jean-Marc Rochette created one of the most suspenseful fantasy strips of the decade with *Le Transperceneige*, on a script by Jacques Lob.

Straight narrative strips continued to flourish in the hands of such practitioners as Denis Sire, Jacques Loustal, Philippe Marcelé, and the Varenne brothers (Alex and Daniel), creators of exciting stories adroitly mixing atmosphere, suspense, and sex. François Boucq, working on a scenario by the noted American novelist Jerome Charyn, drew a haunting tale of betrayal and terror with *The Magician's Wife*. The Belgian Didier Comès (Dieter Hermann) evoked a world midway between reality and legend in such works as *Silence*, and his compatriot François Schuiten, a trained architect, built futuristic cities in *The Walls of Samaris* and *The Tower*. From Switzerland Bernard Cosey contributed *In Search of Peter Pan*, while Gregor Rosinski came all the way from Poland to Brussels to create, in partnership with scriptwriter Jean Van Hamme, the fantasy series *Thorgal, Son of the Stars*.

This period has also seen the development of the "adult" (in the American sense) or erotic comic strip. Although the phenomenon can be dated back to *Barbarella*, it only gained its current dimensions in the late 1970s. Among its most artistically articulate practitioners special mention should be given to

Georges Pichard, whose many creations are often as humorous as they are titillating (*Blanche Épiphanie, Paulette*, etc.). Gérard Leclaire, Georges Lévis, and Philippe Cavell are a few other artists who have managed to transcend the limitations of this somewhat disreputable genre.

In the waning years of the 1980s French comics have clearly come to the end of an era. Whether they will continue their slow decline, or whether there are new talents, new concepts waiting to be born along with the closing decade of the twentieth century remains to be seen.

FRENCH COMICS IN THE UNITED STATES

Prior to 1950 French-language comics were for all intents and purposes virtually unknown to the American public (there had been some desultory attempts in the late 1940s to syndicate a *Tintin* newspaper strip in the original in order to encourage young readers to learn French). Prompted by the worldwide success of the *Tintin* books, Golden Press in the early 1950s started publishing a series of American-translated Tintin titles; there were six books in all (now eagerly sought by collectors) before the publishers decided sales didn't meet their expectations. Only a decade later was the series picked up again, by Atlantic-Little, Brown, which unfortunately chose to use the stuffy British translation provided by Hergé's English publisher, Methuen. Despite this drawback the series has been well received by the American public, and of the twenty-three Tintin adventures published in the original, twenty-one are currently in print on the U.S. market (leaving out only the first two, *Tintin in the Land of the Soviets* and *Tintin in the Congo*).

The growing acceptance of the comics as a genuine twentieth-century artform on both sides of the Atlantic in the 1960s resulted in further intercontinental activity in the field. Spurred on by the success of the *Barbarella* movie, Grove Press in 1966 brought out an American version of the French comic strip, on which the film was based; and the same publisher later came out with additional books of European comics, including Guy Pellaert's *Jodelle* in 1967. In the course of the decade Tintin's major European competitor, Astérix, was also brought to the United States, by publishers William Morrow, among others, and there briefly was an *Asterix* newspaper strip. Unlike Hergé's juvenile hero, the feisty little Gaul never seemed to take hold in this country, however.

The real breakthrough, as far as French comics are concerned, occurred in 1977 when the first issue of *Heavy Metal* magazine came out in the United States; initially an American version of the French *Métal Hurlant*, it later diversified to include works by other French and European, and later American, creators. A monthly when it first appeared, it is now a quarterly far removed from the popularity it enjoyed during its heyday in the late 1970s and early 1980s; it was, however, the first American publication to reveal the work of prominent French comic-strip artists, notably Moebius, Druillet, and Bilal, to a large public.

Heavy Metal's initial success may have inspired Dargaud to establish its own publishing company in the United States under the name Dargaud International. It began operation in the early 1980s and lasted only a few years, plagued as it was by inept management and a basic misreading of the American comics-buying public. During its short existence it nevertheless popularized a number of its properties, such as the already familiar *Astérix* in addition to *Lucky Luke* and *Valérian*.

Started about the same time as Dargaud International, Catalan Communications (originally an offshoot of the Barcelona-based publisher Toutain) proceeded along a much more cautious path and as a result is still very much alive and prospering to this day. The wide range of "graphic novels" Catalan publishes encompasses comics from virtually every major producing country: from France they have issued, among others, Boucq and Charyn's *The Magician's Wife*, Loustal's *Love Shots*, and the major works of Enki Bilal. In 1989 they started publishing a number of volumes aimed at a more juvenile public, using the Comcat imprint (to distinguish it from their main line of books, which are more suited to adult tastes); it eventually intends to publish all of the *Blake and Mortimer* stories, as well as Roger Leloup's popular *Yoko Tsuni* series, among other titles. All these Catalan volumes additionally benefit from high production values and generally good translations.

After Catalan came the flood, as American publishers, big and small, started to realize that there existed a strong sales potential in foreign comics, with French-language comics figuring prominently in the growing tide of imports. The small NBM company (which is mainly a reprint house) brought out Schuiten's *The Great Wall of Samaris*, and is currently in the process of issuing the entire *Roxanna* series by Régis Loisel and Serge Le Tendre—in rather shoddily produced books, unfortunately; while Donning has been distributing Van Hamme and Rosinski's *Thorgal* fantasy strip in a series of nicely designed books. Even Marvel Comics has gotten into the act in its Epic Comics line of graphic novels: under the umbrella title *Moebius: The Collected Fantasies of Jean Giraud* it has been issuing a truly superb collection of the French master's most celebrated works (six volumes have appeared so far), with comments and notes by the artist; additionally it has put out, in a three-volume set, the entire *Incal* saga by Moebius and Jodorowsky. Finally, the newly formed Amusement Comics has started (in 1988) to bring out Charlier and Gir's *Lieutenant Blueberry* series, as well as Charlier's *Buck Danny* (in the version drawn by Francis Bergèse, who took over the strip following Victor Hubinon's death).

While the aforementioned titles have all come out either in hard-cover books or in trade paperback format, a number of French-language comics have also appeared in the U.S. in the standard comic-book size, whether on their own or as part of an anthology title. This is the case, for instance, with Jean-Marc Lelong's caustic humor strip *Carmen Cru*, which was reprinted in a number of comic books under the title *French Ice*, and of *Hollywood Eye* ("Le Privé d'Hollywood") by François Rivière, Jean-Louis Bocquet, and Philippe Berthet, which is featured in the comic book *Aces*. As foreign (and especially French) comics become better known in this country, there are indications that their availability in the English language will increase accordingly.

The panorama of French-language comics published in the U.S. is quite impressive: while the early manifestations of the form are still largely ignored (with the exception of the prewar *Tintin*), the production of the last two decades is fairly well represented—and it is hoped that the gaps still existing will be filled in the near future. Thus the scholar or enlightened amateur wishing to study the field of French comic art is happily confronted with a wealth of primary sources easily available in this country. (An extensive bibliography is provided at the end of this chapter.)

SOURCES AND REFERENCES

There are unfortunately few places in the United States where one can consult the abundant bibliography of and about French-language comics; even specialized libraries such as the Russel B. Nye Library at Michigan State University, or the James Branch Cabell Library at Virginia Commonwealth University in Richmond, or even the otherwise well-stocked Popular Culture Library of Bowling Green State University of Ohio, have little material related to French and Belgian comics, outside the obvious *Tintin* and *Astérix* items. The Museum of Cartoon Art at Rye Brook, New York, has a number of publications but is short on research material, as is the San Francisco Academy of Comic Art.

To gain a meaningful insight into the very complex world of French comics, one has to turn to institutions in France and Belgium which in the last two decades have made a serious and laudable effort at collecting and preserving material pertaining to comics in their own and other countries. The periodicals annex of the Bibliothèque Nationale at Versailles is a good place to start—though their collection of comics publications is often spotty because of theft and neglect. There are other institutions, however, that the researcher may find even more helpful: in France the Centre de l'Image in Angoulême, connected with the city's yearly International Comics Salon, and the comics department of the Public Library in Marseilles have a great deal of documents and research material as well as a knowledgeable staff; in Belgium the University of Louvain has a collection second to none in that country. As a general rule most universities would have at least a fund of comics-related material, with Paris-Sorbonne, Bordeaux, and Grenoble in possession of some important collections. At the government level there is a comics section at the Ministry of Culture, and a commission on comics at the Centre National des Lettres, both in Paris: inquiries can be made to them. In addition there is a number of private and semiprivate organizations throughout the country which also have important resources, while collections maintained by private collectors are sometimes even more rewarding (but often difficult to access).

REFERENCE WORKS

The overwhelming bulk of reference books on the comics published in the United States contain only passing reference (if any) to foreign comics and are therefore, from the point of view of studying French comics, virtually useless. Originally published in conjunction with a major exhibition of comic art at the Louvre, *A History of the Comic Strip* by Pierre Couperie and Maurice Horn (with contributions by others) offers, in the words of the distinguished popular culture scholar M. Thomas Inge, "some of the most provocative comments yet ventured on the aesthetics, structure, symbolism, and themes in comic art" (*Handbook of American Popular Culture*). In this work the French contributions to the field are understandably well represented. Similarly, *Comics: Anatomy of a Mass Medium*, written by the German team of Reinhold Reitberger and Wolfgang Fuchs, also provides a broad view of the variety and versatility of French comics in this international survey (unfortunately marred by an inadequate and ponderous translation).

In his lavishly illustrated anthology, *Masters of Comic Book Art*, the English writer P. R. Garriock presents ten insightful studies of as many internationally acclaimed modern practitioners of the form, including Druillet and Moebius. *The World Encyclopedia of Comics*, edited by Maurice Horn, provides over 100 bio-bibliographical entries on French and Belgian comics and their creators, most of them written by the editor. The companion *World Encyclopedia of Cartoons* contains information on an additional number of artists who, while they may be better noted for their work in animation or cartooning, have also contributed to the French comics scene. Other works by Horn, notably *Comics of the American West, Women in the Comics, Sex in the Comics*, study a number of French comics from the vantage point implicit in their respective titles.

In view of the paucity of works available in English, anyone interested in the vast literature and iconography of French comics must turn to works in the original language. Here, the chief impediment is not that of scarcity but of overabundance: there have probably been more books, treatises, surveys, anthologies, guides, articles, and doctoral theses written on comics in France (and Belgium) than in any other country in the world. Judicious, if ruthless, pruning must therefore be applied, with only works of substance and merit being considered (with availability a secondary factor). Researchers looking for a less selective bibliography may consult Wolfgang Kempkes' *International Bibliography of Comics Literature* (which unfortunately has received no update since the year of first publication, 1974) or John Lent's *Comic Art: An International Bibliography* (1987), with an updated edition currently in preparation. The most extensive bibliography, however, is that provided by Jean-Louis Tilleuil in *La Bande dessinée à l'université . . . et ailleurs* (discussion of this work can be found below).

Among general reference works on the comics *L'Encyclopédie des bandes dessinées*, edited by Marjorie Alessandrini, can be used to supplement the information supplied in Horn's encyclopedias, since the number of entries devoted to French comics is understandably greater—they are, as a rule, short on insight, however. Francis Lacassin was one of the founders of the movement for the rehabilitation of comics in the early 1960s, and in *Pour un neuvième art: la bande dessinée* he has gathered the sum of his thoughts on the narrative form he chooses to call "the ninth art." His arguments are always thoughtful and his points generally cogent, but his apologia gets a trifle strident at times. Michel Pierre tried a more objective approach to the problem in his book simply titled *La Bande dessinée*, but his style is rather dry and his information not always unimpeachable. Jacques Sadoul is a frequent writer on the comics as well as a professional journalist, and his account in *Panorama de la bande dessinée* is perhaps longer on anecdote than on facts, but it is always entertaining and often informative. On the other hand, Annie Baron-Carvais's excellent little book, *Les Bandes dessinées*, is crammed full of facts, figures, charts, and statistics, and is seldom dull; the contents are well organized to give the reader a synoptic view of the state of the medium at the beginning of the 1980s. Jean-Claude Faur, the founder and curator of the comics department at the Library of Marseilles, has contributed a number of incisive essays and enlightening interviews to the comics literature: quite a few of these have been gathered in *À la rencontre de la bande dessinée*, where they can be read with profit as well as enjoyment.

The French are nothing if not a people of explainers, and there are accordingly a fair number of analytical dissections of the comics medium from about as many points of view as there are analysts. Pierre Fresnault-Deruelle is a college professor and respected semiologist with a special interest in the comics. His two more accessible exercises in semiotic analysis are *La Bande dessinée: essai d'analyse sémiotique* and *Récits et discours par la bande, essais sur les comics*; they have brought fresh perspectives in the way one looks at comics, though some of the author's conclusions may seem highly debatable. Jean-Bruno Renard in *Clefs pour la bande dessinée* has also written an analytical work, though more sociologically slanted: his conclusions are on the main positive despite a certain ambivalence as to the cultural merits of the medium. This underscores the fact that, for all their seeming acceptance by intellectual and academic circles, the comics still meet with a number of demurs and reservations on esthetic and societal grounds. These doubts are well outlined by Alain Rey in *Les Spectres de la bande: essai sur la BD*, where the balance of tone and argument, even when negative, never gets shrill. More controversial is Georges Pernin's *Un monde étrange, la bande dessinée*, in which the argumentation is often *ad hominem*.

For some years now the French have had the equivalent of Bob Overstreet's yearly *Comic Book Price Guide* in their own biennial *Trésors de la bande dessinée*, edited by Michel Béra, Michel Denni and Philippe Mellot. While it is mainly for the use of collectors (with a price guide every bit as controversial as Overstreet's), it also gives a bird's eye-view of the wealth of comic material available in French. Philippe Bronson's *Guide de la bande dessinée* fills the same function, although it tends to be more didactic. For an iconographic supplement to these two guides (which only use small black-and-white cuts as illustrations) one may turn to Jérôme Peignot's profusely illustrated account of visual nostalgia, *Les Copains de votre enfance* (The Pals of Your Childhood), which contains well-chosen examples of major and not so major French comics classics. *Les Chefs-d'oeuvre de la bande dessinée*, edited by Jacques Sternberg, Michel Caen and Jacques Lob, aspires to be universal while Peignot's approach was provincial: it fails in this endeavor but can be usefully consulted for additional iconic information on French comics.

Themes and Variations

Over the years a number of histories have seen the light of print, with varying degrees of authority. Jacques Marny's *Le Monde étonnant des bandes dessinées* and Gérard Blanchard's *Histoire de la bande dessinée* are both general histories and both came out at the end of the 1960s, when the debate over the social and esthetic value of the comics was at its peak. Blanchard's is by far the better account: it gives all the facts in a clear and concise way, and weighs the arguments pro and con with a great deal of impartiality. Marny is much more fragmentary in his approach, and in his eagerness to be comprehensive he doesn't always check his sources with the necessary rigor (particularly in his chapters on distribution and readership). Coming much later, *Histoire mondiale de la bande dessinée*, edited by Claude Moliterni, is worth consulting chiefly for its illustrations; yet the chapters, each devoted to a different country, are not especially illuminating—and the chapter on American comics, signed "Robert Kane," is particularly inept. Moliterni has also edited a more interesting work on French and Belgian comics, *Histoire de la bande dessinée d'expression française*, which gives a creditable account of the subject from the vantage of the 1970s. *Histoire de la BD en France et en Belgique*, edited and published by Jacques Glénat et al., gives a better sense of perspective and provides more up-to-date (to 1984) information. Finally, there is *Beyond the Seventh Art: History of the Belgian Strip Cartoon* by Danny De Laet and Yves Varende, which provides an excellent chronicle of the comics production from Belgium's two parts (French and Flemish); published under the auspices of the Belgian Ministry of Foreign Affairs, the book in its English version can be obtained from the Belgian Consulate General in New York.

The history of French comics is so rich and eventful that many books covering only a particular publisher or decade have appeared. Henri Filippini's *Les Années cinquante*, on the 1950s, and Bruno Lecigne's *Avanies et mascarades: l'évolution de la bande dessinée en France dans les années 70* deal with the more recent past; while Édouard François nostalgically recalls the "golden age" of the pre–World War II years in *L'Âge d'or de la bande dessinée*. Among books devoted to a single comics publisher, mention should be made of Filippini's two studies, *Histoire de Pilote et des éditions Dargaud* and *Histoire du journal et des éditions*

Vaillant; of Philippe Brun's *Histoire du journal Spirou et des publications des éditions Dupuis* and of the complementary *L'Âge d'or du journal Spirou* by François-Xavier Burdeyron; and especially of Pierre Ory's *Le Petit Nazi illustré* (The Little Illustrated Nazi) which chronicles the history of the infamous children's weekly *Le Téméraire* put out to propagate Nazi ideology during the years of the German occupation. Of special interest are reminiscences written by insiders: Odile Choron, wife of the former editor of *Hara-Kiri* and *Charlie*, wrote *La Petite Histoire de Hara-Kiri et Charlie Hebdo*; Jacques Dumas ("Marijac") told of the early days of the publication he founded in *Histoire de Coq Hardi 1944–45*; while *Happy Birthday Mickey!: 50 ans d'histoire de Mickey* was authored by this publication's former editor, Michel Mandry. Finally, Yves Frémion, long-time columnist with *Charlie*, has painted an acerbic portrait of that and other "new wave" comics publications in *Les Nouveaux Petits Miquets*, later supplemented by an even more caustic look at the contemporary scene in *L'ABC de la BD*.

Once we move away from more general works and come to monographs, the bibliography becomes almost endless: there seems to be no corner in the vast field of comics literature, no matter how small, that the French have left untouched. In *Vroom, tchac, zowie: le ballon dans la bande dessinée* the noted movie critic Robert Benayoun has been among the first to explore the significance, narrative and symbolic, of the comics' more celebrated convention, the speech balloon; while with *Le Noir et blanc dans la bande dessinée* Couperie has contributed an excellent aesthetic study of the daily strip. *À la rencontre des super-héros* by Gérard Courtial is interesting since it offers a distinctly Gallic perspective on that most American of comic-book clichés, the superhero. As could be expected, the field of sexy and erotic comics has received special attention from the French. Jacques Sadoul was first to labor in that particular vineyard with a sparkling anthology, *L'Enfer des bulles* (a title that can be literally translated as "The Balloon Inferno," but that would not do justice to its very French connotations). With *Érotisme et pornographie dans la bande dessinée*, Michel Bourgeois was even more comprehensive and explicit but, unfortunately, not half as witty as Sadoul. The most voluminous study on the subject has come from the well-known authority Joseph-Marie Lo Duca, author of *Luxure de luxe* (which covers illustration as well as comics).

On individual authors and their works there is an even more staggering mass of literature, with some artists eliciting a greater degree of inspiration and insight from their biographers and critics than others. Nineteenth-century Swiss pioneer Rodolphe Töpffer gets his due in A. Blondel's thorough biography of the man and his work, rightly titled *Rodolphe Töpffer, l'écrivain, l'artiste et l'homme*. In his study of Christophe (simply titled *Christophe*), François Caradec lovingly but incisively retraces the somewhat paradoxical career of the artist later turned scientist whom the French hail as "the inventor of the comics": he wasn't that, but he certainly was the creator of some inspired comic characters, and Caradec puts his work in its proper perspective. In his *Pellos* Pierre Pascal gives us a portrait of yet another "grand old man" of French comics (of the twentieth century this time), in a concise yet illuminating account. No comics creator has garnered as much commentary, exegesis, and appreciation (sometimes bordering on hagiography) as Hergé. The classic account of the Belgian artist's greatest creation remains Pol Vandromme's voluminous study *Le Monde de Tintin*: in perceptiveness and sweep it stands unsurpassed. Benoît Peeters in his almost similarly titled *Le Monde d'Hergé* extended Vandromme's analysis beyond Tintin to include some of the artist's more obscure creations; while Numa Sadoul (not to be confused with Jacques Sadoul) in *Entretiens avec Hergé* traced an affectionate but revealing portrait of the man through a series of interviews he conducted with him. In *Les Héritiers d'Hergé* Bruno Lecigne paid particular attention to the artistic and narrative tradition Hergé founded, a tradition still carried on by Hergé's "heirs" of the so-called Brussels school. Among these, E. P. Jacobs was undoubtedly the most famous and received an excellent study in Claude Le Gallo's *Le Monde d'E. P. Jacobs* (there *is* a sameness in all those titles).

Tintin's only rival in the little world of French comics is Astérix. The character and his national significance were well documented in André Stoll's *Astérix, l'épopée burlesque de la France*, while Goscinny, the strip's co-creator, was the subject of a revealing monograph, *René Goscinny*, by C. J. Philippe. Jean Giraud is unarguably the best-known of current French comics creators (under the twin personas of Gir and Moebius), and he has accordingly received much critical and biographical attention. Numa Sadoul has given us a lively study of the artist's work in his ironically titled *Mister Moebius et Docteur Gir*, and this can be supplemented by the no less entertaining *Les Carnets volés du major* (The Major's Stolen Notebooks) by Thierry Smolderen.

Other biographies of interest are Faur's excellent *Tillieux, écrivain, dessinateur et scénariste* and the remarkable *Tardi* by Thierry Groensteen, the editor of the monthly *Les Cahiers de la bande dessinée*. In addition, a number of cartoonists have written memoirs or autobiographies. The more noteworthy are Jacobs' *Trente années de bandes dessinées* and *Un opéra de papier* (A Paper Opera, the title referring to the artist's early career as a baritone at the Brussels opera house), Uderzo's lavishly illustrated *De Flamberge à Astérix*, and Franquin and Gillain's *Comment on devient créateur de B.D.* In a class by itself is Saint-Ogan's *Je me souviens de Zig et Puce et de quelques autres*, wherein the author shares his fond memories of the characters he created and of the Paris scene in the prewar years.

In *Bande dessinée et culture* the sociologist Évelyne Sullerot related the comics to France's broader cultural context, pointing out that the form has enjoyed the strong support of some of the most distinguished members of the cultural elite (Picasso, Cocteau, Barthes, to name a few). One of the comics' staunchest (and earliest) supporters has been the filmmaker and member of the French Academy René Clair, whose thoughts on the subject were later collected in *Notes sur les bandes dessinées*. All this advocacy eventually prompted educators (hitherto vociferous in their rejection of the comics) to reevaluate their position. Antoine Roux's *La Bande dessinée peut être éducative* (Comics Can Be Educational) was the first step toward acceptance (or perhaps resignation). More specialized studies on the pedagogical possibilities of the comics have since appeared, notably Pierre Masson's illuminating *Lire la bande dessinée*, as well as *Lecture et bande dessinée* and *Histoire et bande dessinée*, both edited by Faur, and many others which can be found in the bibliography. To crown the entire edifice there is the gargantuan *La Bande dessinée à l'Université . . . et ailleurs* (Comics in the University . . . and Elsewhere), an invaluable sum of knowledge compiled by Pierre Massart, Jean-Luc Nicks, and Jean-Louis Tilleuil, which goes well beyond the topic of comics in college into a general discussion of comics in society (the "and elsewhere" of the title). This is absolute "must" reading if only for its voluminous bibliography (over 150 pages long!); for the researcher it is a good place to start—and for this writer a good place to conclude.

BIBLIOGRAPHY

Alessandrini, Marjorie, ed. *Encyclopédie des bandes dessinées*. Paris: Michel, 1979.

Apostolidès, Jean-Marc. *Les Métamorphoses de Tintin*. Paris: Seghers, 1984.

Baron-Carvais, Annie. *Les Bandes dessinées*. Paris: Collection "Que sais-je?" Presses Universitaires de France, 1985.

Benayoun, Robert. *Vroom, tchac, zowie: le ballon dans la bande dessinée*. Paris: Balland, 1968.

Béra, Michel; Denni, Michel; and Mellot, Philippe. *Trésors de la bande dessinée*. Paris: Éditions de l'Amateur, 1988.

Blanchard, Gérard. *Histoire de la bande dessinée*. Verviers, Belgium: Marabout, 1969.

Blondel, Auguste. *Rodolphe Töpffer: l'écrivain, l'artiste et l'homme*. Geneva: Slatkine, 1976.

Bourgeois, Michel. *Érotisme et pornographie dans la bande dessinée*. Grenoble: Glénat, 1978.

Bronson, Philippe. *Guide de la bande dessinée*. Paris: Temps futurs, 1984.

Brun, Philippe. *Histoire du journal Spirou et des publications des éditions Dupuis*. Grenoble: Glénat, 1975.

Burdeyron, François-Xavier. *L'Âge d'or du journal Spirou*. Marseilles: Bédésup, 1988.

Caradec, François. *Christophe*. Paris: Grasset, 1956.

Choron, Odile. *La Petite Histoire de Hara-Kiri et Charlie Hebdo*. Paris: Menges, 1983.

Clair, René. *Notes sur les bandes dessinées*. Paris: Institut de France, 1974.

Couperie, Pierre. *Le Noir et blanc dans la bande dessinée*. Paris: Serg, 1972.

Couperie, Pierre, and Horn, Maurice. *A History of the Comic Strip*. New York: Crown, 1968.

Courtial, Gérard. *À la rencontre des super-héros*. Marseilles: Bédésup, 1985.

Davis, Allen F., ed. *For Better or Worse: The American Influence in the World*. Westport, Conn.: Greenwood Press, 1981.

De Laet, Danny, and Varende, Yves. *Beyond the Seventh Art: History of the Belgian Strip Cartoon*. Brussels: Ministry of Foreign Affairs, 1979.

Duc, B. *L'Art de la bande dessinée*. Grenoble: Glénat, 1982–83.

Dumas, Jacques (Marijac). *Histoire de Coq Hardi 1944–45*. Paris: Éditions de Château-dun, 1981.

Durand, Marion, and Gérard, Bertrand. *L'Image dans le livre pour enfants*. Paris: L'École des Loisirs, 1975.

Eco, Umberto. *Travels in Hyperreality*. New York: Harcourt Brace Jovanovich, 1986.

Escarpit, Denise. *Les Exigences de l'image dans le livre de la première enfance*. Paris: Magnard, 1973.

Faur, Jean-Claude, ed. *À la rencontre de la bande dessinée*. Marseilles: Bédésup, 1983.

———. *Histoire et bande dessinée*. Marseilles: Bédésup, 1979.

———. *Lecture et bande dessinée*. Aix: Édisud, 1977.

———. *Tillieux, écrivain, dessinateur et scénariste*. Marseilles: Bibliothèque de Marseille, 1983.

Filippini, Henri. *Histoire de Pilote et des éditions Dargaud*. Grenoble: Glénat, 1977.

———. *Histoire du journal et des éditions Vaillant*. Grenoble: Glénat, 1978.

———. *Les Années cinquante*. Grenoble: Glénat, 1977.

François, Édouard. *L'Âge d'or de la bande dessinée*. Paris: Serg, 1971.

Franquin, André, and Gillain, Joseph. *Comment on devient créateur de B.D.*. Verviers, Belgium: Marabout, 1969.

Frémion, Yves. *L'ABC de la BD*. Tournai, Belgium: Casterman, 1983.

———. *Les Nouveaux Petits Miquets*. Paris: Le Citron Hallucinogène, 1982.

Fresnault-Deruelle, Pierre. *La Bande dessinée: essai d'analyse sémiotique*. Paris: Hachette, 1972.

———. *Récits et discours par la bande, essais sur les comics*. Paris: Hachette, 1977.

Garriock, P. R. *Masters of Comic Book Art*. New York: Images Graphiques, 1978.

Glénat, Jacques, et al. *Histoire de la BD en France et en Belgique*. 2d ed. Grenoble: Glénat, 1984.

Groensteen, Thierry. *Tardi*. Brussels: Magic Strip, 1980.

Henriot, Jean-Jacques. *L'Enfant, l'image et les médias*. Dammarie-les-Lys: SDT, 1982.

Horn, Maurice. *Comics of the American West*. New York: Winchester Press, 1977.

———. *Sex in the Comics*. New York: Chelsea House, 1985.

———. *Women in the Comics*. New York: Chelsea House, 1977.

Horn, Maurice, ed. *The World Encyclopedia of Cartoons*. New York: Chelsea House, 1980.

———, ed. *The World Encyclopedia of Comics*. New York: Chelsea House, 1976.

Informations & Documents (France), May 1, 1967. Special issue devoted to comics.

Informations & Documents, August 1974. Special issue devoted to comics.

Inge, M. Thomas, ed. *Handbook of American Popular Culture*. 3 vols. Westport, Conn.: Greenwood Press, 1978–81.

Jacobs, Edgar-P. *Un opéra de papier*. Paris: Gallimard, 1981.

———. *Trente années de bandes dessinées*. Paris: Littaye, 1973.

Kempkes, Wolfgang. *International Bibliography of Comics Literature*. New York: R. R. Bowker, 1974.

Lacassin, Francis. *Pour un neuvième art: la bande dessinée*. Paris: Plon, 1971.

Lecigne, Bruno. *Avanies et mascarades: l'évolution de la bande dessinée en France dans les années 70*. Paris: Futuropolis, 1981.

———. *Les Héritiers d'Hergé*. Brussels: Magic Strip, 1983.

Lecigne, Bruno, and Tamine, Jean-Pierre. *Fac-similé*. Paris: Futuropolis, 1983.

Le Gallo, Claude. *Le Monde d'E. P. Jacobs*. Brussels: Lombard, 1984.

Leguèbe, Eric. *Le Voyage en ballon*. Marseilles: Bédésup, 1984.

————. *Voyage en Cartoonland*. Paris: Serg, 1977.

Leguèbe, Wilbur. *La Société des bulles*. Brussels: La Vie Ouvrière, 1977.

Lent, John A. *Comic Art: An International Bibliography*. Drexel Hill, Penna.: John A. Lent, 1987.

Les Lettres Françaises (France), June 30, 1966. Special issue devoted to comics.

Livres Hebdo (France), December 8, 1981. Special issue devoted to comics.

Lo Duca, Joseph-Marie. *Luxure de luxe*. Paris: Dominique Leroy, 1983.

Mandry, Michel. *Happy Birthday Mickey!: 50 ans d'histoire de Mickey*. Paris: Éditions du Chêne, 1984.

Marny, Jacques. *Le Monde étonnant des bandes dessinées*. Paris: Le Centurion, 1968.

Massart, Pierre; Nicks, Jean-Luc; and Tilleuil, Jean-Louis. *La Bande dessinée à l'Université . . . et ailleurs*. Louvain: Presses Universitaires de Louvain, 1984.

Masson, Pierre. *Lire la bande dessinée*. Lyon: Presses Universitaires de Lyon, 1985.

Moliterni, Claude, ed. *Histoire de la bande dessinée d'expression française*. Paris: Serg, 1972.

————. *Histoire mondiale de la bande dessinée*. Paris: Pierre Horay, 1980.

Ory, Pierre. *Le Petit Nazi illustré*. Paris: Albatros, 1979.

Pascal, Pierre. *Pellos*. Angoulême: Sodieg, 1977.

Passamonick, Didier. *L'Expo 58 et le style atome*. Brussels: Magic Strip, 1983.

Peeters, Benoît. *Le Monde d'Hergé*. Tournai: Casterman, 1983.

Peignot, Jérôme. *Les Copains de votre enfance*. Paris: Denoël, 1963.

Pernin, Georges. *Un monde étrange, la bande dessinée*. Paris: Clédor, 1974.

Philippe, Claude-Jean. *René Goscinny*. Paris: Seghers, 1976.

Pierre, Michel. *La Bande dessinée*. Paris: Larousse, 1976.

Reitberger, Reinhold, and Fuchs, Wolfgang. *Comics: Anatomy of a Mass Medium*. Boston: Little, Brown, 1971.

Renard, Jean-Bruno. *Clefs pour la bande dessinée*. Paris: Seghers, 1978.

Rey, Alain. *Les Spectres de la bande: essai sur la BD*. Paris: Minuit, 1978.

Roux, Antoine. *La Bande dessinée peut être éducative*. Paris: Éditions de l'École, 1970.

Sadoul, Jacques. *L'Enfer des bulles*. Paris: Pauvert, 1968.

————. *Panorama de la bande dessinée*. Paris: J'ai lu, 1976.

Sadoul, Numa. *Portraits à la plume et au pinceau*. Grenoble: Glénat, 1976.

————. *Mister Moebius et Docteur Gir*. Paris: Michel, 1976.

————. *Entretiens avec Hergé*. Brussels: Casterman, 1983.

Saint-Ogan, Alain. *Je me souviens de Zig et Puce et de quelques autres*. Paris: La Table Ronde, 1961.

Smolderen, Thierry. *Les Carnets volés du major, ou les aventures de Moebius*. Paris: Schlirf Book, 1984.

Soriano, Marc. *Guide de la littérature pour la jeunesse*. Paris: Flammarion, 1975.

Sternberg, Jacques; Caen, Michel; and Lob, Jacques. *Les Chefs-d'oeuvre de la bande dessinée*. Paris: Planète, 1967.

Stoll, André. *Astérix, l'épopée burlesque de la France*. Paris: Éditions Complexes, 1978.

Sullerot, Évelyne. *Bande dessinée et culture*. Paris: Opera Mundi, 1966.

Tabuche, Bernard. *À la découverte des bandes dessinées occitanes*. Nîmes: Marpoc, 1987.

Tibéri, Jean-Paul. *La Bande dessinée et le cinéma*. Paris: Regards, 1981.

Uderzo, Albert. *De Flamberge à Astérix*. Paris: Philippsen, 1985.
Vandromme, Pol. *Le Monde de Tintin*. Paris: Gallimard, 1959.

Periodicals

L'Année de la bande dessinée (annual), Paris, 1981–83; Grenoble, 1984–.
Bédésup (quarterly), Marseilles.
Les Cahiers de la bande dessinée (monthly), Brussels.
Le Collectionneur de bandes dessinées (monthly), Paris.
Hop (quarterly), Aurillac.

Reprints and Anthologies (in English)

Bartier, Pierre, and Pellaert, Guy. *The Adventures of Jodelle*. New York: Grove Press, 1966.
Bilal, Enki. *Gods in Chaos*. New York: Catalan Communications, 1987.
———. *The Woman Trap*. Catalan, 1988.
Bilal, Enki, and Dionnet, Jean-Pierre. *Exterminator 17*. Catalan, 1986.
Bretécher, Claire. *Frustration*. New York: Grove Press, 1987.
Cazamayou, Philippe (Caza). *Escape from Suburbia*. New York: NBM, 1987.
Charyn, Jerome, and Boucq, François. *The Magician's Wife*. New York: Catalan Communications, 1988.
Christin, Pierre, and Mézières, Jean-Claude. *Ambassador of the Shadows*. New York: Dargaud, 1984.
———. *Heroes of the Equinox*. Dargaud, 1984.
———. *Welcome to Alflofol*. Dargaud, 1984.
———. *The World without Stars*. Dargaud, 1984.
Culliford, Pierre (Peyo). *The Astrosmurfs*. New York: Random, 1982.
———. *The Smurfs and the Howlibird*. Random, 1983.
Forest, Jean-Claude. *Barbarella*. New York: Grove Press, 1966.
Forest, Jean-Claude, and Gillon, Paul. *Lost in Time*. New York: NBM, 1986.
Giraud, Jean (Moebius). *Moebius: The Collected Fantasies of Jean Giraud*. 6 vols. New York: Marvel Entertainment Group, 1987–88.
Giraud, Jean, and Jodorowsky, Alexandro. *The Incal*. 3 vols. Marvel, 1988.
Goscinny, René, and Uderzo, Albert. *Asterix and the Great Crossing*. New York: Dargaud, 1984.
———. *Asterix and Cleopatra*. Montreal: Dargaud Canada, 1978.
———. *Asterix in Britain*. Dargaud Canada, 1979.
———. *Asterix the Gaul*. Dargaud Canada, 1978.
———. *Asterix the Gladiator*. Dargaud Canada, 1979.
Greg, Michel. *Walter Melon*. New York: Dargaud, 1981.
Hergé, *see* Rémi, Georges.
Leloup, Roger. *Vulcan's Forge*. New York: Comcat, 1989.
Loisel, Régis, and Le Tendre, Serge. *Roxanna and the Search for the Time Bird*. 4 vols. New York: NBM, 1988–89.
Paringaux, Philippe, and Loustal, Jacques. *Love Shots*. New York: Catalan Communications, 1988.

Rémi, Georges (Hergé). *The Black Island*. Boston: Atlantic, Little-Brown, 1975.

————. *The Blue Lotus*. Atlantic, 1984.

————. *The Broken Ear*. Atlantic, 1978.

————. *The Calculus Affair*. Atlantic, 1976.

————. *The Castafiore Emerald*. Atlantic, 1975.

————. *The Crab with the Golden Claws*. Atlantic, 1974.

————. *Destination Moon*. Atlantic, 1976.

————. *Explorers on the Moon*. Atlantic, 1976.

————. *King Ottokar's Scepter*. Atlantic, 1974.

————. *The Land of Black Gold*. Atlantic, 1975.

————. *Prisoners of the Sun*. Atlantic, 1975.

————. *Red Rackham's Treasure*. Atlantic, 1974.

————. *The Secret of the Unicorn*. Atlantic, 1974.

————. *The Seven Crystal Balls*. Atlantic, 1975.

————. *Tintin in America*. Atlantic, 1979.

————. *Tintin and the Picaros*. Atlantic, 1978.

Schuiten, François, and Peeters, Benoît. *The Great Wall of Samaris*. New York: NBM, 1987.

Turk, Philippe, and DeGroot, Bob. *Leonardo Is a Genius*. New York: Dargaud, 1984.

Van Hamme, Jean, and Rosinski, Gregor. *Thorgal, Child of the Stars*. Virginia Beach, Va.: Donning, 1986.

————. *Thorgal: The Archers*. Donning, 1987.

————. *Thorgal: The Sorceress Betrayed*. Donning, 1988.

3

Detective/Mystery/ Spy Fiction

FRANZ G. BLAHA

Detective fiction is arguably the most widely read subgenre of popular literature in France. Because of the great variety of media through which detective fiction is presented to the public—ranging from the highly literary *nouveaux romans policiers* of Alain Robbe-Grillet and Michel Butor to the comic-strip detectives of the pulp magazines—the consumers of detective fiction in France are not limited to a narrow socioeconomic range. According to Josée Dupuy (*Le Roman policier*), 25 million copies of mystery and suspense novels were sold in France in 1970; 60 percent of the volumes in lending libraries were novels, of which half belonged into the mystery/suspense category. Dupuy cites further studies (G. Jean; A. Mareuil) which show that detective novels are the preferred leisure reading material in France among all age groups, occupations, and educational groups: "Thus socio-cultural barriers, generation gaps . . . seem to disappear as far as the reader of detective fiction is concerned." In *Les Mots*, Jean-Paul Sartre confesses that he prefers detective novels from the *Série noire* to the works of Wittgenstein. This popularity becomes even more evident if one includes detective films and television programs in the scope of investigation. France has played a leading role in the history of the film detective, lending the name *film noir* to films based on novels by writers of the American "hardboiled" school of the 1930s and 1940s and culminating in filmed versions of the French *romans noirs* of the post–World War II era.

In spite of the popularity and the venerable tradition of French detective fiction, critical attention to the genre does not begin until the 1940s. Moreover, most critical works written in French do not devote themselves to a detailed study of French detective fiction, but are for the most part histories of the genre at large, devoting most of their attention to Anglo-American writers and giving little attention to any French authors, except to those (Gaboriau, Leroux, Leblanc,

Simenon) who are acknowledged international masters of the genre. Most studies of detective fiction written in English limit themselves to a discussion of these same authors; thus, material for the study of all but the internationally famous French mystery writers has to be gathered from a slowly increasing number of articles and "special issues" of French literary journals, as well as from fan magazines like *Enigmatika, Les Amis du crime, Bulletin 813, L'Almanach du crime: L'Année du roman policier* (after 1985 published as *L'Année du polar*).

While information about French detective fiction is sparse in the English language, a number of excellent studies on the subject have been published in German and Italian.

HISTORICAL OUTLINE

Prehistory

Scholars of detective fiction have tried for half a century to make the genre more respectable by giving it venerable ancestors, preferably dating back to Classical antiquity and the Bible. It will suffice here, for the purpose of this historical overview of French detective fiction, to mention only those historical sources which affect the creation of the first French mystery novels, that is, those of Émile Gaboriau and his successors.

The history of the detective novel is intricately connected with the development of police forces. In this regard, France played a leading role in Europe by establishing in 1667 the Haute Police of Paris under the direction of Général de La Reynie. This new police force kindled the public interest through its role in the famous poisoning cases of the Marquise de Brinvilliers (1676) and of Madame Monvoisin (1679), which feature prominently in the *Causes célèbres et intéressantes* (1734) by François Gayot de Pitaval. Pitaval's "true" stories of sensational crimes and their discovery became as popular, both with legal experts and the general reading public, as they were despised by literary critics. Subsequent editors of the more than twenty volumes of the *Causes célèbres* "improved" Pitaval's style and, as one of them, François Richer, confessed, took care "to arrange the material in such a way that the reader cannot spot at once how a case will end and what verdict will be pronounced. He will remain in a state of uncertainty during the development of the action and in that way, I believe, each case will become more gripping, with the reader's attention captivated to the end." This creation of suspense, combined with the growing popularity of the puzzle story (e.g., Voltaire's *Zadig*, 1747), established the Pitaval story as the prototype for crime literature in France and all of Europe.

Crime stories up to the nineteenth century were based almost exclusively on historical crimes and criminals, as well as on the exploits of real law enforcement figures, with the latter being given only secondary billing. After the turn of the century, novels featuring fictional criminals began to grow in number: we find criminal main characters in several novels by Honoré de Balzac and, more popularly, Ponson du Terrail's character Rocambole. At the same time, the figure of the fictional detective begins to make his appearance in France: it is significant that the stimulus comes from a criminal turned policeman—Eugène François Vidocq (1775–1857).

Given to criminal exploits even as a child, Vidocq spent some time in the army, was convicted of forgery in 1796 and sentenced to eight years in prison. After escaping, he joined a group of bandits, whom he later betrayed to the police. He offered his services as informer to the Paris police and was appointed head of the Brigade de Sûreté in 1812. After initial triumphs, his co-workers and his methods came under increasing attack, forcing him to resign in 1825. His *Mémoires* (1828–29) became a great popular success, mainly because Vidocq described in great detail his successes as detective and the methods he used to solve his cases. Vidocq's technique was based on his intimate knowledge of the criminal milieu, his physical strength, and his ability to disguise himself, more than on brilliant analysis. While his *Mémoires* have been exposed as self-serving and mendacious, their influence on the development of detective fiction is beyond doubt. Edgar Allan Poe made his detective, C. Auguste Dupin, a Frenchman and had his exploits take place in Paris. Eugène Sue (*Les Mystères de Paris*, 1842–43) gave a suspenseful panorama of the Parisian underworld, as did Alexandre Dumas *père* in his novel *Les Mohicans de Paris* (1854), whose detective, Jackal, is a mixture between Vidocq and Gaboriau's Monsieur Lecoq, according to Régis Messac. In this novel, the famous phrase "Cherchez la femme" was used for the first time.

Classical Detective Fiction

In 1846 the French public was introduced to Poe's Dupin stories in a translation by Charles Baudelaire; paradoxically, their effect on the French detective novel was more immediate than even in England or the United States. Émile Gaboriau (1832–73) acknowledged his debt to Poe's detective stories, but it was Gaboriau who transformed the American author's "philosophical tales" into full-blown detective novels. At the time of Baudelaire's translation, the long serial novel was the most popular form of literature in France—Gaboriau started as assistant to Paul Féval, one of the most famous writers of *romans feuilletons* (serial novels) at the time. In 1859 Gaboriau launched his own literary career with several serial novels; in his eighth novel, *L'Affaire Lerouge* (1866) (The Widow Lerouge), he introduced police detective Monsieur Lecoq, still inferior to the amateur Père Tabaret in this book, and created the first detective *novel* in world literature. Gaboriau is responsible for shifting the interest of the French reading public from the figure of the criminal to that of the police detective, a significant feature of French detective fiction which has much less interest in private/amateur detectives than its Anglo-American counterpart, as evidenced by the most popular French term for the genre: *(roman) policier*. This growing fascination with the policeman as protagonist can be seen in Gaboriau's subsequent novels in which

Père Tabaret (the direct descendant of C. Auguste Dupin) recedes into the background and Lecoq takes center stage (*Le Dossier no. 113*, 1867 [File No. 113]; *Le Crime d'Orcival*, 1867 [Crime at Orcival]; *Les Esclaves de Paris*, 1868 [The Slaves of Paris]; *Monsieur Lecoq*, 1869; *Le Petit Vieux de Batignolles*, 1876).

Gaboriau's novels were read widely all over the world: Chekhov acknowledged the author's influence on his own *A Hunting Tragedy*, and Bismarck was an enthusiastic Gaboriau reader. In France, Fortuné du Boisgobey (1821–91) and Pierre Zaccone (1817–95) became the most popular of the many Gaboriau imitators; lesser proselytes are Jean Bruno and Simon Boubée. Conan Doyle's first Sherlock Holmes novel, *A Study in Scarlet*, is an exact structural copy of Gaboriau's novels, and E. F. Bleiler correctly states that "If Poe's Dupin was the father of Tabaret and Lecoq, Tabaret and Lecoq are the father and godfather of Sherlock Holmes."

Many French detective novels after Gaboriau's appeared only in serial form in the newspapers and are thus no longer accessible to the general reader. Information about the works and the authors is sparse, and names like Jules Mary, Paul Bellet, Albert Bizouard, Gustave Graux, Édouard Gachot, Alfred Blamont, and A. de Chamarande (all listed in Olivier-Martin, "Origines secrètes du roman policier français") are no longer household words. Today the detective story is considered all over the world predominantly an Anglo-American product; yet in 1889 there was no doubt in Robert Louis Stevenson's mind that detective fiction was "a lady of French origin."

After the turn of the century, the main influence on French detective fiction changed from Gaboriau to Conan Doyle and his brother-in-law, Ernest Hornung (1866–1921). Hornung's charming gentleman thief Raffles serves as the model for the equally famous Arsène Lupin of Maurice Leblanc (1864–1941). Lupin, like Raffles, does not steal from avaricious motives: his greatest challenge and pleasure is to dupe the police, represented by Inspector Ganimard. His outstanding talent is disguise. Under the pseudonym of Monsieur Lenormand he even manages to act as head of the Sûreté for four years, conscientiously trying to catch Arsène Lupin! Lupin figures in some thirty books by Leblanc and has been resurrected by Boileau-Narcejac in the 1970s.

A more sinister French cousin of Raffles is Fantômas, the protagonist of a large number of novels, often in "pulp" format, written by Marcel Allain (1885–1969) and Pierre Souvestre (1874–1914). Fantômas is the king of criminals; he is a phantom who takes the law into his own hands, often in sadistic fashion. The French surrealists saw in him the incarnation of Nietzsche's "superman," unburdened by moral scruples. Fantômas appears to have proletarian roots; his popularity with the masses stems from his ability to break the rules of the social order which favor the rich, and to be able to do so without being punished. Allain and Souvestre took three days to plan a novel, three further days to write it, and four days for corrections. Thus every ten days a Fantômas novel appeared until Souvestre's death slowed down the output. The Fantômas series and its imitators, notably Léon Sazie's "Zigomar" novels, discredit the romantic nineteenth-century notion that crime does not pay and are, with their proletarian bias and their often uncomfortable cruelty, particularly toward women, a preview of the vision of the hardboiled *romans noirs* of the second half of the twentieth century.

The era between World Wars I and II is often called "The Golden Age" of detective fiction. It is a period of middle-class complacency, already nostalgic, which wants to see itself reflected in literature as stable, moral, intelligent, rational, and tasteful. It looks with distaste at proletarian muckrakers and would rather overlook the obvious urbanization and mechanization of contemporary life. Crime is seen as a personal and psychological phenomenon rather than a social one, and the protagonists of the moral fantasies of the public are educated, upper-middle-class pillars of society. In France the models for the detective novel of the "Golden Age" are Conan Doyle and the early masters of the "orthodox" or "classical" detective stories, such as Agatha Christie, Dorothy L. Sayers, S. S. Van Dine. It is the only period in French detective fiction that features a significant number of amateur detectives, most of them patterned after Sherlock Holmes or his French counterpart, Joseph Joséphin "Rouletabille," the creation of Gaston Leroux (1868–1927).

Leroux's masterpiece is the novel *Le Mystère de la chambre jaune*, 1907 (*The Mystery of the Yellow Room*), a locked-room mystery that involves the young journalist-detective in an Oedipal adventure which continues into the sequel, *Le Parfum de la dame en noir*, 1908 (*The Perfume of the Lady in Black*). These novels popularized the "classical" detective story in France by severing the connection between the serial novel and the mystery and by introducing the French reading public to the *roman-problème*, the puzzle novel à la Sherlock Holmes. After 1927, the collections of detective fiction edited by the major French publishing houses experienced a tremendous surge in readership. The leading collection was *Le Masque*, edited by Albert Pigasse and started in 1927. The competing collection, *L'Empreinte*, edited by Alexandre Ralli, acquainted French readers with such masters of classical detective fiction as Freeman Wills Crofts, R. Austin Freeman, Ellery Queen, and Anthony Berkeley. The main significance of both these series is that they provided models for French mystery writers. In addition, Pigasse created additional incentives for French mystery authors to compete with the foreign masters by creating the Prix du Roman d'aventures in 1930. The winners of this literary award constitute the Hall of Fame of French detective fiction between the World Wars: Pierre Véry, Stanislas-André Steeman, Jean Bommart, Yves Dartois, Pierre Apestéguy, and Noël Vindry. Although most of them do not adhere strictly to the "rules" laid down by S. S. Van Dine, Ronald Knox, and W. H. Auden—Vindry is the exception—the Anglo-American influence is evident in all of them. Only Georges Simenon was able to create an authentically French detective during that period; his Maigret series began to appear in 1931. Astonishingly, he wrote nineteen Maigret novels in only nineteen months and published them between 1931 and 1934: ten (!) in 1931; seven in 1932; and one each in 1933 and 1934. After putting Maigret aside for a decade, he revived the famous police inspector once more after World War II and wrote approximately two to four Maigret novels a year until 1973. Altogether, some eighty Maigret stories have been published.

Maigret is the exact opposite of Sherlock Holmes. He is a milieu sleuth; that is, when he is called upon to solve a case, he first acclimatizes himself to the environment, visits local pubs, and strikes up conversations without really investigating. Only when he is thoroughly familiar with the milieu does he proceed to the details of the case. Thomas Narcejac correctly traces Maigret's parentage to Balzac rather than to Poe or Conan Doyle. Simenon's detective novels move the French *roman policier* still further away from the orthodox puzzle/mystery novel and stimulate the growth of the psychological milieu mystery which has replaced the classical detective novel in most Western countries. Colin Dexter's Inspector Morse, Friedrich Dürrenmatt's Kommissar Bärlach, and Sjowall-Wahlöö's Martin Beck are all descendants of Jules Maigret.

It should not be forgotten that, as in England and America, a number of renowned French "mainstream" authors wrote respectable detective novels. Alexandre Arnoux (*Rêveries d'un policier amateur*, 1951), Georges Bernanos (*Un crime*, 1935), Claude Aveline (*La Double Mort de Frédéric Belot*, 1932, and *Voiture 7, place 15*, 1937), as well as Léon Bloy can serve as examples, and it is an ill-kept secret that President Edgar Faure wrote detective novels under the pseudonym of Edgar Sanday.

"Hardboiled" Detective Fiction

According to Boileau-Narcejac, the classical mystery novel is a product of peacetime. It assumes an essentially hale world dominated by reason. This view of a sane, rational world is destroyed in Europe by World War II, which, contrary to World War I, was a war of civilian horrors which, according to Boileau-Narcejac, destroyed the very idea of peace and reason. The resulting climate of disillusionment, fear, and despair shattered the myth of the logical investigation with its resultant inevitable solutions. Thus the popular formula that epitomizes the myth of a rational, intact world, that is, the orthodox detective novel, had to give way to a more appropriate moral fantasy. This transition can be seen in the disappearance of the popular French detective series, like Ralli's *L'Empreinte* and Gallimard's *Le Scarabée d'Or*, and their replacement by Marcel Duhamel's famous *Série noire*.

The model for the new detective novel is the American "hardboiled" thriller of the 1930s. In France, however, the models for the new *roman noir* are not Dashiell Hammett and Raymond Chandler but the "fake Americans" Peter Cheyney and James Hadley Chase. The American hardboiled detective novel portrays society as inherently corrupt, crime as ubiquitous, and logic and reason as inadequate opponents for brutality, perversion, and greed. Hence, crime is no longer an individual, isolated act of a brilliant or, as in Simenon's work, of a diseased mind, but a symptom of a diseased out-of-joint world, where the laws of the jungle govern the battle for power and material goods.

> The unwary reader should take heed: the volumes in the *Série noire* cannot be put into everybody's hands without risk. The devotee of puzzles à la Sherlock Holmes will not always get his money's worth, nor will the chronic optimist. . . . There will be policemen more corrupt than the criminals they pursue. The congenial detective will not always solve the mystery. Sometimes there will not be a mystery. And sometimes, there won't be any detective at all. . . .
>   Then what's left? . . . There is also love—preferably wild—there is unbridled passion, hate without mercy, all feelings which are given voice only rarely in a well-policed society but which are common currency here and which are mostly expressed in a nonacademic language always dominated by HUMOR, black or rosy.

Marcel Duhamel's introduction to Gallimard's *Série noire* (my translation) expresses the change in approach in the new French detective novel. Although the collection, started in 1947, at first published only American authors, French writers were soon added to the series but counseled to write under American pseudonyms. The best-known are Terry Stewart (pseudonym of Serge Laforest) and John Amila (pseudonym of Jean Meckert). The *roman noir*, particularly as published in the *Série noire* and later in the *Fleuve Noir* collection, dominated the French market until the late 1950s, when readers began to tire of the repetitive brutalities of the hardboiled genre, probably in connection with the postwar economic boom.

Contemporary Detective Fiction

Since the late 1950s the French detective novel is characterized by a synthesis of the *roman noir* with the psychological *roman-problème* in the style of Simenon's Maigret novels. This tradition has its origins in the novels of Jacques Decrest and Léo Malet, who are considered the godfathers of contemporary French detective fiction. Malet in particular created French *romans noirs* with the scurrilous private eye Nestor Burma, which were in all regards the equal of the works of Cheyney and Chase, but the public demanded American writers. Malet became famous with his series *Les Nouveaux Mystères de Paris*; his plan was to write one detective novel for every *arrondissement*, or district, of Paris, but he managed to finish only sixteen volumes before abandoning the project.

The acknowledged masters of the contemporary French detective novel are Frédéric Dard, Albert Simonin, and Alfred Le Breton. Their works are characterized by an intensification of the use of slang. Simonin in particular poses language problems even for French readers in his *grisbi* (slang term for "money") novels *Touchez pas au grisbi* (1954) and *Grisbi or not grisbi* (1955). A similar approach is used in Le Breton's *Du rififi chez les hommes* (1953), which is widely known outside of France through the film version.

Dard is easily the most popular writer of the contemporary French *polar* (the slang term for *roman policier* now popularly used in France). His detective hero, Commissaire San-Antonio, has even replaced Dard as the "author" on the title page of his books—in the style of Ellery Queen: the detective now tells the stories as "author." He is the hero of more than seventy widely read novels (over 100 million copies sold by 1984!) and has become a cult figure in French popular culture; a very expensive luxury edition of his collected works has been published, a tribute only very few mystery writers can claim. San-Antonio resembles Cheyney's Lemmy Caution and Fleming's James Bond: he is witty, audacious, attractive to all women, promiscuous, and patriotic. In Frédéric Dard/San-Antonio, the French detective novel has finally found its own national formula and has successfully cast off the culturally uncomfortable Anglo-American models.

The French detective novel of the 1970s and 1980s follows Dard's model; that is, it continues the literary tradition of the *roman-problème*, mixing it with the stringent social criticism of the French *roman noir*, and using a lively language suffused with contemporary argot. After the 1968 uprisings, the French detective novel has taken on distinct political overtones, with much of the dominant ideology provided by the Left. Thus the *néopolar français*, as some critics call it, is characterized by a pessimistic and combative mood and populated by young leftist anarchists. The best-known author of this group of "angry young men" is Jean-Patrick Manchette, who has described his form of detective fiction as "a very violent novel of social intervention." His antiheroes, in open warfare with their society, are urban guerrillas, contemporary "public enemies No. 1." Generally, this post-May '68 new wave in French detective fiction is closely tied to the *films noirs* of Philippe Fourastié, Costa-Gavras, Claude Chabrol, and Alain Corneau.

Espionage Fiction

Just as the development of detective fiction is tied to that of the policeman/detective, the history of the spy story is related to the changing role and the public image of the activity of spies. "Espionage can never be tolerated," exclaims Montesquieu. "It could only be tolerable if it were practiced by honest people, but the infamy required of the people allows us to measure the infamy of the activity itself." A hundred years later, General Baron Étienne-Alexandre Bardin concedes that spies might act from patriotic motives, and in the wake of World War II the significance of espionage for the outcome of the war is made public by histories and memoirs of intelligence operatives. Spies appeared as dramatis personae in classical detective stories (e.g., Agatha Christie's *The Mysterious Affair at Styles*), but the adventures of the heroes were still mainly light-hearted, as for example those of Capitaine Benoît in the adventure series written in the 1930s by Robert-Charles Dumas.

The first French espionage novelist of note is Pierre Nord (pseudonym for André Brouillard). Of his more than seventy books, several have won awards and a number of them have been made into films. His protagonist is Colonel Dubois, chief of French Counterintelligence, whom Nord introduced in his first novel, *Double Crime sur la ligne Maginot* (1936). Nord's characters are not yet the sadistic professional killers of the Cold War period. The main feature of his works is his satiric wit, which irreverently pokes fun at Americans, Russians, and mainly the French. This light-hearted face of the spy novel between the wars changes drastically after 1945 for reasons explained cleverly by Danielle Corbel in her doctoral dissertation "Roman d'espionnage et science politique" (1963), quoted in Hoveyda, *Histoire du roman policier* (1965). She asserts that before World War II, there was a very tentative link at best between the spy novel and political reality, which serves only as a faint background in prewar spy fiction. After World War II, Corbel continues, the spy novel begins to distance itself from the traditional adventure novel, to integrate itself into the political consciousness of the readers, and to parallel their view of international political reality. The spy novel becomes a propaganda weapon in the Cold War. An analysis of pre– and post–World War II novels of writers like Nord and Jean Bommart bears out Corbel's thesis.

The years after 1945 witness the growing popularity of the spy series, that is, the publication of a series of spy novels around a recurring spy hero. While Ian Fleming's James Bond has gained the greatest international following, several French spy heroes became at least as popular as their British colleague. Once again, as in the case of *Le Masque* and the *Série noire*, it is a publisher's collection which starts the new trend in France; this time it is *Le Fleuve Noir*, edited for the Presses de la Cité by Armand de Caro and launched in 1950.

The first popular French spy novelist in the *Fleuve Noir* series is Jean Bruce (pseudonym of Jean-Alexandre Brochet), whose fictional hero, Hubert Bonisseur de la Bath, is significantly a colonel in the CIA, known by the code name of OSS 117. Hoveyda considers the work of both Bruce and Paul Kenny (pseudonyms for Paul Libert and Gaston Gandenpanhuyse) inferior to that of Antoine Dominique (pseud. for Dominique Ponchardier), which features Le Gorille as hero. The Gorilla is, in Hoveyda's opinion, the equal of James Bond; his mission is usually the rescue of Western civilization from international gangsters by assassinating them.

Since 1960 the spy novel has clearly overtaken the detective novel in popularity, at least in France. As Boileau-Narcejac diagnosed correctly, the spy novel has become the illustrated journal of the present. It pretends to represent reality by authenticating every little detail, down to the street names and cigarette brands. Consequently, many of the contemporary spy novels pretend to be real intelligence material and the jargon is borrowed from the obfuscating language of Defense Ministry press releases. The spy novel has frozen into a much more rigid formula than the most formulaic detective novel—because of the frozen positions of the Cold War—and only a massive change in Western social or political structure could lead to a more flexible pattern in spy fiction. This inflexibility has logically invited parodies, such as those by Charles Exbrayat;

this tendency is certainly evident in the later filmed versions of James Bond novels, which no longer take themselves seriously.

It is interesting to note that the contemporary masters of spy fiction—Fleming, Kenny, Bruce, Ponchardier, Deighton, Le Carré—are British and French, not American as one might assume. It is in the activity of their fictional spy heroes that the readers in these countries can still maintain the illusion of playing an important role in the chilling chess game between East and West.

GUIDE TO THE LITERATURE

Background Works

No comprehensive history of French detective/espionage fiction is available in the English language. Indeed, this short survey is the only study in English devoted exclusively to the subject. For the student or scholar interested in a detailed study of detective fiction in general, the best starting point is Timothy Johnson's *Crime Fiction Criticism: An Annotated Bibliography*, although it omits some of the more theoretical scholarly works of recent years, particularly those employing a semiotic approach to the genre. Johnson lists approximately 2,000 works in English dealing with the subject. The reader interested specifically in French detective/espionage fiction will be disappointed.

There exists a large number of reference works dealing with detective fiction in general, most of them written in English. Detective/espionage fiction has become respectable as a subject of academic investigation in the last twenty years, and a substantial number of publications on the history, philosophy, typology, and sociology of the genre have been added to the less sophisticated material addressed mainly to the general reader.

The main source for finding titles of detective novels published in English is Hagen's *Who Done It? A Guide to Detective Mystery and Suspense Fiction*, which has been corrected and updated by Allen Hubin in his journal, *The Armchair Detective*, since the early 1970s. Hagen and Hubin's updates are an excellent source for British and American publications, but neglect all but the most prominent non-Anglo-American authors. Even less thorough—mainly because of its admitted personal preferences—is Barzun and Taylor's *A Catalogue of Crime*; though it is annotated with often amusing and incisive comments by the authors, it is by now a badly dated supplement to Hagen's work; updates have also been published regularly in *The Armchair Detective*. More contemporary but equally flawed is H.R.F. Keating's *Whodunit? A Guide to Crime, Suspense, and Spy Fiction* (1982). Useful reference works which include biographies of the best-known mystery writers are Steinbrunner et al.'s *Detectionary* (1977), *Encyclopedia of Mystery and Detection* (1976) by the same author, and Reilly's more thorough *Twentieth-Century Crime and Mystery Writers* (1986). Again, French authors are not represented well in any of the three.

The stimulus for many early critical studies of detective fiction was provided by Frank Chandler's monumental *The Literature of Roguery* in 1907. Since then, there have been a number of excellent historical surveys of detective fiction available to the general reader. Benvenuti's *The Whodunit: An Informal History of Detective Fiction* pays considerable attention to the French contribution to the genre, while Symons' *A Pictorial History of Crime: 1840 to the Present* favors the Anglo-American authors, as does the same author's extremely readable *Mortal Consequences: A History from the Detective Story to the Crime Novel*. Woeller and Cassiday's *The Literature of Crime and Detection* is an excellent historical account of the genre and is particularly valuable for its thorough study of the sources of French detective fiction. Though published in 1958, Murch's *The Development of the Detective Novel* is still worth reading for a good historical overview which gives due credit to the early French masters like Gaboriau, Leroux, and Leblanc.

Interesting studies of special theoretical aspects or important historical periods include Cassiday's *Roots of Detection: The Art of Deduction before Sherlock Holmes*, which deals mainly with the literary sources of detective fiction and includes material about French writers. Madden's *Tough Guy Writers of the Thirties* contains essays on the American hardboiled school of detective fiction; Panek's *Watteau's Shepherds* illustrates the orthodox mystery between the World Wars as a nostalgic and pastoral literature; and Routley sees the classical detective story as a product of the Puritan imagination in *The Puritan Pleasures of the Detective Story*.

In addition, there are a number of worthwhile discussions of the techniques of the genre, many of them addressed to the aspiring writer of detective fiction. Some of the earliest are Rodell's *Mystery Fiction: Theory and Technique* and Haycraft's *The Art of the Mystery Story*, while Patricia Highsmith's *Plotting and Writing Suspense Fiction* is a more recent work written by a successful practitioner of the genre. Freeman's *The Murder Mystique: Crime Writers on Their Art* presents a technical analysis of the writing of several masters of detective fiction, none of them French, as does John C. Carr's *The Craft of Crime: Conversations with Crime Writers*.

Studies of French Detective/Espionage Fiction

As mentioned before, no comprehensive scholarly study of French detective/ spy fiction exists in the English language; even more surprisingly, none could be found even in French. Although a number of French authors have written on the subject, their works deal to a substantial degree with Anglo-American mystery writers. In the bibliography included in a special number of *Littérature* (February 1983), Uri Eisenzweig, the issue editor, mentions only ninety French studies and deplores the fact that so little has been written on the subject by French authors, whereas there are some 2,000 studies in English and, according to Eisenzweig, the best theoretical material on the genre has been written in German. While the number of French studies on detective fiction had grown to some 150 by 1989, much of the material continues to be published in "fanzines" and lacks scholarly depth. Many of the studies since 1983 have appeared in special issues of scholarly and pedagogical literary journals. Even so, many of the articles in *Le Français dans le Monde* (1984), *Europe* (1976), and *Littérature* (1983) are nothing but a rehash of material dealt with more thoroughly in German and English publications. All three of these special issues, however, are easily accessible in American university libraries for the reader with a decent command of the French language. The best (and only) survey of French detective fiction in English is provided by the 25-page introductory essay in Hale's *Great French Detective Stories* (1984), which summarizes each writer's most significant contribution and draws comparisons between each writer and the equivalent Anglo-American authors of the same period.

The most significant French contribution to scholarship on detective fiction is still Messac's monumental work *Le Détective-novel et l'influence de la pensée scientifique* (1929). Messac provides a detailed source book for the origins of detective fiction and sees the beginnings of the genre as rooted in the transition from Romanticism to the scientific-materialist worldview of the mid-nineteenth century. There is rarely a work, in any language, on detective fiction that does not refer to Messac. Fosca's *Histoire et technique du roman policier* (1937), the first historical survey in French, repeats the often-made comment that detective novels are written "backwards"; that is, the author starts with the solution and fills in the clues, a technique reportedly first used by William Godwin in *Caleb Williams*. Roger Caillois' *Le Roman policier* (1941) demonstrates that the development of detective fiction has closely followed that of mainstream literature in becoming more and more exclusively self-conscious as a genre. Narcejac's *Esthétique du roman policier* (1947) is the first French study to analyze the poetics of the genre. Hoveyda's *Histoire du roman policier* is a highly subjective reader's recollection, which is valuable mainly because it mentions names and titles—mostly without dates or publishers—which can be found in no other source. Lacassin's two-volume *Mythologie du roman policier* contains nothing more than a series of chapters on individual mystery writers, French, English, and American, which is useful particularly because of its bibliography and film-ography sections. Dupuy addresses her 1974 *Le Roman policier* mainly to educators, but lists useful consumer and distribution statistics. The study quoted most frequently, Boileau-Narcejac's *Le Roman policier* (1964), is a fine, if episodic, history of detective fiction with substantial attention paid to the French mystery novel, but it loses much of its appeal because of the authors' insistence on using the study to demonstrate the superiority of their own version of detective fiction, the *roman-suspense*, as they themselves call it.

At present, the most useful and informative works of French detective fiction are *L'Almanach du crime* (called *L'Année du polar* since 1985), edited by Michel Lebrun since 1980, an annual summary of fiction and critical works published in France, and *Le Guide du polar*, published in 1987. Most of the works above include a short section on espionage fiction (for example, Dupuy, Boileau-

Narcejac, and Hoveyda), but the best treatment of the subject is Paul Bleton's "Mystère, secret et tromperie: sur la généalogie du roman d'espionnage français." Lance K. Donaldson-Evans' "The Anatomy of a Spy Novel: Gérard de Villiers and the Modern French *Roman d'espionnage*" is the only study touching on the subject in English.

RESEARCH COLLECTIONS AND CENTERS

No collections of primary or secondary literature on French detective fictions are known to exist in England or the United States. In France, however, the Bibliothèque des littératures policières (BILIPO) was opened to the public in 1984. It contains some 40,000 volumes in a collection dedicated to gathering the complete opus of literature and criticism of detective fictions published in French. Inquiries should be directed to BILIPO, 74–76, rue Mouffetard, 75005 Paris.

POSSIBILITIES FOR FUTURE RESEARCH

French detective and espionage fiction is in all respects the qualitative equal of its British, American, and Continental counterparts. However, while British and American detective fiction is routinely translated into French, even when the quality of the material is dubious, the reverse is not true even of first-rate French mystery and spy authors. Apart from encouraging publishers of detective fiction to translate the best of the French material into English, a complete bibliography of French detective and spy literature available in English (both British and American editions) needs to be compiled.

No comprehensive study of French detective/spy fiction has been published in the English language, in spite of the undeniable influence of French authors like Gaboriau, Leroux, Leblanc, and Simenon on detective fiction in other countries. Most of the material for such a survey already exists in French books and articles, but even in these the focus is frequently not on French writers. Interesting studies in comparative popular literature could and should be made on the sociology, aesthetics, and politics of French detective fiction vis-à-vis the American/British/German detective novel. Such studies might include the comparative analysis of themes, of the moral landscape, and of the social climate. One might investigate how the upheavals of May 1968 are reflected in popular literature, or look at popular views of the French global political role as mirrored in popular French espionage fiction.

Finally, it might be profitable to examine a possible role for the French detective and spy literature in the teaching of French language, literature, and culture in the United States. Foreign popular literature, particularly science fiction and detective literature, is increasingly used in German and British classrooms. In France, school editions of some classics of detective fiction are already being published: in the series Lectoguide, we find such works as Agatha Christie's *Les*

Dix Petits Nègres (American title: *And Then There Were None*), Leroux's *Le Mystère de la chambre jaune* (*The Mystery of the Yellow Room*), Simenon's *L'Affaire Saint-Fiacre*, and the Dupin stories of Edgar Allan Poe.

There is certainly a wealth of interesting and instructive material to be made available to the English-speaking reader and scholar for whom French detective and spy fiction has so far had to remain, for linguistic and bibliographical reasons, a well-guarded secret.

BIBLIOGRAPHY

Abiteboul, Maurice. "Hamlet aujourd'hui: du drame élisabéthain au roman policier moderne." *Caliban* 23 (1986): 27–40.

Achard, Marcel. "Sophocle et Archimède, pères du roman policier." *Les Nouvelles Littéraires*, November 3, 1960.

Adamov, Arkadi. *Der Kriminalroman, mein Lieblingsgenre*. Moscow: Lumina, 1980.

Albert, Walter, ed. *Detective and Mystery Fiction: An International Bibliography of International Sources*. Madison, Ind.: Brownstone Books, 1985.

Alewyn, Richard. "Das Rätsel des Kriminalromans." *Definitionen: Essays zur Literatur*. Frankfurt: Insel, 1963.

Alexandre, Paul. "Ambiguïté du roman policier." *Combat*, June 23, August 18, August 20, 1960.

Allard, Yvon. *Paralittérature* 1, Cahiers de Bibliographie, Collèges 6, Centre de bibliographie du Centre des Bibliothèques. Montreal, 1975.

Alter, Jean. "L'Enquête policière dans le nouveau roman." In *Un nouveau roman: rechercher la tradition*. Paris: Minard, 1964.

Arnold, Armin, and Schmidt, Josef, eds. *Reclams Kriminalromanführer*. Stuttgart: Reclam, 1978.

Astier, Colette. "La Tentation du roman policier dans *Un crime* de Georges Bernanos et *Le Rocher de Brighton* de Graham Greene." *Revue de Littérature comparée* 44 (1970): 224–43.

Aveline, Claude. "Double Note sur le roman policier." In *La Double Mort de Frédéric Belot* (postscript). Paris: Émile-Paul, 1947.

———. "Le Roman policier est-il un genre littéraire?" *Revue des Conférences françaises en Orient* 11/5 (May, 1947).

Barnes, Melvyn P. *Best Detective Fiction: A Guide from Godwin to the Present*. Hamden, Conn.: Linnett Books, 1975.

Barzun, Jacques, and Taylor, Wendell Hertig, eds. *A Catalogue of Crime*. New York: Harper & Row, 1971.

Baudou, Jacques. "Les Petits-Maîtres du roman policier français." *Europe* 571–72 (1976): 150–54.

Baudou, Jacques, and Gayot, Paul. "L'École française des années 30." *Le Français dans le Monde* 187 (1984): 22–25.

Benstock, Bernard, ed. *Art in Crime Writing: Essays on Detective Fiction*. New York: St. Martin's Press, 1983.

Benvenuti, Stefano. *The Whodunit: An Informal History of Detective Fiction*. New York: Collier, 1981.

Benvenuti, Stefano; Rizzoni, G.; and Lebrun, M. *Le Roman policier*. Nantes: L'Atlante, 1982.

Bleton, Paul. "Mystère, secret et tromperie: sur la généalogie du roman d'espionnage français." *Orbis Litterarum* 39 (1984): 65–78.

Bloch, Ernst. "Die Form der Detektivgeschichte und die Philosophie." *Neue Rundschau*, 1960.

―――. "A Philosophical View of the Detective Novel." *Discourse* 2 (Summer 1981): 32–51. Translation of "Philosophische Ansicht des Detectivromans." *Verfremdungen I*. Frankfurt: Suhrkamp, 1961.

Boileau, Pierre. "L'Art du roman policier." *La Revue des Deux Mondes*, July 15, 1951.

Boileau-Narcejac. *Le Roman policier*. Paris: Payot, 1964.

Brecht, Bertolt. "Über die Popularität des Kriminalromans." In his *Schriften zur Literatur und Kunst*. Berlin: Suhrkamp, 1967. Vol. 2.

Caillois, Roger. *The Mystery Novel*. Bronxville, N.Y.: The Laughing Buddha Press, 1984. Limited collector's edition of *Le Roman policier*. Buenos Aires: Éditions des Lettres françaises, 1941.

Care, Jean-Marie, and Maiffredy, Jean. "La Bande dessinée policière." *Le Français dans le Monde* 187 (1984): 46–50.

Carr, John C. *The Craft of Crime: Conversations with Crime Writers*. Boston: Houghton Mifflin, 1983.

Cassiday, Bruce, ed. *Roots of Detection: The Art of Deduction before Sherlock Holmes*. New York: Ungar, 1984.

Cawelti, John G., and Rosenberg, Bruce. *The Spy Story*. Chicago: University of Chicago Press, 1987.

Cazals, Henri. "Le Roman policier est-il un genre littéraire?" *L'Éducation nationale* 21 (June 3, 1965).

Cellard, Jacques. "San-Antonio." *Le Français dans le Monde* 187 (1984): 33–34.

Chandler, Frank W. *The Literature of Roguery*. Boston: Houghton Mifflin, 1907.

Charney, Hanna K. "Pourquoi le 'Nouveau Roman' policier?" *French Review* 46 (1972).

Chassaing, H. *De Zadig au rififi, ou du roman policier*. Montpellier: Imprimerie de la Charité, 1959.

Chastaing, Maxime. "Le Roman policier classique." *Europe* 571–72 (1976): 26–50.

Chimera: A Literary Quarterly. Special Issue: Detective Fiction. 4 (Summer 1947).

Colin, Jean-Pierre. "De l'approche stylistique d'un mauvais genre littéraire: le roman policier." *Linguistique et littérature*, 1968.

―――. "Lire le roman policier." *L'Esprit créateur* 26 (1986): 26–36.

Deleuze, Gilles. "Philosophie de la Série noire." *Arts et loisirs* 18 (1966).

Deloux, Jean-Pierre. "Le Nouveau Polar à la française." *Le Français dans le Monde* 187 (1984): 42–44.

Denning, Michael. *Cover Stories: Narrative and Ideology in the British Spy Thriller*. London: Routledge & Kegan Paul, 1987.

De Porla, Jean. "Chronique du polar." *Le Français dans le Monde* 198 (1986): 13.

―――. *Encore un coup d'arquebuse, Roman policier collectif expérimental*. Suivi de *Qui a tué Victor? Écrire collectivement un roman policier?* Paris: B.E.L.C., 1982.

Diebolt, Évelyne. "Du roman populaire au roman policier." *Le Français dans le Monde* 187 (1984): 8–14.

Di Manno, Yves. "Roman policier et société." *Europe* 571–72 (1976): 117–25.

Donaldson-Evans, Lance K. "The Anatomy of a Spy Novel: Gérard de Villiers and the Modern French *Roman d'espionnage*." *Clues: A Journal of Detection* 2 (1981): 28–36.

Dubeux, Albert. "Le Roman policier." *La Revue des Deux Mondes*, August 15, 1959.

Dumortier, Jean-Louis. *Georges Simenon*. Brussels: Labor, 1985.

Dupuy, Josée. *Le Roman policier*. Paris: Larousse, 1974.

Eisen, Claude. "Du roman policier au roman noir." *La Nouvelle N.R.F.* 3 (March 1953).

Eisenzweig, Uri. *Autopsies du roman policier*. Paris: Bourgois, 1983.

———. "Genèse et structure du roman policier. Hypothèses de travail." *Degrés* 16 (1978).

———. "Chaos et Maîtrise: le discours romanesque de la méthode policière." *Michigan Romance Studies* 2 (1982).

———. *Le Récit impossible: forme et sens du roman policier*. Paris: Bourgois, 1986.

———. "L'Instance du policier dans le romanesque: Balzac, Poe et *Le Mystère de la chambre jaune*." *Poétique* 51 (1982): 279–302.

———. "Madness and the Colonies: French and Anglo-Saxon Versions of the Mysterious Origins of Crime." *L'Esprit créateur* 26 (1986): 3–14.

Europe, Revue littéraire mensuelle. Special Issue: "La Fiction policière," November-December 1976.

Europe, Revue littéraire mensuelle. Special Issue: "Arsène Lupin." August-September 1979.

Europe, Revue littéraire mensuelle. Special Issue:"Gaston Leroux," June-July 1981.

Europe, Revue littéraire mensuelle. Special Issue: "Pierre Véry," April 1982.

Fabre, Jean. "De la littérature policière." *Des Cahiers de la Cinémathèque* 25 (1978).

———. *Enquête sur un enquêteur: Maigret. Un essai de socio-critique*. Montpellier: Université Paul Valéry, 1980.

Ferri, Enrico. *Les Criminels dans l'art et la littérature*. 4th ed. Paris: F. Alcan, 1913.

Fosca, François. *Histoire et technique du roman policier*. Paris: Nouvelle Revue Critique, 1937.

Le Français dans le Monde. Special Issue: "Spécial Roman Policier." 187 (August-September 1984).

Freeman, Lucy, ed. *The Murder Mystique: Crime Writers on Their Art*. New York: Ungar, 1982.

Gattegno, Jean. "Criminels et détectives ou la préhistoire du roman policier à propos d'un livre de Ian Ousby." *Études Anglaises* 3 (1976): 188–97.

Gaudin, Nicolas V. "Interventions digressives du narrateur, ou l'élaboration de San-Antonio." *The French Review* 58 (1984): 58–67.

Goyot, Paul, and Badov, Jacques. "Quand l'énigme fait peur: le suspense." *Le Français dans le Monde* 187 (1984): 38–41.

Grivel, Charles. "Observation du roman policier." In *Entretiens sur la paralittérature*. Paris: Plon, 1970.

Guérif, François. *Le Cinéma policier français*. Paris: Veyrier, 1981.

Hagen, Ordean A. *Who Done It? A Guide to Detective Mystery and Suspense Fiction*. New York: R. R. Bowker, 1969.

Hale, T. J., ed. *Great French Detective Stories*. New York: Vanguard, 1984.

Hankiss, Jean. "Littérature 'populaire' et roman policier." *Revue de Littérature Comparée*, July 1928.

Haycraft, Howard, ed. *The Art of the Mystery Story: A Collection of Critical Essays*. New York: Simon and Schuster, 1946.

———. *Murder for Pleasure: The Life and Times of the Detective Story*. New York: Appleton-Century, 1941.

Highsmith, Patricia. *Plotting and Writing Suspense Fiction*. Boston: Writer, 1966.

Hoveyda, Fereydoun. *Histoire du roman policier*. Paris: Le Pavillon, 1965.

Huet, Marie-Hélène. "Enquête et représentation dans le roman policier." *Europe* 571–72 (1976).

Jacobs, Gabriel. "A Pseudo Roman Policier of the Early Thirties: *La Double Mort de Frédéric Belot.*" *Forum of Modern Language Studies* 20 (1984): 143–53.

Jaubert, Jacques. "Du rififi dans les polars." *Le Figaro littéraire*, April 6, 1974.

Johnson, Timothy W., et al., eds. *Crime Fiction Criticism: An Annotated Bibliography*. New York: Garland, 1981.

Keating, H. R. F., ed. *Whodunit? A Guide to Crime, Suspense, and Spy Fiction*. New York: Van Nostrand Reinhold, 1982.

Lacassin, Francis. *Mythologie du roman policier*. 2 vols. Paris: Union générale d'éditions, 1974.

Lacombe, A. *Le Roman noir*. Paris: Bourgois, 1975.

L'Âme: Le magazine freudien. Special Issue: "Le Roman policier." 14 (1984).

Lanoux, Armand. "Connaissez-vous Gaboriau?" *Les Nouvelles Littéraires*, December 1, 1960.

Lebrun, Michel, ed. *L'Almanach du crime*. Annual Volume. Paris: Veyrier, 1980–84.

———. *L'Année du polar*. Annual Volume. Paris: Ramsay, 1985–.

———. "Les Alchimistes du roman policier." *Europe* 542 (1974): 138–43.

Lebrun, Michel, and Schweighaeuser, Jean-Paul, eds. *Le Guide du polar*. Paris: Syros, 1987.

Lemonnier, Léon. "Edgar Poe et les origines du roman policier en France." *Mercure de France* 186 (October 15, 1925).

———. *Edgar Poe et les conteurs français*. Paris: Montaigne, 1947.

Littérature. Special Issue: "Le Roman policier." 49 (February 1983).

Locard, Edmond. *Policiers de roman et policiers de laboratoire*. Paris: Payot, 1924.

Madden, David, ed. *Tough Guy Writers of the Thirties*. Carbondale: Southern Illinois University Press, 1968.

Magazine Littéraire. Spécial Polar: "Vingt ans de littérature policière." 49 (April 1983).

Marcel, Gabriel. "Romans policiers." *L'Europe Nouvelle*, October 1, 1932.

Maublanc, René. "Romans policiers et romans populaires." *La Pensée* 13 (1947).

Mesplède, C., and Schleret, J. J. *S. N.: Voyage au bout de la Noire*. Paris: Futuropolis, 1985. Updated edition of the 1982 original.

Messac, Régis. *Le Détective-novel et l'influence de la pensée scientifique*. Paris: Honoré Champion, 1929.

Mille, Pierre. "Du roman policier." *Les Nouvelles Littéraires*, May 21, 1932.

Miller, D. A. "From Roman Policier to Roman-Police: Wilkie Collins' *The Moonstone.*" *Novel: A Forum on Fiction* 13 (1980): 153–70.

Morand, Paul. "Réflexions sur le roman policier." *Revue de Paris* 1 (1934): 4.

Morin, Edgar. "Le Roman policier dans l'imaginaire moderne." *N.R.F.* 16 (1959).

Murch, A. E. *The Development of the Detective Novel*. Westport, Conn.: Greenwood Press, 1958.

Narcejac, Thomas. *Esthétique du roman policier*. Paris: Le Portulan, 1947.

————. "Le Roman policier." "Encyclopédie de la Pléiade," *Histoire des littératures.* Paris: Gallimard, 1975. 3:1644–70.

————. *Une machine à lire: le roman policier.* Paris: Denoël, 1975.

Neveu, Erik. *L'Idéologie dans le roman d'espionnage.* Paris: Presses de la Fondation nationale des Sciences politiques, 1984.

Olivier-Martin, Yves. "Le Trio fatidique: Fantômas, Lupin, Rouletabille." *Le Français dans le Monde* 187 (1984): 15–18, 21.

————. "Origines secrètes du roman policier français." *Europe* 571–72 (1976): 144–49.

————. "Structures de la fiction policière." *Europe* 643–44 (1982): 47–55.

Oms, Marcel. "L'Image du policier dans le cinéma français." *Des Cahiers de la Cinémathèque* 25 (Spring/Summer 1978).

Panek, Leroy. *Watteau's Shepherds: The Detective Novel in Britain, 1915–1940.* Bowling Green, Ohio: Popular Press, 1979.

Peské, Antoinette, and Marty, Pierre. *Les Terribles: Maurice Leblanc, Gaston Leroux, Marcel Allain.* Paris: Chambriand, 1951.

Poupart, Jean-Marie. *Les Récréants: essai portant, entre autres choses, sur le roman policier.* Montreal: Éditions du Jour, 1972.

Raabe, Juliette. "Le Phénomène Série noire." In *Entretiens sur la paralittérature.* Paris: Plon, 1970.

Radine, Serge. *Quelques aspects du roman policier psychologique.* Geneva: Mont-Blanc, 1961.

Rapoport, Herman. "Literature and the Hermeneutics of Detection." *L'Esprit créateur* 26 (1986): 71–81.

Reilly, John M., ed. *Twentieth-Century Crime and Mystery Writers.* New York: St. Martin's Press, 1985.

Rice-Sayre, Laura. "Le Roman policier et le nouveau roman: entretien avec Michel Butor." *The French-American Review* 1 (1977): 101–14.

Richard, Jean-Pierre. "Petites Notes sur le roman policier." *Le Français dans le Monde* 50 (1967).

Rivière, Françoise. "La Fiction policière ou le meurtre du roman." *Europe* 571–72 (1976).

Rodell, Marie F. *Mystery Fiction: Theory and Technique.* New York: Hermitage House, 1952.

Routley, Erik. *The Puritan Pleasures of the Detective Story.* London: Gollancz, 1972.

Scheibenreif, H. "Nouveau roman und Detektivroman." Dissertation. See *Dissertation Abstracts International* 42/2 (1981): Item 1560C.

Schulz-Buschhaus, Ulrich. *Formen und Ideologien des Kriminalromans: Ein gattungsgeschichtlicher Essay.* Frankfurt: Athenaion, 1975.

Schweighaeuser, J.-P. *Le Roman noir français.* Paris. Presses Universitaires de France, 1984.

Simsolo, Noël. "De'polar'isation." *L'Arc* 90 (1984): 52–55.

Smith, Robert P., Jr. "Chester Himes in France and the Legacy of the *Roman Policier.*" *College Language Association Journal* 25 (1981): 18–27.

Steele, Timothy. "Matter and Mystery: Neglected Works and Background Materials of Detective Fiction." *Modern Fiction Studies* 29 (1983): 435–50.

Steinbrunner, Chris, et al., eds. *Detectionary.* Woodstock, N.Y.: Overlook Press, 1977.

————. *Encyclopedia of Mystery and Detection.* New York: McGraw-Hill, 1976.

Symons, Julian. *A Pictorial History of Crime: 1840 to the Present*. New York: Crown, 1966.

———. *Mortal Consequences: A History from the Detective Story to the Crime Novel*. New York: Harper & Row, 1972.

Tani, Stefano. *The Doomed Detective: The Contribution of the Detective Novel to Post-modern American and Italian Fiction*. Carbondale: Southern Illinois University Press, 1984.

Thomson, H. Douglas. *Masters of Mystery*. London: Folcroft, 1931.

Todorov, Tzvetan. "Typologie du roman policier." In *Poétique de la prose*. Paris: Seuil, 1971.

Tourteau, J. J. *D'Arsène Lupin à San-Antonio. Le Roman policier français de 1900 à 1970*. Paris: Mame, 1970.

Vareille, Jean-Claude. "Culture savante et culture populaire: brèves remarques à propos des horizons idéologiques, des structures et de la littérarité du roman policier." *Caliban* 23 (1986): 5–19.

———. *Filatures. Itinéraires à travers les cycles de Lupin et Rouletabille*. Grenoble: Presse Universitaires de Grenoble, 1980.

Vincent, Bruno. "Les Français de la série noire." *Le Magazine littéraire* 78 (July-August 1973).

Vogt, Jochen, ed. *Der Kriminalroman*. 2 vols. Munich: Fink, 1971.

Woeller, Waltraud, and Cassiday, Bruce. *The Literature of Crime and Detection: An Illustrated History from Antiquity to the Present*. New York: Ungar, 1988. Translation of *Illustrierte Geschichte der Kriminalliteratur*. Frankfurt: Insel, 1984.

Zeltner, Gerda. "Robert Pinget et le roman policier." *Marche Romane* 21 (1971).

Žmegač, Viktor, ed. *Der wohltemperierte Mord*. Frankfurt: Athenäum, 1971.

4

Editorial/Political/Gag Cartoons

JEAN-CLAUDE FAUR

It may seem paradoxical that one of the countries that gave the world such a great number of world-renowned graphic artists does not really have a word equivalent to the Anglo-Saxon "cartoon," other than by certain periphrases such as *dessin de presse* (press drawing) or *dessin d'humour* (humor drawing). These appellations are the most widely used, although *illustration, dessin politique, dessin éditorial* (illustration, political cartoon, editorial cartoon), or even "strip"—directly translated or taken from American English—count only for the printed image, as if the "animated cartoon" did not also come from the same discipline.

In the publishing and press fields, the profession itself—where common techniques prevail by far over differences in medium—has not always found a clear and definitive designation that would be accepted by all. For instance, we still speak of some professional journalists or some part-time stringers as *reporters dessinateurs* (reporters-drawers)—note here again the term's English etymology—even when it is rather rare to see a press artist actually go on a professional trip in order to do real "reporting."

HISTORICAL OUTLINE

With these reservations in mind and whatever terminology is used (it will vary with the circumstances), it appears that the press drawing, like the comic strip or graphic art in general, goes back in France to the very origins of human creativity.

Prehistoric sites discovered in France are legion, we know, and make it the true and uncontested cradle of the image civilization, well before the invention of any writing. Pech-Merle, Combarelles, Pont de Gaume, Oullins, Le Mas d'Azil, and of course the caves at Niaux or Lascaux testify to the creative genius of our distant ancestors as early as protohistory, even if only, as Gérard Blanchard has noted, by the "more or less advanced stylizations of the signs for the male and female sexes"—stylization being the very principle of caricature.

If we keep to a strictly historical and geographical framework (Celtic and Druidic as well as Greek and Roman), France has hardly kept sites comparable, say, to those at Herculaneum and Pompeii, where random volcanic catastrophe has allowed the conservation on the city walls of the moving, almost journalistic traces of numerous drawings or graffiti inspired by the great moments of daily life. Electoral battles among municipal notables or fans' passions for some gladiator of that time—real "show business" personalities—are naturally the most frequent themes used by these anonymous street artists.

We can, however, find intact in France, from the Middle Ages on, graphism's uninterrupted thread thanks to such manuscripts, and their illuminations, as the famous *Hortus Deliciarum* by Herade of Lansberg (1185). These manuscripts are real art that will know its apogee in the fourteenth and fifteenth centuries. For example, the Karlsruhe Manuscript, at the early beginning of the fourteenth century, which represents the life in images of Raymond Lulle—justly recognized as "the most productive publicist of his time" (Charles Langlois, quoted in Blanchard)—is already an authentic drawn reportage.

Furthermore, based on the drawings done in the margins of the minutes of Joan of Arc's trial, how can we not see in her anonymous portraitist the real ancestor of our current courtroom artists and even the first "reporter-drawer" of the modern era? Actually, the entire Middle Ages bathes in the *visual*. "The cathedral, that temple of the image," to quote Francis Lacassin's felicitous phrase, through its sculptured as well as painted representations and through its stone friezes and Ways of the Cross, is a permanent invitation to the figurative representation of both the real and the imaginary, and here the gargoyle is every bit as good as the votive statue. Indeed, the technique of exception, like embroidery exemplified by the famous Bayeux tapestry, which relates the conquest of England by William the Conqueror and the various events of the Battle of Hastings, also obviously falls in this category. Gérard Blanchard can thus correctly qualify the Bayeux work as "embroidered reportage" and even speak of its "political slant."

Nevertheless, it is true that the impact of these means of expression was exclusively limited to a small public either of fortunate owners of rich illuminated manuscripts or of the faithful and tourists. In fact, it was the invention and then the general use of the printing press that allowed the *distribution* of the image to an ever-increasing population. This printing press, as we too often forget, was first exclusively *xylograhic*, that is, devoted to the reversed reproduction by contact in a hand press of wood engravings crudely, then artistically, chiseled and reproduced on a variety of media, including manuscript vellum, before the industrial production of rag paper. The oldest known xylography (1370) is the famous "Protat Wood," now at the library of the University of Strasbourg.

Believed to have been used to print fabrics, it shows the common use of a "phylactery," or thin, unrolled ribbon, coming out of the characters' mouths and on which were written the words they spoke.

Prior to the Gutenberg press (which xylography survived long after), these xylographic incunabula presented the important advantage of offering the artist great flexibility of execution, since image and text could be combined in the same graphic solution of continuity, even when typographical composition imposed its own rules. *The Dance of the Dead* (1485) by Guyot Marchant or Charles VIII's coronation and entrance into Paris by Pierre Le Caron in 1498 can be considered true press drawings. Paradoxically, it is Gutenberg's invention of movable type and, in 1456, his famous forty-two-line Bible that caused the almost complete disappearance of images from printed production, insofar as the text gathered in rigid lines in the typesetter's stick had to come out of the illustration to go underneath as caption.

With rare exceptions, therefore, the engraver was no longer the main author of a work but just a supernumerary craftsman, and the typographical book soon became synonymous with graphic austerity. Wood engraving, now incompatible with metal typography printing, disappeared or became once again an artistic discipline reserved for special works. The development of other engraving methods, etching in particular, made this disappearance at the industrial level complete. Finally and necessarily, large print runs crushed the lead, tin, and antimony mixture, hence a fortiori wood engravings as well. It is not surprising then that, in the sixteenth and seventeenth centuries, the history of caricature emphasized the artists who chose etching as their medium: Robert and Jean Jacques Boissard and their *Masquerades* (1597), Jacques Callot with his *Balli di Sfessania* and his *Gobbi* (1622), Jacques Lagniet, the publisher of *The Most Illustrious Proverbs* (1657), or Nicolas de Larmessin and his *Costumes grotesques* (1695), in which each profession is shown with its particular accessories—all these testify to illustration's and caricature's artistic durability. Nor should the role of "occasionals" printed and sold on the occasion of important events or extraordinary rumors be neglected. The taking of Naples in February 1495 by Charles VIII was the occasion of a real illustrated reportage. The "beast of Gavaudan" easily provided sensational representations encouraged by popular credulity. These "occasionals" circulated widely, sold like hotcakes, and then, by their very nature, disappeared. An excellent discussion of this subject is presented by Jean-Pierre Seguin, former curator in chief of the Print Department of the Bibliothèque Nationale and currently director of the Pompidou Center.

In 1631 the first "gazettes" appeared. These periodical information sheets are at the origin of modern journalism, and the 1785 engraving portraying the vendor of one of these gazettes is quite significant, since under the banner headline of "Aerial Voyage" is the drawing of a hot air balloon rising from the ground. Moreover, the power of suggestion of these "occasionals" is such that they would remain popular until the end of the nineteenth century and coexist happily alongside the industrial press. These *canards* (rags, but literally ducks),

as they were then nicknamed, in mocking allusion to the imperial eagles dec-
orating the daily bulletins of Napoleon's Grand Army, for a long time continued
to be engraved on wood like their xylographic ancestors, and certain well-known
engravers, like Garson, Delalu, or Cordonnier, single-handedly created hundreds
of canards.

If, however, they remained anonymous, these canards also were characterized
by their subjects, whether of an anecdotal, exaggerating, or bloodcurdling nature.
An 1886 canard, for example, does not hesitate to title its front page "60-Year-
Old Man Cut in Pieces." The subtitle further points out with little subtlety but
great delight that he was then "boiled in a stewing pot and fed to pigs by his
brother and sister-in-law." The "reporter-drawer" of the time shows us the poor
man being murdered with an ax and a butcher knife, while three or four limbs
of the victim already lie on the floor.

Very different in their spirit and layout are the "images d'Épinal," which
proliferated at the same time, although they too derived from the same desire
to inform and to fill with wonder. In 1773, on succeeding his bookseller-publisher
father, established in Épinal, Jean-Charles Pellerin understood the financial opportunity of selling popular representations in a series of small prints of similar
size on a single folio or plano page. At the beginning, it was a question of
retelling stories known to all, generally taken from the Gospels or from the most
popular saints' lives, in eight, twelve, or sometimes sixteen drawings with short
captions. Thus the mostly illiterate public of the time could grasp the general
meaning of each plate and mount them, as later with chromos, on the walls of
the main room.

Using the same formula, Pellerin, a fervent supporter of Napoleon I, helped
spread the legends of the imperial epic with the help of his engravers, among
whom were François Georgin and Antoine Réveillé (himself a former soldier of
the emperor's Old Guard). Thrown in jail under Louis XVIII, Pellerin put back
into circulation his most seditious images, though not without first obliterating
in black or red the all too Napoleonic symbols. He thereby actively contributed
to the return of the exiled future Napoleon III. Later, after abandoning wood
engraving for modern lithographic presses in 1854, the Pellerin factory permanently turned toward the colored-print trade for children—for which it is still
famous today.

Also at the same time, books of the Romantic era, in the area of "noble
publishing," broke with Classical typographical tradition and increasingly welcomed illustrations. Indeed, the fashion of the day consisted of innumerable
travel stories that developed a respectable exoticism where, in certain pages, the
text proper was reduced to a few lines in order to give more space to pictures
of palm trees and minarets worthy of the *Thousand and One Nights*. A gleeful
Francis Lacassin cites as a French predecessor to the Swiss Rodolphe Töpffer,
François Aimé Louis Dumoulin, who, as early as 1805, proposed an adaptation
of *Robinson Crusoe* in a series of 150 etchings.

However, the development of illustration and caricature in the nineteenth century was unquestionably linked to that of the industrial press, made possible by the advent of the machine and the replacement of human or animal energy, first with steam and then with electricity. In 1814 the London *Times* still "only" printed 1,100 sheets an hour. In 1863 the Marinoni rotative press made it possible for *Le Petit Journal* to print 6,000 sheets an hour and, in 1869, to have a daily run of over 450,000 copies. The era of the mass-market press had arrived.

Henceforth, reporters-drawers would see new outlets open, mainly in fashion and social periodicals aimed at women . . . and at men, and in political papers created during troubled times. This occurred despite the invention of photography and its possible competition, although as Töpffer noted in 1841, "Daguerre's plate gives similarity instead of likeness." (In the end, drawers were in fact replaced by photojournalists.)

In 1830, Charles Philipon, himself a former drawer, founded *La Caricature*, which, following a series of ruinous trials brought by July Monarchy governments, he replaced with *Le Charivari* two years later. This newspaper "publish[ed] a new drawing every day" and would appear until 1878. Such a remarkable success was due in large part to the quality of Philipon's collaborators, who were the best graphic artists of the period.

Among them was the Marseilles-born Honoré Daumier, who had already received a six months' prison sentence for having represented King Louis-Philippe as a Rabelaisian monster in his "Gargantua" (1831). From 1836 to 1838, in the wake of the adventures of the protagonist of the *Auberge des Adrets* play, popularized by the great actor Frédérick Lemaître, Daumier created the "Robert Macaire" series. Macaire is a shameless swindler, in turn journalist, merchant, physician, or lawyer, always on the lookout for a new swindle that will bring him a fortune. The drawings are a barely veiled satire of the era's growing capitalism and of Émile de Girardin, the William Randolph Hearst of the time. Daumier later worked with Victor Hugo to illustrate *Les Châtiments*, a collection of poems against Napoleon III. He remains the most incisive of the nineteenth-century French caricaturists and has inspired a long line of artists.

Another great collaborator of Philipon's was Guillaume Sulpice Chevalier, signing as Gavarni. After his start at Girardin's *La Mode*, he devoted himself fully to satirical drawing, making fun of the budding bourgeoisie's mores, before collecting them in such series as "Les Lorettes" and "Fourberies de Femmes." Last must be named Jean Ignace Isidore Gérard, known as Grandville, the famous illustrator of La Fontaine, Swift, and Defoe. He revealed himself to be a true graphic fabulist, especially in his "Scenes of the Public and Private Lives of Animals," where he gave animal heads to human characters, before creating "Another World" (1844), a visionary work whose incredible modernity would later be praised by the surrealists.

It is from this current that *Le Musée Philipon* came out in 1842, of which Cham (né Amédée de Noé) made a real French *Mad* magazine before its time. Here was proof of Philipon's success: when *Punch* began publishing in 1841, it called itself "The London *Charivari*." It was, as Michel Melot pithily notes, because *Le Charivari* "was then of the extreme left, but intended for the most progressive middle-class" (quoted in Béchu). In this same spirit Hetzel founded *La Revue comique* in 1848, which was entirely aimed against the future Emperor Napoleon III, before the 1851 coup d'état forced Hetzel into exile. *La Revue comique* gathered the pens of Quillenbois, Bertall, Johannot, and especially Félix Tournachon, alias Nadar, whose "Monsieur Réac" became the prototype of the eternal opportunist. Nadar then joined in 1849 the *Journal pour rire* (later changed to *Journal amusant*) of the omnipresent Philipon.

There, Nadar found Gustave Doré, the great illustrator of Rabelais, Balzac, Cervantes, Dante, and future author of the "Political, Romantic and Caricatural History of Holy Russia" and of the "Parisian Zoo" (1854). He collaborated as well on the *Musée franco-anglais*, for which he invented the "drawn reportage" by sketching scenes of the Crimean War without ever leaving his Paris apartment. Also working at the *Journal pour rire* were the tireless Cham, Bertall, Alfred Grévin, and Albert Robida. Robida had his start at the *Journal* in 1866 before moving on to *La Vie parisienne*, then creating his own periodical, *La Caricature*, in 1874, and finally going into science-fiction illustration, notably with "War in the Twentieth Century" (1887), full of premonitory touches that give him increasing recognition from modern collectors.

The Commune of 1870 saw a flowering of satirical sheets with often evocative titles: *La Carmagnole, Le Grelot, La Flèche, La Fronde illustrée*. These were short-lived indeed, for the Third Republic soon rang their death knell. Symbolically, Honoré Daumier, now blind, stopped contributing satire in 1872.

It then became fashionable to publish journals of manners, like Marcelin's *La Vie parisienne*, or reviews of *portraits-charges*, like *L'Hydropathe*, founded in 1879 by Émile Cohl—one of the future inventors of the animated cartoon. Also of interest were *Le Trombinoscope, L'Éclipse, La Lune rousse* (all three by André Gill), and *Les Hommes d'aujourd'hui*. The height of technical refinement is arguably *Le Titi*, which from 1878 to 1880 published drawings done in invisible ink that came out only when heated. The entire philosophy of the time could be stated in André Gill's famous formula: "I have never seen M. Thiers; I drew him 500 times: I have instead considered his legend and given the public a silhouette more true to its preconceived ideas" (quoted in Lethève). At least it is an honest admission.

The law of July 29, 1881, on freedom of the press, by deleting in particular the "prior approval" clause which favored censorship, brought about an extraordinary proliferation of press enterprises, thus making the years 1880–95 the real "golden age" of caricature in France. In 1882 there were 3,800 newspapers and periodicals; in 1892 there were more than 6,000, of which 2,000 were in Paris alone! This period coincided with all kinds of technical advances. The use of the rotary press was widespread, lithogravure was replaced by photogravure, then by color runs, and the telephone, finally, allowed the editor to order his "topics" long distance.

The most prestigious of the era's titles, *Le Chat noir*, was founded precisely in 1881 by Rodolphe Salis, the owner of the famous nightclub whose sign was designed by Alexandre Steinlen himself. A friend of Aristide Bruant, Steinlen then collaborated on *Le Chambard socialiste, Le Rire, L'Assiette au beurre* and created in 1910 the society of "Humorists," a group of twelve artists among whom were included Jean-Louis Forain, Adolphe Willette, Léandre.

At Steinlen's side at *Le Chat noir* were Willette, who later led *Le Courrier français*, then *L'Assiette au beurre*; Emmanuel Poiré alias Caran d'Ache, before contributing his regular drawing to Monday's *Le Figaro*; the ever-popular André Gill; Émile Cohl, already mentioned; and many others. Quickly, *Le Chat noir* became "the *New Yorker* of the turn of the century." Steinlen, the illustrator of Bruant, Anatole France, Guy de Maupassant, is the drawer par excellence of the disinherited. Indeed, the unemployed, orphans, minors, and prostitutes forcefully appear in the pages of *Le Chat noir*, while Steinlen contributed under a pen name to many other papers.

Another famous review of the time, *Le Courrier français*, was founded in 1884 by Jules Roques. Advertisements from the pharmaceutical industry (for instance, Géraudel lozenges or Dubonnet quinine tonic wine) brought him a large readership which greatly enjoyed Willette's drawings of Mimi Pinson and Pierrot. (As a matter of fact, Willette created in 1888 his own *Pierrot*, a four-page journal of which he was the sole administrator, editor, and artist.) Along with him, *Le Courrier* also published Villon, Beardsley, Valloton. As for *Le Rire*, founded in 1894, it welcomed to its ranks, besides Willette, again, numerous talented artists of the time: Gyp, Charles Léandre, Jossot, Abel Faivre, Steinlen, Forain, and even Toulouse-Lautrec and Van Dongen, for many painters did not disdain contributing to satirical reviews, often with self-caricatures like Toulouse-Lautrec's. The reverse is also true, since drawers, like Forain, whose "Parisian Comedy" appears in 1892, did not hesitate to exhibit next to Manet or Degas.

However, the most prestigious review of the period, until World War I, was unquestionably *L'Assiette au beurre*. Founded in 1901, each issue it published centered on a particular theme, often with a provocative purpose, generally entrusted to a single drawer. The greatest liberal artists contributed to it, such as Félix Édouard Valloton, who illustrated in 1902 the theme of "Crime and Punishment," after working for a long time at *Le Rire* and *Le Cri de Paris*, and also at *La Revue blanche*, *L'Escarmouche* (founded by Georges Darien), *The Chap Book* (Chicago), and *Pan* (Berlin). He was also a member of the "Nabis" group that included Toulouse-Lautrec, Bonnard, Maillol. Gustave Henri Jossot, after his debut at *Le Cycle* and *Le Rire*, created between 1901 and 1907 some 300 drawings for *L'Assiette au beurre* while working for the liberal press (*Le Diable, Les Temps nouveaux*). He completely abandoned satirical art when he converted to Islam, although his cartoons were regularly reprinted in the anarchist or antiestablishment press, including today's *L'Enragé, Libération*, and *Le Monde libertaire*.

Among the other names found in *L'Assiette au beurre*'s pages we should mention Jules-Félix Grandjouan, founder in 1899 of the *Libertaire*, who died in jail of tuberculosis (1912); the Czech-born Frantisek Kupka, who illustrated the issue on "Money" before devoting himself to abstract painting with Picabia and Kandinsky; Adolphe Willette, Abel Faivre, Alexandre Steinlen. (Thanks to Stanley Appelbaum, a fair sample of the best of *L'Assiette au beurre* was published by Dover in 1978.)

The passion for caricature, then, is such that most great dailies are enriched with illustrated weekly, often autonomous, supplements. *Le Petit Journal, La Libre Parole illustrée, Le Gaulois du dimanche* summarize or review the news of the past week. Similarly, after *Le Journal de la jeunesse*, founded by Hachette in 1872, numerous illustrated periodicals appeared aimed at the young, a brand-new phenomenon in the French press.

Le Petit Français illustré, from 1889 on, opened wide its pages to Georges Colomb, who facetiously signed Christophe. There he created the famous series of "Le Savant Cosinus," "Le Sapeur Camember," and "La Famille Fenouillard," which, it has just been learned, was greatly enjoyed by the future Queen Elizabeth II. In the same vein, *La Jeunesse illustrée*, beginning in 1903, *L'Illustré* in 1904, *La Semaine de Suzette* in 1905, *L'Épatant* in 1908, and *L'Intrépide* in 1910 are some of the many mainstays for the ancestors of modern comic strips, as Maurice Horn points out in a previous chapter.

Benjamin Rabier became renowned as an unsurpassable animal drawer with his duck Gédéon, and his "Laughing Cow" is still today the logo of a famous cheese brand. Caumery and Pinchon created the character of Bécassine, still very popular with elderly readers; and Louis Forton invented the celebrated "Pieds-Nickelés," the oldest French comics characters to have adventures to this day.

This appropriately named Belle Époque was also filled with poverty. Although the bright lights of the capital hid the abuses and conflicts of a largely rural society, spattered by the Dreyfus Affair and the Panama Canal scandal, the era ended in World War I and gave rise to a patriotic "sky blue," where the "sacred union" mobilized soldiers as well as drawers, quick to attack those safe at the rear—just as during the Commune, numerous suitable sheets made their appearance with suggestive titles like *Le Rire rouge* with Willette; *La Baïonnette* with Léandre, Gus Bofa, Jacques Nam; *Le Mot* with Paul Iribe, Sem, and a certain Jim, who was none other than Jean Cocteau himself; *La Grimace*; or finally *Le Canard enchaîné*, the only one still to survive today.

It was the period of "brainwashing," the ancestor of our "psychological warfare," when children were pictured with their hands cut off by the hated "Boches" (Germans), who, no doubt about it, no longer respected anything. Military newspapers were encouraged by the General Staff since they helped prop up the troops' morale. "La Borne" (the milestone), a drawing by Forain published in the May 22, 1916, issue of *Le Figaro*, would even be printed in thousands of copies to be scattered by plane over German lines! Peace marked an unavoidable slowing down of the satirical press, at least until the return of the great scandals and events: the League of Nations, Stavisky, February 6, 1934, the war in Ethiopia, or the Franco-Soviet accord.

Most of the large dailies made it a point of honor to have their own comic artist. Alain Saint-Ogan for a long time contributed gentle cartoons, captioned by the local editor, to *La Dépêche du Midi*, before he created in *Le Dimanche illustré* his characters of Zig, Puce, and Alfred, who would bring him an almost international success in the 1930s. Jean Pennès, aka Sennep, was the pillar of *L'Écho de Paris* from 1924 to 1938, before working at *Le Figaro* from 1945 to 1967. Maurice Henry had his start at *Le Petit Journal* in 1932 before drawing some 30,000 cartoons in 160 periodicals like *L'Œuvre*, *L'Express*, *Carrefour*, etc. François Lejeune, signing Jean Effel, began in 1933 in *Le Rire* before working for *France Soir* or *L'Express*, then *L'Humanité*, while doing *La Création du monde* (1952), a delightful animated cartoon that would be translated into sixteen languages. Albert Dubout contributed first to *Pêle Mêle*, *Le Rire*, and *Le Journal amusant*, before increasingly devoting himself to funny illustrations of rather serious authors like Boileau or Edgar Allan Poe, without, however, neglecting Dumas, Rabelais, or Marcel Pagnol. Finally, *Paris-Soir* showed originality by simultaneously opening its pages to artists of opposing political viewpoints.

It was especially in its political or satirical newspapers, however, that the period between the wars saw new talent emerge. Ben, Roger Chancel, Paul Iribe, Ralph Soupault, and Bib signed their works in *L'Ami du peuple*, *Gringoire*, *Le Charivari*. *Le Canard enchaîné*, which had about 200,000 readers in 1934, welcomed the likes of H. P. Gassier, Jean Effel, Raoul Guérin, Pol Ferjac, Monier, Moisan, Maurice Henry. Established by Eugène Merle in 1919, the most popular paper by far was *Le Merle blanc* which, with a 1922 circulation of 812,000 copies, "siffle et persifle le samedi" (whistles and hisses and satirizes every Saturday) with the help of Gassier, Laforge, or Marcel Arnac. The year 1938 saw the birth of the amazing *Os à moëlle*, "the official organ of crackpots," founded by the humorist Pierre Dac, in which appeared many artists from *Le Canard enchaîné*. Happily, its wacky nonsense has lost none of its flavor.

World War II had in turn its share of humorous drawings—restrictions and the black market were the main themes—and of propaganda illustrations whose inventory remains to be done. There was also an astounding proliferation of leaflets and stickers, sometimes against Freemasons, sometimes clandestine, but without an actual publishing history, except for the juvenile weekly *Le Téméraire*. After the war, under the pressure of various factors (chief among which was television), there occurred a slow but ineluctable disappearance or at least a merging of the large national and regional dailies (there are no more than a dozen Parisian and national papers), at the same time that photography and advertising invaded the magazines.

Besides Sennep, already mentioned above, we should take note of such great contemporary drawers as Tim, gone from *L'Humanité* (1952–57) to *L'Express* (since 1957), and well known to readers of *Newsweek, Time*, the *New York Times*, and so on; Jean Bosc, who joined *Paris Match* in 1952 and also worked at *Punch* and *Esquire*; Maurice Sinet, who signed ''Siné'' in *Le Canard enchaîné, Elle, France Soir, L'Express* and whose humorous series of ''Chats,'' by punning on the phonemes, gained a wide audience. Falling into other categories are Jacques Faizant and René Pellos. First at *Jours de France* (1945–57), then as Sennep's successor at *Le Figaro* (since 1957), in addition to *Le Point*, Faizant is the author of an amusing series on old ladies, as well as the only drawer to be a member of the editorial board of a large national newspaper (*Le Figaro*). Furthermore, his name has been mentioned for the French Academy. Pellos has not only continued in worthy fashion Forton's Pieds-Nickelés adventures, but is one of the rare great professionals to have specialized in sports drawings, notably the Tour de France bicycle race which he followed for *L'Aurore, L'Équipe*, or *Miroir Sprint*, after a stint in the 1930s at *L'Intransigeant*.

Many more deserve to be included here for various reasons: Piem, Cabu, Plantu and his editorial cartoons in the daily *Le Monde*, Copi for his ''Sitting Woman'' that was one of the charms of *Le Nouvel Observateur*, Claire Bretécher who has succeeded him in that weekly, or Sempé and his faithful partner, René Goscinny, the founder of *Pilote*.

A special place should be reserved for Chaval, the pen name of Yvan Le Louarn. He contributed to *Le Figaro* and *Punch*, to *Paris Match*, where he excelled in nonsensical ads touting tube products like toothpaste or mustard. He also was an informed illustrator of such difficult writers as Nietzsche, Swift, and Flaubert, as well as the creator of *Les Oiseaux sont des cons* (Birds Are Assholes), an unanswerable animated cartoon dated 1965. This born pessimist killed himself in 1968.

Chaval's death almost passed unnoticed in the vast social and political tidal wave that shook France in May of that year, when a whole school of caricaturists was literally established, having had its first tests in the satirical magazine *Hara-Kiri* from 1959 on. Its skills were next sharpened during the *Pilote* crisis in 1968 itself and finally in the firebrand periodical titled *Charlie Hebdo*, famous for its merciless covers. One of these, on the death of President De Gaulle, did not hesitate one bit to print the headline: ''Tragic Ball at Colombey: One Dead''— an obvious allusion to the tragedy in which 150 young people had died in a ballroom fire in the small town of Saint-Laurent-du-Pont. Among these irreverent artists we can list Georges Wolinski, since then editorial cartoonist for *L'Humanité* and *Le Nouvel Observateur*; Cabu, now at *Le Canard enchaîné*; Gébé; and the late Reiser. All have had great influence on a new generation of caricaturists, including those on the right of the political spectrum where less media-conscious artists, like Pinatel, Chard, Hoviv, Aramis, or Trez, have their no less faithful public.

A sign of the times is that today, many French cities are fighting for the privilege of housing public or private collections of satirical drawings or comic strips: Épinal, of course, but also Angoulême, Tourcoing, Marseilles, Metz, and others still—revealing yet another proof of a passion for a quasi-official recognition of this full-fledged art.

CRITIQUE OF THE LITERATURE

There exist in France—and close by in Brussels—important documentation centers that make high-level cartoon research possible. But, with some exceptions mentioned in the bibliography, few truly "scientific" works have appeared until now because of four principal pitfalls which, if avoided, would improve the quality of studies on the subject.

Verbose Dissertations

Too many university studies (from master's essays to doctoral theses) remain at a superficial level of analysis. They believe it indispensable to repeat yet again the same historical review before getting to the point. As to the subject itself, it is often a pretext for philosophical or semiological overflows where Deleuze and Guattari are quoted every other page, while one uneasily feels, in these thick tomes, the absence of a real iconic culture and the methods of comparative (graphic) literature. Finally, most authors give the impression of not knowing the technical and professional data concerning illustration and press drawing, and their special constraints, thus often falsifying the analysis.

Poor Operation of the Collections

Elsewhere I wrote that for a blind person the *Mona Lisa* is at most a painting, even, perhaps, only oil on canvas. Some specialized collections pride themselves on computerizing their documents but leave badly trained, even incompetent, staff in charge, with only crude thesauruses that come close to confusing press drawing, animated cartoon, comic strip, and so on. How then can one bring up, for a given document, the "Marey effect" in chronophotography, for example?

At a 10,000-volume specialized collection, the retrieval system was asked to look up the technical term of Italian origin "doppo bomba," then its common French equivalent, "après bombe." The computer fell into an alarming silence. After vainly selecting the term "post atomique," I eventually discovered the existence of two expressions unused in the profession: "BD post catastrophe" and "BD post cataclysme." Not only is it hard to see what differentiates these two, but the two rubrics each supplied only one book title, and a different one at that. The unreliability of this collection's computerization will remain so as long as it is not based on a specialized thesaurus appropriate for the field.

Lack of a Critical Apparatus

Too many works of popularization, catalogues, even dissertations, do not bother with a critical apparatus: listing of sources, bibliographies, or quite simply an index of names—which reduces considerably their practical usefulness. The 1989 *De De Gaulle à Mitterrand: 30 ans de dessins d'actualité en France*, though published by the Musée d'histoire contemporaine and BDIC, does not avoid this pitfall. Yet it would be a precious tool with the addition of a simple index of the eighty-odd principal contemporary artists presented, many of whom are still little known. It is true that the Centre National des Lettres, which has recently decided no longer to subsidize thesis publication, sets the example by forcing publishers to eliminate from their dissertation manuscripts any reference that could remind the reader of their university origin; footnotes and austere bibliographies become especially incongruous in a work of popularization. Such practice is not the smallest paradox for an organization whose function is supposed to encourage the publication of "difficult" texts for a limited readership.

Extreme Specialization

Underlined at the beginning of this article was the ambiguity in French about the notion of "cartoon." Consequently, according to various sensibilities, around the different designations of *dessin de presse, bande dessinée, illustration pour enfants*, and so on, a partitioning has been created between specialists which particularly frustrates any reasoned attempt at synthesis.

Here again is an up-to-date example: Claude-Anne Parmegiani's *Les Petits français illustrés, 1860–1940*, published by Éditions du Cercle de la Librairie with the aid of CNL, places the apogee of the children's French illustrated book in 1930 with *Babar* by Jean de Brunhoff.

Actually, the problem is not that far removed when one consults the name index (which this time does exist). Félix Lorioux, the principal adapter in France of Walt Disney's *Silly Symphonies*, receives ten full pages, whereas Alain Saint-Ogan is barely mentioned, not having "left any undying memory": a sad oversight of his many contributions to press drawing (*La Dépêche, Le Parisien libéré*), and also of the general passion for *Zig et Puce*, heroes of plays and radio programs, school blotters, dolls, and so many other "merchandising products," and even involved in Lindbergh's epic flight. How to explain the absence in this same book of Saint-Exupéry's quasi-universal *Little Prince*, except by this overspecialization that forces one to take from a graphic artist only what, out of his entire production, fits within such and such an arbitrarily defined category?

This observation is just as valid for all the other graphic "disciplines" thus defined to the detriment of the cartoonists' artistic sensitivity. The best French comics catalogue does not hesitate to amputate an artist like Pellos of one of his little masterpieces—*Mali l'hippopotame*—ignored by the children's illustration specialist for the reason that René Pellos is mainly a creator of comics; the same is true for *Les Aventures de Paillasson*, a delightful children's story illustrated, at the beginning, by Maurice Tillieux. It is as if Leonardo da Vinci's purely graphic work were dissociated from his paintings, or the work of Burne Hogarth, the quasi-creator of *Tarzan*, were cut off from his *Dynamic Anatomy*.

Everything, Therefore, Remains to Be Done

The principal pitfalls eliminated, a feeling arises that everything still remains to be done because, simply, by often putting the cart before the horse, the essential has been omitted in any truly "scientific" research: to *first* provide oneself with the indispensable tools, that is, rigorous monographs on the French press that closely examine without prejudices and preconceptions contents, themes, contributors, circulation figures, formats, sale prices, layouts, and even the "iconic presence index" (as it was rigorously defined by a University of Montpellier team about the universe of the drawer Jacques Martin) of the entire French press.

Indeed, a few famous titles have benefited with varying fortunes from this *analytical* treatment before any particular thematic study: *La Semaine de Suzette, Le Téméraire, Garth, L'Assiette au beurre*, on which it is now possible to work with relative confidence. There remain exceptions, however. It is true that this type of research is specially tedious and hardly rewarding to those not used to this kind of exercise. It is also true that this kind of ascesis, knowing there will always be some opportunist to climb shamelessly on another's results, can discourage all vocations beforehand.

But Everything Can Begin to Be Done

Without a doubt, it is Alain Beyrand who has best shown the way. After studying the distribution of the Marten Toonder series in the regional daily press in France, Beyrand has tackled "forty years of comics in the *N.R.*," a title too limited since the *whole* graphic production in *La Nouvelle République du Centre Ouest* (1946–88), a daily newspaper established in Tours, is being compiled, including illustrations of popular novels, daily strips, drawn movies, humor drawings (by Faizant, Chen, Chaval, Tetsu, etc.), graphic advertisements, and even children's drawn games.

The thoroughness of this remarkable work includes an authors' index, a listing and publication chronology of their contributions, and the precise identification of pen names, showing the present status of research, using collections of old newspapers bought by the pound! The only drawback is that this publication, mimeographed at the author's expense, is limited to twenty-three copies for friends and a twenty-fourth for the Culture Minister, to encourage him to further the development of cartooning in the French press.

Following this status report, the hope remains for the implementation of a complete research project on the history of the cartoon in France, all genres together, once the cartoonist is recognized as a true artist in our society.

RESEARCH COLLECTIONS AND CENTERS

Angoulême: Uniting the graphic art collections of the municipal museum and the library in superb, brand-new premises specifically built for it, the Centre national de la bande dessinée et de l'illustration (CNBDI; National Comics and Illustration Center) henceforth houses 15,000 albums, 1,000 reference works, 800 original comic-strip pages, and about twenty dissertations on comics. Since 1985 it receives the *dépôt légal* (copyright registration) of comic strips appearing in France and has published a professional catalogue. The CNBDI wishes to encourage any research dealing with the children's press. Contact J. P. Mercier or P. Laloi, 121 Route de Bordeaux, 16000 Angoulême.

Épinal: The Musée de l'Imagerie Pellerin and the Centre du Dessin de Presse (Press Drawing Center), which seem to be reorganizing, did not respond to our questionnaire. See below the Musée National des Arts et Traditions Populaires (Paris).

Grenoble: Last born in this field, the Centre de Recherche sur la Littérature Graphique (CRLG: Graphic Literature Research Center) maintains 5,000 books and albums, 800 files, 2,000 periodicals, 400 works, and 400 strip pages or advertising posters (in collaboration with the Salon européen de la BD). Current director: Christian Alberelli, 25 rue des Résistants, 38400 Saint-Martin d'Hères.

Marseilles: The Comics Department of the Municipal Library (38 rue du 141e R.I.A., 13003 Marseilles) did not respond. With approximately 1,000 reviews since 1890, about 7,000 to 8,000 books and albums, almost 2,000 brochures and 500 pages or posters, it is the oldest and richest cartoon collection in Europe. Numerous catalogues on Tillieux, Hogarth, Jean Ache, Jean Cocteau, and so on.

Paris: The Musée de la Publicité de l'Union Centrale des Arts Décoratifs, 18 rue de Paradis, 75010 Paris, owns some 50,000 old posters or lithographs from the entire world, an important library specializing in graphic arts, and more than 20,000 slides. Numerous catalogues on posters and advertising are available. Current director: Jean-Louis Capitaine.

Paris: The Carnavalet Museum (23 rue de Sévigné, 75003 Paris) has 300,000 etchings, some 10,000 drawings, and an important poster collection. A phototheque is open to the public. Current curator-in-chief: B. de Montgolfier.

Paris: The Musée National des Arts et Traditions Populaires (National Popular Arts and Traditions Museum) is located at 6 avenue du Mahatma Gandhi, 75016 Paris. It owns around 50,000 plates of Épinal images and about a thousand drawings and caricatures published in Épinal. The museum is eager to encourage scholars wishing to do research on the origins of comic strips and caricature in France.

Paris: The Public Information Library (The Pompidou/Beaubourg Center cannot "follow up on the many requests it gets. . . . To receive [short] answers to [simple] questions, you can contact our Minitel 36.15 LIBE''). Current assistant to the director: Jacques Bourgoin. Telephone: 42.77.12.33.

Paris: The Bibliothèque de l'Arsenal, 1 rue de Sully, 75004 Paris, has all the humorous magazines published in Paris from 1880 to 1914 and owns an important documentation on press drawing and comics to 1980. Current curator-in-chief: J. C. Garreta.

Tourcoing: The Cultural Center at 100 rue de Lille, 59200 Tourcoing, has for its goal the creation of a European Center for Humor and Communication in the wake of its 5th European Humor Festival held April-June 1989. Collecting old and new documents, cataloguing them on videodiscs, and communicating them (including abroad) are on the current director's (J. L. Schell) agenda.

Roubaix: The Municipal Library (B.P. 737, 59066 Roubaix Cedex 1), which owns a collection on press drawing, including original drawings, has published catalogues on Teel and Cuvelier, two regional artists. It also sponsors *Au Vrai Polichinelle*, a review that studies the marionette and takes press drawing and comics into account. The current director is Bernard Grelle.

Rouen: The Municipal Library possesses quite a rich collection in eighteenth- and nineteenth-century caricatures, along with incomplete collections of satirical newspapers of the nineteenth and early twentieth centuries (e.g., *Le Charivari, La Caricature, L'Assiette au beurre*), as well as posters. Current assistant director: Valérie Neveu, 3 rue Jacques Villon, 76043 Rouen Cedex.

That documentary resources on graphic art are abundant and varied can easily be seen. However, until now, little truly scientific scholarship has been accomplished; too often instead, we have general studies or syntheses which, for all that, repeat each other. Although university dissertations are multiplying, they only rarely contribute to our knowledge of the genre. The history of most publications and periodicals still remains to be done from a strictly bibliographical viewpoint, and we should especially require—at least for university researchers—the inclusion of complete bibliographies and indexes of cited authors and titles.

BIBLIOGRAPHY

Adhémar, Jean, ed. *Dessin d'humour du XVe siècle à nos jours*. Paris: Bibliothèque Nationale, 1971.

Alexandre, Arsène. *L'Art du rire et de la caricature*. Paris: Librairies-Imprimeries Réunies, 1892.

Appelbaum, Stanley, ed. *French Satirical Drawings from "L'Assiette au beurre."* New York: Dover Publications, 1978.

Auclert, Jean-Pierre. *La Grande Guerre des crayons:... 1914–1918*. Paris: Laffont, 1981.

Bachollet, Raymond. "Paul Iribe 'témoin' de son temps." *Le Collectionneur français* 184 (1981): 7–8.

———. "Le Catalogue des journaux satiriques: *Le Mot.*" *Le Collectionneur français* 195 (1982): 10–11; 196 (1982): 7–8; 197 (1983): 5–7.

Baeque, Antoine de. *La Caricature révolutionnaire*. Paris: Presses du CNRS, 1988.

Bayard, Émile. *La Caricature et les caricaturistes*. Paris: Delagrave, 1900.

Béchu, Jean Pierre. *La Belle Époque et son envers*. Paris: André Sauret, 1980.

Benayoun, Robert. *Le Nonsense: de Lewis Carroll à Woody Allen*. Paris: Balland, 1977.

Bertrand, Simone. *La Tapisserie de Bayeux*. St. Léger-Vauban: Zodiaque, 1966.

Blanchard, Gérard. *Histoire de la bande dessinée*... Rev. ed. Verviers, Belgium: Marabout, 1974.

Cahiers de l'art mineur. Paris, 1975–. Numerous issues on Grandville, Caran d'Ache, Callot, Cham, Steinlen, Robida, Doré, Johannot, Daumier, Jossot, etc.

Caricature, presse satirique: 1830–1918. Paris: Bibliothèque Forney, 1979.

Champfleury (Jean Fleury). *Histoire de la caricature moderne.* Paris: Dentu, 1885.

Cuno, James B. "Charles Philipon and La Maison Aubert: The Business, Politics, and Public of Caricature in Paris, 1820–1840." Dissertation, Harvard University, 1985.

Daumier, Honoré. *Les 100 Robert Macaire.* Paris: Pierre Horay, 1979.

Dixmier, Élizabeth. *L'Assiette au beurre.* Paris: Maspero, 1974.

Duflo, Pierre. *Constantin Guys, fou de dessin, grand reporter, 1802–1892.* Paris: Seydoux, 1988.

Duhem, Pierre. *Un écho de la Révolution: Au pays des Gorilles.* Paris: Beauchesne, 1989.

Edelman, Jean. *Gus Bofa et les illustrateurs de l'entre-deux-guerres.* Paris: Musée-galerie de la SEITA, 1983.

Effel, Jean. *De la troisième République à la seconde Restauration.* Paris: Temps actuels, 1981.

Farwell, Beatrice. *French Popular Lithographic Imagery, 1815–1870.* 12 vols. Chicago: University of Chicago Press, 1981.

Halimi, André. *Ce qui a fait rire les Français sous l'Occupation.* Paris: Lattès, 1979.

Histoire générale de la presse française. 5 vols. Paris: Presses Universitaires de France, 1969.

Horn, Maurice, ed. *The World Encyclopedia of Cartoons.* New York: Chelsea House, 1980.

Jones, Philippe R. *La Presse satirique illustrée entre 1860 et 1890.* Tours: Institut français de presse, 1956.

Lacassin, Francis. *Pour un 9e art, la bande dessinée.* Paris: Union générale d'éditions, 1971.

Langlois, Claude. *La Caricature contre-révolutionnaire.* Paris: Presses du CNRS, 1988.

Larkin, Oliver W. *Daumier: Man of His Time.* New York: McGraw-Hill, 1966.

Lethève, Jean. *La Caricature et la presse sous la IIIe République.* Paris: Colin, 1961.

Melcher, Edith. *The Life and Times of Henry Monnier, 1799–1877.* Cambridge, Mass.: Harvard University Press, 1950.

Morin, Violette. "Le Dessin humoristique." *Communications* 15 (1970).

Politique et polémique: La Caricature française et la Révolution, 1789–1799. Paris: Bibliothèque Nationale, and Los Angeles: University of California at Los Angeles, 1988.

Ragon, Michel. *Les Maîtres du dessin satirique.* Paris: Pierre Horay, 1972.

Revel, Jean-François. "L'Invention de la caricature." *L'Oeill* 109 (1964): 12–21.

Romi. *Histoire des faits divers.* Paris: Éditions du Pont Royal, 1962.

Schwarz, Heinrich. "Daumier, Gill and Nadar." *Gazette des Beaux-Arts* 19 (1957): 89–106.

Seguin, Jean-Pierre. *Canards du siècle passé.* Paris: Pierre Horay, 1969.

———. *Nouvelles à sensation: canards du XIXe siècle.* Paris: Colin, 1959.

Soulas, Philippe. *Dessins politiques mai 68–mai 74.* Paris: Balland, 1974.

Traits tirés sur l'actualité. Le Champ du possible, 1978.

Vaissière, Pascal de la, ed. *L'Art de l'estampe et la Révolution française.* Paris: Musée Carnavalet, 1977. Exhibition catalogue.

Vincent, Howard P. *Daumier and His World*. Evanston Ill.: Northwestern University Press, 1968.

Wechsler, Judith. *A Human Comedy*. Chicago: University of Chicago Press, 1982.

To keep up with current activities related to this topic the following publications are very useful:

Bédésup, B.P. 14, 13234 Marseilles Cedex 4.

Un Bon Dessin vaut mieux qu'un long discours, B.P. 192, 75160 Paris Cedex 04.

WittyWorld, P.O. Box 1458, North Wales, Penna. 19454.

Translated by Pierre L. Horn

5

Film

SYBIL DELGAUDIO

At the time of this writing, French cinema has been experiencing a dark interval in a history of countless bright moments that include the likes of Jean Renoir, Abel Gance, Jean-Luc Godard, and François Truffaut, among many others. Concerned observers have called it *la crise*, a bleak period of nonart which has among its culprits and results the significant drop in attendance figures at French movie theaters (due in part to the high cost of tickets and the proliferation of minute, multiplex screens), the large number of movies aired on recently expanded French television (without the commercials that have traditionally been a part of the filmgoing experience), and the ''banalization'' of the French cinema, an artistic decline which has produced primarily lower-quality comedies and police thrillers, but few of the attempts at serious fimmaking that have long characterized French films for English-speaking audiences.

There is some good news in the popular success of higher-quality films such as Claude Berri's *Jean de Florette* and *Manon of the Spring*, and Jean-Loup Hubert's *Le Grand Chemin*, all of which suggest that there is probably an artistic middle ground between the popular but vapid police thrillers and the less popular, more revered tradition of the *auteur*. But the best news of all for the future of French cinema may be Jack Lang's reinstatement as Minister of Culture, Communication and Great Works. Lang, an energetic chauvinist who disdains American influence on French culture, was restored to the position he had held from 1981 to 1986 when the Socialists returned to power in May 1988. A long-time cinephile, Lang has announced an $11.5 million grant to renovate French movie theaters as well as a regulation limiting the number of movies that can be shown on prime-time television. If Lang's strategy works, perhaps the financiers of future French film productions will be more willing to risk money on fresh ideas and new talent, with less worry about blockbuster potential and the lowest common denominator.

Historically, French cinema has struggled more with the disjunction between art and entertainment than have other national cinemas. In fact, this duality has undoubtedly stimulated more quality films than could ever have been possible in the single-minded, commercially obsessed United States film industry. Both cinemas began with a studio-controlled system, but since the 1920s the studio system in France has ceased to exist, whereas it remained the dominant mode of production in America until the 1960s. American cinema, while struggling under the rule of powerful, profit-driven producers, became a commercial entertainment medium, providing audiences with escapist fare that often reflected popular needs, dreams, and drives in images of high glamour. When the French cinema broke free of its studio control, the way was cleared for individual artists to dominate, and it is partly this tendency toward the primacy of the director as *auteur* that has encouraged France's contribution to the art of world cinema. In addition, the desire to free itself from Hollywood domination, both as its model and in its market, led to the creation of a richly developed alternate cinema, a crucial contributor to the growth of film as art.

HISTORICAL OUTLINE

The struggle between cinema as art and cinema as entertainment began with the birth of the movies, and movies—the commercial exploitation of cinema— were born in France. When the Lumière brothers opened the first movie theater at Paris' Grand Café in 1895, they exhibited a prototypical film style that would continue to be at the core of ensuing theoretical and aesthetic debates about the essence of cinema. For the filming of their *actualités*—everyday events such as a baby eating breakfast or a train arriving at a station—these pioneering "realists" were exploring the potential of this new medium to fascinate and inform, to entertain and instruct. In addition to introducing a new form of popular entertainment, they had also discovered a new art. The Lumières even experimented with rudimentary narratives, and their short film *L'Arroseur arrosé* was a classic comedy of mischief and reprisal. Though their subject often appeared to be randomly chosen slices-of-life, the Lumières revealed their artistry in the meticulousness of their cinematic choices and their ability to recognize the artistic perception of the camera eye. Still, at least in terms of subject matter, the Lumières were more recorders than creators, and it was not until one of their first-night audience members began his experiments that cinema's ability to create magic and illusion was fully explored.

Georges Méliès was the cinema's first great artist. Méliès used his experience with theatrical techniques to create a cinema of magical tricks, dreams, and fantasies that fascinated audiences who were beginning to look beyond cinema's potential to re-create reality. His world of illusion became the artistic model for the theories that stressed that film art was the result of differences between physical reality and cinematic reality. Artistically and theoretically the Lumières and Méliès discovered the dualistic nature of cinema's essence (its ability to capture a moment of reality and its ability to create a world of illusion) while exploring its popular appeal as a form of mass entertainment. But it is their discovery of cinema's relationship to both filmmaker and audience, that is, cinema as art/cinema as entertainment, that became their greatest contribution to the ensuing position of film in French popular culture.

The popularity of Méliès' films from 1896 to 1905 was challenged, however, by two studios, Pathé-Frères and Gaumont, the former taking over Méliès' Star Film Company in 1908 and ultimately forcing him out of filmmaking by 1913. Both studios had their own "geniuses"; at Pathé-Frères, Ferdinand Zecca made outdoor chase films, melodramas, and farces that departed from Méliès' stage-bound theatrical pieces; while at Gaumont, Louis Feuillade took the everyday events discovered by the Lumières and used them to evoke the dreams of Méliès. Feuillade was most associated with a detective serial film based on a popular novel about a master criminal known as Fantômas. In this serial, Feuillade combined a keen understanding for what the public wanted with a sharp artistic eye for the details of film direction; his approach to film art stressed the details of composition over the combined images of montage, highlighting yet another of cinema's great theoretical/aesthetic debates, later expressed in the formative theories of Sergei Eisenstein and the realist theories of André Bazin.

In 1908 the *film d'art* movement made a conscious attempt to attract more middle-class audiences to the cinema by increasing its artistic and intellectual appeal. Using talent and material from France's most respected theaters (e.g., the Comédie Française), the *film d'art* movement brought art to the masses, encouraging a new, more educated audience, while convincing producers that there was popular appeal in highbrow entertainment. *Films d'art* were rarely more than static reproductions of staged scenes, and while their output proved that movies could exceed one reel in length, and convinced directors that acting for films required very different skills from those used for theater, the movement was soon supplanted by the more exclusively cinematic language associated with D. W. Griffith and the demand for American films. French domination of the international motion picture industry decreased markedly after 1910 with the meteoric rise of Hollywood production.

The *film d'art*, though it disappeared, had paved the way for the contributions of intellectuals as filmmakers in France. After World War I, Paris became the center of such artistic movements as surrealism, dadaism, and cubism, and practitioners of these movements, as well as critics of film, became fascinated with the possibilities of film to explore the concepts of avant-garde art. Chief among these intellectuals was Louis Delluc, the first editor of the film journal *Cinéma*, who was interested in creating a cinema that would be completely "French," while elevating it to the level of the other arts. Delluc gathered many young filmmakers to form the first avant-garde, or "impressionist" school, including such talents as Jean Epstein, whose background had been in poetry and philosophy; Marcel L'Herbier, who had been a poet and film critic; and Germaine Dulac, who had been a musician. While some of the impressionist filmmakers, especially Epstein, explored Lumières' concerns (a fascination with everyday events, ordinary people, and natural locations) and attempted to combine art with more popular appeal (Georges Sadoul has termed this quality in French cinema *populisme*), this first avant-garde was primarily limited in its appeal to the intellectual. Only Abel Gance, whose association with the impressionists was brief, combined poetic images with developed narratives to produce films of intense power and artistic genius (*La Roue* in 1922 and the technically stunning *Napoléon* in 1927 are specific examples), which would influence generations of French filmmakers to follow.

The dramatic decline in the popularity of French films—due in part to the split between intellectual and popular appeal following the *film d'art* and impressionist movements, and in large measure to the loss of an international market following the war—allowed for the dominance of American films in France during the twenties and until the coming of sound. However, while the French cinema struggled to define its own character, the movement to combine popular cinema with art and intellectualism continued. Influenced by the impressionists, French film criticism began to develop, encouraging daily film reviews in newspapers, as well as sparking the birth of film journals and ciné-clubs, all of which contributed to a rich and growing field of cinema studies and film theory. Writers like Léon Moussinac (*Naissance du cinéma*, 1925) began to treat film as an art form as important as painting or music, and ciné-clubs maintained the creative and intellectual tradition of French cinema while providing a ready-made audience for foreign films (specifically German and Soviet) and for the second avant-garde movement of the late twenties (in films by Man Ray, Jacques Feyder, Luis Buñuel, Fernand Léger, and Jean Cocteau). With roots in dadaism and surrealism, the second avant-garde made nonnarrative films that appealed primarily to the senses and explored cinema's essential purity, divorced from traditions that had bound it to literature. René Clair, who began his career in the second avant-garde movement, most successfully bridged the gap between the cinema of high art and the more commercial cinema, when, in 1927, he made the successful *Italian Straw Hat*, and when he experimented in later films with sound and popular genres such as the musical. Jean Vigo was also an important figure in early French sound cinema; in *Zéro de conduite* (1933) and *L'Atalante* (1934) he combined poetry with politics, prefiguring the concerns of France's Golden Age filmmakers.

Other than for Vigo and Clair, the early sound era was not artistically or financially rich for French cinema. Hollywood dominated French screens with its rush of sound films, Pathé and Gaumont both faced bankruptcy, and production dropped from 160 to 120 films per year. Ironically, these factors contributed to the development of independent production, which led to the most artistically rich period in the history of French cinema. Known as "poetic realism," this movement combined the Lumière interest in naturalism with lessons learned from the entire tradition of French filmmakers to produce films that found poetry in the ordinary and encouraged the work of great film artists such as Jacques Prévert, Julien Duvivier, Marcel Carné, Marcel Pagnol, and the remarkable Jean Renoir.

As the most important and influential of the poetic realists, Renoir combined techniques of realism with a social conscience, struggling with the dual appeal of intellectualism and popularity in films which were critically acclaimed but often not commercially successful (of his first two films, *La Chienne* and *Boudu Saved from Drowning*, both made in 1932, only the first was commercially successful, while his masterpiece, *Rules of the Game* released in 1939, was thought to be too inaccessible a work for French popular taste).

It was during this period, often called France's Golden Age of Cinema, that French production became increasingly more splintered, relying on the rather small output of numerous independents that produced an average of one-and-a-half films per year. Audiences in the provinces, which accounted for 90 percent of the commercial market, attended films on a regular, weekly basis, rarely altering their habits based on a film's quality—a rigidity which, ironically, secured a loyal following among the French cinema public throughout the thirties and until the Occupation. The thirties also witnessed the decline of the ciné-clubs and film journals as the more intellectual cinephile was replaced by the popular moviegoer. It was a period in which the great works of art by Renoir, Carné, and Jean Grémillon alternated with the mediocre efforts of the likes of Christian-Jaque, a director who made twenty-five films in ten years, consistently modifying his style to the desires of popular taste. After a brief association with politics in the years of the Popular Front (1936–38), French cinema in the Golden Age was actually a conglomeration of artists and hacks that encouraged the output of mediocre films while it permitted the director to emerge as the dominant figure of creativity in the filmmaking process. Unlike Hollywood's studio system, which gave primary power to the producer, the French system, with its numerous independent companies, allowed each project its own individual character and each director his own autonomy.

In 1940, when France fell to the Germans, French cinema came under government control. Vichy created its own agency (the Comité d'Organisation de l'Industrie Cinématographique, which survives today as the CNC) for the purpose of financing French production and wresting control from "corrupt" independents. Since American films were not imported during this period, competition was reduced and French films enjoyed a period of record-high attendance. While several of the greatest directors (Clair, Duvivier, Max Ophuls, Feyder, and Renoir) left the country to work in other parts of Europe or in America, the way was also cleared for new directors, giving opportunities to Robert Bresson, Jacques Becker, and Henri-Georges Clouzot among others.

Following the war the French film industry was dominated by filmmakers who shifted between public popularity and critical acclaim. Jean Delannoy, while not a favorite of French critics, was enormously popular with audiences, while

Christian-Jaque continued to make commercially successful films that provided audiences with escapist entertainment. Several of these postwar directors had roots in the avant-garde (Claude Autant-Lara and Yves Allégret) and made films that were often political as well as artistic. The emphasis on a film of the working class was beginning to be replaced by the emphasis on personal expression, as a new vitality was beginning to emerge in film journals, ciné-clubs, and the film product itself. Jacques Tati, Jean Cocteau, Robert Bresson, and Jean-Pierre Melville began their own, individual approaches to cinema, giving rise (along with a change in CNC policy that no longer subsidized producers based on previous box-office successes, but considered instead the proposed script the most important criterion for subsidy) to a system that began to encourage new filmmakers with original ideas.

The New Wave emerged in the late fifties, partly as a result of economic and policy shifts within the industry, partly as a result of the need to infuse new blood into a failing industry and artform. Louis Malle, Roger Vadim, and Marcel Camus provided a transition based on their own inexpensively shot, first-film successes (Malle's *Ascenseur pour l'échafaud*, 1957; Vadim's *Et Dieu créa la femme*, 1956; and Camus's *Mort en fraude*, 1957) while other young cinephiles, several of whom began as critics for the journal *Cahiers du Cinéma*, devoured the films of Henri Langlois's Cinémathèque Française, absorbing all they could of the visual styles of American directors. Stylistically, the early New Wave films were reactions against the Hollywood aesthetic of content over style, stressing personal vision and highlighting the choices that foregrounded the techniques of cinema. Often using portable equipment, hand-held cameras and improvisational acting, the New Wave directors challenged basic assumptions about the cinema, considering its political implications, questioning traditional narrative, and preferring the everyday problems of human existence to those that had been the subject of earlier filmmakers. Ushered in by François Truffaut's *The 400 Blows* (financed by Truffaut's father-in-law) and Jean-Luc Godard's *Breathless* (financed with the money Truffaut had made on *The 400 Blows*), the New Wave (whose other young stars included Jacques Rivette, Claude Chabrol, and Éric Rohmer), in stressing a personal attitude toward filmmaking not possible in large, studio-controlled systems, foregrounded the director as creator of the film while expressing a commitment to cinema as art. Others, who formed the more radical Left Bank group (Agnès Varda, Alain Resnais, Chris Marker), developed personal styles which left them less open to the later mainstreaming that eventually subsumed Truffaut, setting them apart from popular appeal. Godard, most specifically, made films which became increasingly more political and intellectual, further limiting the mass audience appeal of his work.

With the publication of the *auteur* theory, the young filmmakers/critics of *Cahiers* elevated American directors like Hawks and Ford to the level of *auteurs* and shifted the emphasis from Hollywood product to personal signature, narrowing the gap in American cinema history that had always existed between art and entertainment. The New Wave's influence was international as well as local, altering not only the style of contemporary American films, but reevaluating the artistry of the efforts of studio directors.

Ironically, as the sixties wore on and the New Wave directors splintered into mainstream and specialized appeal, French cinema widened the gap between art and popular entertainment, its annual output emphasizing police and comedy genres and actor vehicles. The events of May 1968, precipitated in part by the firing of Henri Langlois as head of the Cinémathèque Française, joined student protesters with workers in a general strike that paralyzed the country and radicalized artists like Godard, who forced the Cannes Film Festival to close, and with thousands of other filmmakers, writers, and technicians, formed an États-Généraux of the French cinema dedicated to the creation of a more socially and politically committed form of filmmaking. But the États-Généraux had difficulty agreeing on a policy that reflected a consensus, and its disorganization gave rise to the development of individual filmmaking collectives which stressed anonymity and directly challenged the supremacy of the *auteur*.

Actually, the most profound impact of May 1968 was in the area of film theory and film journals. *Cahiers du Cinéma* became more radicalized, and *Cinéthique* was established in 1969. While *Cahiers* still explored mainstream cinema from a position now influenced by Marxism and the psychoanalytic theories of Jacques Lacan, *Cinéthique* (inspired by the theories of Louis Althusser) denounced the mainstream, offering the avant-garde as the only true "materialist" cinema and shifting analysis away from pure aesthetics to explore relationships between aesthetics and ethics. Both journals allied against what they perceived as the antitheoretical approach of *Positif*, which had published articles attacking the followers of Christian Metz and semiotics as obscure and pretentious. (See Sylvia Harvey's *May '68 and Film Culture* for a detailed analysis of the events of May 1968, their impact on film theory and culture, and the various political positions taken by the aforementioned journals.)

With the infusion of new spirit into the French film industry engendered by the events of May 1968, it is particularly disappointing to chart the years that followed. The promise of an invigorated cinema was lost again in a diffusion of spirit and confusion of goals, many of them still commercial, and the real revolution of ideas was left to film theory and the work by people such as Christian Metz in cinema semiotics—work which has significantly altered the way in which cinema is perceived as well as the way in which its history and aesthetics have been taught throughout the world.

While May 1968 permitted some experimentation in films by Marguerite Duras, Alain Robbe-Grillet, Jacques Rivette, and others, the gap between art and entertainment has continued to widen. By 1971, André Astoux, then head of CNC, declared in response to a dwindling box office that French films must be more geared toward entertainment if an audience was to be brought back. In 1976, censorship was abolished, giving rise to the popularity of the pornographic film (*Emmanuelle* was the number-one box-office hit); French film journals, previously engaged in backbiting, joined forces to request the formation of a

National French Film Institute. Their proposal called for a library and an accessible archive for the study of cinema, clearly an attempt to rescue a film culture that was quickly disappearing.

By the late seventies, American films, always popular, were becoming increasingly dominant, and while some New Wave directors continued to make films, they were, except for Godard, becoming more distracted by commercial concerns. But the struggle to achieve an art cinema continues in France through the work of individual filmmakers and the attempt to reconstruct a national filmmaking tradition based on government support and the encouragement of individual expression. In its battle against Hollywood domination, the French film industry's acknowledgment of a common enemy may yet unify the commercial and artistic factions of French cinema to forge and strengthen a film industry and culture that is both indigenous and artistically rich.

REFERENCE WORKS

Because so much has been written in the field of film history, theory, and criticism, reference works, while useful for capsulized and superficial information, are normally encouragements to look further.

Several encyclopedic works contain better than average essays on film personalities. David Thomson's *A Biographical Dictionary of Film* contains informative critical essays on nine hundred directors, actors, and producers, and, unlike many works of this sort, Thomson's book manages to express, in each essay, a point of view that is worth consideration. Georges Sadoul's *Dictionary of Film Makers* (and its companion, *Dictionary of Films*—both also available in French) contains brief biographies of directors, producers, writers, cinematographers, and composers. Since Sadoul is French, he gives particular attention to important figures in the history of French cinema. When the English edition was published, the translator revised Sadoul's original work by adding new entries for directors who established reputations beginning in the sixties. Both Thomson's and Sadoul's books contain filmographies for each entry, but it is important to note that such information is limited to covering years before the books' publications (1972 for Sadoul; 1981 for Thomson). Other filmographies can be found in James Robert Parish's *Film Directors Guide—Western Europe*, published in 1976.

For the best critical dictionary on film, the researcher should consult Richard Roud's two-volume *Cinema: A Critical Dictionary*. Roud's work contains extended critical essays on selected filmmakers (most of them directors) who have contributed to the development of cinema. Essays have been written by various contributors, some of them experts in their particular subject. In addition to its many fine essays on French filmmakers, the work also covers unusual subjects which may be of interest to the researcher in French cinema. There is an excellent essay on the origins of French cinema by Henri Langlois as well as essays on some of the important figures in the history of French cinema, including Marguerite Duras and Jean Eustache, among many others not covered by the more popularly influenced choices of Thomson or Sadoul.

Less astutely critical, but also useful is Leslie Halliwell's frequently revised *The Filmgoer's Companion*, containing not only brief biographies of popular film personalities but also rather offbeat topics that list films about bullfights, explorers, and politics, as examples. Another recent volume, *The Illustrated Who's Who of the Cinema*, edited by Ann Lloyd and Graham Fuller, combines attractive illustrations with its biographical material, primarily on performers.

In French, there are several good encyclopedic works that cover cinema history. Roger Boussinot's one-volume *L'Encyclopédie du Cinéma* is a useful compilation of brief essays on actors, directors, and films, including published critical opinions with each entry, as well as sections devoted to specific subjects such as the New Wave and Chinese cinema. Jean Mitry's six-volume *Filmographie universelle* covering France and Europe is helpful to the researcher who is looking for chronologically arranged information. Volume 1 (*Index historique des techniques et industries du Film*) is a year-by-year history (1860–1962), listing important events, discoveries, and releases arranged by date, while Volume 2 (*Primitifs et Précurseurs—France et Europe*) contains essays on early filmmakers and producers. Later volumes cover cinema history with essays on filmmakers, movements, and discoveries. René Jeanne and Charles Ford's six-volume *Histoire encyclopédique du cinéma* is divided into countries and covers the years from 1895 to 1955. This is a comprehensive work, but its original 1947 publication, even with a 1970 revision, makes it somewhat dated. Also dated is Ford's *Histoire populaire du cinéma* (1955), though it contains very good sections on early film history and national cinemas.

WORKS OF HISTORY AND CRITICISM

For general histories of cinema with sections devoted to the various movements in French cinema history, the researcher can consult several works in English. David Cook's *A History of Narrative Film* covers France chronologically, containing sections on cinema origins, avant-garde impressionism, poetic realism (with a separate section devoted to Jean Renoir), the Occupation and postwar cinema, and the French New Wave and its major figures. Information from books such as this should always be supplemented by more detailed studies of particular directors (researchers are referred to bibliographies listed in Cook et al., since space limitations preclude such listings here) and periods in French cinema history. Also useful is Gerald Mast's *A Short History of the Movies* which, in addition to similar material contained in Cook, includes a section on "The New Internationalism" dealing with changes in film commerce since the mid–1960s. The recently published *The Cinema Book*, edited by Pam Cook, divides cinema study into five major sections: history, genre, authorship, history of narrative, and narrative and structuralism, authored by writers who approach film theory and criticism from different perspectives. It is particularly useful in its treatment of the period from the sixties through the seventies, when film studies underwent a transformation to include theories influenced by structuralism and psycho-analysis, subjects barely mentioned by either David Cook or Gerald Mast. In French, the most comprehensive history of cinema is Georges Sadoul's six-volume *Histoire générale du Cinéma*, which, while it concludes with a volume on Hollywood and the end of the sound era, contains an important first volume on the prehistory of cinema, covering the years 1832–97. Jean Mitry's *Histoire du cinéma* is an important work which has been frequently updated since its first publication in 1967.

There are several useful histories of French cinema, some of which are general and cover cinema's entire history, while others deal with specific periods. *French Cinema*, by Roy Armes, is a comprehensive study of French cinema from its inception through the eighties. Given the difficulty of producing a one-volume study of a national cinema as rich as that of France, Armes has done an admirable job in presenting the ways in which filmmakers, through their work, responded to economic, social, and cultural conditions in France, as well as to changing theories of the cinema. Less detailed is Marcel Martin's slim volume, *France*, more of an index or guide to important directors, actors, technicians, and film titles. Georges Sadoul's *Le Cinéma français, 1890–1962* covers major move-ments and personalities, with a useful alphabetical listing of filmmakers and filmographies, as well as a chronological listing by date of important events in cinema history. James Reid Paris' *The Great French Films* and Anthony Slide's *Fifty Classic French Films: A Pictorial Record* are primarily picture books; yet both contain synopses and commentary, and Paris' book begins with an intro-duction by François Truffaut. Robin Buss's recent *The French through Their Films* is more sociological than some of the aforementioned works, dividing its approach into categories such as "politics and religion," and "provincial and rural life," for example, to present a picture of French society through its films. Included is a very helpful filmography of those films covered by the book, containing useful pieces of researched information about each film not easily found anywhere else. In a similar vein, Allen Thiher's *The Cinematic Muse: Critical Studies in the History of French Cinema* covers French film from 1928 to 1966, relating films to other areas of French culture.

There are many excellent books dealing with particular periods in French cinema history. Richard Abel's impressive *French Cinema: The First Wave, 1915–1929* is among the outstanding works on a national cinema. In his coverage of both the dominant film industry and the alternate cinema network, Abel has written a detailed, unique perspective on French cinema. A more conventional, yet serviceable follow-up to the years covered by Abel is John W. Martin's *The Golden Age of French Cinema, 1929–1939*. Written for the respectable, mul-tivolume Twayne Series on the history of filmmaking, the book concentrates on the achievements of those filmmakers (especially Duvivier, Feyder, Grémillon, and Pagnol) whose work, until then, had not been dealt with adequately in English. Another important contribution to the scholarship of the early period in French cinema is Mary Lea Bandy's *Rediscovering French Film*, a collection of important essays by both filmmakers and film scholars. This volume grew out of the retrospective on early French cinema presented by the Museum of Modern Art from 1981 to 1983 and contains an extensive bibliography of works (in both French and English) covering this period. David Bordwell's *French Impressionist Cinema: Film Culture, Film Theory, and Film Style* examines the period from 1918 to 1928 through an analysis of thirty-six films of the period and is filled with Bordwell's usual insights. Elizabeth Strebel's *French Social Cinema of the 1930's: A Cinematographic Expression of Popular Front Consciousness* examines why French cinema rose to international prominence in 1935, focusing on the interaction between film and society. Roy Armes's two-volume *French Cinema Since 1946* is auteurist in its approach, dealing in Volume 1 with directors in "The Great Tradition" (including Clair, Renoir, Clouzot, Grémillon, Tati, etc.) and in Volume 2 with directors who can be categorized in terms of "Personal Style" (including Franju, Melville, Varda, and the rest of the New Wave). Another auteurist approach to French cinema can be found in John J. Michalczyk's *The French Literary Filmmakers*, which covers filmmakers who have made their reputations in both literature and film, and includes sections on Sacha Guitry, Jean Giono, and others not covered elsewhere. André Bazin's *French Cinema of the Occupation and Resistance*, while not a comprehensive study, since Bazin did not begin writing about the period until it was half over, is a collection of essays compiled by François Truffaut, dealing with specific films and filmmakers and representing, as Truffaut has put it, the birth of Bazin's own critical aesthetic. Since Bazin's contribution to cinema studies has been so important, the researcher should also consult his two-volume theoretical work *What Is Cinema?*, as well as Dudley Andrew's biography, *André Bazin*. André Bazin is also the subject of Volume 9, No. 4 of the film journal *Wide Angle*. In *The New Wave*, Peter Graham has collected important essays on the New Wave, written, during that period, primarily by the critics of *Cahiers du Cinéma* (Godard, Chabrol, Truffaut) and *Positif*. Other essays by *Cahiers* critics have been collected and translated in *Cahiers du Cinéma: The 1950's, Neo-Realism, Hollywood, New Wave*, edited by Jim Hillier. A second volume, *Cahiers du Cinéma: 1960–1968. The New Wave, New Cinema and Re-evaluating Hollywood*, is useful in introducing changing approaches of the *Cahiers* critics. James Monaco takes a completely auteurist approach in *The New Wave*, defining the movement simply in terms of "Truffaut, Godard, Chabrol, Rohmer, Rivette," in chapters that deal with each of those filmmakers. Raymond Durgnat's *Nouvelle Vague: The First Decade*, one of the first books on the subject, is nevertheless still the best.

Several general works on cinema contain useful sections on France. Paul Monaco's *Cinema and Society* deals with the social aspects of film in France and Germany during the 1920s, covering such topics as the economics of the film industry, relationship with the government, and ways in which films reflected national character. *The Film Industry in Six European Countries*, published jointly by the London Film Center and Unesco, contains a section on France but is dated by its 1950 publication. By far the most useful collection of essays and information on the French film industry, however, has appeared in Peter Cowie's annual *International Film Guide*. Begun in 1967, each year's edition has included an essay on the current state of the French film industry, with up-to-date information on archives, magazines, and cinema bookshops. The 1985 version contains an invaluable "Dossier on France," an in-depth survey of developments, trends, and major personalities in and associated with the post–New Wave era. More theoretical essays on French cinema are collected in Janet Staiger and Ben Lawton's *1976 Film Studies Annual*, a sampling of film scholarship from a film conference held at Purdue University. Robin Wood's *Second Wave* is a collection of pieces on the post–New Wave era, containing articles on filmmakers such as Jean-Pierre Lefebvre and Jean-Marie Straub, who are rarely covered in other books. Finally, and most recently, Melinda Camber Porter's *Through Parisian Eyes: Reflections on Contemporary French Arts and Culture* covers a wide spectrum of figures in philosophy and the arts, with a section on contemporary French filmmakers that includes essays on Resnais, Malle, Tavernier, and others.

Several film journals have devoted complete issues or major sections to a study of French cinema. *Wide Angle*, Volume 4, No. 4 (1981), is a special issue on French cinema, while "Classic French Film," is covered in a special section of *American Film* (1981). The French journal *L'Avant-Scène du Cinéma* has a special double issue (Nos. 279–80, January 1–15, 1982) covering early French cinema and based on the film collection of the Cinémathèque Française.

In French, Francis Courtade's *Les Malédictions du cinéma français. Une histoire du cinéma français parlant (1928–1978)* is a comprehensive study of crises faced by the French film industry throughout its history, including chapters on financing, censorship, technology, and the influence of television. Charles Ford's *Histoire du cinéma français contemporain, 1945–1977* includes chapters on documentary film and the commercial cinema, subjects rarely treated in other works on French cinema.

The influence of French philosophical, cultural, and psychoanalytic thought on film theory, scholarship, and the cinema itself has been immeasurable, and the amount of material available too enormous to deal with here. The researcher is referred specifically to the work of Christian Metz, whose books on cinema semiotics (*Film Language* and *The Imaginary Signifier*) provide invaluable introductions to contemporary film theory as influenced by such thinkers as Claude Lévi-Strauss, Roland Barthes, Jacques Derrida, Maurice Merleau-Ponty, Michel Foucault, and Jacques Lacan, among many others. Also useful in its analysis of the history and impact of French film theory is Edward Loury's *The Filmology Movement and Film Study in France*.

Periodical articles on French cinema published after 1973 are indexed annually in *The Film Literature Index* and the *International Index to Film Periodicals*. The latter also contains useful annotations. Articles published prior to 1973 are indexed in Richard Dyer MacCann and Edward Perry's *The New Film Index* and Gerlach and Gerlach's *The Critical Index*.

RESEARCH COLLECTIONS

Film scholarship has always been complicated by the difficulty of obtaining materials for viewing, although the recent explosion of available video materials has helped somewhat. A good collection of French cinema on video can be found through Facets Video, 1517 West Fullerton Avenue, Chicago, Illinois 60614. Films can be either purchased or rented by mail, and the researcher is advised to send for their catalogue.

Those who prefer to view films in their original or 16mm formats should turn to the limited number of American archives which continue to collect and preserve films as well as exhibit films in special series. Since 1975, the Museum of Modern Art in New York City has been running a "Perspectives on French Cinema," an annual exhibition of current and historical films often accompanied by a discussion with the filmmaker. MOMA also houses an extensive collection of French cinema from the silent through the contemporary era. Other, smaller collections that include French films are contained at the Library of Congress in Washington, George Eastman House in Rochester, the Film Archives at UCLA, and the collection at the State Historical Society of Wisconsin in Madison. The Anthology Film Archives in New York City houses a good collection of French avant-garde films. All of the above provide viewing facilities for scholarly research.

In France, the Cinémathèque Française, in the Palais de Chaillot in Paris, houses the largest collection of French cinema. While its reputation for assisting scholars has been less than stellar, its recent reconciliation with the French government bodes well for a shift toward greater accommodation. Smaller collections of French cinema may be found at the Bois d'Arcy (whose Service des Archives de Film du Centre National de la Cinématographie also contains print materials such as stills, posters, and scripts), the Cinémathèque Universitaire (Paris), and the Cinémathèque de Toulouse.

Print materials in the United States are available at the Library and Museum of the Performing Arts at Lincoln Center, New York City. Its Theater and Film collection is among the best in this country and contains a variety of materials in both French and English, from books and magazines to clippings, reviews, posters, and stills. Also invaluable to the researcher is the print collection at the Museum of Modern Art's Film Study Center and Library. The center's material on French cinema is found primarily in clippings folders (their collection of materials on the French avant-garde is particularly impressive), while books and nonrecent periodicals are housed in the library. The Film Study Center's staff provides generous and invaluable assistance to researchers. Other, less extensive collections of print materials on French cinema are available at the Library of Congress and the Doheny Library of the University of Southern California.

In France, research libraries containing print materials related to the cinema are located at the Bibliothèque Nationale, the Bibliothèque de l'IDHEC, the Bibliothèque de la Cinémathèque Française, and the Bibliothèque de l'Arsenal, all located in Paris. Print materials can also be located at the Cinémathèque de Toulouse.

The bibliography lists books and articles on French cinema, periods in its history (e.g., the Occupation) and major movements (e.g., the New Wave). Not included here, for reasons of space, are books and articles which deal with specific directors, individual films, and more focused material.

The inclusion of journal articles has been limited mostly to those published since 1973. For earlier articles, the researcher is referred to Gerlach and Gerlach, *The Critical Index: A Bibliography of Articles on Film in English, 1946–1973*, which indexes twenty-three film journals, and *The New Film Index*, edited by Richard Dyer MacCann and Edward W. Perry, which indexes several standard journals, such as those indexed in *The Reader's Guide*, as well as numerous film journals.

BIBLIOGRAPHY

Abel, Richard. *French Cinema: The First Wave, 1915–1929*. Princeton, N.J.: Princeton University Press, 1984.

———. *French Film Theory and Criticism*. 2 vols. Princeton, N.J.: Princeton University Press, 1988.

Adair, G. "Gilbert Adair from Paris." *Film Comment* 15, 4 (1979): 4, 6.

Agel, Henri; Bazin, André; et al. *Sept ans de cinéma français (1945–1951)*. Paris: Éditions du Cerf, 1953.

Allombert, G.; Merigeau, P.; Lefèvre, R.; and Grelier, R. "Le Mélodrame." *Image et Son* 336 (1970): 32–50.

———. "Vers une nouvelle modification de la structure économique du cinéma français." *Image et Son* 301 (1975): 45–50.

Amengual, B., et al. "Un étrange cinéma dans une drôle d'époque." *Écran* 8 (1972): 2–17.

American Film. Special issue on classic French film. 17, 6 (1981).

Andrew, Dudley. *André Bazin*. New York: Oxford University Press, 1978.

Armes, Roy. *French Cinema*. New York: Oxford University Press, 1985.

———. *French Cinema Since 1946*. Vol. 1, *The Great Tradition*. New York: A. S. Barnes, 1970.

———. *French Cinema Since 1946*. Vol. 2, *Personal Style*. New York: A. S. Barnes, 1970.

———. *French Film*. New York: Dutton, 1970.

Auty, M. "French Cinema in the Seventies." *Focus on Film* 36 (1980): 38–42.

L'Avant-Scène du Cinéma. Special issue devoted to treasures of the French Cinémathèque. 279–80 (January 1–15, 1982).

Bandy, Mary Lea, ed. *Rediscovering French Film*. New York: Graphic Society, 1983.

Bardèche, Maurice, and Brasillach, Robert. *Histoire du cinéma français*. Paris: Martel, 1948.

Barrot, O. "Génériques d'avant-guerre." *Cinématographe* 114 (1985): 68–69.

Bazin, André. *French Cinema of the Occupation and Resistance: The Birth of a Critical Esthetic*. New York: Ungar, 1981.

———. *What Is Cinema?* 2 vols. Berkeley: University of California Press, 1971.

Bertin-Maghit, J.-P. "Propagande sociologique dans le cinéma français de 1940–44." *Image et Son* 329 (1978): 71–84.

Beylie, C. "Perpignan à la recherche du cinéma perdu." *L'Avant-Scène du Cinéma* 335 (1984): 89–92.

———. "Un prince de la comédie mondaine: Yves Mirande." *Cinématographe* 102 (1984): 56–63.

Bordwell, David. *French Impressionist Cinema: Film Culture, Film Theory, and Film Style*. New York: Arno, 1980.

Boussinot, Roger, ed. *L'Encyclopédie du Cinéma*. 2 vols. Paris: Bordas, 1970.

Buss, Robin. *The French through Their Films*. New York: Ungar, 1988.

Carcassonne, P. "Visages de l'autre." *Cinématographe* 49 (1979): 26–28.

Carcassonne, P., et al. "Dossier: le 'cinéma' français." *Cinématographe* 85 (1983): 1–30.

Cébé, G. "Pour en finir avec une certain tendance du cinéma français . . . " *Image et Son* 357 (1981): 58–62.

Cervoni, A. "La Loi de l'offre et de la demande." *Cinéma* (Paris) 212–13 (1976): 52–62.

———. "Twenty-Five Years of Reflection." *Film Society Review* 7 (1972): 37–50.

Cheray, J. L. "Dossier d'une crise." *Image et Son* 324 (1978): 13–15.

Chevallier, J. "Mai 68 . . . et après." *Image et Son* 326 (1978): 67–84.

Chevrie. M. "L'Internationale et la voix." *Cahiers du Cinéma* 358 (1984): viii–ix.

Chirat, R. "Théâtre et cinéma des années trente: l'acteur en mutation." *Cinéma d'aujourd'hui* 10 (1976): 19–27.

———. "Le Cinéma des années noires." *Avant-Scène* 127–28 (1972): 80–83.

Ciment, M. "Une tendance certaine du cinéma français." *Positif* 144–45 (1972): 103–9.

"Le Cinéma français au présent: réalités et perspectives." *Cinéma d'aujourd'hui* 12–13 (1977): 7–233 (special issue).

"Le Cinéma français se meurt . . . mais ne se rend pas." *Cinéma* (Paris) 163 (1972): 30–122.

"Le Cinéma militant dans l'histoire en France." *Cinéma d'aujourd'hui* 5–6 (1976): 19–31.

Colpart, G. "Cinéma populaire? Ouvrir des brèches." *Téléciné* 213 (1976): 26–27.

Cook, David. *A History of Narrative Film*. New York: Norton, 1981.

Cook, Pam, ed. *The Cinema Book*. New York: Pantheon, 1985.

Cornand, A., et al. "Cinéma des minorités ethniques." *Image et Son* 293 (1975): 17–86.

Costa-Gavras. "Dossier d'une crise." *Image et Son* 325 (1978): 17–18.

Courtade, Francis. *Les Malédictions du cinéma français. Une histoire du cinéma français parlant (1928–1978)*. Paris: Moreau, 1978.

Cowie, Peter, ed. *International Film Guide*. Published annually, 1967–present. London: Tantivy.

Cros, J.-L., et al. "Le Cinéma français des années soixante-dix." *Image et Son* 356 (1980): 90–124.

Cuel, F. "Le Pire Groupe." *Cinématographe* 85 (1983): 22–23.

DeMattos, A. "French Serials." *Films in Review* 31, 4 (1980): 252 (letter).

Desrues, H. "Les Français et le cinéma." *Image et Son* 304 (1976): 22–25.

"Dossier permanent du cinéma français." *Cinéma* (Paris) 209 (1976): 82–97.

"Dossier: retour à la qualité française?" *Cinématographe* 71 (1981): 1–42.

Durgnat, Raymond. *Nouvelle Vague: The First Decade.* Loughton, England: Motion Publications, 1966.

"1895–1910: Les Pionniers du cinéma français." *L'Avant-Scène du Cinéma* 334 (1984): 2–23, 25–37, 40–89.

Fieschi, J. "Doit-on le dire?" *Cinématographe* 85 (1983): 2–4.

Film Comment 17, 6 (1981): 33–47 (special section on classic French cinema).

The Film Industry in Six European Countries. London: London Film Center/Unesco, 1950.

Fofi, G. "The Cinema of the Popular Front in France (1934–38)." *Screen* 13, 4 (1972–73): 5–57.

Ford, C. "The French Serials 1913–28." *Films in Review* 30, 1 (1979): 21–29.

Ford, Charles. *Histoire populaire du cinéma.* Paris: Mame, 1955.

———. *Histoire du cinéma français contemporain, 1945–1977.* Paris: Éditions France-Empire, 1977.

Fowler, Roy. *The Film in France.* London: Pendulum, 1946.

Franju, G. "De Marey à Renoir, trésors de la Cinémathèque Française 1882–1939." *L'Avant-Scène du Cinéma* 279–80 (1982): 3–5, 7–60, 62–88.

Frayling, C. "Six Characters in Search of an Auteur." *Listener* 50, 3 (1985): 15–17.

Gevaudan, F. "Un tiercé bien français . . . " *Cinéma* (Paris) 169 (1972): 53–58.

Graham, Peter. *The New Wave.* Garden City, N.Y.: Doubleday, 1968.

Guérif, François. *Le Cinéma policier français.* Paris: Veyrier, 1981.

Halliwell, Leslie. *The Filmgoer's Companion.* New York: Avon, 1984.

Harvey, S. "Les Bonnes Femmes." *Film Comment* 17, 6 (1981): 40–47.

Harvey, Sylvia. *May '68 and Film Culture.* London: BFI, 1980.

Haustrate, G. "Ambiguïtés d'un certain cinéma français." *Cinéma* (Paris) 217 (1977): 6–17.

———. "Les Interrogations du mois." *Cinéma* (Paris) 195 (1975): 6–7.

Hennebelle, G. "La Grande Trahison du cinéma français de 1945 à nos jours." *Écran* 21 (1974): 14–26.

Hillier, Jim, ed. *Cahiers du Cinéma: The 1950's, Neo-Realism, Hollywood, New Wave.* Cambridge, Mass.: Harvard University Press, 1985.

———. *Cahiers du Cinéma: 1960–1968. The New Wave, New Cinema and Re-evaluating Hollywood.* Cambridge, Mass.: Harvard University Press, 1986.

Jeancolas, J.-P. "Fonction du témoignage (les années 1939–45 dans le cinéma de l'après-guerre)." *Positif* 170 (1975): 45–60.

———. "Le Cinéma des Français (1)." *Jeune Cinéma* 76 (1974): 1–12.

———. "Le Cinéma des Français (2)." *Jeune Cinéma* 78 (1974): 15–28.

Jeanne, René, and Ford, Charles. *Histoire encyclopédique du cinéma.* 6 vols. Paris: Laffont, 1947–62.

———. *Dictionnaire du cinéma universel.* Paris: Laffont, 1970.

Juin, Hubert, et al. "1900 la belle époque." *Cinéma* (Paris) 246 (1979): 27–42.

La Fond, J.-D., et al. "Points de repère pour un cinéma." *Image et Son* 331 (1978): 27–94.

Langlois, Henri. "French Cinema: Origins." In Richard Roud, ed., *Cinema: A Critical Dictionary*, vol. 1. New York: Viking, 1980.

Lassa, H., and Allombart, G. A. "Dossier d'une crise." *Image et Son* 322 (1977): 4–6.

Lejeune, Paule. *Le Cinéma des femmes d'expression française*. Paris: Atlas, 1987.

Le Pavec, J.-P. "Images d'en France." *Cinéma* (Paris) 209 (1976): 87–89.

Leprohon, Pierre. *Cinquante ans de cinéma français (1895–1945)*. Paris: Éditions du Cerf, 1954.

Lévy-Klein, S. "Sur le cinéma français des années 1940–44, (I) L'organisation." *Positif* 168 (1975) 21–30. (II) *Positif* 170(1975): 35–44.

Lloyd, Ann, and Fuller, Graham. *The Illustrated Who's Who of the Cinema*. 2d ed. New York: Portland House, 1987.

Loury, Edward. *The Filmology Movement and Film Study in France*. Ann Arbor, Mich.: UMI Research Press, 1982.

Magny, J. "Beau fixe sur la Croisette?" *Cinéma* (Paris) 317 (1985): 2.

Martin, John W. *The Golden Age of French Cinema: 1929–1939*. Boston: Twayne, 1983.

Martin, Marcel. *France*. New York: A. S. Barnes, 1971.

———. "Le Ciné est aussi un art." *Écran* 34 (1975): 2–3.

———. "Vingt ans après: une certaine constante du cinéma français." *Écran* 21 (1974): 33–36.

Mast, Gerald. *A Short History of the Movies*. New York: Macmillan, 1986.

Masterworks of the French Cinema. New York: Harper & Row, 1974.

Mayer, Michael. *Foreign Films on American Screens*. New York: Arco, 1965.

Ménil, A. "Images sans marques." *Cinématographe* 85 (1983): 8–10.

Mérigeau, P., and Serceau, D. "L'Auteur." *Image et Son* 364 (1981): 63–96.

Metz, Christian. *Film Language*. New York: Oxford University Press, 1974.

———. *The Imaginary Signifier*. Bloomington: Indiana University Press, 1977.

Michalczyk, John. *The French Literary Filmmakers*. East Brunswick, N.J.: Art Alliance Press, 1980.

Mitry, Jean. *Filmographie universelle*. vols. 1–3: France and Europe. Paris: Institut des Hautes Études Cinématographiques, 1963.

———. *Histoire du cinéma*. 5 vols. Paris: Éditions Universitaires, 1967–80.

Monaco, James. "French Film Now: An American Perspective." *Stills* I, 1 (1980): 18–26.

———. *The New Wave*. New York: Oxford University Press, 1976.

Monaco, Paul. *Cinema and Society: France and Germany During the Twenties*. New York: Elsevier, 1976.

Noëll, R. "Histoire du spectacle cinématographique à Perpignan." *Cahiers de la Cinémathèque* 8 (1973): 3–19.

Oms, M. "Le Charme discret du cinéma de Vichy." *Cahiers de la Cinémathèque* 8 (1973): 66–69.

Overbey, David. "Journals: David Overbey from Paris." *Film Comment* 17, 6 (1981): 6, 8.

Oxenhandler, Neal. "The Dialectic of Emotion in New Wave Cinema." *Film Quarterly* 27, 3 (1974): 10–19.

Paris, James Reid. *The Great French Films*. Secaucus, N.J.: Citadel, 1983.

Parish, James Robert, et al. *Film Directors Guide: Western Europe*. Metuchen, N.J.: Scarecrow Press, 1976.

Petat, J. "L'Avant-garde française des années vingt." *Cinéma* (Paris) 217 (1977): 18–31.

Pithon, R. "Le Cinéma français de la drôle de guerre." *Écran* 40 (1975): 7–10.

———. "Le Cinéma français et la montée des périls." *Cahiers de la Cinémathèque* 18–19 (1976) 93–105.

Porter, Melinda Camber, ed. *Through Parisian Eyes: Reflections on Contemporary French Arts and Culture*. New York: Oxford University Press, 1986.

Prédal, René. "Dossier permanent du cinéma français: les téléphones blancs du cinéma français." *Cinéma* (Paris) 208 (1976): 68–81.

———. "La Génération de 70 du cinéma français." *Jeune Cinéma* 150 (1983): 22–29.

———. "La Génération de 70 du cinéma français. Les deux courants du nouveau cinéma." *Jeune Cinéma* 151 (1983): 20–22.

———. *La Société française (1914–1945) à travers le cinéma*. Paris: Colin, 1972.

———. *Le Cinéma français contemporain*. Paris: Cerf, 1984.

Rashish, P. "Another Wave: French Film in the 80's." *Stills* I, 3 (1981): 15–19.

Robson, E. W., and Robson, M. M. *The Film Answers Back: An Historical Appreciation of Cinema*. London: John Lane, 1939.

Roud, Richard, ed. *Cinema: A Critical Dictionary*. Vols. I and II. New York: Viking, 1980.

Roura, P., ed. "Cinéma de Vichy." *Cahiers de la Cinémathèque* 8 (1973): 3–70. Special issue.

Sadoul, Georges. *Chroniques du cinéma français, 1939–1967: Écrits. 1*. Paris: Union Générale d'Éditions, 1977.

———. *Dictionary of Film Makers*. Berkeley: University of California Press, 1972.

———. *Dictionary of Films*. Berkeley: University of California Press, 1972.

———. *French Film*. London: Falcon, 1953.

———. *Histoire générale du Cinéma*. 6 vols. Paris: Denoël, 1948–75.

———. *Le Cinéma français, 1890–1962*. Paris: Flammarion, 1962.

Sellier, G. "Flash-back: ces singuliers héritiers du cinéma français des années trente." *Cinéma* (Paris) 268 (1981): 4–26.

Slide, Anthony. *Fifty Classic French Films: A Pictorial Record, 1912–1982*. New York: Dover, 1987.

"Spécial Cinéma Français." *Cinéma* (Paris) 212–13 (1976): 18–234.

Staiger, Janet, and Lawton, Ben, eds. *1976 Film Studies Annual*. West Lafayette, Ind.: Purdue University Press, 1976.

Strebel, E. "Flashback sur 'ciné-liberté.' " *Écran* 44 (1976): 3–4.

———. *French Social Cinema of the 1930's: A Cinematographic Expression of Popular Front Consciousness*. New York: Arno, 1980.

Talon, G. "Regards critiques sur la production et la réalisation des films: au temps du Front populaire." *Cinéma* (Paris) 194 (1975): 34–57.

Thiher, Allen. *The Cinematic Muse: Critical Studies in the History of French Cinema*. Columbia: University of Missouri Press, 1979.

Thomson, David. *A Biographical Dictionary of Film*. 2d ed. New York: Morrow, 1981.

Védrès, Nicole. *Images du cinéma français*. Paris: Chêne, 1945.

Viot, P. "The *Journal* Looks at the French Film Industry Today." *Journal of the Producers Guild of America* 19, 1 (1977): 3–9.

Viviani, L., et al. "Le Cinéma du sam'di soir." *Cahiers de la Cinémathèque* 23–24 (1977): 14–129.

Wide Angle 4, 4 (1981). Special issue devoted to French cinema.

Wide Angle 9, 4 (1987). Special issue devoted to André Bazin.

Williams, D. D. "Films in Paris: Lotte H. Eisner." *Cinema Journal* 14, 3 (1975): 68–74.

Wood, Robin, ed. *Second Wave*. New York: Praeger, 1970.

6

Food and Wine

PIERRE L. HORN

After love, the French view food and wine as perhaps the most important elements of their lives. Indeed, they enjoy talking about them as much as their actual consumption. Above all, the meal is a social activity, which may explain the expansive French mealtimes: conversing while pleasing the palate is considered essential to daily life. The French will go to some lengths, therefore, to assure that even a moderately priced meal meets their standards.

In the last two decades, however, two conflicting situations have developed. On the one hand, with the invasion of (mostly American) fast-food chains and a lunch period reduced to one hour in large cities, the French have begun to eat less well and more hurriedly; they now spend, according to Roger Sue, 1.7 hours per meal at the table (compared to 1.2 in the United States). On the other hand, as concern over cholesterol and liver and heart ailments has risen, they increasingly are questioning the healthfulness and value of their food, demanding better quality and controls.

This latter development has brought about salad bars and vegetarian restaurants, in addition to a lower consumption of wine. Despite many wine bars and cafés, annual wine consumption has gone down from 172 liters in 1940 to 104 liters in 1976, with 10 percent of the population not drinking any wine. Instead, fruit juices and mineral water are preferred (although sales of soda, not the healthiest of beverages, have tripled between 1968 and 1973, especially Coca-Cola, with sales of 114 million liters in 1975). Yet, for the vast majority of French men and women, the two-hour lunch of four or five courses and the copious Sunday family gathering are essentially unchanged, except that they now eat much less bread and fewer potatoes. Furthermore, larger quantities of canned meals (for instance, *cassoulet, quenelles*, couscous), frozen foods, meat (a third of the food budget), and sugar in all its forms are eaten. At the same time, new and exotic food and drink are constantly being added to the table, whether corn (in cans), palm hearts, yams, kiwi, or California wines.

HISTORICAL OUTLINE

Food

France's culinary art did not truly begin until the sixteenth century, when Catherine de' Medici came from Italy to marry King Henri II and brought some of her best chefs with her. Even so, there already existed a fine tradition of food preparation, necessitated either by the need to add variety during the many Lent and meatless days imposed by the Church or by a desire to emulate Roman cuisine. While at first cooks used red wine to enhance their cooking, spices (from the Middle East and India) as well as herbs were soon added to boiled and roasted dishes. Usually stuffed and covered with sauces and gravies, game (which was plentiful), fish (of which herring from Denmark was king), pork, eggs, and poultry, along with vegetables, cheeses, and fruits, appeared on the medieval table of a rich or noble house.

The poor, relying mostly on eggs, vegetables, and legumes, sometimes complemented by lard or chicken, were undernourished and often died of hunger. The large stewpot hung in the fireplace was continually replenished with new food items and leftovers: many "casseroles" (a French word), such as *choucroute garnie, pot-au-feu*, oxtail soup, *bouillabaisse* were thus concocted. Each meal was correctly described *à la fortune du pot* (pot luck).

During the Renaissance, with the introduction of Italian cooking and foods like pasta and cantaloupe, quality and delicacy were emphasized over quantity, and gastronomy, "cette science de gueule" (Montaigne), replaced mere gluttony. French chefs quickly learned and improved on their colleagues' lessons, so much so that French cuisine became known throughout Western Europe for its refined sophistication. Besides Italy and the Orient, newly discovered America sent its bounty as well, from tomatoes and strawberries to cane sugar. As more interesting menus were elaborated, the best ingredients were sought out, which resulted in local regions acquiring to this day a national, even international, reputation for their produce and specialties.

While the sixteenth century introduced fine eating to France, it was the age of Louis XIV that raised it to an art, as the royal family and the nobles took pride in their chefs, who often became superstars. Chief among them was La Varenne, the Marquis d'Uxelles's *écuyer de cuisine*, who not only created exquisite dishes but also was a prolific writer of cookbooks. Discussions soon arose about the best and most sumptuous tables in Paris, which sometimes led to dishonor, as in the case of Vatel, who, on discovering that there might not be enough fish for the king's feast, committed suicide (1671).

The eighteenth century saw two separate culinary movements. One involved an even more complicated and *recherché* cuisine, where dishes were shown off to provide visual pleasure. All of them were brought at once from distant kitchens and placed on buffet tables for everyone's admiration, resulting in their being quite cold by eating time. (This is referred to as *service à la française*.) In addition, since there was no passing around of platters and guests ate only the food placed closest to them (served by their own staff), seating arrangements indicated position and status. The other movement represented a reaction to this superrefinement by stressing freshness, simplicity, and lightness—in short, a kind of *nouvelle cuisine*.

It was during this period that, for example, mayonnaise, meringue, pâté de foie gras, and baba au rhum (credited to King Stanislas Leszczynski) were invented, as well as many of the sauces now part of the French repertoire. Also, as in the previous century, dishes were more and more frequently named after patrons or would-be patrons (crème Chantilly, sauce béchamel), for producing regions (duck Montmorency [cherries], potage Argenteuil [asparagus]), with aristocratic connotations (bouchée à la reine, mousseline de poisson à la maréchale) and poetic qualifiers (suprême de volaille, salade mimosa), or from their preparation (civet de lapin à la farigoulette, poireaux gratinés à la savoyarde). During the Revolution, the tomato was introduced into Parisian and hence national cooking by southern soldiers; the potato, which had been imported from America several centuries before, now became popular thanks to severe food shortages and the tireless efforts of Antoine Parmentier, who had long advocated its cultivation and use by humans.

Antonin Carême (1784–1833), who served in the best houses of Europe, continued the tradition of expensive and elaborate cooking, culminating in his creations of *pièces montées* (set pieces) that were marvels of architectural design and ingenuity. In contrast, he simplified sauces, the foundation of French cooking, while inventing hundreds of variations on the basic three (béchamel, velouté, and espagnole). The uncontested leader of French classical cuisine, he influenced nineteenth- and twentieth-century practitioners through his numerous cookbooks. Auguste Escoffier, in particular, put many of Carême's principles into practice and constantly sought imaginative innovations or combinations, first in his luxury hotel restaurants, then in his books, some of which became the bible of modern Parisian *haute cuisine*.

In the 1960s a group of young chefs rebelled against this still very complicated style to create what restaurant critics Henri Gault and Christian Millau called *nouvelle cuisine*—in the fashion, no doubt, of *nouveau roman* and *nouvelle critique*. More interested in simple preparation, appealing to the eye, of course, but without heavy sauces, cream, or butter, these chefs built their menus around seasonal products and happy finds at the market. Their names read like a who's who of contemporary culinary creativity: Paul Bocuse, whom President Giscard d'Estaing decorated with the Legion of Honor in 1975 for "spreading the art of fine French food throughout the world," Roger Vergé, the Troisgros brothers, Raymond Oliver, Michel Guérard. Later, others adapted these ideas in their own establishments, although today there seems to be a return to a less plain cuisine, perhaps in reaction to some of this movement's excesses (if this is the right term).

As mentioned above, books dealing with food preparation and service appeared early, first in Latin, then in French. The oldest compendium of kitchen advice in French, *Enseingnemenz qui enseingnent a appareiller toutes sortes de viandes*, was written around 1300 as an appendix to a medical work and concerned food preparation (*viande* meant food in general). At the end of the fourteenth century, the anonymous *Ménagier de Paris* gave instructions in morals, housekeeping, and cooking to bourgeois ladies of the house; Taillevent's *Le Viandier* is very technical and is addressed to cooks of the high nobility. Alongside the refined cuisine of the 1600s, numerous books were published mostly for the upper classes. La Varenne was not only a famous adept in the kitchen, but also a best-selling author who shared his recipes, rules, and methods, starting in 1651 with *Le Cuisinier français*; in the next century the two most important culinary writers were François Marin and Menon. Both, shunning the bother and expense of "aristocratic" cooking, wrote specifically for the bourgeois household. Marin's *Les Dons de Comus* (1758) and Menon's *Nouveau Traité de la cuisine* (1739) and *La Cuisinière bourgeoise* (1746) were frequently reprinted and revised and greatly influenced later chefs in Europe and post-Revolutionary America. At the same time, gastronomic and culinary periodicals began to appear (e.g., *Journal des Dipnosophistes* and *Les Nouvelles de la Grappe*). Many did not enjoy much circulation or reader interest, unlike *Le Gazetier du comestible*, an early shopper newspaper (1767), giving prices of various foods and recommendations for purchase.

It was in the nineteenth century, however, that a veritable cookbook explosion occurred. From the pens of Beauvilliers and Carême (ideological competitors) to those of Dubois and Favre, literally hundreds of cookbooks were published, many of which quickly became classics. It was also then that leftovers were formally acknowledged thanks to Antoine Gogué's 1856 *Secrets de la cuisine française* and Baron Brisse's own collections (1867). Moreover, weekly or monthly periodicals gave recipes and tips and offered suggestions for menus and marketing. Of these, the most interesting are *L'Art culinaire* (1883–1939), whose aim was "the Progress of Culinary Art" and to which such greats as P. Gilbert, A. Tavenet, and A. Escoffier contributed, and *Le Pot-au-feu* (1893–1940). Unlike so many cookbooks and magazines of the period, this biweekly targeted the housewife who wanted to learn to cook but lacked the necessary background around the kitchen; it thus emphasized practical techniques and knowledge (e.g., how to select pots and pans or fresh vegetables).

The proliferation of cookbooks has continued into the twentieth century, when it seems that anyone with a typewriter (or word processor) is writing a book of recipes. Although traditional cuisine is still the main focus of either gastronomes (Curnonsky and Courtine, chief among them) or practitioners (Escoffier and Montagné, for example), regional and/or provincial cooking and house specialties are more and more the subject of interest from Curnonsky and Rouff's *La France gastronomique* to Benoît's *La Cuisine lyonnaise*, and from Point's *Ma gastro-nomie* to Bocuse's *La Cuisine du marché*. Periodicals, too, split along specialized lines. While *La Revue culinaire* (1920–   ) is a scholarly defense and illustration of the culinary arts, *Elle* presents recipes (with its conveniently detachable cards) for the modern woman. Others still, like the weekly *Guide cuisine* ("40 recettes pour la semaine"), are solely devoted to providing easy recipes for nutritious and inexpensive meals.

The French ate at home, and frequented the various inns set up in important market centers and relay stations only for business reasons or during their travels because, for one thing, the food usually ranged from mediocre to bad. Despite the poor quality of the fare and the fixed *table d'hôte*, some well-located Paris eateries of the late Middle Ages and sixteenth century, such as "L'Épée royale," "Le Grand Cerf," "L'Écu d'Orléans," acquired a certain reputation among merchants and the local citizenry. However, the restaurant concept was not born until 1765 when, over the hue and cry of the caterers' guild, a certain M. Boulanger (onomastics is destiny) established a shop where he sold different *restorative* dishes. The first real restaurant, as we understand the term today, actually opened in 1782. Antoine Beauvilliers' "La Grande Taverne de Londres" not only offered a menu from which diners could choose, but he also emphasized the palate over the eye, as when he introduced steak, especially filet mignon, to Parisians.

Seeing his success, other putative restaurateurs quickly followed suit and competed with each other in and around the Palais-Royal district. A few of the great establishments were Véry, Véfour, Les Frères provençaux (which was the first to serve meridional cooking), Méot (gourmet eating in a luxurious setting), Le Rocher de Cancale ("the eighth wonder of the world," a seafood restaurant appropriately owned by a M. Balaine), and the Café des Mille-Colonnes (where Madame Romain, the most beautiful woman in Paris and the owner's wife, presided). Nineteenth-century restaurants continued their development, as dining out became increasingly fashionable, but the axis shifted to the Grands-Boulevards, where the Café Anglais (with Adolphe Dugléré of Proustian fame as its chef) and Café Riche reigned supreme well into the Belle Époque, and to the Champs-Élysées, where Ledoyen opened its doors. Foyot, Louis-Philippe's chef, started his restaurant after the royal family went into exile; Voisin, at the height of the Second Empire, offered one of the best tables in Paris; Brébant, founded in 1865, reached its apogee in the 1880s, closing down in 1889 ("My heart shrank," wrote Achille Ozanne in *L'Art culinaire*).

Magny offered its wonderful *dîners* to the Goncourts, Flaubert, George Sand; La Tour d'Argent, which began in 1582 as a left-bank tavern, became a full-fledged restaurant in 1860 and continues to this day to serve its world-renowned *canard au sang*. In the early 1860s, Peter's, where Pierre Fraisse created his *homard à l'américaine*, was the first to offer each week the same menu on the same day. Maxime Gaillard opened on May 21, 1894, a renovated Maxim's on rue Royale, which was to be for a long time the very symbol of *haute cuisine* and elegant high society. (It is now owned by Pierre Cardin.) Also in mid-century, the French style of serving was replaced by what is called *service à la russe*. Credited to Urbain Dubois, this way allowed the staff to apportion the various dishes in the kitchen itself and serve them hot and in sequence directly to the guests.

Beside these temples of gastronomy appeared, during the July Monarchy (1830–48), many eating establishments that were only a nuance above soup kitchens. Cheap and of poor quality, they offered *prix fixe* meals to a growing population of poor industrial workers. Bouillons Duval, established in 1855, soon became a chain all over Paris and competed with others just as well known: La Table d'hôte and Californie, with its gold-rush connotations. The 1862 edition of the *Paris-Guide* recommended these quite seriously to its slumming readers, tired of *écrevisses à la bordelaise* or *selle d'agneau Richelieu*.

Very little has changed in the twentieth century, except that Paris is no longer the only center for fine cuisine and that, both in Paris and the provinces, many good regional, ethnic, and specialized restaurants have found a niche next to the great restaurants, old and new. Among the new places of great reputation outside the capital, special mention should be made of La Pyramide, owned by Mme. Mado Point, the first woman ever chosen "Meilleur Ouvrier de France" (1974).

Just as literature and theater had their reviewers, food providers soon had theirs as well, starting with Grimod de La Reynière (1758–1838). For almost ten years, he wrote his *Almanach des gourmands* in a witty and lively style, sharing recipes and discoveries, listing the best suppliers, neither afraid to name names of those owners who did not have their clients' interest at heart, nor shy about enthusiastically recognizing those who did. Given his success, it was understandable that he would be imitated.

Honoré Blanc's *Le Guide des dîneurs*, however, can be considered the first real restaurant guide (1815). Alphabetically arranged, it lists the most important restaurants in Paris, with menus and prices, and makes recommendations both about dishes and which places to avoid for their inflated prices, bad service, mediocre food, or skimpy portions. Other nineteenth-century restaurant guides continued the pattern found in Blanc's "indispensable work." Among the more interesting are Gardeton's *Nouveau Guide des dîneurs* (1828) and Briffault's *Paris à table* (1846).

Yet it was Michelin, a tire company, that saw its commercial future in the link between motoring and dining out. To encourage traveling, Michelin distributed a free guide to some of its recommended provincial inns and restaurants. The first edition came out in 1900 and gave information on some 1,200 towns. With the *Guide*'s popularity, improvements were added to make selections more useful: in 1926, a single-star rating system; in 1931, a two- and three-star scheme. As the book's introduction explains, one star means "a very good restaurant in its category"; two stars, "excellent cooking; worth a detour"; and three stars, "exceptional cuisine; worth a special journey." The 1990 edition lists nineteen three-star establishments, of which fourteen are in the provinces. Totally impartial, the book quickly became the standard both in the profession and among the dining public; as such it carries considerable influence, although few commit suicide, à la Vatel, over the loss of a star.

Since the end of World War II, other guides have successfully copied the Michelin formula, whether with red roosters (*Guide Kléber-Colombes*, another tire company) or chef's hats (*Guide Julliard de Paris*, edited by Gault and Millau). The *Guide des Relais Routiers*, often called the poor man's Michelin, is a gold mine of reasonably priced places mostly frequented by truck drivers. In addition, most of the large daily newspapers and national magazines publish restaurant reviews that are often just as influential, in their timeliness, as the annual guides.

Considering such passionate interest in food, it was natural that gastronomic associations evolved over the centuries, possibly beginning with Rabelais's fictional *Gastrolâtres*. Founded in 1683, the Ordre de la Méduse, perhaps the oldest eating society, was soon followed by the Société de l'Aloyau. In the eighteenth century, Henrion de Pansey was the first to conceive of an Academy of Gastronomes modeled after the French Academy, an idea Grimod de La Reynière implemented later with his Société des mercredis, which met at Legacque's, while the eighteen-member Club des grands estomacs gathered first at Pascal and then at the more fashionable Philippe. On the eve of World War I, *Le Matin*'s Louis Fourest founded the Club des Cent, still probably the most famous of all contemporary societies. Mention must also be made, if only for its whimsical mission, of the Confrérie des Chevaliers du Goûte-Boudin located in Mortagne-au-Perche, the center of black pudding country.

Next to restaurants, cafés play an important role in French life. Originally, as the word indicates, cafés served only coffee, imported by the Dutch in the mid-1600s and gradually reaching into France under Louis XIV. Procope (né Francesco Procopio dei Coltelli) opened his "*maison de café*" in 1686 on rue des Fossés Saint-Germain (rue de l'Ancienne-Comédie), where it still operates today. In a very pleasant atmosphere, people could sit and drink coffee, read newspapers, talk about art and literature, play chess. So popular were such establishments that, according to Gottschalk, by 1723 they numbered over 300 and by 1789 some 2,000, doubling to 4,000 within twenty years. The better-known were the Café de la Régence (Robespierre's favorite), the Café de Foy, and the Café du Croissant, which gave its name to that Paris street. Soon, wine was served as well, and cafés changed with fashions, mores, and clientele. Today, Fouquet's and the Café de la Paix, for instance, cater to a rich clientele, while the Flore and Deux Magots still retain something of their postwar existentialist connections.

Mealtimes, too, have changed. The medieval *dîner* and *souper*, respectively eaten at 9 A.M. and 5 P.M., were served in the seventeenth century around noon and 8 P.M., making the midday meal the more important of the two. When, in the next century, *dîner* was pushed back to 2 or 3 P.M. and *souper* to 9 or 10 P.M., a morning collation, usually consisting of milk and coffee, was added. In the aftermath of the Revolution, deputies were required to attend National Assembly meetings from 1 to 6 P.M. and were, therefore, skipping their *dîner*. The modern noontime *déjeuner* of grilled meats was thus invented, *dîner* was served after 6 P.M., *souper* disappeared (though it came back temporarily to indicate the meal taken after the theater), and the collation became the *petit déjeuner* (continental breakfast).

Wine

Until the Romans invaded Gaul, bringing wine with them, barley beer was the population's drink of choice. Quickly, however, wine replaced this drink, especially after being stored, like beer, in wooden casks rather than in amphoras, thereby gaining a fine aged taste. Emperor Charlemagne, considered by many the earliest French gastronome, encouraged viticulture to such an extent that by the fourteenth century vineyards had been planted all over France, including within Paris proper. The three most important regions, then as today, were Bordeaux, the southwest area around Cahors, and Burgundy. In fact, the Burgundy production was often so high that royal ordinances required bad vines be eradicated.

Wine, which was mostly red, appeared on rich and noble tables, of course, although a low-quality homemade *piquette* was drunk by the lower classes or used for marinating and cooking. A need developed, then, to acquire and sell wine by the barrels: the first recorded wine fair, organized along the lines of regional grain markets, took place in 1214 in Mâcon, where, every May, it is still held today. (Paris holds its prestigious fair in March.)

As good eating evolved during the Renaissance and the seventeenth century, the French consumed great quantities of wine, both at home and in taverns. *Vins à la mode et cabarets du 17e siècle* lists over a hundred drinking establishments, some of which, like Le Mouton blanc and La Pomme de pin, were famous for welcoming artists and writers. It was also in the seventeenth century that Dom Pierre Pérignon, a Benedictine monk and cellarer, invented around 1670 a process which turned still white champagne into a sparkling—and festive—wine that has never lost its deserved popularity. While most wines could be stored in their casks (if possible, made of the fine Tronçais oak), it soon appeared that glass bottles were much more convenient and could help in the maturing, too. Warner Allen dates the idea of such aging, quite appropriate for a Château Lafite, to 1797, but it was probably already being done by clever English importers of claret.

Sales statistics for 1800 to 1850 show a marked preference for Burgundy over Bordeaux, as well as a high volume of imported wines, especially from Germany. Moreover, the figures indicate that *vin ordinaire* consumption greatly increased in working-class homes thanks to efficient rail transportation and the opening of the Nicolas chain of low-priced wine stores during the early years of the July Monarchy. What could not be helped, however, were the various vine diseases, and particularly the almost total devastation caused in the 1870s by the American phylloxera, with the consequence that vineyards had to be replanted with American root stock and largely brought under control by 1887.

This epidemic cemented the existing relationship between the governing bodies and wine producers in that tax abatement and subsidy legislation were enacted and protectionist tariff barriers erected. Starting in 1905, under the pressure of wine lobbies (for example, the powerful Confédération Générale des Vignerons), a series of laws against misrepresentation of the place of origin were passed, delineating (sometimes with disastrous results) "the name of the *cru* to a territory clearly defined by tradition" and requiring that "the wine come only from noble vines (*cépages*) to the exclusion of direct productive hybrids." Today, these laws are enforced by the Direction de la Répression des Fraudes and the Institut National des Appellations d'Origine, as in the case of the Cruse scandal: The Cruse brothers and several other Bordeaux wine wholesalers and shippers were caught in mid-1973 adulterating wine and falsifying labels. Another important development in wine categorization occurred in 1855 with subsequent and often as controversial changes as the legislation on *appellations contrôlées*. The Official Bordeaux Classification divided the sixty great wines into five growths (*crus*), later adding Graves (1953 and 1959) and Saint-Émilion (1955), but still omitting Pomerol.

Despite reduced production and consumption in France (though exports continue to grow), wine's presence in daily life is still very strong. Whether drinking the year's Beaujolais Nouveau or one of the vintages of old, connoisseurs learnedly argue over the merits of Burgundy over Bordeaux (and vice versa) and literally go into rapture as they rhapsodize over "bottled velvet" or "supreme magnificence" and speak of the "art of drinking wine." Given such comments, it is no wonder that on the one hand all books give their idiosyncratic—or consensus—judgment of wines and specific years, and on the other that drinking and tasting societies have flourished, from the Ordre des Coteaux during the reign of Louis XIV to the contemporary Confrérie des Chevaliers du Tastevin and the Connétablie de Guyenne.

REFERENCE AND HISTORICAL WORKS

By far the most complete source, if dated (1890), is Georges Vicaire's *Bibliographie gastronomique*. Not limited to France, it mentions, usually with explanations, printed materials regarding food and drink, including plays, miscellany, decrees. Katherine G. Bitting, too, provides a good annotated *Gastronomic Bibliography* of books (1939) about food and related subjects published in all Western languages. In 1953, André L. Simon, the late founder and president of the Wine and Food Society, edited *Bibliotheca Gastronomica: A Catalogue of Books and Documents on Gastronomy*, which unfortunately stops in 1861 (date of Mrs. Beeton's book on household management). Based on the Society's important collection, the entries are often introduced by a short paragraph on the author or the text.

The basic cooking reference work remains the frequently updated *Larousse gastronomique* for its wealth of information and practical advice, not to mention wonderful recipes presented by Prosper Montagné (1938 edition) and Robert Courtine (1984). Also very useful is Escoffier et al.'s *Guide culinaire: Aide-mémoire de cuisine pratique*, for, as the subtitle implies, it explains terms and gives succinct reminders for more than 5,000 items. *Le Grand Dictionnaire de cuisine* (1873), by Alexandre Dumas, is interesting for its literary as well as fanciful value, providing amusing etymologies of foods and dishes, real or invented, and origins of utensils and professions. Joseph Favre's four-volume *Dictionnaire universel de cuisine* is more serious and informative (1894).

Thanks to its particular mystique, wine receives the most attention from reference-book publishers. Gérard Debuigne's *Nouveau Larousse des vins* (2nd edition, 1979) is a handy book on the subject, enhanced by illustrations and maps. The *Hachette Guide to French Wines*, edited by André Vedel, is the best in its genre: it not only lists and briefly rates thousands of wines, but also gives twenty pages of useful addresses and an index keyed to wines and producers/shippers. Lichine's *Encyclopedia of Wines and Spirits* and Clarke's *Essential Wine Book* are, for their part, packed full of information on wines from around the world.

There are too many histories of food and wine to be considered here; however, the following are highly recommended. *Histoire de l'alimentation et de la gastronomie depuis la Préhistoire jusqu'à nos jours* by Alfred Gottschalk (1948) and *Histoire pittoresque de notre alimentation* by G. and G. Blond (1960) are both good panoramic surveys of the subject, as are *A History of Wine* by H. Warner Allen and *The Delectable Past* by Esther B. Aresty, even if they are not limited to France. In 1985 Stephen Mennell published an excellent and well-documented monograph on "eating and taste in England and France from the Middle Ages to the present," which expands on the work of Jean-Paul Aron, particularly *Le Mangeur du XIXe siècle* (1973; translated as *The Art of Eating in France*, 1975).

Specialized aspects are discussed in a variety of books: cafés in Fosca's *Histoire des cafés de Paris* (1934); restaurants in Andrieu's *Histoire du restaurant en France* (1955); food industries in Vasseur's 1966 fine little book; chefs in Page and Kingsford's *The Master Chefs: A History of Haute Cuisine* (1971; mostly on France) and Blake and Crewe's *Great Chefs of France* (1978). Relations between wine producers and the government are masterfully analyzed by Charles K. Warner in his 1960 *Winegrowers of France and the Government since 1875*. Very useful statistics on French eating habits are interestingly presented in Jean-Claude Toutain's *La Consommation alimentaire en France de 1789 à 1964* (1971) and Henri Dupin's *L'Alimentation des Français* (1978).

With the increased emphasis on nutrition and health, a number of best sellers have come out in the last twenty years. The noted food critic Robert Courtine published *L'Assassin est à votre table* (The Murderer Is at Your Table) in 1969, appropriately with an introduction by Albert Simonin, a famous *Série noire* author. His book was soon to be followed by such frightening titles as *L'Alimentation suicide* (Gérald Messadié, 1973) and *La Pollution dans votre assiette* (Élisabeth Venaille, 1974).

Finally, no scholar can embark on a study of food or wine without first consulting *Physiologie du goût* by Anthelme Brillat-Savarin (1755–1826). While not strictly a reference book, this 1826 masterpiece offers in a series of delightful anecdotes and digressions the author's "méditations" on all subjects related to gastronomy and the culinary arts. Indeed, some of his aphorisms have attained the level of proverbs: "A meal without wine is like a day without sunshine" and "Tell me what you eat, I'll tell you what you are," to quote but two.

RESEARCH AND RESOURCE CENTERS

Besides the great libraries in Paris, there are other organizations interested in fostering research. These include:

Trade Associations

Chambre syndicale de la Haute Cuisine française, 123 rue des Dames, Paris 17e.

Chambre syndicale de la Restauration, 22 av. de la Grande-Armée, Paris 17e.

Chambre syndicale des Industries et Commerces en gros des Vins, 3 pl. des Vosges, Paris 4e.

Confédération française des Hôteliers, Restaurateurs et Cafetiers, 2 rue Barye, Paris 17e.

Confédération nationale des Vins d'Appellations d'origine contrôlées, 21 rue François Ier, Paris 8e.

Fédération internationale des Vins et Spiritueux, 103 bd Haussmann, Paris 8e; plus many regional winegrowers' associations.

Fédération mondiale des Sociétés de Cuisiniers, 3465 Rankin Ave., Windsor, Ont., Canada.

Government Organizations

Institut national des appellations d'origine, 138 av. des Champs-Élysées, Paris 8e.

Office international de la Vigne et du Vin, 11 rue Roquépine, Paris 8e. Houses a 3,000-volume library on viticulture and enology.

Gastronomic Societies

Association mondiale de la Gastronomie, 7 rue d'Aumale, Paris 9e.

Club des Cent, 31 rue de Penthièvre, Paris 8e.

Club Prosper Montagné, 45 rue St-Roch, Paris 1er.

Confrérie des Chevaliers du Tastevin, Nuits-St-Georges (Côte d'Or).

International Wine and Food Society, 108 Old Brompton Rd., London S. W., England. This worldwide nonprofit organization believes that "an intelligent approach to the pleasures of the table is more than the mere satisfaction of appetite." Its 4,000-volume library contains an important collection of books, manuscripts and incunabula, laws and decrees.

Museums

Château Mouton-Rothschild, Pauillac (Gironde). A beautiful collection of art with a wine theme, including tapestries by Jean Lurçat.

Musée de l'Art culinaire, rue Escoffier, Villeneuve-Loubet (Alpes-Maritimes). Located in Auguste Escoffier's house, the collection includes art about food, a reconstructed Provençal kitchen, chefs' papers and mementos, menus.

Musée du Vin, 5 sq. Charles-Dickens, Paris 16e. Provides an overview of wine production and lore through tools, artifacts, presses, documents.

Musée du Vin de Bourgogne, rue de l'Enfer, Beaune (Côte-d'Or). Gives an excellent background of the industry.

Universities

Although specializing in the scientific grape cultivation and wine production, the Viticulture and Enology Department, California State University, in Fresno, and the Institut d'Œnologie, Université de Bordeaux, both have extensive library holdings. For food and restaurant management in general, the School of Hotel Management, Cornell University, Ithaca, N.Y., itself has an excellent library.

SUGGESTIONS FOR FUTURE RESEARCH

Despite an abundance of books on food and wine, many exciting possibilities for future research still exist. One such possibility could consist in studying certain organizations from their founding onward to examine their special influence and/or contribution: Établissements Nicolas as vintner, wholesaler, shipper, and retailer is a good example of vertical integration. The Confédération Générale des Vignerons, founded in 1907, the most important pressure group before World War I, and Édouard Barthe, deputy from Hérault and chairman of the powerful Commission des Boissons and related legislative committees, both merit a study, since Maurice Caupert's thesis on the CGV dates back to 1921. The work of the Institut national des appellations d'origine since its creation in July 1935 can also lead to interesting discoveries, and so would an in-depth reading of *L'Art culinaire*, the leading journal of its kind for almost forty years.

Other worthy sociohistorical topics may include cafés before and during the turbulent years of the French Revolution, luxury restaurants under Napoleon III or during the Belle Époque, the rise and fall of three-star restaurants since the award's inception in 1931, or the mutual exchanges between the United States and France, especially in light of the "fast-food invasion." There is a need as well for biographical work on such figures as Baron Brisse, the gastronome and culinary journalist, or chefs past or present. Finally, the way food and wine have been depicted in art and literature remains an excellent source for scholarly pursuits.

BIBLIOGRAPHY

Allen, H. Warner. *A History of Wine*. New York: Horizon Press, 1961.

————. *The Wines of France*. London: Fisher Unwin, 1924.

Andrieu, Pierre. *Histoire du restaurant en France*. Montpellier: La Journée vinicole, 1955.

Arbellot, Simon. *Curnonsky, prince des Gastronomes*. Paris: Productions de Paris, 1965.

Aresty, Esther B. *The Delectable Past*. New York: Simon & Schuster, 1964.

Aron, Jean-Paul. *Le Mangeur du XIXe siècle*. Paris: Laffont, 1973.

Audot, Louis-Eustache. *La Cuisinière de la campagne et de la ville*. Paris: Audot, 1829.

Barthes, Roland. *Mythologies*. Translated by Annette Lavers. New York: Hill & Wang, 1972.

Beauvilliers, Antoine. *L'Art du cuisinier*. 2 vols. Paris: Pilet, 1816.

Bitting, Katherine G. *Gastronomic Bibliography*. San Francisco, 1939.

Blake, Anthony, and Crewe, Quentin. *Great Chefs of France*. New York: Abrams, 1978.

Blanc, Honoré. *Le Guide des dîneurs*. Westmount, Quebec: L'Étincelle, 1985.

Blond, Georges and Germaine. *Histoire pittoresque de notre alimentation*. Paris: Fayard, 1960.

Bocuse, Paul. *La Cuisine du marché*. Paris: Flammarion, 1976.

Bouton, Victor. *La Table à Paris*. Paris, 1845.

Bréjoux, Pierre. *Les Vins de Loire*. Paris: Éditions techniques et commerciales, 1956.

Briffault, Eugène. *Paris à table*. Paris: Hetzel, 1846.

Brillat-Savarin, Anthelme. *Physiologie du goût*. Paris: Flammarion, 1982.

Brisse, Baron. *Le Calendrier gastronomique pour l'année 1867*. Paris: Bureaux de "La Liberté," 1867.

Carême, Antonin. *L'Art de la cuisine française au XIXe siècle*. 5 vols. Paris, 1833.

————. *Le Maître d'hôtel*. Paris, 1822.

Carter, Youngman. *Drinking Bordeaux*. New York: Hastings House, 1966.

Cassagnac, Paul de. *Les Vins de France*. Paris: Hachette, 1927.

Castelot, André. *L'Histoire à table*. Paris: Plon, 1972.

Caupert, Maurice. *Essai sur la C.G.V.* Montpellier: L'Économiste méridional, 1921.

Chappaz, Georges. *Le Vignoble et le vin de Champagne*. Paris: Larmat, 1951.

Charpentreau, Jacques, and Kaës, René. *La Culture populaire en France*. Paris: Éditions Ouvrières, 1962.

Châtillon-Plessis. *La Vie à table à la fin du XIXe siècle*. Paris: Firmin-Didot, 1894.

Chavette, Eugène. *Restaurateurs et restaurés*. Paris: Le Chevalier, 1867.

Clarke, Oz. *The Essential Wine Book*. New York: Viking, 1985.

Clos-Jouve, Henri. *Le Livre d'or des maîtres-queux et cordons bleus de France*. Paris: La Revue française, 1970.

Cocks, Charles, and Féret, Claude. *Bordeaux et ses vins*. Bordeaux: Féret, 1969.

Coquet, James de. *L'Appétit vient en lisant*. Paris: La Table ronde, 1973.

———. *Lettre aux gourmets, aux gourmands, aux gastronomes et aux goinfres*. Paris: Simoën, 1977.

Courtine, Robert J. *L'Assassin est à votre table*. Paris: La Table ronde, 1969.

———. *Mes repas les plus étonnants*. Paris: Laffont, 1973.

Curnonsky, and Marcel Rouff. *La France gastronomique. Guide des merveilles culinaires et des bonnes auberges françaises*. Paris: Rouff, 1921.

Curnonsky, and Gaston Derys. *Gaietés et curiosités gastronomiques* (Paris: Delagrave, 1933).

Curnonsky, and Austin de Croze. *Le Trésor gastronomique de France*. Paris: Delagrave, 1933.

Danflou, Alfred. *Les Grands Vins bordelais*. Paris, 1867.

Darenne, E. *Histoire des métiers de l'alimentation*. Meulan: A. Réty, 1904.

Debuigne, Gérard. *Nouveau Larousse des vins*. Paris: Larousse, 1979.

Delvau, Alfred. *Cafés et cabarets de Paris*. Paris: Dentu, 1862.

Dion, Roger. *Histoire de la vigne et du vin en France*. Paris, 1959.

Dubois, Urbain, and Bernard, Émile. *La Cuisine classique*. 2 vols. Paris: Dentu, 1856.

Dumas, Alexandre. *Le Grand Dictionnaire de cuisine*. Paris: Veyrier, 1978.

———. *Histoire de la cuisine*. Paris: Waleffe, 1967.

Dumonteil, Fulmert. *La France gourmande*. Paris: Librairie universelle, 1906.

Dupin, Henri. *L'Alimentation des Français*. Paris: ESF, 1978.

L'École parfaite des Officiers de bouche. Paris, 1662.

Enseingnemenz qui enseingnent a appareiller toutes sortes de viandes. Ca. 1300; B. N. Fonds Latin No. 7131.

Escoffier, Auguste, with Gilbert, Philéas, and Fetu, Émile. *Le Guide culinaire: Aide-mémoire de cuisine pratique*. Paris: Flammarion, 1921.

Favre, Joseph. *Dictionnaire universel de cuisine*. 4 vols. Paris: Librairie des Halles, 1894.

Fondation Française pour la Nutrition. *Les Français et leur alimentation*. Paris: FFPN, 1978.

Forest, Louis. *L'Art de boire*. Paris: Établissements Nicolas, 1927.

Fos, Léon de. *Gastronomiana*. Paris: Rouquette, 1870.

Fosca, François. *Histoire des cafés de Paris*. Paris: Firmin-Didot, 1934.

Galet, Pierre. *Cépages et vignobles de France*. 4 vols. Montpellier: Imprimerie du Paysan du Midi, 1956–64. A completely revised and updated edition is being prepared: Montpellier: Déhan, 1988–.

Garard, Ira D. *The Story of Food*. Westport, Conn.: AVI, 1974.

Gardeton, César. *Nouveau Guide des dîneurs*. Paris: Bréauté, 1828.

Gault, Henri, and Millau, Christian. *Guide gourmand de la France*. Paris: Hachette, 1970.

———. *Guide Julliard de Paris*. Paris: Julliard, 1963–.

Gaussel, Alain. *Je veux savoir ce que je mange*. Paris: Pavillon, 1973.

Gilbert, Philéas. *La Cuisine à l'usage des familles*. Paris: Librairie de l'enseignement technique, 1900.

Girard, Alain. "Le Triomphe de *La Cuisinière bourgeoise*: Livres culinaires, cuisine et société en France aux 17e et 18e siècles." *Revue d'Histoire moderne et contemporaine* 24 (1977): 497–523.

Gogué, Antoine. *Les Secrets de la cuisine française*. Paris: Hachette, 1856.

Gottschalk, Alfred. *Histoire de l'alimentation et de la gastronomie depuis la Préhistoire jusqu'à nos jours.* 2 vols. Paris: Éditions Hippocrate, 1948.

Goudeau, Émile. *Paris qui consomme.* Paris: Béraldi, 1893.

Grimod de La Reynière, Alexandre-Balthazar-Laurent. *Almanach des gourmands.* Paris: Maradan, 1803–12.

———. *Écrits gastronomiques.* Edited by J.-C. Bonnet. Paris: U.G.E., 1977.

———. *Manuel des Amphytrions.* Paris: Capelle & Renand, 1808.

Guide Kléber-Colombes. Paris: Taride, 1949–.

Guide Michelin. Clermont-Ferrand: Michelin, 1900–.

Guide des Relais Routiers. Paris: SEJT, 1977–.

Hachette Guide to French Wines. Edited by André Vedel. New York: Knopf, 1986.

Hamp, Pierre. *Mes métiers.* Paris: Gallimard, 1930.

Hémardinquer, Jean-Jacques, ed. *Pour une histoire de l'alimentation.* Paris: Colin, 1970.

Henish, B. A. *Fast and Feast: Food in Medieval Society.* University Park: Pennsylvania State University, 1976.

Herbodeau, Eugène, and Thalamas, Paul. *Georges-Auguste Escoffier.* London: Practical Press, 1955.

Héron de Villefosse, René. *Histoire et géographie gourmandes de Paris.* Paris: Éditions de Paris, 1956.

Institut National de la Statistique et des Études Économiques. *Enquête permanente sur la consommation des Français.* Annual reports.

Johnson, Hugh. *The Story of Wine.* London: Mitchell Beazley, 1989.

Journal d'un bourgeois de Paris sous Charles VI et Charles VII. Paris, fifteenth century.

Lachiver, Marcel. *Vin, vigne et vignerons en région parisienne du XVIIe au XIXe siècles.* Pontoise: Société historique de Pontoise, 1982.

La Fizelière, Albert de. *Vins à la mode et cabarets du 17e siècle.* Paris: Pincebourde, 1866.

La Reynière (R. J. Courtine). *Cent Merveilles de la cuisine française.* Paris: Seuil, 1971.

Larousse gastronomique. Paris: Larousse, 1984.

Laurent, Robert. *Les Vignerons de la Côte d'Or au dix-neuvième siècle.* 2 vols. Paris: Les Belles-Lettres, 1957.

La Varenne, François-Pierre de. *Le Cuisinier français.* Paris, 1651.

———. *Le Pâtissier français.* Paris, 1653.

Lebault, Armand. *La Table et le repas à travers les siècles.* Paris: Laveur, 1910.

Leslie, Eliza. *Domestic French Cookery.* Philadelphia: Carey & Hart, 1832.

Lichine, Alexis. *Encyclopedia of Wines and Spirits.* New York: Knopf, 1977.

———. *Wines of France.* New York: Knopf, 1974.

Lombard, Léandre-Moïse. *Le Cuisinier et le médecin.* Paris: Curmer, 1855.

L. S. R. (Le Sieur Robert). *L'Art de bien traiter.* Paris, 1674.

Marie de Saint-Ursin, P. J. *Journal des gourmands et des belles.* Paris, 1807.

Marin, François. *Les Dons de Comus.* Paris: Pissot, 1758.

Maurial, Ludovic. *L'Art de boire, connaître et acheter le vin.* Paris: Librairie du "Petit Journal," 1865.

Ménagier de Paris, Le. 2 vols. Ca. 1393; Geneva: Slatkine, 1982.

Mennell, Stephen. *All Manners of Food.* Oxford: Blackwell, 1985.

Menon. *La Cuisinière bourgeoise.* Paris: Temps actuels, 1981.

———. *Nouveau Traité de la cuisine.* Paris: David, 1739.

Messadié, Gérald. *L'Alimentation suicide.* Paris: Fayard, 1973.

Mlle. Léontine. *La Cuisine hygiénique*. Paris: Desloges, 1856.

Monselet, Charles. *Gastronomie. Récits de table*. Paris: Charpentier, 1874.

Montagné, Prosper. *Le Grand Livre de la cuisine*. Paris: Flammarion, 1929.

Mordacq, Philippe. *Le Menu. Une histoire illustrée de 1751 à nos jours*. Paris: Laffont, 1989.

Nicolardot, Louis. *Histoire de la table*. Paris: Dentu, 1868.

Nostradamus. *Excellent et moult utile opuscule (. . .) de plusieurs exquises recettes*. Paris, 1555.

Oliver, Raymond. *The French at Table*. London: Wine and Food Society, 1967.

Page, Edward B., and Kingsford, P. W. *The Master Chefs: A History of Haute Cuisine*. New York: St. Martin's Press, 1971.

Pasquelot, Maurice. *La Terre chauve*. Paris: La Table ronde, 1971.

Perpillou, Aimé V. *Le Ravitaillement des grandes villes*. Paris: Centre de documentation universitaire, 1967.

Pestel, Henri. *Les Vins et eaux-de-vie à appellations d'origine contrôlées en France*. Mâcon: Buguet-Comptour, 1959.

Pidoulx, Pierre. *Le Grand Cuisinier de toute cuisine*. Paris, 1540.

Point, Fernand. *Ma gastronomie*. Paris: Flammarion, 1969.

Promenade gastronomique dans Paris par un amateur. Paris: Dondey-Dupré, 1833.

Rabaudy, Nicolas de. *Guide des meilleurs restaurants de France*. Paris: Lattès, 1976.

Ray, Georges. *Les Industries de l'alimentation*. Paris: Presses Universitaires de France, 1948.

———. *Les Vins de France*. Paris: Presses Universitaires de France, 1957.

Revel, Jean-François. *Un festin en paroles*. Paris: Pauvert, 1979.

Ricard, Jules. *À prix fixe et à la carte*. Paris: Calmann-Lévy, 1895.

Root, Waverley. *The Food of France*. New York: Vintage, 1966.

———. *Paris Dining Guide*. New York: Atheneum, 1969.

Scott, James M. *Vineyards of France*. London: Hodder & Stoughton, 1950.

Simon, André L., ed. *Bibliotheca Gastronomica: A Catalogue of Books and Documents on Gastronomy*. London: Wine and Food Society, 1953.

Sue, Roger. *Le Loisir*. Paris: Presses Universitaires de France, 1980.

Taillevent (Guillaume Tirel). *Le Viandier*. Edited by Terence Scully. Ottawa: University of Ottawa Press, 1988.

Tannahill, Reay. *Food in History*. New York: Stein & Day, 1973.

Terrail, Claude. *Je suis restaurateur*. Paris: Conquistador, 1955.

———. *Ma Tour d'Argent*. Paris: Stock, 1974.

Thomazi, Auguste. *Histoire de la pêche des âges de la pierre à nos jours*. Paris: Payot, 1947.

Thonnat, Nicole. *L'Alimentation en question*. Paris: Desclée, De Brouwer, 1973.

Toutain, Jean-Claude. *La Consommation alimentaire en France de 1789 à 1964*. Geneva: Droz, 1971.

Vasseur, Léon. *Les Industries de l'alimentation*. Paris: Presses Universitaires de France, 1966.

Venaille, Élisabeth. *La Pollution dans votre assiette*. Paris: Calmann-Lévy, 1974.

Vicaire, Georges. *Bibliographie gastronomique*. Paris: Rouquette, 1890.

Warner, Charles K. *The Winegrowers of France and the Government since 1875*. New York: Columbia University Press, 1960.

Wason, Betty. *Cooks, Gluttons and Gourmets: A History of Cookery*. New York: Doubleday, 1962.

Wells, Patricia. *The Food Lover's Guide to Paris*. New York: Workman, 1988.

7

Leisure

ROGER SUE

Paradoxically, while all the activities usually grouped under the generic term "leisure" do not stop developing in quantity and intensity, the study of leisure as a phenomenon characteristic of modern and even postmodern societies remains on the fringes, far from the discourses that serve as the basis for today's social representation and that are on this subject in flagrant contradiction to reality itself.

Is this because it is difficult to ascribe a specific field to leisure and then constitute it into an object of study? Yet the phenomena of work, family, religion, culture, all objects of formal scrutiny, suffer from the same definition and conceptualization problems, since the object always exceeds the theory elaborated, thereby producing new knowledge.

Is it, then, leisure's subjective character that would make of it a psychological state specific to each individual (leisure as pleasure) rather than an object for sociological study? But how can we deny the importance of social conditions of production in such a state or states?

Or is it as a consequence of refusing to see in leisure anything other than the product of labor and its statutory and/or manipulative effects (leisure as consumption)? But how can we ignore leisure's liberating character and productive dimension?

Could it be the inability of traditional thought systems (positivism, institutionalism) or current ones (sociology of everyday life, constructivism, ethnomethodology) to give an account of leisure? But is this not itself (considering its objective importance) an extraordinary revealer as well as explainer of the crisis and possible overshooting of modern thought?

Perhaps it is simply that leisure is "revolutionary" (Dumazedier) in the sense that it introduces a societal break that saps the foundations of power of those in power, said foundations resting on a social work ethic and its morality (Max Weber).

To understand the importance of these questions and the social "repression" of which some are the object, as well as the major stakes they cover for our societies' transformation and the interpretation of that transformation, it is useful to survey the principal stages of the theorization of leisure in the French context; to consider its present theoretical development from other viewpoints; and to indicate some perspectives that are opening in the very near future.

SUBJECTIVE HISTORY OF THE THEORIZATION OF LEISURE

Founding Myths of Greek Civilization

Greek civilization continues to cross the centuries, constituting itself into a "myth of eternal return" (Nietzsche) as it reappears in various forms throughout history, such as the myth of Prometheus "the industrious." Regarding industry's opposite—leisure—one would refer to the myth of Dionysus, "the Dionysian spirit" in Nietzsche, or, closer to us, "the shadow of Dionysus" in Maffesoli. But from the standpoint of a theorization of leisure, it is less mythology and its various figures than it is the interpretations of the Greek conception of leisure (Vernant, Foucault) which still play today—and perhaps more strongly than yesterday—the role of founding myth, a kind of "lay" myth always present in the theorization of leisure.

At least three great dimensions in this founding myth can be distinguished. The first dimension—*idleness*—defines leisure as a *state* (idle individual), a social condition, the intrinsic character of an order, the very nature of Greek citizenship. In this conception, idleness is not the opposite of work (itself not a homogeneous category) but is instead the state of servitude characterized by things "domestic" (*oikos*, which will later give us the word *economy*), reserved to women and slaves. We should remember that the foreigner Aristotle, by exceptional favor, each year had to pay a tribute of twelve drachmas to avoid the domestic condition and being sold at the slave market.

This question of idleness, sometimes validated, sometimes condemned—often both—crosses the centuries. Found in the successive positions, contradictory debates, and accommodations of the Church about contemplative life/life of work, it is central in the oppositions and class struggle where the exploiter-capitalist is stigmatized as being an idle stockholder (Saint-Simon, Marx); it is picked up again and illustrated in the United States by Veblen, who showed both the relation and the break between the idle class and what he called the "leisure class," giving leisure a much more modern concept. It reappears in the twentieth century in the 1950s and 1960s in industrial society's accelerated development phase, supported by another myth, that of the *abundant* society (Riesman).

Meanwhile, the notion of leisure replaced that of idleness due to the latter's increasingly pejorative connotation with the development of industrial society, assimilating idleness to "do-nothingness," a negative and highly distorted view of its original concept ("time in order to do"), and especially due to the generalization and uniformization (payment by salary) of work. In this new context, leisure no longer defines a "state" by opposition to work but rather as its *product* (Dumazedier). Actually, this distinction is artificial, for the Greeks' idleness was indeed "fed" by the work of slaves and artisans (*techne*) on which it depended. What changes, and it is of course a radical change, is the generalization of work and leisure for all in an alternating rhythm.

This idleness myth, conceived in its modern form as "leisure civilization" of "free time society" (Dumazedier, Sue), has totally been overshadowed by the economic crisis from the 1970s on. However, with the increased reduction of work time (of which unemployment is only a variant at the societal level), the progressive inversion of the inactive/active ratio, the more and more real prospects of production and labor automation (robots as new slaves), the idleness myth is unarguably "returning" once again. The weight of work as a dominant representation of society's production (Touraine) is such that it forbids any conceivable and *a fortiori* realistic alternative reflection. It is useful, therefore, to again find the meaning of the idleness myth in its positivist version, that is, not as a simple "negative" of work, but as a thought creating new categories of social activities and values—still called "work"—provided work is given a very broad meaning in relation to industrial society's reductive conception. In fact, the other dimensions of the original leisure myth are even more understandable from the viewpoint of their positivity and functionality in modern society.

Indeed, the *second dimension of the myth* is linked to education: one of the possible translations of the notion of Greek "leisure" is the word *skole* from which "school" is derived (Lanfant). But the meaning of skole exceeds by far that of school, including schools of thought. Close to its original meaning is the notion of freedom. The skole-ed individual is first a free man always in opposition to the state of servitude qualified as *askole*. In this sense, the skole is very close to, but unlike, idleness, which is a state, a "gift of the Gods" (Vernant), and freedom is less a given than an *acquisition process*.

This freedom is one of and by the mind, acquired only through a long "labor" of education all during life to arrive at knowledge, with discourse as the method. Greek "leisure" supposes idleness, but an objectified idleness, which bears within itself its finality, namely, one's education, self-knowledge, in its most finished form, the knowledge of nature and the world. Idleness is indivisible from the relationship to oneself, from a self alienated as object of knowledge reached by a labor of self-education that is at the same time its realization, whose maieutics furnishes the best example in Plato.

This time, from the point of view of education, a similar problematic is again encountered in Carl Rogers' "freedom to learn," in the sense that education arises first from work on oneself (self-desire). Thus in leisure can be seen in the sense of skole not only freedom, but freedom as a means of education—education turned toward self-realization as accomplishment of nature. This theme is found again in "the care of the self" of Foucault, who describes the search of "the intensity of the relations to self" that is both a therapeutic (for "philosophying is the best care one can bring to oneself") and a mode of knowledge ("to learn how to live one's whole life," Seneca).

Clearly found in the history of the modernity of leisure is the mark of those fundamental themes linked to the founding myth. The progressive liberation from work, gained or granted, was frequently demanded in the name of the right to learn. Objectively, at the level of social times (*temps sociaux*), time for education was the first to benefit from the relaxing of the organization of labor—and this occurred long before the first laws making schooling mandatory.

The first laws regarding work-time reduction concerned restrictions on child labor. The people's schools and popular education's first steps brought a legitimate support to these restrictions (Léon, Poujol, Cacéres). It is one reason why the study of leisure theorization in France is inseparable from that of popular education.

The institutionalization of mandatory education sought at once to reduce work's hold and to dissociate education in the strict sense of leisure insofar as it is constrained time. This dissociation will increase with the affirmation of a more and more evident cohesion between the educational and productive systems and with the improvement of the educational level as an essential factor in the economic growth process. A few exceptions aside, and despite the goodwill present in numerous pedagogical statements, leisure as education or education as leisure are rejected into the extracurricular or the noncurricular.

In the postmodern period in which we live, the conditions exist for a reactivation of the educational leisure dimension according to the original myth: for instance, the schools' progressive opening onto resources that are external to them; the multiplication of "parallel schools" (Porcher); the development of continuing education which, even when focused on professional training, reintroduces the acquisition of fundamental knowledge and a certain pedagogy through leisure (company-sponsored internships); the development of educational leisure and of cultural industries, etc.

In brief, many scholars think that industrial society's move toward a society dominated by free time and leisure will introduce a new cultural (in the broad sense) era, where the cultural (strict sense) debate will be central (Zeldin) against a background of a society qualified as "educational" (Dumazedier) or "pedagogical" (Beillerot). Since the educational effort is less and less centered on its relation to work as a homogeneous model essential to everyone, it will give room to a plurality of heterogeneous models based on the quest for self-realization and, therefore, on a permanent self-education.

The third dimension of the founding myth is the concretization of the previous two under the form of *citizenship* as understood by the Greeks. That is, citizenship as supreme accomplishment of the qualities of Greek identity, maintaining privileged relationships (proximity) with the gods. This citizenship, not a state but a citizenship "in actuality," presupposes idleness and its dimension of objective freedom in a labor of self-education which enables the citizen to rise to the dignity of the philosopher, who finds a kind of consecration in handling the city's affairs, that is, in "managing" destiny. Thus, leisure finds a superior form of realization in the full exercise of citizenship. This is a recurrent theme in leisure theorization that explains why leisure sociology is so close to a sociology of action opening onto a political sociology.

Soon, however, the conquest of economic rationality through utilitarian thought will extend and generalize the domestic sphere (in the sense of *oikos*) and transform everyone into a servant of work whose finality will, little by little, escape from him to become a finality in itself. In short, the philosopher will give up his place to the economist, a new philosopher albeit without a philosophy.

Work and its organization will become the "public business" par excellence, whereas leisure will be rejected into the private sphere, "deprived" of social representation, in the name of an individual freedom and almost entirely submitted to the work sphere. The paradox, as Marx pointed out, is that this reversal could have happened in the name of freedom, by referring to work as a source of liberty and equality in the ideology of the bourgeois revolution of 1789.

According to Marxist structuralist perspective, however, this ideology is a condition necessary for the intermediate stage (socialist society), where the generalization of labor and equality in its production conditions will cause its overshooting toward a "leisure" or free work society according to everyone's needs. This free work or this leisure essentially turned toward satisfying "superior needs" (education, culture) is also dedicated to the collective management of city affairs, in perfect concordance with the Greek mythology on which Marx based himself, though most often not explicitly.

While there are strong differences about the means of achieving this ideal society, most nineteenth-century French socialist thinkers share this long-term view, a view that will always be an important element of leisure theorization. The modernity of the "leisure-citizenship" theme is today perhaps the least evident of the leisure dimensions inspired by Greek mythology. Yet it is also perhaps the most important, for any decisive advance toward new social organization forms presupposes a public recognition (political) as a means of action and, above all, as a convergent point of social representations or ideology.

Hence, a new paradox emerges: whereas we have never been so close to a leisure society (objectively from the viewpoint of social times), public discourse about work as ideology is practically unchanged since the nineteenth century. Discourse about work and its economy remains the founding discourse, the discourse of government, that is, the one that allows the exercise of power. Consequently, work remains the basis of the social order, even if the gap between this representation and the lived reality continues to become more pronounced and to reach absurd limits, as shown by the emptiness of political discourse and the generalized disaffection it provokes. For the moment, for lack of a structuring discourse, there are juxtaposed social movements (Touraine) that sometimes recall May 1968 but which for all that do not form a social movement cemented by a common ideology.

Latin Etymology and Additions in Meaning

The analysis of leisure meanings from Greek mythology, with a few nuances, could be transposed to the Roman world. The same basic dimensions would still be found in leisure theorization. However, the greater proximity of Latin roots in French permits the specification and completion of various meanings involved in the modern leisure concept. Thus, *loisir-oisiveté* (leisure-idleness) directly derives from the word *otium*; the concept of this idleness is very similar to the Greeks', but it seems, according to Latin scholars, that there can be in *otium* a nuance of demonstration illustrated by an effect of "consumption."

The Roman otium is a distinctive mark which qualifies the citizen and identifies him socially, but this otium-idleness needs to be marked, remarked, demonstrated by giving tangible signs of consumption. Wealth is no longer only an inner state of freedom and available time, but must also flaunt itself in an unbridled consumption that needs to be "outside the norms" (so it will not be confused with vulgar consumption) and is all the more actualized in that it supposes a considerable accumulation of work to produce this wealth, which is itself ostensibly scorned. Extravagant overconsumption is the sign of an idleness all the more valued because it translates itself by the "wasting" of wealth, hence of integrated work. This theme is crucial to Veblen's research through the idea of "ostentatious consumption." It is also found in all analyses of the "consumption society" (from Baudrillard to Bourdieu) in which economic rationality increasingly compares leisure to a pure consumption phenomenon indicative of social distinction.

Today, this question remains fundamental insofar as, like the other themes discussed here, it can reveal a societal change, an entry into a postmodern society, that is, in our context, a society oriented more toward Being than Having (E. Fromm). Progression of immaterial consumption, consumption and production of signs (information, education), cultural consumption and production, and search for new social experiences and new life-styles are but a few examples.

Even closer, etymologically, is the opposite of otium: *neg-otium* which gives the French word *négoce* (trade, commerce). Those who are without otium and its attributes must literally sell goods or themselves (slaves of work), and their condition, or status, is destined to create the exchange value. (We should not forget that the word *travail*, work, comes from *trepalium*, a Roman torture device.)

The root of the word *loisir* (leisure) comes from the Latin *licet, licere*, which means "it is permitted to," "it is all right to." In its modern interpretation, this *loisir* is synonymous with authorization: it has a moral connotation and is assumed freed from constraints. It is a *deserved* leisure after obligations are fulfilled, which means both having accomplished one's "work" and one's "social duty" as conditions of one's liberation. Yet, if kept to the original meaning, a totally different interpretation can be given. *Licere* can be understood in the sense of a right for those who precisely have a right to leisure by their very condition as Roman citizens.

In this light, licere is no longer the opposite of duty, it is itself a duty, the "duty to be," inherent in the condition of the man of leisure. A negative (by opposition to a moral) content becomes positive, as it creates an ethic for man, now moral in leisure. This meaning will reappear later in Wolfenstein's notion of "fun morality," a new leisure ethic that seems much more suited to a post-modern society. Furthermore, from licere comes *licence* in French. He who has *licence* (sixteenth-century French) has the *right to teach*, a strong reminder of the link between leisure and education.

In a broader sense, licence is a right, a social recognition of an exercising right, the right to be a citizen. However—and here is a basic ambiguity in all conceptions of leisure—licence—which is a right—also contains the possibility of its subversion, its own excess and immorality in "licentiousness." Thus, licence can be a "duty to be" as well as its "perversion/subversion." In concepts of leisure, this ambivalence regarding leisure is seen as an idealized duty to be, on the one hand, and as a possibility of upsetting the moral and social order on the other. This recalls Freud's idea of the "pleasure principle."

To oversimplify, leisure, which imposed itself as duty to be and self-fulfillment of superior man in Antiquity, has little by little taken the meaning of "licentiousness" with the rise of the work ethic. The whole question today is to establish a new "leisure license," a new ethic for modern times, a new education of the citizen, for, as Gide wrote, "nothing excellent is done save in leisure."

Finally, by association more than by derivation, leisure has been connected with *ludic* (from *ludere*, to play). Leisure in the sense of play is synonymous with futility and pastime and occupies a secondary place in the social value order. It is the opposite of the "spirit of seriousness" (Weber), foundation of rationality, necessary for progress and good social order. Play, as a kind of necessary social release or vestige of infantilism, is only tolerated and often condemned as a waste of time and money. It acts as a negative counterpoint to the myth of sole rationality founded on the possibility of a scientific and technical organization of society.

While not at all the Romans' or Greeks' idea of leisure as play, two essential elements can be extrapolated. First, play is related to the "puerile" sphere and is the privileged form of children's education. In a word, it is pedagogy—a new link between leisure and education (Mauriras-Bousquet). We can consider this meaning in its simple form of introduction into the real world, the world of adults, but also more basically as characteristic of the educational act and of any thinking activity, that is, literally "mind game" in the sense understood by Nietzsche in the "joyous game" which is the way to know and to appropriate the world by "Joyful Wisdom."

Second, society itself can be defined as play. For man is only "the toy of the gods'' who manipulate his destiny; consequently, the human world is only a game to the extent that it is only a reflection, a *mime*, an imitation (mimesis), a distorted reproduction of the universe of the gods, an illusion (*illusio*, from *ludere*). At the same time, play is a human trait, ''homo ludens,'' as Huizinga calls it. Play is man's tragic dimension, but precisely if he knows to recognize it as such, play can also allow him to attain the knowledge (education) of the gods, who are themselves very ''playful'' since they have created man as a demigod; the difference is that the gods master the game whereas humans are only stakes (*enjeu*). This is why, as Caillois showed in his definition of play, it mobilizes man's very essence in *alea, agon, ilynx,* ''mimicry.'' It is by giving in to the vertigo of play, that is, by being profoundly human, that man (object of the game) will be able to have an idea of the divine and of what separates him from it, that is, the mastery of the game.

Generalization of Work as Condition of Leisure Production for All in the Nineteenth Century

If studies on the notion and conception of leisure in Antiquity can lead us to a reflection on postmodernity, we must analyze as well theorizations that lead to the modernity in which we are still engaged. With the nineteenth century there occurred a dominant paradigm (positivist thought) whose keystone, a new representation of work (salaried or not) as a *global* mode of production of the new society (industrial), is still at the basis of the principal schemata of today's social thought. This is illustrated in the study of leisure progressively linked to its exclusive relation to work, to the point of being overshadowed as object of specific research or of being perceived as the simple negative of work.

The nineteenth century heralded a production society founded on general work (''measure of value'') whose accumulation in the form of overwork and increment values would allow for the extension of financial and industrial capital (''crystallized labor''), generating rapid progress in production and productivity. The period of rapid accumulation of capital necessary for the ''economic takeoff'' assumed both very intense work (17- to 19-hour workdays in factories or mines were common) and a work product that was, to the detriment of salaries and consumption, essentially allocated to profit-investment. Under these conditions, leisure was extremely reduced, even nonexistent, a simple reproduction of perseverance in work (physiological time).

Yet it was this work extension and formalization that, under the double requirement of granting a few social demands and freeing a minimum time for consumption, would give rise to leisure in its modern sense, that is, as a *product of work, accessible to all.* But—very often forgotten or overshadowed—this work ideology is also, in most theorizations, an ideology of leisure as an ultimate finality of this work, a hidden side of the period's theories which the invasive economic rationality would little by little push aside (Naville). It is in such a context that, citing a few authors, we can quickly review the main elements of a still-current theorization of leisure.

Saint-Simon, thinker par excellence of this burgeoning industrial society and often called an "industrialist socialist," defends the principle and necessity of a "scientific" organization of work founded on technical progress, whose key figure follows Saint-Simon's own profession of engineer, and which provides the sole path for economic and *social* progress. By this account, he denounces leisure, but leisure as he understands and observes it is very close to idleness.

This idleness is by definition unproductive, it is a source of waste (of time and property), it is contrary to the morality of the effort needed for the industrial society's advancement, and it is mostly the fundamental factor of social inequality, for it derives from the work and sweat of the immense majority. Consequently, faithful to the spirit of the Enlightenment, Saint-Simon pleads not only for a right to work but also for an obligation to work, first step toward a certain social equality, the necessary condition for a "general mobilization" to make the industrial society a reality.

If this aspect of his thought remains alive today, we have somewhat "forgotten" in what design it used to lie. We have kept the "industrialist" Saint-Simon, promoter of the modern economy, but we have forgotten the socialist. For Saint-Simon, the technical and industrial society's finality is not work or even the accumulation of wealth but its equitable distribution among all "producers" in order to build a brotherly society.

Saint-Simon is not thinking of a "postindustrial" stage but of this society's achievement itself, its vocation, of the sense of history. It is quite logical that industrial society's goal is to progressively relieve work, thanks to technical improvements, and to free man from it, at least in its constricting part, thanks to an abundance of produced goods that at the same time would benefit all. Saint-Simon did not explicitly speak of a "leisure society," whose connotation is too negative in his view, but of freely consented work, more in the spirit of the socialism of his time.

In Paul Lafargue (Karl Marx's son-in-law), we have a rather good illustration of Marxist theories of leisure mixed with certain ideas derived from French socialism. Lafargue published *Le Droit à la paresse* in 1884, a book considered (quite wrongly, I believe) as the first classic of leisure sociology in the modern sense. Actually, as with Saint-Simon and Marx, Lafargue's leisure is a "bourgeois" category, very close to the aristocratic idleness with which the "new masters" dream of identifying themselves regardless of their own morality.

Lafargue describes very incisively how the bourgeois must do "violence" to himself to display his status through idleness and overconsumption, which are from then on inextricably linked. The bourgeois is a man with an "unhappy conscience" not only because of his lower-class origins but because he turns his back on the fulfillment of universal conscience, in the sense of history. Initial progress, at once moral and economic, comes from the bourgeois "going back" to work, which supposes that workers apply a "right to laziness" less as a right to leisure than as a subversive weapon meant to force the bourgeois to work in order to maintain his capital's profitability and to reinforce productive investments by eliminating overconsumption.

As in Marx and Saint-Simon, we remain in an ideology of work and its extension as necessary condition for liberation from it and for social equality. There is no positive vision of leisure in industrial society, since these authors remain in a Judaeo-Christian morality concerning effort and work, rejecting leisure in a perpetual "beyond." It is an "all or nothing" doctrine: as long as there will be work (both alienation and original sin), there cannot really be leisure (reconquest of the divine in man).

In its application, the "right to laziness" can be understood in Lafargue either as a progressive weapon, foreshadowing somewhat our "work-to-rule," or as a radical weapon similar in its ultimate form to the general strike (a great myth of French anarcho-syndicalism), or to the preparation of the "grand evening" in the Marxist problematic.

It is with an American, Thorstein Veblen, that we can close this survey of nineteenth-century theorizations of leisure. In *Theory of the Leisure Class* (1899), Veblen applied himself to dismantling and illustrating, more as an ethnologist than a sociologist, the mechanisms that make of leisure a class symbol. Starting from an evolutionist instinct theory close to the Darwinian model, Veblen opposes the peaceful "workmanship instinct" to the warlike "predatory instinct." It is the predatory instinct that is prevalent in capitalists, new "captains" of industry. This predatoriness finds its favorite place in leisure, whose raison d'être is to provoke a statutory effect by designating the individual's dominant social position.

Breaking with all functionalist explanations, Veblen shows that leisure is a very sophisticated series of signs intended to prove that the individual is not subjected to work (for example, the fashion of wearing white gloves) and that he can ostensibly subject the work of others to his benefit (a large domestic staff all the more valued that it is in part useless, vicarious leisure).

From this perspective, leisure is associated with "ostentatious consumption," which must be understood as consumption of time, the most unproductive of consumptions (see Ben Franklin's "Time is money"), as consumption of the most useless objects and activities possible, which precisely gives it its value, or also as extravagant consumption all the more prized that the incorporated worth is great (of the *potlatch* type).

If Veblen's book remains an indisputable work for leisure sociologists, most particularly in France, it is because it opens an area of research in several simultaneous directions. It is the first to make leisure and its representations revealing of social relationships, the very object of class relationships. In this sense leisure is more than a symbol: it is the symbol of symbols. Leisure is at once symbol and object of symbol. This is a great opening for culturalist interpretations of the social, for through its deliberately nonfunctionalist interpretation it shows the cultural system's autonomy and opens a breach into the positivist system. The essential place given the notion of *consumption* in all its forms indicates the modernity of all the analyses that will later focus on the consumer society.

Moreover, Veblen's analysis of leisure as a consumer phenomenon is not ordered along a simple dualism between those who have leisure on one side and those who do not on the other. Breaking with the interpretation of leisure as idleness, he shows that leisure can be understood as an organizing principle of social classes among themselves, less by the effect of opposition than by sometimes subtle *differentiations* among the classes. Here, leisure is the favored locus of "distinction" (Bourdieu) which reveals a class symbolic.

But Veblen also senses that the distinction he is analyzing from a predatory and rivalry instinct (today, we would say competitive) is a fundamental force for the consumption race necessary to feed the capitalist system. From this point of view he is one of the best interpreters of the change from production society to consumer society that will characterize capitalism's new age, the twentieth century.

Modernity: Leisure and the Consumer Society

With the twentieth century, we enter the era of modernity characterized by a very strong development of productive forces as the apogee of the industrial system, which means as well its decline or, better, its overshooting. This period finds its consecration with the *trente glorieuses* (the period of economic growth in Western Europe following World War II [Fourastié and Dahrendorf]) and rests notably on a very strong capitalistic intensity and a continuous rise in education and qualification levels, which have made considerable productivity gains possible (sixfold in France since 1936). This law of productivity is the objective basis of modern leisure; it finds its expression both in increased production and revenues and in continuously reduced work time, that is, the appearance of real leisure time for all.

This is why the contrast work/leisure dear to the nineteenth century is abandoned in favor of a conception making leisure the product of work. Also, leisure loses its negative image to become a socially valued time, even the symbol of a new society that no longer rejects rewards and bonuses from work into a hypothetical beyond but authorizes its immediate enjoyment. It can even be individually perceived as a symbol of social success to the extent that having leisure is being able to "buy" leisure activities, of which the car and vacation provide the first ingredients and the first statutory marks in conformity with Veblen's analysis.

During this period the problematic of leisure is indissociable from what is called the consumer society. First, this is because the reduction in working time was not done in the name of free time only or out of purely humanitarian motives, but for a production logic that, arrived at the mass production stage, presupposes mass consumption and therefore increased free time. Then, the dominant conception of leisure is objectivized in activities and things that presuppose consumption to such a point that leisure and consumption will be practically confused; we no longer speak of *leisure* (time) but of *leisure activities* (consumption). From this viewpoint, leisure (time for consumption) and leisure activities (objects of desire "satisfied" through consumption) are essential forces of the consumer society.

To this dominant approach illustrated by a vast sociological literature (from Morin to Baudrillard) can be contrasted those seeking a leisure sociology not reducible to its own consumption. From this viewpoint, we could not reduce leisure to a pure market logic, even if this logic is permanently in effect. First, many leisure activities consume little. On the contrary, we can easily show the *productive* character of many leisure activities (family activities, cultural and educational activities, practical activities) for oneself, for others, for the general economy. Furthermore, no activity is reducible to its consumption, for there is always a cultural specification process that in certain cases and in various degrees favors a raised self-consciousness and even the ability to criticize one's own consumption. In an optimistic view of social development the actual consumption stage (material consumption) is only a stage opening to a higher kind of "consumptions" that can transform the market logic.

Finally, for some (e.g., Gorz), it is appropriate to emphasize the new contradiction of the production system between the need to work more in order to earn more and engage in new leisure activities and the need to have more and more time available to enjoy and develop these activities. This contradiction still benefits work to the extent that the distribution of the productivity gain was done in favor of purchasing power rather than free time, but the increasingly marginal satisfaction drawn from additional gain compensates less and less the lack of time. It is from this problematic, which links society's new production conditions (economic logic) and modern leisure analysis—sometimes congruent with this logic but never reducible to it—that we can order our reading of the main authors of new theorizations about leisure.

The first important current comes from the United States, which more quickly entered into the consumption society (intra-social distribution is easier than in Europe). Leisure is at the confluence of a series of studies that in France will have a lasting influence on the emerging sociology (as scientific field) of leisure. In this current one author is undoubtedly prominent and is a somewhat symbolic figure for the French: David Riesman. Mainly inspired by Mayo's empirical studies showing the importance of life outside work on work itself, Riesman published *The Lonely Crowd* in 1950. Oddly, this is not a book of sociology but of social psychology and deals little with leisure as such, but with the production conditions (that seem to him to be set in place) of a "new" individual, the other-directed man.

Riesman starts from a rather positive view of the consumption society, owing less to the increase in living standards it provides than to the state of *abundance* it provides (that seems to him very near) and especially to the individual's liberation both from work and from material consumption, allowing for the advent of a new culture. Leaning mostly on J. K. Galbraith's thesis (*The Affluent Society*), Riesman believes that the conditions are present to attain humanity's third stage, a "third man" he defines in opposition to the tradition-directed man and the industrial society's inner-directed man, dominated by an internalized work ethic.

The "new," other-directed individual can be considered a man of leisure who replaces the man of work. Leisure is seen in an active and positive mode as a new human investment in man. His intrinsic definition rests on his quality as a "communicating individual," creating himself and creating new social experiences and a new culture in this permanent communication, which structures him and is a permanent creation. Here again, we have a highly optimistic view based on the positiveness of the development of mass communication media and on the expansion of socialization made possible by liberation from work. We see the precursory character of Riesman's thought, which will go alongside or far beyond leisure sociology through the sociology of (inter)action, cultural development, and of course communication as seen in the media by McLuhan or in philosophy by Habermas.

Yet, since the evolution of reality does not prove (quickly enough?) the theses of *The Lonely Crowd* right, the time came for disillusionment, the less well-known second phase of Riesman's thought. In *Abundance for What?* he notes that economic and material progress has not liberated man, but on the contrary has corrupted him in a system that perpetuates consumption greed, with its effects of show, where the object replaces the relation, where leisure, as leisure, is killed to answer conformity's demands, where work and destructive competition remain society's main forces. Why this failure? Why this "error" in prediction?

Essentially, according to Riesman, for lack of "maturity" on the part of man, who does not yet have the required ability for "other-directedness." A long *education* at the *societal level* is necessary, for man is unaware of the manipulations of which he is literally the *object* in a system of "inverted network" (Galbraith). Only education will be able to reverse the present network, which conditions the individual to the very center of his leisure activities, and get him to reach an actor's status. Riesman offers a theory in two steps (optimism-pessimism and illusion-disillusion) that will appear again, like a rhetorical device, in most leisure sociologist writings, since the "leisure society" always refers to an ideal and inaccessible myth, sometimes preventing objective measuring of the reality of social change.

The problematic of leisure in France rests on slightly different bases than in the United States, from where it will take a certain time to cross the Atlantic. In France, it is much more tied to an omnipresent work sociology, itself under considerable Marxist influence. The first author to sense the importance of a leisure sociology is Georges Friedmann, one of the noted work sociologists in France. In his early studies, Friedmann tried to show the negative, even destructive, effects of the conditions of modern work, dominated by the ideology of scientific and technical organization ("one best way") inspired by Frederick W. Taylor. He noticed, too, that because of reduced work time, the leisure sphere continued to develop and widen to cover all workers, who found in it a relaxation-investment in opposition to forced work. There is here almost a "dual personality" phenomenon, showing that workers can not be destroyed by their work and can find in their leisure activities "compensations" that make work bearable. This *compensation theory*, first step of a leisure sociology, can be interpreted in different ways.

In a strictly Marxist view, it can be considered a new form of alienation within a framework of a widened reproduction of the perseverance in work. Such is not Friedmann's conception. On the contrary, for him it can be considered a form of liberation by which the worker again finds spaces of autonomy and possibilities of realizing a potential ignored by the world of work. However, from this perspective, leisure activities remain strictly dependent on the kind of profession conditioning them. Finally, with progressively increasing free time, it can constitute a sphere more and more independent from work and serve as the basis for a new cultural development that will not be without retroactive effect on the work sphere itself.

It seems that Friedmann's view fluctuates between the second and third interpretations of the compensation theory. Yet, toward the end of his life (*La Puissance et la sagesse*), faithful to his theoretical origins, he believed that no profound change was possible without transforming work itself, for work determinism remained the strongest by its mechanical action as well as by the dominant symbols ("puritan work ethic") it conveyed. Leisure could not be considered an alternative, providing substitute values: it remained in the compensation range and was subject to work determinism. With analyses based more on economics, Jean Fourastié would develop a problematic whose line (from *40.000 heures* and *Le Grand Espoir du XXe siècle* to *Des loisirs pour quoi faire?*) is not without analogies to Friedmann's thought.

The constitution of a sociology of leisure in the true sense, that is, as a specific and autonomous field of social sciences, fell to Joffre Dumazedier, a Friedmann disciple. He is world-renowned not only for his studies (*Vers une civilisation du loisir* is translated into thirty-three languages) but also for his activities in the education and popular culture milieus and on behalf of a sociology of action based on a praxis.

The *seminal* character of his contributions to leisure sociology occurs at several levels. The most important lies in his epistemological break vis-à-vis his predecessors. According to Dumazedier and the best rules of Durkheim's method, one must establish leisure as specific object (in itself) and start from the *viewpoint* of this object to analyze the dialectic of its relationships with the other social times. The break occurs in this *reversal*, which favors leisure as center of reflection and mode of analysis instead of making it a simple result of determinisms that are external to it. This reversal is decisive and conditions his entire thought.

Consequently, leisure is no longer an assembly of "activities outside work" that could be accounted for from a socioprofessional status or from statutory effects (consummatory or not), manipulated (or not) by the dominant ideology. Leisure has its own existential *dynamic*, its own functionality, its own levels of specific representation, and above all—and this is an essential aspect for Dumazedier—its own logic for creating new values. Of course, this specific creative logic of leisure must be conceived in the multiplicity of its links with the other social times; but the growth of leisure time, becoming prevalent time, tends to reinforce the active influence of leisure practices and values on the whole of social behaviors. What is involved, and this is a major element for the sociological explanation, is the shift in the social dynamic's "center of gravity." This shift is itself understandable only if leisure is linked to a problematic of development and cultural action.

It is this cultural aspect in leisure that Dumazedier favors, for he is best able to explain the evolution of social behaviors. Leisure opens the field and recognizes popular culture and movements to allow all to have access to quality leisure activities. In Dumazedier's view, leisure is inseparable from a movement of continuing education that is not solely reducible to professional training and is materialized by a development in self- and hetero-education. The leisure society is above all an "educational society," which brings us back to the Greek concept of leisure. The educational aspect of leisure rests on an implicit axiology that emphasizes (qualitatively at least) the cultural forms in leisure. This again poses the problem of the meaning of culture and, retroactively, of education.

Dumazedier is also one of the first to have seen the emergence of what he will call an "innovative social subject." At variance with structuralist interpretations (Marxist or not) of society, he believes that the widening of the leisure sphere produces the conditions for a strengthened autonomy of the subject, who more and more tends to escape from institutional constraints and their deterministic explanations, starting with work but also with religion or the family, to affirm his identity and his growing capability of action on his own life along with greater free time.

Lastly, the conviction of Dumazedier's ideas is supported by his obstinacy in defending an *empirical* sociology grounded in facts, observations, and investigation results in order to create and demonstrate the relevance of his theses. The best illustration of this is his diachronic study of the cultural dynamic in the French city of Annecy, inspired by the example of Muncie, Indiana, studied by Robert Lynd and his wife (*Middletown*, 1929). Annecy, a highly privileged city in its cultural leisure activities, compared to the average, seems to him not only an example to ponder but also a probable illustration of the future.

Beside this current, which is the only one to explicitly treat leisure as such, the prevalent sociological approaches focus on the analysis of consuming phenomena as essential illustrations of modernity, of which leisure offers a favored symbolic form. In this light, leisure is at once reduced to its sole consumption, negated in other potentialities (specific time, cultural values), or thrown back to the myth of libertarian illusions. These analyses partake of the great disenchantment of the modern world (Max Weber), whose consumer—hence, leisure—society represents a higher stage.

Baudrillard's works in particular illustrate this position rather well. Basically, it proceeds from extending the notion of *alienation* to the area of consumption. In modern society the individual is doubly alienated—as worker-producer and more so as worker-consumer. These two kinds of modern alienation reinforce each other and create a productional system. In this concept, leisure is far from being a liberation; instead, it reinforces alienation and enslavement to a merchandise system. Much influenced by what he calls the "Veblen effect," Baudrillard believes that consumption, hence leisure, is accomplished on the basis of the object's exchange value, that is, on its sign (both monetary and class) and not on its use value: "The sign is the apogee of merchandise." Consumption functions on the basis of an inexhaustible rhetoric of signs, which feeds on an insatiable desire, since no consumption can ever "fulfill" that desire. This is the production system's ultimate trick to ensure its durability, since in the end its purpose is not to answer needs but to create them.

In this view, merchandise, changed into signs (whose production is limitless), invades the entire social space and "mediatizes" the totality of social relationships by reifying them and by indicating their trade value. This analysis leads us, of course, to a system of immaterial production (information, education, culture, leisure) that is now only sign production, whose material support is, strictly speaking, "insignificant" but continues nonetheless to function according to the logic of merchandise. This is the height of alienation, since the individual can no longer have any critical distance either toward his consumption or himself (which is the same thing), to the extent that thought itself, as a semiotic production, is subjected to the symbolic code of the merchandise.

Thus this system, in which the actors are dissolved, closes onto itself, alienation is everywhere, and reality is no more than a gigantic sham in which merchandise-signs reign supreme. This impasse, even this nihilism, to which this reflection on consumption and leisure leads us, has the merit of underlining the totalitarianism of the concept of alienation, an ambiguous concept, as soon as alienation is no longer linked only to a mode of production (work) but also to a mode of consumption (leisure) which in this illustrative case is a mode of existence.

Paradoxically, it is Marxist thinkers who have a less radical and totalitarian view of alienation and of leisure as culmination of its process. For Lefebvre, Marxist analysis can no longer be limited to the sole analysis of work as a modern mode of production. Everyday life exceeds by far the work universe, and one cannot reduce the individual to his condition as worker only, since in order to understand it one must also analyze the multiple facets of the "extracurricular" in everyday life.

Does this mean that leisure can escape the alienation produced by work? Yes and no. No, because daily life is a privileged place for observing the multiplicity of "partial alienations," and even is their *concretization*. In this sense, as in Baudrillard (much influenced by Lefebvre), leisure is an illusion of liberation and is wholly in a "factitious" universe, an imaginary universe that overshadows reality and the need to transform it. But in Lefebvre, the proliferation of partial alienations does not produce *total alienation*. In fact, it remains partial, for leisure reveals a series of contradictions in the production system of the types work-leisure, consumption-self-realization, etc. At once, leisure holds a "potential" revolutionary ferment that can progressively help in reunifying a consciousness misled by work alienation and by the ideology it produces and in shaping a "transition man" who will become Marx's "total man" when he has overcome his contradictions.

Pierre Naville, like Lefebvre, considers that Marxist analysis has been unfairly reduced to that of work, whereas Marx tried to think going beyond it and its opposite in free time. According to his interpretation, the root of alienation lies in constrained work, of which leisure is only a facet so long as it remains subject to work. But in a rather structuralist interpretation of Marx, Naville thinks that the production system tends more and more to deny what produced it, that is, precisely, work, because of the development of automation and of the substitution of capital for work.

Hence a qualitative reversal can occur that will open the way to a leisure society, to a found-again "enjoyment." Naville's analysis is not without ties to the later Marcuse, who relied still more on a Freudian and Reichian problematic to explain the "decisive break" by the reversal of social times in which the May 1968 French students would so much believe. But unlike Lefebvre, for Naville, who is a work sociologist, alienation (as a negative global concept of leisure) will remain as long as work subsists as society's essential mode of production.

Postmodernity: The "Meaning" of Social Times

The period 1970–80 was dominated by the persistent theme of the economic crisis (compared to the 1950s and 1960s) with the consequent focusing on work and overshadowing of leisure sociology (which seemed almost an "indecent" subject) as well as a new maturing/maturity of this sociology. In fact, this "crisis," even if not yet evident today, will help leisure sociology, for it is above all a *work crisis* despite an uninterrupted though less strong growth. This emphasizes all the more the continual tendency of production societies always to produce more always with less work, whether this reduction appears in the form of longer schooling and permanent training, early retirement, uncertainty of work, or unemployment.

A synthetic figure can summarize these observations: The daily working time in 1986 for the entire French population aged 15 or more represented 2 hours 31 minutes a day. At the same time, outside-work activities do not in general stop expanding, even if they favor TV watching (40% of free time). Also, the notion of leisure no longer explains this submersion of new or old activities, which become overdominant in the life cycle. This is why the idea of "free time" succeeded little by little that of leisure, even if for some (e.g., Dumazedier) one must distinguish, in free time, the leisure of family, sociopolitical, or religious activities.

This semantic shift (from leisure to free time) causes a major theoretical consequence. By stressing temporality, it revives a practically forgotten sociological current, that of *social times*. From proponents of the Durkheim school of thought (Halbwachs), it was partly taken up by Hubert, then by Gurvitch. According to this approach, social times can be a privileged mode for observing social matters and their changes to the extent that these times are a product of the different activities they regulate, as well as the framework for their organization and mainly their representation. Better, the structuring of these various social times in their different relations can act as a society's identification mode (as some ethnologists have seen) and can even place them in an historical development context.

This observation is, naturally, decisive for our societies where the dynamic of social times, marked essentially by the trilogy of education time, work time and free time, is in rapid evolution. The concept of dominant time, pivot time, or structuring time seems central to this sociology. It means that a time analyzed on several levels (quantitative, qualitative, representations, and values) conditions and, to some extent, organizes the other social times. So it was of religious time in the Middle Ages (Le Goff), so it is of modern work time, so it will be of free time in the postmodern era.

The future may already be *de trop* for, according to many, free time is already dominant time, notably on the quantitative level, on the level of individual and collective values, on the level of society's production mode. Yet it is sure that there is still today a missing level, perhaps the most decisive, that of social representation and of those responsible for representing it, which we must distinguish from collective representation.

For lack of having reached this level, many analyses remain captive of the paradigm of modernity (that is, of work) without being able to account for the new production conditions of today's society. It is precisely the task undertaken today by a still-growing free time sociology in its postmodern version. For if it is easy to show how work as dominant social time was able to organize modern society in its production and representation (witness *all* the classical and neoclassical sociologies functioning around the same *categories* arising from work), it is much less obvious—since they need to be constructed—to validate new categories that show the new society's dynamic.

Furthermore, the sociological approach of free time, on the basis of a social time theorization, is confirmed by a general evolution of the main sociological paradigms and of the social interpretation models deriving from them. Important questions are raised by currents issued from classical, neoclassical, or Marxist sociology, based on the dominant work paradigm and an institutional approach of society. Very quickly, these highly "deterministic" currents evolve toward a *real* interactionism that, under various conditions, gives visibility and new weight to the notions of agent, subject, actor, individual.

It is also noticed in the institutionalist approach which proposes new analytical modes of the institutionalizing-institutionalized relation, in education sociology (Charlot), and even in the sociology of work (in the literal sense) with the latest studies by Crozier and Sainsaulieu. These sociologies which, in their most advanced form, can go as far as a sociology of action (Touraine), give a more important part to the *constructionalist* dimension in the social analysis, which brings them close to the observation of truly lived *times* and, therefore, to the influence exercised by the entire times liberated from work.

All these openings, even modest ones, are getting close (that is the very logic of social reality's evolution) to a free time sociology founded on the principle of a liberation-determination through outside-work activities, introducing a new representation of the actor whose interactions with his environments no longer obey a stable hierarchy. Parallel to these progressive evolutions of "classical" sociology, a radical and critical approach is developed, which stresses the effect of *deconstruction* of the social in our postmodern societies. It is the end of the great paradigms and great interpretation systems provoking a global crisis of rationality. From this perspective, the social is explained by what it is not anymore, and introduces us into "an era of void" (Lipovetsky, Mendel) that is also a theoretical "void."

To the Weberian "disenchantment of the world" would correspond the disenchantment of theory. In general, this negative critique is done on behalf of a subject become unseizable because of the multiplicity of his *adherences*, which is a global nonadherence where permanent change and the subjection to the effects of fads and artifices dominate. Such an analysis recalls somewhat Baudrillard's. But the explanation is not to be sought in some alienation or other, since alienation is "consumed," so to speak. Besides, the causal or essentialist explanation is no longer possible, since the individual is no longer explained by the social from which he continuously escapes in order to re-create it elsewhere, in the ephemeral (*L'Empire de l'éphémère*, by Lipovetsky).

Rather, it is from the individual on (*L'Ère de l'individu*, by Renaut) that the social could be accounted for. We understand the turning around, but we see, too, the impasse that is the powerlessness to account for the individual starting from the new social conditions of his production. That this analysis is considered "impossible" by the subject's very irreducibility is a philosophical position that takes us out of a sociological problematic which, in turn, must try to operate constructs, even partial and/or ephemeral, because the necessity of the meaning is essential in order to escape from nihilism. Besides, this approach necessarily avoids it and seems much more relevant when it refers to the notions of play, to media influences, to underlying cultural logics that "nevertheless" have a structuring collective effect.

Such is the case for Paul Yonnet (*Jeux, modes et masses*), who, in his empirical studies of play, trifecta, house pets, jogging, or rock music, tries to show the original meaning and the values produced by these activities, which have an unknown social structuring effect because most of the time they are not studied or they are reduced to simple epiphenomena dependent on *a priori* constructs (logic of work, of classes, of alienation). The interest of these approaches lies, therefore, in these "updates" of free time activities as creation loci of a new social order and/or a new individual.

A similar inspiration, though on different theoretical bases, is found in *everyday life sociology* illustrated by authors like Maffesoli and Ferraroti following the work of Lefebvre and Certeau. The theoretical origins of this sociology are at the junction of phenomenology (Husserl, Merleau-Ponty), of Weber's comprehensive sociology and Simmel's "formal" frame of reference. "Everyday life" is not defined *a priori* or structured according to a logic of activities that could be organized into a hierarchy or according to a time logic. It is actually everyday life which "makes" the sociology, for what matters is the meaning the actors give their actions and not one preestablished by the sociologist. The sociologist would instead be a "spokesman" of the lived and the existential where the total meaning is offered and cannot be reduced to theoretical constructs. The importance of this everyday life is expressed by the rise of a new *social experience* in relation to self and to others, which gives the social its true sense.

This sociology notices an intensifying of this social experience through the return of Dionysus, a new hedonistic and pleasure morality (fun morality?), a network socialization that multiplies the number and diversity of contacts and relationships. Obviously, this new social experience happens essentially during the free time taken as a liberation from all normative systems sociologists vainly try to construct.

All these "new" sociologies share a major common feature with free time sociology. They treat the same object but without knowing it and without recognizing it; they believe, as does free time sociology, that there is a shift in the centricity in our societies that no longer rests on work and its organization as a major productive dynamic and of which the ensuing theories cannot precisely give account. However, for lack of theorizing this shift and explaining it in its objective dimensions (social time reversal, new values, new modes of economic and social production), they refrain from understanding the conditions of their own appearance, production, history. They remain either in a critical dimension—what is called the "effect of deconstruction" of the social—or in a subjectivism that ignores the effects of structure. There needs, henceforth, to be an effort at clarification for a confrontation with free time sociology which has, for its part, clearly opted for the paradigm of free time following that of work time, in the historical context of evolution-revolution of social times.

BIBLIOGRAPHICAL REVIEW

There are numerous bibliographies about the different leisure practices in France, from sports and tourism to arts, culture, and communication, to name a few. It is impossible to mention all such sources here; however, an encyclopedic survey of leisure topics can be obtained in *L'Univers des loisirs* (1990), which reads like a dictionary, with more than two hundred authors listed.

Concerning the study of leisure itself, the author of reference remains Joffre Dumazedier, who has been the true initiator of leisure sociology in France. The work that made him famous, and his best-known, is titled *Vers une civilisation du loisir*; first published in 1962, this book has been constantly revised and is translated into thirty-three languages. His fundamental studies include, among others, *Sociologie empirique du loisir* (1974), as well as his last work, *Révolution culturelle du temps libre, 1968–1988* (1988), which extends the concept of leisure toward the more general one of free time.

If knowledge of the history of leisure theories as I have tried to present in this chapter is desired, then Marie-Françoise Lanfant's *Les Théories du loisir* (1972) is to be consulted first. For a highly critical response to this theoretical approach, *La Sociologie du temps libre* (1974), by Marie-Charlotte Busch, presents a very good introduction.

Many scholars, all well known in France, have been interested in leisure from a theoretical viewpoint, but without making it the focus of their research. Among the best-known is Georges Friedmann, whose book *La Puissance et la sagesse* was published in 1972. Jean Fourastié's *Des loisirs pour quoi faire?* (1972) must also be mentioned.

With respect to a relationship between leisure and social stratification, especially among social classes, it would be good to refer to the 1982 study by Christian Lalive d'Épinay, *Temps libre: culture de masse et cultures de classes aujourd'hui*. Concerning a link between leisure and the young population within the framework of education, two monographs are particularly recommended: *7 mois de loisir, ou la face cachée de l'éducation*, by Jean-François de Vulpillières (1981), and *Théorie et pratique ludiques*, by Martine Mauriras-Bousquet (1984).

The study of leisure in France has frequently been considered from the popular culture point of view; on this subject, two books stand out. They are Antoine Léon's *Histoire de l'éducation populaire* (1983) and Geneviève Poujol's *L'Éducation populaire en France: histoires et pouvoirs* (1981).

For an admittedly sketchy study of certain leisure activities highly characteristic of French customs, one should look at *Jeux, modes et masses, 1945–1985* (1985), by Paul Yonnet. In this work the author proposes to show that so-called minor activities, such as bingo or trifecta, actually very much structure contemporary social and everyday life.

The latest theoretical developments in free time sociology point out that some researchers are now oriented in a more encompassing fashion toward the study of the various social times, of which free time obviously represents an essential part today. If we want to favor an historical perspective, the book by Nicole Samuel and Madeleine Romer, titled *Le Temps libre, un temps social*, is a must.

A more general approach is used in two fine collections of essays: *Temps et*

Société, edited by Gilles Pronovost and Daniel Mercure (1989) and *Les Temps sociaux*, edited by Daniel Mercure and Anne Wallemacq (1988).

Finally, to conclude this quick survey of a few basic works, two scientific journals need to be added since their main topic of research is leisure and free time. One, *Temps libre*, is a French review published in Paris; the other, *Loisir et Société/Leisure and Society*, housed at the Université de Trois-Rivières in Quebec and edited by Max D'Amours and Gilles Pronovost, publishes articles in French and English. This excellent publication has an international scope and is virtually the only outstanding scientific journal on the subject of leisure.

BIBLIOGRAPHY

Althusser, Louis. *Pour Marx*. Paris: Maspero, 1968.
Baudrillard, Jean. *La Société de consommation*. Paris: Denoël, 1970.
———. *Le Système des objets*. Paris: Gallimard, 1986.
———. *Pour une critique de l'économie politique du signe*. Paris: Gallimard, 1972.
Beillerot, Jacky. *La Société pédagogique*. Paris: Presses Universitaires de France, 1982.
Bourdieu, Pierre. *La Distinction*. Paris: Minuit, 1979.
———. *Choses dites*. Paris: Minuit, 1987.
Bourdieu, Pierre, and Passeron, Jean-Claude. *La Reproduction*. Paris: Minuit, 1970.
Busch, Marie-Charlotte. *La Sociologie du temps libre*. Paris: Mouton, 1974.
Cacéres, Benigno. *Histoire de l'éducation populaire*. Paris: Seuil, 1967.
Caillois, Roger. *L'Homme et le sacré*. Paris: Gallimard, 1950.
Certeau, Michel de. *Inventer le quotidien: Arts de faire*. Paris: U.G.E., 1980.
Charlot, Bernard. *La Mystification pédagogique*. Paris: Payot, 1980.
Crozier, Michel. *L'Acteur et le système*. Paris: Seuil, 1981.
Dahrendorf, Ralf. *The Modern Social Conflict*. London: Weidenfeld & Nicolson, 1988.
Dumazedier, Joffre. *Vers une civilisation du loisir*. Paris: Seuil, 1962.
———. *Sociologie empirique du loisir*. Paris: Seuil, 1974.
———. *Révolution culturelle du temps libre, 1968–1988*. Paris: Méridiens, 1988.
Duvignaud, Jean, ed. *Sociologie de la connaissance*. Paris: Payot, 1979.
Ferraroti, Franco. *Le Paradoxe du sacré*. Paris: Éperonniers, 1987.
Foucault, Michel. *Histoire de la sexualité*. Paris: Gallimard, 1984. Vol. 3.
———. *Cours au Collège de France, 1970–1982*. Paris: Julliard, 1989.
Fourastié, Jean. *Les 40.000 heures*. Paris: Laffont, 1965.
———. *Le Grand Espoir du XXe siècle*. Paris: Gallimard, 1971.
———. *Des loisirs pour quoi faire?* Paris: Casterman, 1972.
Friedmann, Georges. *Où va le travail humain?* Paris: Gallimard, 1953.
———. *Le Travail en miettes*. Paris: Gallimard, 1964.
———. *La Puissance et la sagesse*. Paris: Gallimard, 1972.
Freud, Sigmund. *Civilization and Its Discontents*. Chicago: University of Chicago Press, 1950.
Fromm, Erich. *To Have or to Be?* New York: Harper & Row, 1976.
Galbraith, John Kenneth. *The Affluent Society*. Boston: Houghton Mifflin, 1958.
Gorz, André. *Adieux au prolétariat*. Paris: Galilée, 1980.
———. *Métamorphoses du travail*. Paris: Galilée, 1988.

Gurvitch, Georges. *La Vocation actuelle de la sociologie*. Paris: Presses Universitaires de France, 1963.

Habermas, Jurgen. *The Theory of Communicative Action*. Boston: Beacon Press, 1984.

Halbwachs, Maurice. *La Mémoire collective*. Paris: Presses Universitaires de France, 1950.

Hegel, G. W. F. *Lectures on the History of Philosophy*. London: Routledge & Kegan Paul, 1968.

Hubert, Henri, and Mauss, Marcel. *Mélanges d'histoire des religions*. Paris: Alcan, 1929.

Huizinga, Johan. *Homo Ludens*. London: Routledge & Kegan Paul, 1949.

Husserl, Edmund. *The Idea of Phenomenology*. The Hague: Nijhoff, 1964.

Kaplan, Max. *Leisure: Theory and Policy*. New York: Wiley, 1975.

Lafargue, Paul. *Le Droit à la paresse*. Paris: Maspero, 1965.

Lalive d'Épinay, Christian. *Temps libre: culture de masse et cultures de classes aujourd'hui*. Lausanne: Favre, 1982.

Lanfant, Marie-Françoise. *Les Théories du loisir*. Paris: Presses Universitaires de France, 1972.

Lefebvre, Henri. *Critique de la vie quotidienne*. Paris: L'Arche, 1958.

Le Goff, Jacques. "Temps de l'Église et temps du marchand." *Annales* 3 (May–June 1960).

Léon, Antoine. *Histoire de l'éducation populaire en France*. Paris: Nathan, 1983.

Lipovetsky, Gilles. *L'Ère du vide*. Paris: Gallimard, 1983.

———. *L'Empire de l'éphémère*. Paris: Gallimard, 1987.

Maffesoli, Michel. *L'Ombre de Dionysos*. 2d ed. Paris: Méridiens, 1985.

———. *La Connaissance ordinaire*. Paris: Méridiens, 1985.

———. *Le Temps des tribus*. Paris: Méridiens, 1988.

Marcuse, Herbert. *Eros and Civilization*. Boston: Beacon Press, 1955.

———. *One-Dimensional Man*. Boston: Beacon Press, 1964.

Marx, Karl. *A Contribution to the Critique of Political Economy*. New York: International Publishers, 1970.

———. *Capital*. New York: International Publishers, 1984.

Mauriras-Bousquet, Martine. *Théorie et pratique ludiques*. Paris: Economica, 1984.

Mauss, Marcel. *Théorie sociologique*. Paris: Presses Universitaires de France, 1975.

Mayo, Elton. *The Human Problems of an Industrial Civilization*. Cambridge, Mass.: Harvard University Press, 1946.

Mendel, Gérard. *La Crise de générations*. Paris: Payot, 1969.

———. *Vers une anthropologie sociopsychanalytique*. Paris: Payot, 1972.

Mercure, Daniel, and Wallemacq, Anne, eds. *Les Temps sociaux*. Brussels: De Boeck Université, 1988.

Merleau-Ponty, Maurice. *Phénoménologie de la perception*. Paris: Gallimard, 1976.

Morin, Edgar. *Sociologie*. Paris: Fayard, 1984.

Naville, Pierre. "De l'aliénation à la jouissance," in *Le Nouveau Léviathan*. Paris: Anthropos, 1967. Vol. 1.

Nietzsche, Friedrich. *The Joyful Wisdom*. New York: Russell & Russell House, 1964. Vol. 10.

Porcher, Louis. *L'École parallèle*. Paris: Larousse, 1974.

Poujol, Geneviève. *L'Éducation populaire: histoires et pouvoirs*. Paris: Éditions Ouvrières, 1981.

Pronovost, Gilles, and Mercure, Daniel, eds. *Temps et Société*. Quebec City: Institut québécois de recherche sur la culture, 1989.

Renaut, Alain. *L'Ère de l'individu*. Paris: Gallimard, 1985.

Riesman, David. *The Lonely Crowd*. New Haven, Conn.: Yale University Press, 1950.

———. *Abundance for What?* Garden City, N.Y.: Doubleday, 1964.

Rogers, Carl R. *Freedom to Learn*. Columbus, Ohio: Charles Merrill, 1969.

Sainsaulieu, Renaud. *Sociologie de l'organisation de l'entreprise*. Paris: Presses de la FNSP/Dalloz, 1987.

Saint-Simon, C. H. de. *OEuvres*. Paris: Anthropos, 1966.

Samuel, Nicole, and Romer, Madeleine. *Le Temps libre, un temps social*. Paris: Méridiens, 1984.

Simmel, Georg. *Épistémologie et sociologie*. Paris: Presses Universitaires de France, 1985.

Sue, Roger. *Le Loisir*. Paris: Presses Universitaires de France, 1980.

———. *Vers une société du temps libre*. Paris: Presses Universitaires de France, 1982.

———. *Vivre en l'an 2000*. Paris: Michel, 1985.

Touraine, Alain. *Production de la société*. Paris: Seuil, 1973.

———. *Le Retour de l'acteur*. Paris: Fayard, 1984.

L'Univers des loisirs. Paris: Letouzey et Ané, 1990.

Veblen, Thorstein. *The Theory of the Leisure Class*. London: Allen & Unwin, 1970.

Vernant, Jean-Pierre. *Mythe et pensée chez les Grecs*. Paris: Maspero, 1971.

Vulpillières, Jean-François de. *7 Mois de loisir, ou la face cachée de l'éducation*. Paris: Presses Universitaires de France, 1981.

Weber, Max. *Economy and Society*. Berkeley: University of California Press, 1978.

Wolfenstein, Martha. "The Emergence of Fun Morality," in *Mass Leisure*. Edited by Eric Larrabee and Rolf Meyersohn. Glencoe, Ill.: Free Press, 1958.

Yonnet, Paul. *Jeux, modes et masses, 1945–1985*. Paris: Gallimard, 1985.

Zeldin, Theodore. *France 1848–1945*. 2 vols. Oxford: Clarendon Press, 1973–77.

Translated by Pierre L. Horn

8

Love, Men, and Women

EDITH J. BENKOV

"L'amour, toujours l'amour." French, as the cliché has it, is the language of love. It is not surprising then that a chapter on love should be found in a volume devoted to French popular culture. The notion of romantic love is itself a cultural construct that found its most clearly articulated expression in the first centuries of this millennium. But is that concept distinct from erotic love? And whose views are reflected in those concepts? That documentation which has been most thoroughly studied and analyzed—historical, literary, plastic and visual arts—concerns a small portion of the population, members of the social elite. If we take popular as meaning "of the people," then the attitudes of the vast majority of French men and women, those who lived during the nearly 800 years of the Ancien Régime, must remain for a large part a mystery. Recent studies in history pioneered by the Annales school, as well as cultural anthropological approaches, have begun to shed some light on the *menu peuple*; yet no complete picture is available.

How then to convey what the concept of love has meant in one culture over a period of nearly a thousand years? This is the dilemma faced by any cultural historian. My approach must perforce be eclectic but will be one which will privilege both literary sources and memoirs. While such texts most often represent the attitudes of a certain literate elite, their influence goes beyond the reading public: for the "high" culture of one era is frequently the popular culture of another.

HISTORICAL BACKGROUND

Romantic Love Invented

No discussion of love in French culture can ignore the weight of history, which places the invention of romantic love in the twelfth century somewhere between the courts of Provence and the courts of England. The love poetry of the early troubadours such as Guillaume IX or Bernart de Ventadour posits the situation of an idealized love object and an aspiring lover. In its quintessential form, the lady on the pedestal is distant, removed, to the point of being unattainable and, most frequently, married. Although the timid lover is frustrated in his efforts to see his lady or to speak to her, he remains faithful, attempting to prove his devotion to his beloved while maintaining a cloak of secrecy that will protect her reputation. These poets create an amorous discourse which remains nearly unchanged until the sixteenth century. It is a poetics based on desire and its deferral.

Whereas troubadour poetry sings most frequently of unconsummated desire, *amour courtois* (courtly love) as expressed in northern lyrics or romances represents a passionate, all-consuming love, often leading to the lovers' death or exile. The northern tradition fuses the Provençal love lyric with legends of marital infidelity, be it Iseult or Guinevere, firmly establishing the triangle of wife/ husband/lover as the model. The key element in this concept of love is that it is love outside of marriage. Marriage, and most particularly marriage among the elite, was not an affective institution. Marriages were arranged without consulting the feelings of the parties involved; they were no more than simple business transactions in which the woman served as currency.

Love in Literature

For the early medieval period, the images we have are largely products of two seemingly distinct cultural milieus, that of the court and that of the city. Yet, while each maintained a separate social identity, the expression of their attitudes toward gender relations, at least on a literary level, appear to be complementary—dividing less along lines of class and environment than along those of "high" and "low" in the sense of serious and comic.

The troubadour lyric has attracted much critical attention, since it is considered the point of origin for the medieval love lyric. Pierre Bec's *Anthologie des troubadours* and his *Burlesque et obscénité chez les troubadours* are well-annotated editions which, when read together, offer nearly the full range of troubadour poetry. Troubadour poetry does indeed have two sides: idealization of the love object on one hand and an overtly erotic and often obscene character on the other. What must be added is *The Women Troubadours*, an anthology with an excellent historical introduction by Meg Bogin. Bogin's work is a necessary corrective to the hegemony of male-voiced poetic discourse, and although the dominant conceits of the troubadour lyric clearly posit a male lover and a female love object, the female lyric must not be overlooked. The studies on love in the works of these Provençal writers are many. The works of René Nelli, especially his *Érotique des troubadours* and the first volume, *La Femme et l'amour* of his *Écrivains anti-conformistes* are indispensable. They are complemented by Jean-Charles Huchet's *L'Amour discourtois*. Topsfield's *Troubadours and Love* is a solid, if somewhat conservative, study of the thematic. Finally Moshé Lazar's *Amours courtois et fin'amors dans la littérature du XIIe siècle* offers a cogent analysis of the origins of troubadour poetry and leads into northern French literature, where *fin'amors* becomes *amour courtois*.

No single complete version of the legend of Tristan and Iseult has survived from the Middle Ages; the earliest of those texts (twelfth century) which remain are fragmentary versions. Yet that myth establishes the theme of romantic love and the conflict between love and marriage in French (and Western) culture. The love between Tristan and Iseult is an adulterous one. Although betrothed to Marc, it is Tristan with whom Iseult falls in love. Such is their passion that they will eventually die for it. The lovers' struggles form the basis of the story which pits desire against obstacles—a pattern which will be repeated throughout French literature. Denis de Rougemont's *L'Amour et l'Occident* presents that myth and its impact on the concept of love filtered through the late nineteenth-century Wagnerian perspective which inextricably links the themes of love and death.

The *Lais* of Marie de France (late twelfth century) are another manifestation of the "courtly" tradition. Hers are short verse tales which deal with both happy and unhappy lovers. Like the legend of Tristan to which she contributes a chapter, her stories are often of Celtic folk-tale origin. Chrétien de Troyes, a writer active at the court of Champagne, composed verse romances of the knights of the Round Table, works which account for the bulk of the canon of Arthurian legends. While his *Lancelot* most clearly fits the adulterous tradition, his romances more frequently break with the established norms to suggest a model for conjugal love. *Érec et Énide* treats the problem of erotic love and social duty within a marriage context, perhaps offering a countermodel to the fatal attraction of the Tristan myth. Peter Noble treats the question of *Love and Marriage in Chrétien de Troyes*. Bezzola's *Le Sens de l'aventure et de l'amour* and Frappier's *Amour courtois et Table Ronde* each attempt to account for Chrétien's unique vision of courtliness. Ménard's study of *"Les Lais" de Marie de France* treats the meaning of love and adventure in the works of that author. Coppin's *Amour et mariage dans la littérature française du nord au Moyen-Âge* also takes up the conflict between marriage and love. This subject was also the theme for a recent colloquium at Amiens, the proceedings of which appear in the collection *Amour, mariage et transgressions au Moyen-Âge* edited by Buschinger.

A number of studies try to analyze the concept of love in twelfth- and thirteenth-century France. Duby's *Le Chevalier, la femme et le prêtre* and his *Que sait-on de l'amour en France au XIIe siècle?*, a series of lectures given at Oxford, and John Moore's *Love in Twelfth-Century France* are analyses based on both literary and historical sources, as is Penny Gold's *The Lady & the Virgin: Image, Attitude, and Experience in Twelfth-Century France*. Jean Leclercq offers a psycho-historical analysis of the ecclesiastic view in his *L'Amour vu par les moines au XIIe siècle*. Penny Sullivan also treats "Love and Marriage in Early French Narrative Poetry," and Rosemarie Jones's *The Theme of Love in the Romans d'Antiquité* analyzes the impact of Ovid, as well as the troubadours, on courtly love while emphasizing the theme of "love as sickness," one of the commonplaces of medieval amorous discourse. Andreas Capellanus' Latin treatise *The Art of Courtly Love*, a lover's manual of how to win a desired woman and then how to cure himself, is typical of the attitudes discussed by Jones. In *La Courtoisie au moyen-âge*, Henri Dupin surveys texts of the twelfth and thirteenth centuries to derive an overview of what "courtly" encompasses, as does Méray's *La Vie au temps des cours d'amour*, courts in which questions of love were supposedly debated in a semi-legalistic fashion with the lady rendering a judgment. Myrrha Lot-Borodine in her *De l'amour profane à l'amour sacré* and C. S. Lewis in *The Allegory of Love* both underline the compatibility of the courtly idea of the perfection of the love object with the spiritual: Lewis from a traditionalist Christian perspective and Lot-Borodine from a psychological point of view. Jean Markale's study *L'Amour courtois ou le couple infernal* leads away from the interpretation of the courtly as spiritual allegory.

Not all representations of love follow the thematic exigencies of "high" literature. The comic possibilities of love, marriage, and infidelity flourish in two genres, the *fabliau* (short verse tale) and the farce. *Fabliaux* such as the "Bourgeoise d'Orléans" (thirteenth century) punish the husband who would prevent his wife's rendezvous with her lover: the wife and lover meet and the husband suffers a sound beating, all the while thinking his wife to be faithful. This comic type, *mari cocu, battu et content* (the contented though beaten cuckold) is a frequent character in the *fabliaux*. Marriage, then, exists, but love, or at the very least sexual pleasure, is firmly planted outside of its boundaries. Indeed, what has often been considered a misogynist attitude in the Middle Ages might be redefined as misogamist. The unhappiness of the husband (albeit because of his wife) reinforces the need to search for love elsewhere. As in the *fabliaux*, farces frequently portray the bleaker side of marriage. In "Le Cuvier" (fifteenth century), for example, husband and wife are engaged in a battle for control. In this case, it is the husband who triumphs. The farce, unlike the *fabliau*, is a more conservative genre and supports the established social order rather than offer possibilities of subversion.

Somewhere between these extremes lies *Le Jeu de Robin et Marion*, Adam de la Halle's fanciful thirteenth-century vision of love among the shepherds. The play draws its thematic inspiration from contemporary *pastourelle* poems: Marion loves Robin but is abducted by a knight, who tries to force his affections on her. She escapes from the knight, and the shepherd and shepherdess are reunited and joined by their friends for a picnic. The first half may well give a clue to the very real danger faced by peasant women, rape by an errant knight, but the idyllic vision of love among the *menu peuple* anticipates the eighteenth-century taste for masquerade among the nobles and the *fêtes galantes* so skillfully painted by Antoine Watteau.

As the Middle Ages waned, love and marriage were still not to be reconciled. Love and marriage are frequent themes in the literature of the Renaissance, although a bifurcation occurs which seems to be linked to the emergence of prose. Love and marriage together dominate prose, as in the novella or the nascent novel, while ideal love, unrequited love, or passionate love finds expression in verse—love as a subject of lyric poetry becomes firmly established.

Sixteenth-century poetry reflects the influence of neo-Platonist thought of such Italian writers as Marsilio Ficino and the equally Italian Petrarchan tradition (itself modeled on troubadour poetry). Festugière's study, *La Philosophie de l'amour de Marsile Ficin*, treats the theories of the philosopher and his all-important influence on Renaissance thought. These influences can be seen in the *Sonnets* of Louise Labé, a member of the artisan class, who exploits the established poetic discourse while reshaping it to express an ideal of sensual love. A similar type of thematic originality can be seen in Pierre de Ronsard's three cycles of love poems. Each cycle matches its tone and thematic variants to the love object it sings. The "Cassandre" sonnets use the voice of the Petrarchan lover; the "Marie" poems addressed to a country girl are more playful and sensual; the "Hélène" poems of his later period are more stylized yet not Petrarchan, characterized by the cynicism that comes with age and experience in love.

There is no shortage of critical literature on the Renaissance love lyric. Minta's *Love-Poetry in Sixteenth-Century France* deals primarily with the works of Marot and Scève. Desonay's *Ronsard, poète de l'amour* remains the authoritative study of love in Ronsard's works, but Gendre's *Ronsard, poète de la conquête amoureuse* is equally recommended. For Labé, Chan's article on the function of the beloved as well as articles by Anne Jones and Rigolot are particularly perceptive. Two studies by Mathieu-Castellani, which deal with themes of Baroque literature and particularly poetry, bridge the period after Ronsard to the early seventeenth century: *Les Thèmes amoureux dans la poésie française 1570–1600* and *Mythes de l'Éros baroque*. Lacy's *26 chansons d'amour de la Renaissance* offers a representative selection of the love lyric.

Of those prose fiction works which treat the themes of love and marriage, the *Heptaméron* of Marguerite de Navarre merits attention. In a conscious attempt to imitate and surpass her model, Boccaccio's *Decameron*, she draws heavily on the ribald traditions of Gallic humor of the *fabliau* and the farce as well as the Italian novella. Marguerite, however, departs from the stock themes of these genre traditions. Ideally, marriage and love are, at least, to be compatible. That is, mutual love should be a part of marriage. The "reality" of the tales told by her characters leads the reader to believe that the ideal put forward in the text is one that is rarely realized. Lucien Febvre's classic study *Autour de "l'Hep-*

taméron'': *amour sacré, amour profane* analyzes Marguerite's varying religious and social ideals.

While the Classical Age is most often remembered for the simplicity and clarity of its theater, the Baroque novel is noted for its length and the complications of its plot which most frequently concerns a couple. Honoré d'Urfé's *L'Astrée*, set in the fifth century, recounts the romance of Celadon and Astrée, while *Le Grand Cyrus* of Madeleine de Scudéry tells of the adventures of Artamène, later revealed as Cyrus, the grandson of Alexander. Aronson's article ''Amour et mariage dans les œuvres de Mlle de Scudéry'' is a useful introduction to the complexities of the theme, and Ehrmann's *Un paradis désespéré. L'Amour et l'illusion dans ''l'Astrée''* treats the underside of the Baroque.

The Classical novel emerges from the Baroque with Madame de Lafayette's *La Princesse de Clèves*, which deals with the consequences of those court intrigues which Brantôme recounted with such flair. Here, marriage, love and its sufferings, passion, and adultery are weighed against peace of mind and reputation. The princess rejects her suitor, the Duke of Nemours, whom she loves and who returns her love, for she will not become just another of his conquests. Jules Brody's article ''*La Princesse de Clèves* and the Myth of Courtly Love'' places the novel within the context of the medieval ideal. *The Motif of the Renunciation of Love in the Seventeenth-Century French Novel*, an interesting if somewhat idiosyncratic study by Sister Jeannine Sassus, posits a stronger influence of Spanish literature and of post-Tridentine spirituality on the protagonists' morals.

The theater presents striking contrasts. Classical tragedy epitomized by Jean Racine's *Phèdre* depicts a world where passion is the dominant and, ultimately, destructive force. In contrast, the primary theme in the comedies of Molière is rarely love, yet as Couvelaire points out in his essay ''Mariage forcé et mariage contrarié dans le théâtre de Molière,'' the subplot of marriage is. The ideal couple is young and joined by love, even in *Le Tartuffe* in which hypocrisy and disguise pit the false love (lust) of Tartuffe for Elvire against the mutual affection between Valère and Mariane. *Dom Juan*, the pluperfect seducer and libertine and literary ancestor of Valmont of *Liaisons dangereuses*, is the ideal's opposite: once married, he prefers to pursue a different ideal, that of love as sexual conquest.

The happy endings of Molière's comedies are closer than one might think to Perrault's *Contes*, fairy tales which again posit a happy union. Love (and passion) within marriage is a viable model, or so the example of Cinderella would have us believe. Even if the *Contes* are nothing but ''mere'' children's stories, they cannot be ignored, since it is these ideals which become part of the cultural expectations. A useful article on this topic is Welch's ''La Femme, le mariage et l'amour dans les contes de fées mondains du XVIIe siècle français.''

In the seventeenth century, not only do we find the possibility of love and marriage coexisting but we also encounter a refinement in the language of love itself. *La préciosité* will leave its mark on expression, only to be parodied and mocked in Molière's *Les Précieuses ridicules*. And the moralists will cast a cold glance at society and decry what they see. Horowitz's *Love and Language* studies the moralists like La Rochefoucauld whose stark realism points to self-love as the motivating force for human actions, a vision also found in the works of Madame de Lafayette. The subject of *préciosité* and love as well as gallantry and love is exhaustively covered in Pelous' study *Amour précieux, amour galant (1654–1675)*, but for a less staid vision Deems Taylor's *The One-Track Mind: Love Poems of the XVIIth and XVIIIth Century in France* is a refreshing introduction to the libertine view of love and sex. Lachèvre's *Les Derniers Libertins* is another anthology that gives some of the flavor of the era. For a critical analysis of sexuality and libertinage, consult Bougard's recent study *Érotisme et amour physique dans la littérature française du XVIIe siècle*.

Love in the eighteenth-century novel, as Vera Lee maintains in her study, is principally a game of strategy (*Love and Strategy in the Eighteenth-Century French Novel*). Her claim is supported by Goodden's recent *The Complete Lover: Eros, Nature, and Artifice in the Eighteenth-Century French Novel*. The same, moreover, could be argued for the theater as well. The Enlightenment as descendant of libertine philosophy would seem to link love and sex more easily than the Classical ideal, which favored chastity or renunciation in love. Indeed, the very title of Marivaux's *Le Jeu de l'amour et du hasard* underscores the lack of fatality in the affective arena. The play itself revolves upon disguise and deceit, a betrothed couple testing their attraction, ending in the announced marriage. Deguy's *La Machine matrimoniale chez Marivaux* is an excellent analysis of the machinations of *marivaudage*.

Love in the novel takes a more risqué turn: Abbé Prévost's *Manon Lescaut* introduces a "femme fatale" as a heroine who brings about her own downfall as well as that of the inexperienced young man who falls in love with her. The novel will stage a battle of the boudoir; for Vera Lee, Laclos's *Liaisons dangereuses* is typical of the century rather than unique. These are novels of gallantry in which moral concerns weigh lightly on the protagonists' heads. Need one be reminded that the works of the Marquis de Sade are also from this century? The dislocation of order which would culminate in the Revolution was evident in all aspects of society.

Two novels, in particular, represent opposite attitudes in love and perhaps, too, the differing visions of the century: Laclos's *Liaisons* and Jean-Jacques Rousseau's *Julie ou La Nouvelle Héloïse*. Both are epistolary novels which place the reader in a position of intimacy—and uneasy complicity—with the characters, but while the vision in *Liaisons* shows love (lust or perhaps simply, pride) as a destructive force, *La Nouvelle Héloïse* posits a model for passion and conjugal fidelity (be it with different partners).

Bellenot in his "Formes de l'amour" analyzes Rousseau's conception of love and takes *La Nouvelle Héloïse* to be exemplary. Ellis' *"Julie ou la Nouvelle Héloïse": A Synthesis of Rousseau's Thought* rejects the theory of passion versus marriage in Julie's feelings for Wolmar and Saint-Preux in favor of a social thesis based on class difference. Babel's article "Jean-Jacques Rousseau et notre temps" emphasizes the applicability of Rousseau's concept of love to our age. Both Diaconoff's *Eros and Power in "Les Liaisons dangereuses"* and Tishkoff's "I Have Created Myself': Sex, Power and Love in Laclos' *Les Liaisons dangereuses"* are concerned with power and its manipulation in the *Liaisons*. Peter Gay's article "Three Stages on Love's Way" treats moral attitudes in the two works. Miller's *The Heroine's Text* offers a feminist reading of *Manon Lescaut, Liaisons dangereuses*, and *La Nouvelle Héloïse* which sees the texts as the fantasy of a male author who puts forth his view of ideal love, a view which would not be shared by the text's heroine.

A frequent and erroneous association reduces the Romantic movement of the early nineteenth century to works dealing with love in which a brooding, dark hero is the central figure. D. G. Charlton's two-volume *The French Romantics* offers a survey of the period which is certain to expand that limited view. It contains essays on drama, poetry, prose as well as history, politics, etc.

This is not to say that Romantic literature was not concerned with love. In his *Méditations*, of which "Le Lac" is perhaps the most famous, Lamartine ponders questions of love and loss. Bouchard's *Lamartine et le sens de l'amour* is a solid analysis of the place of love in Lamartine's poetry. But poetry was not the most frequent forum for love. Balzac's *Lys dans la vallée*, which again opposes conjugal fidelity to fulfillment, presents the nearly "classic" affair between Félix and Madame de Mortsauf, a case of love at first sight which will never be consummated. For an analysis of the scene of encounter of the lovers, Rousset's *Leurs yeux se rencontrèrent* is highly recommended. Rousset analyzes the mutual glance as a "forme fixe" and draws parallels through French and other literatures.

In a completely different view are works by Stendhal and Fourier. *Le Nouveau Monde amoureux* is Fourier's utopian socialist vision of sexual freedom, satisfied desire, and amorous bliss. On the other hand, Stendhal's essay *De l'amour* is an almost scientific analysis of love, which he divides into four categories: *amour-passion* (passionate love, of which Héloïse and Abélard are the perfect representatives); *amour-goût* (dalliance); *amour de vanité*, in which the lover is an item to be shown off, much as any other possession; and *amour physique*, sexual pleasure. Stendhal also puts forth his theory of "crystallization" which tends to reinforce the idea of the perfection of the love object. Although many of his views are traditional (for example, love as a malady), the work offers an important, if highly subjective, vision of love at the beginning of the Romantic period. Levowitz-Treu's *L'Amour et la mort chez Stendhal* is a study deserving of attention.

The heroine in the nineteenth century has many guises. George Sand, whose own love affairs find their way into many a pulp history, offers a different view of Romanticism in *Lélia*, in which she rewrites the Romantic hero as a woman. But it is surely Gustave Flaubert's *Madame Bovary*, undeniably one of the greatest works of French literature, which, through the struggles of its heroine, most vividly depicts the conflict between the ideal of passionate, romantic love and the banality of everyday life. The novels of adventure and chivalry Emma read in her adolescence are the direct descendants of the Tristan legend and Chrétien de Troyes. That Emma finds disillusionment not only in marriage but in her adulterous liaisons comments on how thoroughly the literary ideal of the twelfth century is integrated into popular views of love.

L'Amour and *La Femme*, two works by the historian Jules Michelet, were designed to reinforce moral values—perhaps as a reaction to the dissolution of morals typified in *Madame Bovary*. Michelet's couple is faithful and married, with the woman subservient to the man, dependent upon the common double standard (e.g., women are more guilty of adultery). Nonetheless, he does conceive of a "true" partnership, held by love, in his discussion of love, and he considers the pleasures of love and intimacy (sexual pleasure). Thus, he admits erotic and spiritual components in love. He is against arranged marriages— mother and daughter should work together to find a partner the daughter wants. Love, for Michelet, can be a powerful force within marriage. Jeanne Calo's *La Création de la femme chez Michelet* provides a thorough analysis of Michelet's conception of women and her role in marriage.

Manon finds her counterparts, male and female, in the novels of the late nineteenth century. Maupassant's *Bel-Ami* is a selfish, unscrupulous hero who exploits the attraction women feel for him to advance socially. In *Nana*, Zola's prostitute heroine uses her clients. Both are products of their society. Naturalism allows for little sentimentality. Love is less an ideal in literature than a longed-for state. Alvado's *Maupassant ou l'amour réaliste* and Bertrand Jennings' *L'Éros et la femme chez Zola* both deal with the loss of the ideal in love.

The closer one gets to the contemporary period, the less easy it is to discern what characterizes the attitudes of love in the period, for rather than an historical object to be described, one enters into the realm of modern society's cultural biases. Twentieth-century French literature did not escape Freud's influence, nor has it found a solution to alienation. But it is still concerned with love.

Apollinaire, the poet of unhappy love, was the herald of surrealism, which followed World War I. Breton's *L'Amour fou* and Paul Éluard's *Capitale de la douleur* are resonant with the surrealist fantasy of woman and love, a woman who recalls the ideal courtly lady—muse and lover. Plouvier's *Poétique de l'amour chez André Breton* and Eglin's *Liebe und Inspiration im Werk von Paul Éluard* treat the conception of love in each poet's work and their sources of inspiration.

Synonymous with existentialism are the names of Jean-Paul Sartre and Simone de Beauvoir. Although their love affair has inspired many a biography (as well as autobiography), the fictional representations of love in their writings are far from the exhuberant vision of the surrealists. Neither the protagonists of Beauvoir's novel *L'Invitée (She Came to Stay)* nor of Sartre's short story "L'Intimité" are individuals who may experience one of the *moments privilégiés* as does Roquentin in *La Nausée*, but happiness in love is ephemeral and perhaps not even desired. Nahas' *La Femme dans la littérature existentielle* uses the myths of woman in French literature as a background to her analysis of the young girl who embarks upon a search for love, which ends either in marriage or in alienation. "Murdering *L'Invitée*" by Evans deals with gender relations in the work. And each author is the subject of a biography dealing with love: Lilar writes *À propos de Sartre et de l'amour* and Claude Francis and Fernande Gonthier have written *Simone de Beauvoir: A Life, a Love Story*.

FAMOUS LOVERS

Whether art imitates life or life imitates art in the case of romantic love and love affairs is a very fine line. Often those works which appear to be "histories" of love in France draw equally from those literary lovers and from historical figures. Nina Epton's *Love and the French* is typical of this genre. A romanticized history that traces love in French society from the troubadours through the post-World War II years, it is useful for the broadness of its treatment, but one should beware of her tendency to rely too much on her sources and of her frequent generalizations. A somewhat similar work in French would be Richard's *Histoire de l'amour en France*, which ends its survey at the Belle Époque.

A second group of histories exists, which might be seen as the precursors to *People* magazine. These works cater to the taste for gossip about the lives of the rich and famous. One of the earliest French manifestations of such a history is Pierre de Brantôme's *Les Dames galantes*, a sixteenth-century history of the morals and, most specifically, the lives and loves of the Renaissance courts. Brantôme's style is that of an amiable raconteur, mixing his own experiences with adventures he has heard from others. *Brantôme, amour et gloire au temps des Valois* by Anne-Marie Cocula-Vallières is an informative study of the writer and his milieu. A century later, the *Histoire amoureuse des Gaules* by Bussy-Rabutin recounts in much greater detail the loves of five notable women, including his own liaison with Madame de Sévigné. The work landed Bussy-Rabutin in jail. Each text is characteristic of its century: Brantôme recalls the novella and indeed speaks with knowledge of the court of François I; Bussy-Rabutin reads like the historical novels of a Scudéry or a Lafayette.

This type of *chronique des scandales* is a genre which continues to enjoy immense popularity, whether the subject is contemporary or historical, as is evident from Claude Dulong's *L'Amour au dix-septième siècle*, which returns the reader to the era of Bussy-Rabutin and draws its conclusions based on literary sources, as does his *La Vie quotidienne des femmes au Grand Siècle* or Jacques Desforges's *Chronique amoureuse de Paris sous la Monarchie de Juillet*, which gathers its tidbits from novels of that era. Joseph Barry's *French Lovers: From Héloïse and Abélard to Beauvoir and Sartre* deals with the relationships of a number of famous couples, including such less orthodox pairs as Toklas-Stein and Cocteau-Marais. André Berry's *L'Amour en France* also tells tales of the boudoir, as does the continuing series of Guy Breton, *Histoires d'amour de l'histoire de France* and Jacques-Henry Bauchy, *Histoires d'amour des provinces de France*. The amorous adventure appears as well as in *The Erotic History of France* by Henry Marchand, a privately printed work dating from the 1930s which covers the period from the Middle Ages to the nineteenth century. Here the emphasis is on the titillating, although the material will undoubtedly seem quite tame to the contemporary reader. Important political figures are frequently subjected to such scrutiny. A typical example would be Bertrand's *La Vie amoureuse de Louis XIV* which is an early (1920s) psychological study.

LOVE LETTERS

Writing about love is not limited to professionals, as Molière so comically points out in his *Bourgeois gentilhomme* when Monsieur Jourdain painstakingly tries to turn the phrase "Belle Marquise, vos beaux yeux me font mourir d'amour" ("Beautiful Marquise, your beautiful eyes make me die of love"), in a manner which will impress his lady fair by its style. How to express emotions was the concern of many. By the Renaissance, there was a proliferation of how-to books on letter writing, including, of course, that most delicate of subjects. François Desrues' *Les Fleurs du bien-dire* is a compendium of examples "recueillies aux cabinets des plus rares esprits" to guide in the expression of passion. There are numerous collections of love letters, from Pillement's *Anthologie de lettres d'amour* to Lacrételle's *La Galerie des amants*. For a more scholarly, though somewhat dated, edition of letters, there is Semerau's *Liebesbriefe aus dem Rokoko*. Lebègue's article "La Sensibilité dans les lettres d'amour au XVIIe siècle" provides a useful historical background to the genre.

The epistolary novel, such as *Les Liaisons dangereuses* or *La Nouvelle Héloïse*, is a fictionalized version of the "real" genre of love letters. Once again, the boundaries between fiction and reality can be slippery, as Bernard Bray shows in his study *L'Art de la lettre amoureuse. Des manuels aux romans (1550–1700)*, which traces the development of the genre. Bray and Landy-Houillon have also compiled an anthology of epistolary novels, including, for example, *Lettres portugaises*. A provocative study of voice in these novels can be found in Susan Carrell's *Le Soliloque de la passion féminine ou le dialogue illusoire*, which deals with the one-sidedness of this correspondence.

Outside of epistolary fiction, there are frequent exchanges of passion by letter as well, the editions of which are far too numerous to begin to list. Two pairs of correspondents might be singled out: Abélard and Héloïse, who are the standard for the love letter, and a recent edition by Françoise Sagan, *Sand & Musset: Lettres d'amour*, since it brings together two famous lovers who are equally accomplished writers. The privileged place they occupy in Romanticism makes their correspondence invaluable.

HISTORICAL/SOCIOLOGICAL APPROACH

Works dating from the last two decades of the nineteenth century and the first decade of the twentieth century were influenced by Darwinism and the Naturalist movement and in their zeal to classify all natural phenomena often turned their eyes on love. Edmond and Jules de Goncourt, themselves novelists, wrote *La Femme au dix-huitième siècle*, which deals with the lives and loves of women at all levels of society, from *salonistes* to shopkeepers. Bergerat's *L'Amour en république* (1889) is a contemporary "sociological" study of love in the Third Republic. Lescure's *La Société française pendant la Révolution. L'Amour sous la Terreur* and Bournand's *L'Amour sous la Révolution* both treat the same period of French history in a fairly comparable manner. Lacroix's study, *Le Dix-huitième Siècle* completes the era.

CULTURAL/HISTORICAL APPROACH

A different type of historical perspective would be that of the contemporary *mentalités* approach. *Histoire de la vie privée*, edited by Ariès and Duby, while not dealing solely with France, is both insightful and provocative, as is Ariès, *L'Enfant et la vie familiale sous l'Ancien Régime* which does concentrate on France, albeit before the modern era. *Culture populaire et culture des élites dans la France moderne*, by Robert Muchembled, again not specifically on love, does offer a background and treats the topic. The author sets up a division in culture between the fifteenth and sixteenth centuries and the seventeenth and eighteenth centuries as the time when popular culture became distinct from culture.

Le Roy Ladurie's *L'Argent, l'amour et la mort en pays d'oc* uses an 18th century novella to examine customs of love and marriage, among other topics, in Languedoc. Like Le Roy Ladurie's other studies, it is thorough and provocative. *Amours illégitimes* by Marie-Claude Phan also deals with Languedoc in the eighteenth century, although her topic is seduction. In the same vein, there is also Jean-Louis Flandrin's *Amours paysannes*, which covers the topics of love and sexuality from the sixteenth to the nineteenth century in the French countryside. Two recent works by Martine Segalen also treat the topics of love and peasant life: *Love and Power in the Peasant Family: Rural France in the Nineteenth Century* and *Amours et mariages dans l'Ancienne France*. The collection of essays edited by Wheaton and Hareven, *Family and Sexuality in French History*, presents a more general view of the subject. *Marriage and Family in Eighteenth-Century France* by James Traer focuses on relations within the family. All of these works have in common an emphasis on the group rather than on the individual and veer away from favoring the nobility as model.

CONTEMPORARY FRENCH SOCIETY

For a general survey on what love is, the "Que sais-je?" series has a volume simply entitled *L'Amour* by Burney. Some other general studies of note are

Solé's *L'Amour en Occident à l'époque moderne*, Lilar's *Le Couple*, a feminist-oriented philosophical analysis, and for an approach based on semiotics and psychology, Kristeva's *Histoires d'amour*.

As an introduction to modern French society and the attitudes of the French, two works by Theodore Zeldin merit attention. *France 1848–1945* is a well-documented analysis of the period leading up to contemporary France. *The French* presents a highly readable view of that nation with the chapters on "Love, Marriage and Family" and "Women" being of particular relevance to the question. Zeldin observes from the outside; less mediated contact with the attitudes of the contemporary French can be found in *La Française aujourd'hui: La Femme et l'amour*, a general study; *Aujourd'hui la vie*, a 1985 survey of "des milliers de téléspectateurs" (thousands of TV viewers) who were questioned on such topics as love, marriage, money, religion, etc.; or *Patterns of Sex and Love: A Study of the French Woman and Her Morals* published by the Institut Français d'Opinion Publique. As a comparison with today, there is also Bauer's *Recensement de l'amour à Paris* which dates from 1922. Also, Marny's *Les Adolescents aujourd'hui* treats the attitudes of youths, and Marroncle's *Aujourd'hui les couples* as well as Ibert and Charles' *Love, the French Way* provide insight into current viewpoints.

FUTURE RESEARCH

As is obvious from this brief overview, much research remains to be done on the question of love in French culture. Not only are there opportunities in cultural history for the earlier periods and the modern era, but feminist studies on love are few. Moreover, the question of erotic love versus romantic love is one which merits further attention. The eighteenth century achieved a tenuous balance between the two, but for the most part they have been separated and, therefore, appear incompatible. Finally, few studies exist on the media, particularly film and television.

Perhaps the best way to start is with a trip to Paris, preferably in the spring.

BIBLIOGRAPHY

Albistur, Maïté, and Armogathe, Daniel. *Histoire du féminisme français*. 2 vols. Paris: des femmes, 1977.

Alexandrian, Sarane. *Les Libérateurs de l'amour*. Paris: Seuil, 1977.

Alvado, Hervé. *Maupassant ou l'amour réaliste*. Paris: Pensée Universelle, 1980.

Apostolidès, Jean-Marie. "Figures populaires, figures mythologiques dans la *Femme du Boulanger*." In *Popular Traditions and Learned Cultures in France*. Edited by Marc Bertrand. Stanford, Calif.: Anma Libri, 1985.

Armstrong, Nancy, and Tennenhouse, Leonard, eds. *The Ideology of Conduct: Essays on Literature and the History of Sexuality*. New York: Methuen, 1987.

Ariès, Philippe. *L'Enfant et la vie familiale sous l'Ancien Régime*. Paris: Plon, 1960.

Ariès, Philippe, and Duby, Georges, eds. *Histoire de la vie privée*. Paris: Seuil, 1986. Vols. 2 and 3.

Aronson, Nicole. "Amour et mariage dans les œuvres de Mlle de Scudéry." *Esprit créateur* 19 (1979) 1:26–39.

Aujourd'hui la vie: des milliers de téléspectateurs témoignent sur l'amour, la chasteté, le mariage . . . Paris: Orban, 1985.

Babel, Henry. "Jean-Jacques Rousseau et notre temps." In *Jean-Jacques Rousseau au présent*. Lyon: Presses Universitaires de Lyon, 1978.

Barbey, Léon. *Martin Le Franc, prévôt de Lausanne, avocat de l'amour et de la femme au XVe siècle*. Fribourg: Éditions Universitaires de Fribourg, 1985.

Barry, Joseph Amber. *French Lovers: From Héloïse and Abélard to Beauvoir and Sartre*. New York: Arbor House, 1987.

Barthes, Roland. *Fragments d'un discours amoureux*. Paris: Seuil, 1977.

Bataille, Georges. *L'Érotisme*. Paris: Minuit, 1957.

Bauchy, Jacques-Henry, et al. *Histoires d'amour des provinces de France*. Paris: Presses de la Cité, 1974–.

Bauer, Gérard. *Recensement de l'amour à Paris*. Paris: "Le Livre," 1922.

Bayne, Sheila. "Women in Seventeenth-Century France." *PFSCL* 8 (1981): 146–56.

Bec, Pierre. *Anthologie des troubadours*. Paris: 10/18, 1977.

———. *Burlesque et obscénité chez les troubadours: le contre-texte au Moyen-Âge*. Paris: Stock, 1984.

Bellenot, Jean-Louis. "Les Formes de l'amour dans *La Nouvelle Héloïse* et la signification symbolique des personnages de Julie et de Saint-Preux." *AJJR* 33 (1953–55): 149–207.

Bergerat, Émile. *L'Amour en république: étude sociologique, 1870–1889*. Paris: Dentu, 1889.

Berl, Emmanuel. *Le Bourgeois et l'amour*. Paris: Gallimard, 1931.

Berry, André. *L'Amour en France*. Paris: La Table Ronde, 1962.

Bertrand, Louis. *La Vie amoureuse de Louis XIV. Essai de psychologie historique*. Paris: Fayard, 1924.

Bertrand Jennings, Chantal. *L'Éros et la femme chez Zola*. Paris: Klincksieck, 1977.

Bessière, Jean, ed. *Figures féminines et roman*. Paris: Presses Universitaires de France, 1982.

Bezzola, Reto R. *Le Sens de l'aventure et de l'amour*. Paris: H. Champion, 1968.

Bogin, Meg. *The Women Troubadours*. New York: W. W. Norton, 1980.

Bosch, Élisabeth. "L'Amour et la mort: Bataille-Duras: Quelques Variations sur le nom de Stein." *Neophilologus* 4 (1983): 377–83.

Bouchard, Marcel. *Lamartine et le sens de l'amour*. Paris: Les Belles Lettres, 1941.

Bougard, Roger G. *Érotisme et amour physique dans la littérature française du XVIIe siècle*. Paris: Lachurie, 1986.

Bournand, François. *L'Amour sous la Révolution*. Paris: Gréthelin, 1909.

Bray, Bernard. *L'Art de la lettre amoureuse. Des manuels aux romans (1550–1700)*. Paris: Mouton, 1967.

Bray, Bernard, and Landy-Houillon, Isabelle, eds. *Lettres portugaises; Lettres d'une péruvienne; et autres romans d'amour par lettres*. Paris: Flammarion, 1983.

Brécourt-Villars, Claudine. *Écrire d'amour: anthologie de textes érotiques féminins, 1799–1984*. Paris: Ramsay, 1985.

Breton, Guy. *Histoires d'amour de l'Histoire de France*. Paris: Noir et Blanc, 1956.

Brody, Jules. "*La Princesse de Clèves* and the Myth of Courtly Love." *University of Toronto Quarterly* 36 (1969): 107–35.

Burney, Pierre. *L'Amour*. "Que sais-je?" Paris: Presses Universitaires de France, 1984.

Buschinger, Danielle, ed. *Amour, mariage et transgressions au Moyen-Âge*. Actes du Colloque d'Amiens de mars 1983.

Cahiers de la Compagnie Madeleine Renaud–Jean-Louis Barrault, 1983. No. 106.

Calo, Jeanne. *La Création de la femme chez Michelet*. Paris: Nizet, 1975.

Carrell, Susan Lee. *Le Soliloque de la passion féminine ou le dialogue illusoire: étude d'une formule monophonique de la littérature épistolaire*. Paris: J.-M. Place, 1982.

Chan, Andrea. "The Function of the Beloved in the Poetry of Louise Labé." *AJFS* 17 (1980) 1:46–57.

Charlton, D. G., ed. *The French Romantics*. 2 vols. Cambridge: Cambridge University Press, 1984.

Chocheyras, Jacques. *Le Désir et ses masques*. Grenoble: Presses Universitaires de Grenoble, 1981.

Cocula-Vallières, Anne-Marie. *Brantôme, amour et gloire au temps des Valois*. Paris: Michel, 1986.

Coppin, Joseph. *Amour et mariage dans la littérature française du nord au Moyen-Âge*. Paris: Argences, 1961.

Coste, Didier, and Zéraffa, Michel, eds. *Le Récit amoureux*. Paris: Champ Vallon, 1984.

Couvelaire, Jean-François. "Mariage forcé et mariage contrarié dans le théâtre de Molière." In *Thématique de Molière*. Edited by Jacques Truchet. Paris: SEDES, 1985.

Cuénin, Micheline. *L'Idéologie amoureuse en France (1540–1627)*. Paris: Aux Amateurs de Livres, 1987.

Darmon, Pierre. *Mythologie de la femme dans l'Ancienne France*. Paris: Seuil, 1983.

Deguy, Michel. *La Machine matrimoniale chez Marivaux*. Paris: Gallimard, 1986.

Desforges, Jacques. *Chronique amoureuse de Paris sous la Monarchie de Juillet, d'après les romans du temps . . .* Paris: Club du Livre, 1964.

Desonay, Fernand. *Ronsard, poète de l'amour*. 3 vols. Brussels: Palais de l'Académie, 1952–59.

Desrues, François. *Les Fleurs du bien-dire*. Paris: M. Guillemot, 1600.

Diaconoff, Suellen. *Eros and Power in "Les Liaisons dangereuses."* Geneva: Droz, 1979.

Duby, Georges. *Le Chevalier, la femme et le prêtre*. Paris: Hachette, 1981.

———. *Que sait-on de l'amour en France au XIIe siècle?* Oxford: Clarendon Press, 1983.

Dudovitz, Resa Lynn. "The Myth of Superwoman: A Comparative Study of Women's Bestsellers in France and the United States." *DAI* 48, 2 (August 1987): 385A.

Dulong, Claude. *L'Amour au dix-septième siècle*. Paris: Hachette, 1969.

———. *La Vie quotidienne des femmes au Grand Siècle*. Paris: Hachette, 1984.

Dupin, Henri. *La Courtoisie au moyen-âge (d'après les textes du XIIe et XIIIe siècle)*. Paris: Picard, 1931.

Duquette, Jean-Pierre. *Colette. L'Amour de l'amour*. Ville LaSalle, Quebec: Hurtubise HMH, 1984.

Eglin, Heinrich. *Liebe und Inspiration im Werk von Paul Éluard*. Bern and Munich: Francke, 1965.

Ehrmann, Jacques. *Un paradis désespéré. L'Amour et l'illusion dans "L'Astrée."* Paris: Presses Universitaires de France, 1963.

Ellis, M. B. *"Julie ou la Nouvelle Héloïse": A Synthesis of Rousseau's Thought.* Toronto: University of Toronto Press, 1949.

Epton, Nina Consuelo. *Love and the French.* Cleveland: World, 1959.

Evans, Martha Noel. "Murdering *L'Invitée*: Gender and Fictional Narrative." *YFS* 72 (1986): 67–86.

Febvre, Lucien. *Autour de "L'Heptaméron": amour sacré, amour profane.* Paris: Gallimard, 1944.

Fein, P. L.-M. *Women of Sensibility or Reason: The Function of the Feminine Characters in the Novels of Marivaux, Diderot, Crébillon fils, Duclos, and Laclos.* Harare: University of Zimbabwe, 1987.

Festugière, J. *La Philosophie de l'amour de Marsile Ficin et son influence sur la littérature de XVIe siècle.* Paris: Vrin, 1941.

Flannigan, Arthur. *Mme de Villedieu's "Les Désordres de l'amour": History, Literature, and the Nouvelle Historique.* Washington, D.C.: University Press of America, 1982.

Flandrin, Jean-Louis. *Les Amours paysannes (XVIe-XIXe siècle).* Paris: Gallimard-Julliard, 1976.

La Française aujourd'hui. La Femme et l'amour. La Nef 1960, New series, No. 5.

Francis, Claude, and Gonthier, Fernande. *Simone de Beauvoir: A Life, a Love Story.* New York: St. Martin's Press, 1987.

Frappier, Jean. *Amour courtois et Table Ronde.* Geneva: Droz, 1973.

Furber, Donald, and Callahan, Anne. *Erotic Love in Literature: From Medieval Legend to Romantic Illusion.* Troy, N.Y.: Whitston, 1982.

Gay, Jules. *Bibliographie des ouvrages relatifs à l'amour, aux femmes, au mariage, et des livres facétieux, pantagruéliques, scatologiques . . .* Paris: Lemonnyer, 1894–1900.

Gay, Peter. "Three Stages on Love's Way." *Encounter* 47 (1957): 8–20.

Gendre, André. *Ronsard, poète de la conquête amoureuse.* Neuchâtel: La Baconnière, 1970.

Gold, Penny Schine. *The Lady & the Virgin: Image, Attitude, and Experience in Twelfth-Century France.* Chicago: University of Chicago Press, 1987.

Goncourt, Edmond and Jules de. *La Femme au dix-huitième siecle.* Paris: Firmin Didot, 1862.

———. *L'Amour au dix-huitième siècle.* Paris: Dentu, 1875.

Goodden, Angelica. *The Complete Lover: Eros, Nature, and Artifice in the Eighteenth-Century French Novel.* Oxford: Clarendon Press, 1989.

Gunn, A. M. *The Mirror of Love: A Reinterpretation of the Romance of the Rose.* Lubbock: Texas Tech Press, 1952.

Haraucourt, Edmond. Preface to *L'Amour et l'esprit gaulois à travers l'histoire du XVe au XXe siècle.* Paris: Martin-Dupuis, 1927.

Hervé-Piraux, F. R. *Les Logis d'amour au XVIIIe siècle.* Paris: Daragon, 1912.

Horowitz, Louise K. *Love and Language: A Study of Classical French Moralist Writers.* Columbus: Ohio State University Press, 1977.

Huchet, Jean-Charles. *L'Amour discourtois.* Toulouse: Privat, 1987.

Ibert, Jean-Claude, and Charles, Jérôme. *Love, the French Way.* London: Heinemann, 1961.

Institut Français d'Opinion Publique. *Patterns of Sex and Love: A Study of the French Woman and Her Morals*. New York: Crown, 1961.

Jadoux, Henri. *Le Théâtre et l'amour*. Paris: Perrin, 1985.

Jones, Anne Rosalind. "Assimilation with a Difference: Renaissance Women Poets and Literary Influence." *YFS* 62 (1981): 135–148.

Jones, Rosemarie. *The Theme of Love in the Romans d'Antiquité*. London: Modern Humanities Research Associates, 1972.

Kelly, Douglas. *Medieval Imagination: Rhetoric and the Poetry of Courtly Love*. Madison: University of Wisconsin Press, 1975.

Kristeva, Julia. *Histoires d'amour*. Paris: Denoël, 1983.

Lachèvre, Frédéric. *Les Derniers Libertins*. Geneva: Slatkine, 1968.

Lacrételle, Jacques de. *Amour nuptial*. Paris: Gallimard, 1929.

———. *La Galerie des amants*. Paris: Perrin, 1963.

Lacroix, Paul. *Le Dix-huitième Siècle, institutions, usages et coutumes, France. 1780–1789*. Paris: Firmin-Didot, 1875.

Lacy, Norris, ed. *26 chansons d'amour de la Renaissance*. Paris: Klincksieck and Lawrence: University of Kansas Press, 1975.

Lazar, Moshé. *Amours courtois et fin'amors dans la littérature du XIIe siècle*. Paris: Klincksieck, 1964.

Lazard, Madeleine. *Images littéraires de la femme à la Renaissance*. Paris: Presses Universitaires de France, 1985.

Lebègue, Raymond. "La Sensibilité dans les lettres d'amour au XVIIe siècle." *CAIEF* 11 (1959): 77–85.

Lebel, Jean-Jacques. *L'Amour et l'argent*. Paris: Stock, 1979.

Lebrun, François. *La Vie conjugale sous l'Ancien Régime*. Paris: Colin, 1975.

Lecercle, Jean-Louis. *L'Amour de l'idéal au réel*. Paris: Bordas, 1971.

Leclercq, Jean. *L'Amour vu par les moines au XIIe siècle*. Paris: Éditions du Cerf, 1983.

Lee, Vera. *Love and Strategy in the Eighteenth-Century French Novel*. Cambridge, Mass.: Schenkman, 1986.

Le Roy Ladurie, Emmanuel. *L'Argent, l'amour et la mort en pays d'oc*. Paris: Seuil, 1980.

Lescure, Mathurin de. *La Société française pendant la Révolution. L'Amour sous la Terreur*. Paris: Dentu, 1882.

Levowitz-Treu, Micheline. *L'Amour et la mort chez Stendhal: métamorphoses d'un apprentissage affectif*. Paris: Nicaise, 1978.

Lewis, C. S. *The Allegory of Love*. London: Oxford University Press, 1936.

Lilar, Suzanne. *À propos de Sartre et de l'amour*. Paris: Grasset, 1967.

———. *Le Couple*. Paris: Grasset, 1963.

Lot-Borodine, Myrrha. *De l'amour profane à l'amour sacré: essai de psychologie sentimentale au Moyen-Âge*. Paris: Nizet, 1961.

Mandrou, Robert. "Pour une histoire de la sensibilité." *Annales ESC*. July-September 1959, 581–88.

Marchand, Henry L. *The Erotic History of France*. New York: The Panurge Press, 1933.

Margerit, Robert. *L'Amour et le temps*. Paris: Gallimard, 1963.

Markale, Jean. *L'Amour courtois ou le couple infernal*. Paris: Imago, 1987.

Marny, Jacques. *Les Adolescents aujourd'hui; culture, loisirs, idoles, amour, religion*. Paris: Centurion, 1965.

Marroncle, Jeannine. *Aujourd'hui les couples*. Paris: Éditions Ouvrières, 1980.

Mathieu-Castellani, Gisèle. *Mythes de l'Éros baroque*. Paris: Presses Universitaires de France, 1981.

———. *Les Thèmes amoureux dans la poésie française 1570–1600*. Paris: Klincksieck, 1975.

Mauzi, Robert. *L'Idée du bonheur au XVIIIe siècle*. Paris: Colin, 1960.

Ménard, Philippe. *"Les Lais" de Marie de France: contes d'amour et d'aventure du Moyen Âge*. Paris: Presses Universitaires de France, 1979.

Méray, Antony. *La Vie au temps des cours d'amour; croyances, usages et moeurs intimes des XIe, XIIe et XIIIe siècles, d'après les chroniques, gestes, jeux-partis et fabliaux*. Paris: Claudin, 1876.

Michel, Arlette. *Le Mariage chez Balzac: amour et féminisme*. Paris: Les Belles Lettres, 1978.

Miller, Nancy K. *The Heroine's Text: Readings in the French and English Novel, 1722–1782*. New York: Columbia University Press, 1980.

Minta, Stephen. *Love-Poetry in Sixteenth-Century France: A Study in Themes and Traditions*. Manchester: Manchester University Press, 1977.

Moore, John Clare. *Love in Twelfth-Century France*. Philadelphia: University of Pennsylvania Press, 1972.

Moreau, Pierre. *Amours romantiques*. Paris: Hachette, 1963.

Muchembled, Robert. *Culture populaire et culture des élites dans la France moderne: XVe-XVIIIe siècles*. Paris: Flammarion, 1978.

Nadal, Octave. *Le Sentiment de l'amour dans l'œuvre de Pierre Corneille*. Paris: Gallimard, 1948.

Nahas, Hélène. *La Femme dans la littérature existentielle*. Paris: Presses Universitaires de France, 1957.

Nelli, René. *L'Amour et les mythes du coeur*. Paris: Hachette, 1975.

———. *Les Écrivains anti-conformistes du Moyen Âge occitan: I. La Femme et l'amour*. Paris: Phébus, 1977.

———. *L'Érotique des troubadours*. Paris: Union générale d'éditions, 1974.

———. *Érotique et civilisations*. Paris: Weber, 1972.

Neuschäfer, Hans Jörg. "Liebe im Feuilletonroman: Das Scheidungsgesetz von 1884 im Spiegel der Pariser Tagespresse." In *Liebesroman, Liebe im Roman*. Edited by Titus Heydenreich and Egert Pöhlmann. Erlangen: Universitätsbibliothek Erlangen-Nürnberg, 1987.

Noble, Peter S. *Love and Marriage in Chrétien de Troyes*. Cardiff: University of Wales Press, 1984.

Pelous, Jean-Michel. *Amour précieux, amour galant (1654–1675)*. Paris: Klincksieck, 1980.

Péret, Benjamin. *Anthologie de l'amour sublime*. Paris: Michel, 1956.

Perrot, Michelle. "The New Eve and the Old Adam: Changes in French Women's Condition at the Turn of the Century." In *Behind the Lines: Gender and the Two World Wars*. Edited by Margaret Randolph Higonnet et al. New Haven, Conn.: Yale University Press, 1987.

Phan, Marie-Claude. *Amours illégitimes: histoires des séductions en Languedoc, 1676–1786*. Paris: CNRS, 1967.

Pia, Pascal, ed. *Dictionnaire des œuvres érotiques*. Paris: Mercure de France, 1971.

Pillement, Georges. *Anthologie des lettres d'amour*. Paris: Le Bélier, 1956.

Plouvier, Paule. *Poétique de l'amour chez André Breton*. Paris: Corti, 1983.

Priollaud, Nicole, ed. *La Femme au XIXe siècle*. Paris: Messinger, 1983.

Richmond, Ian, and Venesoen, Constant, eds. *Présences féminines: littérature et société au XVIIe siècle français*. Paris: Papers on French Seventeenth Century Literature, 1987.

Riordan, Sister Francis Ellen. *The Concept of Love in the French Catholic Literary Revival*. New York: AMS Press, 1969.

Regan, Mariann S. *Love Words: The Self and the Text in Medieval and Renaissance Poetry*. Ithaca, N.Y.: Cornell University Press, 1982.

Richard, Guy. *Histoire de l'amour en France: du Moyen-Âge à la Belle Époque*. Paris: Lattès, 1985.

Rigolot, François. "Gender vs. Sex Difference in Louise Labé's Grammar of Love." In *Rewriting the Renaissance*. Edited by Margaret W. Ferguson, Maureen Quilligan, and Nancy J. Vickers. Chicago: Chicago University Press, 1986.

Rougemont, Denis de. *Comme toi-même; essais sur les mythes de l'amour*. Paris: Michel, 1961.

———. *L'Amour et l'Occident*. Paris: Plon, 1939.

Rousset, Jean. *Leurs yeux se rencontrèrent. La Scène de première vue dans le roman*. Paris: Corti, 1981.

Rouveyre, André. *Amour et poésie d'Apollinaire*. Paris: Seuil, 1955.

Sassus, Sister Jeannine. *The Motif of the Renunciation of Love in the Seventeenth-Century French Novel*. Washington, D.C.: Catholic University Press, 1963.

Segalen, Martine. *Love and Power in the Peasant Family: Rural France in the Nineteenth Century*. Chicago: University of Chicago Press, 1983.

Segalen, Martine, and Chamarat, Josselyne. *Amours et mariages dans l'Ancienne France*. Paris: Berger-Levrault, 1981.

Semerau, Alfred, trans. and ed. *Liebesbriefe aus dem Rokoko*. Berlin: Hyperionverlag, 1915.

Solé, Jacques. *L'Amour en Occident à l'époque moderne*. Paris: Michel, 1976.

Solignac, Pierre, and Serrero, Anne. *La Vie sexuelle et amoureuse des Français*. Paris: Trévise, 1980.

Sollers, Philippe. "Le Toit," in his *Logiques*. Paris: Seuil, 1968.

South Carolina, University of. College of Humanities and Social Sciences. *Eroticism in French Literature*. 1983. A special colloquium issue.

Stewart, Philip. *Le Masque et la parole: le langage de l'amour au XVIIIe siècle*. Paris: Corti, 1973.

———. "Representations of Love in the French Eighteenth Century." *Studies in Iconography* 4 (1978): 125–48.

Sullerot, Évelyne. *Histoire et mythologie de l'amour*. Paris: Hachette, 1974.

Sullivan, Penny. "Love and Marriage in Early French Narrative Poetry." *Trivium* 19 (1984): 85–102.

Taylor, Deems., trans. and ed. *The One-Track Mind: Love Poems of XVIIth and XVIIIth Century France*. New York: Library Publishers, 1953.

Tishkoff, D. " 'I Have Created Myself': Sex, Power and Love in Laclos' *Les Liaisons dangereuses*." *TSJSNW* 15 (1984): 73–85.

Topsfield, L. T. *Troubadours and Love*. Cambridge: Cambridge University Press, 1979.

Traer, James. *Marriage and Family in Eighteenth-Century France*. Ithaca, N.Y.: Cornell University Press, 1980.

Viallaneix, Paul, and Ehrard, Jean, eds. *Aimer en France 1760–1860*. Actes du Colloque

International de Clermont-Ferrand. 2 vols. Clermont-Ferrand: Faculté des Lettres et Sciences Humaines de l'Université de Clermont-Ferrand II, 1980.

Les Visages de l'amour au XVIIe siècle: 13ème Colloque du CMR 17 sous le patronage de la Société d'études du XVIIème siècle. Toulouse: Université de Toulouse-le Mirail, 1984.

Welch, Marcelle Maistre. "La Femme, le mariage et l'amour dans les contes de fées mondains du XVIIe siècle français." *PSCFL* 10 (1983): 47–58.

Wheaton, Robert, and Hareven, Tamara K., eds. *Family and Sexuality in French History.* Philadelphia: University of Pennsylvania Press, 1980.

Zeldin, Theodore. *France 1848–1945.* 2 vols. Oxford: Clarendon Press, 1973–77.

———. *The French.* New York: Pantheon, 1982.

Zumthor, Paul. "Le Sens de l'amour et du mariage dans la conception classique de l'homme." *Archiv* 181 (1942): 97–109.

9

Newspapers, Magazines, Feminine Press

JOSEPH MARTHAN

In 1989, the year of the Bicentennial of the French Revolution and the Declaration of the Rights of Man and the Citizen, the press took on a very particular importance. An impressive series of exhibitions, colloquia, books, press articles were devoted to it. Indeed, the people's struggle for democracy and newly won freedom of the press cannot be dissociated, for a true democracy guarantees freedom of the press and vice versa. And any history of the press is closely linked to other histories: cultural, social, economic, technical, political. The press reflects society's evolution but is also the agent of this evolution; its history is also the history of its influence. To cite just one famous example, it is obvious that Émile Zola's articles in *L'Aurore* concerning the Dreyfus Affair not only inform us about this historical episode but have contributed to influencing its development as well. We understand, therefore, the historian's multiple interest in those daily archives.

HISTORICAL OUTLINE

If the prehistorical press can be dated back to Antiquity—for any structured society needs news that circulates, even if only at the administrative level—press history could only begin with the invention of the printing press. Starting in the sixteenth century, the great movements, whether scientific, intellectual, religious, or economic, combined their effects to create a need and a thirst for information. Thus the Renaissance and the Reformation, the discovery of new continents, increasing commercial exchanges, wars, material progress all attracted new readers. The French Revolution also gave an extraordinary impetus in the proliferation and dissemination of newspapers. In the nineteenth century, as progress occurred in education and democracy, in transportation and postal delivery, in the development of capitalism and the introduction of advertising, there could be seen a mass journalism parallel to the substantial decrease of the cost of daily papers. Today the written press has lost its information monopoly. Shaken by the explosion of the electronic media, it must, in order to affirm its uniqueness in the media environment, quest for innovation and original formulas.

From the Origins to the End of the Second Empire

From the Printing Press to the Revolution

Before printed matter, news circulated at a very high price on manuscript sheets which could reach only a limited public of princes and rich merchants. Gutenberg's invention gave access to information to a much less restricted audience. For instance, the impact of the Lutheran or Calvinist message cannot be imagined without the printed medium. Wars, foreign or civil, scourges, cataclysms, New World curiosities, court life, and a partiality for what is called sensational news gave rise to a rash of printed flyers: *occasionnels* and *canards*. Militants of every stripe waged guerrilla warfare on each other through satirical tracts. Lampoons and notices, usually of a seditious nature, proliferated during the religious wars. The Fronde provoked thousands of *mazarinades* (printed attacks on Cardinal Mazarin). However, missing from all these publications was a fundamental element, that of periodicity. This is precisely the novelty Théophraste Renaudot was to introduce. Historians agree on 1631, the year of *La Gazette*'s founding, as the periodical press's birthdate in France. Physician and historiographer to the king, Renaudot was an original man, a visionary. A great traveler, gifted with an immense intellectual curiosity, he had the occasion to observe the foreign press. Before anyone else in France, he felt the need for information and for a periodical press whose great power he already foresaw. Subsidized and protected by Richelieu and Louis XIII, who perceived very well the importance of the press in transmitting their political message, he received the exclusive privilege for *La Gazette*.

The first issue had four pages roughly 9 by 6 inches; a few months later it had eight pages, then twelve in 1642. To foreign news, Renaudot added national news from the sixth issue on. News about the armies and the royal courts abroad and in Paris got the lion's share. More than three centuries before Robert Hersant, Renaudot published monthly supplements which completed *La Gazette* with analyzed information. The success of his periodical was immediate, as the repeated attacks of his adversaries, the praise of his supporters, and the numerous imitations and pirated editions can attest. Every year the *Gazette* issues were gathered into a bound volume. Renaudot added remarkable prefaces that still today are of great topicality. He continually emphasized the mission of the journalist who must, above all, passionately seek the truth, even if he cannot always find it. *La Gazette*, having become *La Gazette de France* and a biweekly in 1762, would dominate along with *Le Journal des Savants* and *Le Mercure* the entire prerevolutionary period.

Le Journal des Savants was founded in 1665, under Colbert's patronage, by Denis de Sallo. It reviewed scientific, theological, and literary works published in France and abroad. At first a weekly, it became a monthly in 1724. Its success was enormous, and it was imitated throughout Europe. In 1672, Donneau de Visé created *Le Mercure Galant*, which became *Le Mercure de France* in 1724 and was essentially a literary sheet. *Le Mercure* also knew a great success and was copied in Europe. Next to this official and authorized press, which held a monopoly and enjoyed royal privilege, public demand and curiosity caused a flowering of newspapers the power structure tolerated in order to better control. Under the Ancien Régime, any printed matter, book and paper alike, was subject to control both from the Church and government. The press was vigilantly watched, censored, and any illicit authors, publishers, and printers were prosecuted. A repressive legislation forced journalists to exercise prudence and self-censorship.

Many specialized periodicals saw the light in the eighteenth century. Among the most famous are *Les Mémoires de Trévoux, Les Nouvelles ecclésiastiques, Le Pour et le Contre, Le Journal encyclopédique, Le Nouvelliste du Parnasse,* and *L'Année littéraire.* They constitute an exceptional document on the Age of Enlightenment and the debates that animated it. Yet they could not, lest they be suspended, question religious and political orthodoxy. In this repressive context, handwritten news and French papers printed abroad and circulated clandestinely offered a breath of fresh air in the atmosphere of a French press smothered by censorship. A publication like *La Gazette de Leyde* was distinguished by its seriousness and the quality of its political news. *Les Nouvelles de la République des Lettres* reviewed numerous works that had been censored in France.

1789: The Press of the Revolution and the Revolution of the Press

It was in this repressive climate that the Revolutionary blast would shake the press structure from top to bottom and establish new newspapers marking a fundamental step in press history. We already see in the spring of 1789, before the taking of the Bastille, a veritable taking of press powers. Under popular pressure, the locks of the Bastille opened de facto. Brissot and Mirabeau would even defy the government and publish their newspapers without prior authorization. Article XI of the Declaration of the Rights of Man (August 26, 1789) proclaimed that "the free communication of thoughts and opinions is one of man's most precious rights; any citizen can therefore speak, write, and print freely. . . . '' Whereas prerevolutionary political papers could be counted on the fingers of one hand, no fewer than 250 papers, of every stripe, Revolutionary or royalist, were started in the last eight months of 1789. This unheard-of flood of politics is one of the outstanding traits of the Revolutionary press. The repressive system of the Ancien Régime fell under the press. Booksellers, printers, publishers, and book peddlers proliferated. As Alain Manévy points out in the

May 2, 1989, issue of *Le Figaro*, "Freedom of the press is the first conquest of the Revolution. Out of 5,279 individuals imprisoned in the Bastille between 1659 and 1789, 1,250 belonged to the world of the printed word: 450 political writers and 199 lampoonists, 162 master printers and booksellers, 200 journeymen and apprentices, 19 master binders and journeymen, 14 line-engravers, 206 peddlers." The Revolutionary press was also a conquest of youth. Newspaper founders were young and enthusiastic. Perhaps never had a journalist been as involved in his writing, as much actor of his time as passionate writer. Let us add to the names already mentioned—Mirabeau and Brissot—those of Marat, Desmoulins, Louvet, Loustalot, Hébert, and Royou. The counterrevolutionary press was not to be outdone, however. The journalists animating it, who included Rivarol, lacked neither talent nor bite. It was during the Revolution that, in the wake of the press, the concept of public opinion arose.

Even if after August 10, 1792, the Terror would muzzle the press again, the wind of liberty would continue to animate the struggle of the journalists out to reconquer their freedom.

From the Convention to the End of the Second Empire

Except for a springtime's duration of found-again freedom in 1848, all the régimes—whether the Convention, Directory, Consulate, First Empire, Monarchy, or Second Empire—would, to curb the press and slow its spread, draw from a rich repressive arsenal: surety bond, tax stamps, prior authorization, printer's license, and finally censorship. Nevertheless, despite the régime's efforts to reduce it, the press continued to expand. Two years after the May 11, 1868, law cancelling the system of warnings and prior authorization and accepted by a weakened Second Empire, the press saw a doubling of its circulation. The abolition of tax stamps on September 5, 1870, by the Third Republic accelerated the movement further. This process culminated in the law of July 29, 1881, which gave the French press one of the most liberal systems in the world and, except during the two World Wars, guaranteed its independence from the government in power. If this law freed the press from political oppression, however, it could not protect it from the far more dangerous power of money, since the press was not totally incorruptible. The secret and ambiguous relations it sometimes maintained with financial circles were for a long time to strain its credibility.

The Press's Golden Age (1871–1914)

Historians agree about placing the golden age of the French press between 1871 and 1914. It is then that the popular and feminine press expanded rapidly and the daily press had considerable growth. A few figures easily show the extent of the phenomenon both in Paris and in the provinces. Circulation of Parisian dailies went from one million in 1870 to 5.5 million in 1914, and that of provincial dailies from 350,000 to 4 million. The development of the periodical press was even faster. The basic causes of the unprecedented growth are the same as for the previous period, but they acted in a more emphatic fashion. Pierre Albert and Fernand Terrou summarize them well: "Generalization of education, democratization of political life, growing urbanization, development of transportation and communication means and, as a direct consequence, broadening of newspaper information areas and of reader curiosity. At the same time, decreased issue prices, . . . aligned with those of popular sheets, and . . . the slow evolution of the masses' average standard of living" (*Histoire de la presse*, p. 56). We should add that the press was the only means of information. Yesterday as today, the development and health of the press are a function of the Westernization of economic and social life. As Jean-François Revel pointedly noted, "We cannot not notice, if we place ourselves in an historical context, the connection of three phenomena: economic development, political democracy, and freedom of the press. These three phenomena are linked everywhere and always" (*Le Débat*, March-May 1986). Never had the press been so involved in its epoch as under the Third Republic and so present at each monent and in every sector of national life. Never had it had so much influence on public opinion and the course of events. It helped fashion the attitudes, tastes, and political ideas of the masses. Never had writers, great or not, participated so much in the life of the press, so that it was in the twentieth century that the legal status of writer became different from that of journalist. This vigor of the press was upheld by the sheer number and variety of titles, reflecting the scope of political and religious affiliations by appealing to different readerships (notably, the young and women) and by increasing specialized columns. During this period four Parisian (therefore, national) dailies reached or passed the million mark: *Le Petit Journal*, *Le Matin*, *Le Journal*, *Le Petit Parisien*. With 1.5 million copies in 1914, the latter had the largest circulation in the world. Like the Paris press, the provincial press knew a proliferation of titles. From 100 titles in 1870 it went in 1914 to 242, and some twenty of them had runs of more than 100,000 copies. It can be said that under the Third Republic newspapers became a common consumer product.

A closer look at the popular press shows its development accelerated in the second half of the nineteenth century. Until the early nineteenth century, the press could only write for a limited social and cultural elite, since newspapers were expensive and the majority of the population was illiterate. In 1836 a yearly subscription cost more than a Paris worker's average monthly salary. A few thousand copies were considered a respectable print run, and total Paris daily circulation barely reached 80,000. We can understand why February 1, 1863, represents a decisive stage in press history. It was on that day that Moïse Millaud launched *Le Petit Journal* at five centimes, then the lowest-priced daily in the world. Émile de Girardin, a pioneer of the popular press, had already blazed the trail by halving the subscription price of his *La Presse*, a daily he founded in 1836. The other competing papers could only follow the trend. Technical progress, which helped reduce production costs, and expansion of advertising allowed for a significant drop in newspaper prices. The press could then reach the popular masses because throughout the nineteenth century subscription prices continued to fall in relative value and the number of illiterates was dramatically falling, too. The popular press had no pretention to seriousness. Above all, it wanted to entertain and please. Thus, *Le Petit Journal* had "the courage to be dumb." In 1870 it already printed 300,000 copies and twenty years later more than one million.

The popular press sensed the tastes and curiosity of a still uncultured public and knew how to cater to them. It exploited sensational news to increase circulation when it covered famous crimes and criminals. Until then relegated to the inside or, worse, to the last page, sensational doings were propelled to the front page. The introduction of serialized novels, which delighted and thrilled, contributed to the popular press's success by creating faithful generations of readers. Alexandre Dumas, Eugène Sue, Ponson du Terrail, among others, enjoyed a tremendous following with the general public. The number of pages increased progressively and, to attract a wider readership, the amount of features increased as well: features devoted to popular sports, especially cycling and soccer, to games, contests, the horoscope, women's interests and concerns. *Le Petit Journal* justified popular papers in this fashion: "They are popularizers and initiators. They chat, expose, and guard against pontificating." The popular press contaminated, so to speak, the great newspapers which, to diversify and increase their audience, added popular columns. Press popularization was accomplished to the detriment of political information which, all during the nineteenth century, would lose its supremacy to nonpolitical columns.

The press under the Third Republic had an exceptional vigor and richness. It offered an extraordinary gamut of journalistic formats and played a role of the first order, teaching the population to read and write and expressing and disseminating ideas and knowledge.

World War I and the Period between the Wars

World War I, though it stimulated the English-language press, created grave difficulties for French newspapers. Lost advertising revenues, newsprint scarcity and expensiveness, and distribution problems all caused a decrease in the number of pages and the disappearance of numerous titles. But graver still was the gap in credibility and confidence encountered by the press during the war. Even if its activity was severely curtailed by civilian and military censorship, it nonetheless shared the responsibility for disinformation. A victim of censorship, it was also its instrument. There is a fascinating contrast between the pitiless reality of the front and the optimistic reporting found in newspapers. The press, with rare exceptions, printed the propaganda provided by military and political authorities. The civilian population had access, therefore, only to filtered and biased information. World War I broke the instinctive trust the public had for the press. Certainly the press would continue to influence public opinion, but it would never again find the power it enjoyed before 1914 in shaping and directing it.

Until then the French press was first in the world in size of circulation. World

War I was to break its dynamism and shake its supremacy to the benefit of the Anglo-American press. After the Great War, the daily press would find competition from the new medium of radio and from specialized periodicals. Regarding the latter, Yves Guillauma, in his remarkable *La Presse en France*, was even to assert that "the birth of abundantly illustrated specialized magazines presented at that time as important an evolution as the birth of the cheap popular press at the end of the 19th century" (p. 16). To confront this double competition, newspapers showed ingenuity in order to attract and keep a more demanding audience. Accelerating a move begun before the war, they diversified their columns: special pages were reserved to sensational news but also to the automobile and aviation, to entertainment and sports, to radio and the movies, to women and fashion, to arts and letters, to games and amusements. Newspapers thus hoped, through their various sections, to reach a broader readership. One result of this move was the newspapers' relative depolitization. Political articles were reduced to make space for the others. Opinion dailies lost their prestige to political weeklies. Left-wing periodicals, like *Marianne* and *La Lumière*, or right-wing, like *Candide* and *Gringoire*, reflected between-the-wars political thought much better than daily papers.

Contrary to the Anglo-Saxon press, which knew a considerable growth, the French press, especially the Paris press, was relatively stagnant between 1914 and 1939, when its circulation went from 9.5 million to 12 million. The greatest success of the daily press of the time was *Paris-Soir*, which did not stop improving its formula: sensational news, of course, but also lots of illustrations, rich and superb sports articles, quality reporting, careful layouts and headlines, a punchy style. It saw its circulation climb from 134,000 to 2 million by the eve of World War II. Yet this success must not hide the noticeable decline of the other Paris dailies, in particular the five great papers (the four "millionaires" already mentioned plus *L'Écho de Paris*).

From World War II to Today

War Years and Liberation

During World War II the press was closely controlled. It was subjected to censorship by the Pétain government and the Occupation authorities. The German Propaganda Office craftily handled writers, journalists, and politicians and knew how to play on their ambitions and rivalries to get them to defend collaborationist policies. There were frankly collaborationist newspapers. But many others preferred to shut down rather than submit to orders from Vichy or the occupying force. A clandestine press also thrived. It was the work of writers, printers, and distributors who, despite the enormous sacrifices and dangers involved—arrest, deportations, and death sentences—had the courage to refuse humiliation and defeat and to inform and get France's voice heard. This shadow press had an extraordinary development (historians count more than 1,000 titles) and exercised a considerable influence on its readers' consciences. The Liberation, in 1944, brought about an upheaval of French press structures, regulated through a series of ordinances passed by the provisional government. Newspapers published under German supervision were banned. The only ones allowed to appear were those shut down during the Occupation, the underground papers, and the new ones subsidized by various Resistance groups. To make press enterprises more ethical, these ordinances also sought to ensure press responsibility and multiplicity.

Characteristics of Today's Press

The number of titles and circulation figures for the general daily news press of Paris show a regular decline since the end of the war. In 1945, it counted 26 titles and a run of 4.6 million copies. In 1988, titles numbered nine and circulation had fallen to 2.8 million. As to the regional daily press, the number of titles for the same period went from 153 to 68, and its circulation seemed to stabilize around 7 million (7,530,000 in 1945, 7,300,000 in 1988). However, if we consider that the French population jumped from 40 million to 55 million, we notice that the penetration rate of the daily press (Paris and provinces) has greatly diminished since 1945, going from 303 copies to 184 per 1,000 inhabitants. This rate puts France at the 31st place in the world but among the last of developed countries, very far behind West Germany, Great Britain, the United States, Canada, Scandinavia, and Japan.

What factors have contributed to this erosion? Often given as the main factor is competition from the electronic media, which broke the information monopoly so long enjoyed by the printed press. The French also have less time available for reading daily newspapers, since each day TV viewers spend an average of 3 hours 26 minutes in front of their set, radio listeners 2 hours 44 minutes, whereas time devoted to reading (papers and books) is only an average 27 minutes a day! The competition facing the press in the near future will be even rougher with electronic media deregulation, television and radio network explosion, satellite and cable broadcasting, computer telecommunication developments, etc. Yet this competition cannot be the sole reason for French disaffection with the daily press. Other advanced countries have kept a strong daily press despite a highly developed electronic sector. In particular, we can cite Japan, which has one of the strongest newspaper penetrations—719 copies per 1,000 people— Britain, whose excellent electronic media do not hinder a dynamic daily press, or the United States, where the daily press has been able to resist teeming electronic media. Other reasons, therefore, must be given. The French daily is the most expensive in the world, and its cost rises faster than anywhere else. From 1970 to 1984, the consumer price index multiplied by 2.75 but the newspaper index by 6. Several reasons explain this. A powerful labor union, the *Syndicat du livre CGT*, strong from its monopoly over printed matter production, has constantly slowed down modernization likely to lower very high production costs; moreover, a lengthy strike can lead a newspaper to bankruptcy. Another major handicap is a weak advertising market. In 1986 France spent $81 per person on advertising, far behind West Germany ($133), Great Britain ($145), and very far behind the United States ($424). If in 1988, at 55.6 percent in advertising expenditures, the French printed press still occupies a dominant position compared to the other media, it is nevertheless in a precarious position because of the increase in new media. Indeed, while television's share of advertising revenues has jumped between 1985 and 1988 by 7.6 points (from 17 to 24.6 percent), the press has lost 3.9 points (from 59.5 to 55.6 percent). It remains to be seen if television will energize the overall advertising market, including the press, as in Italy, or continue its expansion to the detriment of the press. Another consequence of this weak advertising market is that advertising constitutes only 40.4 percent of total press revenues, behind the other Western countries where this ratio is never less than 50 percent.

The French distribution system, however efficient, also adds to the cost of a newspaper, especially a daily. Thus, for a national daily, distribution expenses amount to slightly more than half the sales price. Furthermore, subscriptions and home delivery, which reduce costs and create a faithful readership, represent, unlike in the United States or Japan, only a small percentage of newspaper sales (most are in fact *bought* daily). The national daily press remains in a precarious financial condition in spite of massive aid from the state.

The press belonging to political parties is no longer profitable. The golden age of the ideological press of the Third Republic is long gone. The number of titles and its circulation have plummeted. Party organs are in chronic deficit and are read solely by members. The French are resisting party newspapers that favor opinion over information. The experience of *Le Matin de Paris* is, in this respect, edifying. Its marked Mitterrandism literally caused it to sink at the same time that the French were reelecting Mitterrand to the presidency. This is why Jean-François Revel in his *Débat* interview (cited above) minimized all the factors contributing to the national daily press's decline save one: the press did not know how to separate opinion from information. It seems that it has finally understood, as evidenced by a revamped *Le Monde* and *Le Figaro*, that this distinction was essential to its survival.

The clear decline of the daily press occurred mainly at the expense of the national Paris press. For a long time snubbed and outranked by Paris newspapers, the daily regional press caught up, with a 1939 circulation of 6 million copies. Today, with 7 million, it dwarfs the Paris press. A regional daily, *Ouest-France*, born at the Liberation, first ousted *France Soir* in 1976 and is now the largest French daily with a run of 839,000, that is, almost 300,000 more than its closest rival, *Le Figaro*. At the same time, the penetration rate of the Paris press in the provinces has continued to decrease. How to explain this domination? If the regional press has resisted the newspaper crisis better than the Paris press, it is because it has known how to adapt to technological developments and regional changes. What makes its strength is its local coverage. It has a close network of local correspondents who know and understand their specific areas. No hamlet or village is without its stringer. The regional paper is bought above all to have local news. So regional dailies have several local editions. *Ouest-France* publishes 44 editions to better cover the twelve *départements* it serves. The regional press provides its readers the feeling of closeness, what sociologists call the feeling of belonging. Taught by the experience that obviously political papers are bound to disappear, the regional press, to attract readers from all opinions and socioeconomic status and to offend no one, adopts a consensus stand and a neutral political tone. We must also emphasize that regional dailies are open to the young, who read them before they would read national papers. For example, *Ouest-France* in 1985–86 published the work of *lycée* students of Cherbourg. *L'Alsace* regularly publishes submissions from students. The large regional dailies, with rare exceptions, have a monopoly position within their area. This results from an increasing concentration of the regional press. This concentration takes various forms: elimination or merger of newspapers, concentration of means of production, distribution agreements (that is, the promise of no direct competition), and even advertising published in common. The regional press will have to face the challenge represented by additional local radio and soon TV stations that may steal readers and advertisers.

A closer analysis of the Paris press shows that its weakness is mainly due to the collapse of working-class dailies. Of the five titles that, before the crisis of the 1970s, had the largest readership, two have disappeared, *Paris-Jour* and *L'Aurore*. Only three are left, *Le Parisien Libéré, France Soir* and *L'Humanité*, which in 1976 had a total run of 839,000 copies, well below what the five papers printed in 1969 (2,363,000). Where is the time between the wars when dailies published a million or more? Even after World War II there were impressive circulation numbers: *France Soir* at more than 1.4 million at the end of the 1950s and *Le Parisien Libéré* close to a million in the early 1970s. This decline of the working-class national daily press, it should be noted, is also visible in the periodical press, though it is in full expansion. Let us look at a 1972 survey (*Histoire générale de la presse française* 5: 376) done about two newspapers, *Le Monde* and the working-class *Le Parisien Libéré*. We notice that almost 60 percent of *Le Parisien Libéré* readers had an eighth-grade education or less, compared to only 8 percent for *Le Monde* readers. Inversely, 49.2 percent of *Le Monde* readers had a college education, while the rate was only 4.4 percent for *Le Parisien Libéré* readers. Does this imply that the higher the population's educational level rises, the more readers the working-class press loses? But then how to explain that a country like Britain, comparable to France in its social and economic development, has working-class dailies with runs in the millions? Does this mean that the French have become reluctant toward the popular press? The editorial content differs also when we examine popular press or *Le Monde* headlines. Sensational news occupies more space in *France Soir* or *Le Parisien Libéré* than in *Le Monde*. To take a specific example, in the July 12, 1984, issue, sensational news covered 25.7, 27, and 3 percent respectively. On the other hand, that same day, *Le Monde* devoted 12.8 percent to foreign affairs compared to *France Soir*'s 1.2 percent and *Le Parisien Libéré*'s 0 percent (*Ex-*

plorer le journal, p. 31). Also, economic, scientific, and literary articles are more developed in *Le Monde*, while sports and game pages are more important in popular-class papers. For Jean-Louis Servan-Schreiber, the mass press has disappeared forever in France: "Industrial logic . . . leads to an elitist press, expensive, of good graphic and intellectual quality, and with a high advertising content, in view of the omnipresent and popular electronic media. The era of a cheap mass press (except for TV weeklies) is long gone" (*Le Débat*, March-May 1986). However, several projects financed by powerful multimedia conglomerates are under study to create a popular national daily of mass appeal like *USA Today*. Perhaps they will find the formula needed to interest and win back a large French audience. But the main obstacle for these projects remains the resistance of the regional press, which fears being sacrificed or at least losing its de facto monopoly.

The periodical press: Contrary to the dailies' decline, the periodical press since the 1960s has experienced a considerable expansion. If the French are keeping away from daily newspapers, they are buying magazines by the truckloads. Eighty-nine percent of the 15-year-old and older population read at least one magazine. France comes in first in the world in magazine copy sales per 1,000 people (1,354). Despite some failures, each year the launching of new magazines belies doomsayers of the magazine press. From 1981 to 1985, 359 periodicals were launched compared to only four dailies. This success is due in part to the almost total lack of true Sunday papers of the Anglo-American type, but also and specially to the adaptive faculty of this particular sector. The magazine press has understood better the social and technological changes and has managed to respond to the needs, interests, and aspirations of the French. One example, among many, of this attention to sociodemographic trends is the dazzling success of the "golden ager" press.

Magazines have also been able to modernize their presentation and style, which explains why they are most sought after by advertisers. In 1986 their advertising market share for all types of periodicals was 38.1 percent against 20.9 percent for dailies and 18.5 percent for television. With an impressive number of titles (900), the magazine press covers practically all aspects of life and reaches all sectors. Its vitality is explained by its diversity and the richness of its features. We have a magazine press for general or economic and financial news, for sports and leisure, for home and family life, for women, the young, etc. It is a specialized press that targets its public well. As Pierre Albert notes, "instead of one public, there are many publics satisfied by the specialized press through its extreme diversity." Magazine entrepreneurs are always on the lookout for new opportunities, for the narrower the target the greater its appeal to advertisers.

We should note that TV magazines enjoy a great popular success and are the biggest in terms of distribution. Thirteen titles, with a 25.5% market share in the magazine press medium, have an average paid distribution of 12.5 million copies (1987 figures). Four of these titles rank among the first ten magazines selling more than a million. It is *Télé 7 jours*, with a 3.2 million printing, that is the overall champion. The TV magazine press has also had a phenomenal growth paralleling a general media explosion. Seven new titles came out between 1982 and 1987. From 1984 to 1987, TV magazine sales have increased by 45 percent or 3.9 million copies. The first three jumps in press circulation figures, for all categories, were realized by TV weeklies.

As was the case for the political daily press, party or partisan magazines with a strong political line have died. The French financial press, even though still weak compared with the Anglo-Saxon or Japanese, has shown an unsuspected vigor in the last few years; since the 1960s several titles were started. Its circulation is rising, in particular the daily press, which has experienced expansion. In 1987 the greatest growth in the daily press came from financial dailies. Long neglected by the general information press, financial columns now enjoy greater coverage, often in the form of a supplement, both in magazines and in dailies. A financial journalist like Jean Boissonnat has a national audience. It seems that money is no longer a taboo subject in France, and the French are now reconciled to the idea of competition, profits, and business. The Bourse is henceforth a popular institution. It is not paradoxical in the least that Socialists, once in power, were responsible for this new attitude.

A phenomenon merits attention: the impressive rise of the free (supermarket) ''throwaway'' press. In 1986, with 523 titles and 40 million copies, it already formed the largest segment of the printed press. Its advertising revenue share was close to 15 percent of revenues for the entire press. This rising trend is continuing, for the market for such papers is far from saturated.

Caught between the rock of electronic media and the hard place of the magazine press, will the national daily press be able to resist this double competition? Yes, it will keep its readers and even attract new ones, if it shows imagination and adaptability. It must pursue the modernization of its production facilities, acquire a finer and more aggressive advertising strategy and, most important, it must enrich its editorial content. The daily will be able to survive and even prosper only if it exploits its unique specificity and originality: breadth of information, appeal to reflection, and involvement of the reader as active subject. A thirty-minute TV newscast represents an information mass of less than what appears on the front page of a newspaper! The daily paper's vocation, therefore, is a double one: investigation without compromise and deepening of information. As Giovannini, president of the Italian Newspaper Publishers Association, pointed out in his 1985 address, ''Despite the enormous time television steals from reading, it does not fulfill the need for information, thoughtfulness, commentary. I would even say that it stimulates it'' (quoted in *Médiaspouvoirs*, September 1987, p. 70). André Fontaine, an acute observer and director of *Le Monde*, brilliantly summarizes what is required to revive the daily press:

Le Monde knew how to reestablish for the public its image of a great independent and modern newspaper, which had weakened somewhat, we must admit, especially among its traditional readership of college students and executives. The investigation by our reporters of what has been called "the Greenpeace Affair" marked a turning point. Indeed, it brought a double demonstration: *Le Monde* owed no allegiance to the government in power, and the *Monde* reporters, far from being asleep, were at the forefront of the investigation, with a lively and independent journalism. Readers made no mistake about it. From this point dates the rise of our circulation numbers. Readers who were coming or returning to us found then a more accessible paper, better presented, more tuned to the news, and which over the following months was to offer them the proof of a constant renewal. In a year and a half, supplements as well as new columns were launched or restarted. The "crisis" has undoubtedly had a salutary effect. It has forced us to remember the fundamental factors that make a paper successful: a well-managed enterprise, a strong identity (the newspaper's soul), a permanent dynamic, including in the editorial content (*Médiaspouvoirs*, September 1987, p. 77).

The *Monde* example is typical of the national daily press in general. Papers are modernizing their format, developing and adding new features, creating thematic supplements. *Figaro Magazine, Madame Figaro, Figaro TV*, and *Figaro Madame* are the pacemakers for the self-same daily. *Le Parisien Libéré* (changed to *Le Parisien* in 1986), in addition to its national edition, covers with twelve local editions all the Greater Paris *départements*. Since March 3, 1989, *Libération* publishes on Fridays a special booklet devoted to Europe.

New Trends

Compared to other developed countries, such as Germany, Britain, or the United States, France has a press characterized by its low degree of concentration. Since the Liberation, legislators have sought to ensure press diversity by limiting concentration. Yet, today, worldwide media competition makes it imperative to foster powerful French conglomerates able to face this competition. It is essential to find a formula that allows concentration while preserving information diversity. These last few years we see the emergence of large press holding companies, themselves part of multimedia and multinational corporations. The largest of these French groups have, in different degrees, invested in electronic media in France and abroad. For instance, the Hersant group, which controls 35 percent of the regional press and 25 percent of the national daily press, has acquired the FUN radio station and controls, with the Italian Silvio Berlusconi, *la 5*, the French TV channel. Moreover, it has interests in foreign press companies, notably in Belgium, Spain, and the United States. The most dazzling example of this media thrust is Hachette's. Hachette is the most diversified and international holding company in France. With its purchase of the American firms of Diamandis and Grolier and, recently, of Spain's Salvat, Hachette now ranks fourth among the world's giant communication conglomerates. It does business in thirty-six countries, and half its turnover comes from abroad. It is the world's top seller of encyclopedias and publisher of magazines. It has succeeded in exporting several of the group's periodicals. *Elle*, in particular, has met a spectacular international success, being published in fourteen countries and thirteen languages, including Chinese. Alongside this French transplant abroad, the large European or American groups have interests in French media companies. In addition to Silvio Berlusconi, Bertelsmann, Maxwell, and Murdoch own interests in French print and electronic media. The English Pearson group paid $140 million to purchase *Les Échos*, although its circulation is no more than 70,000 copies.

The forthcoming United States of Europe will accelerate this synergy (a fashionable word) of the media, which know less and less the meaning of frontiers. On May 11, 1990, The Maxwell group, for instance, began publishing a European newspaper aptly titled *The European*!

The Feminine Press

The history of the feminine press reflects that of French society. It evolves beside society's democratization in general and women's improved status in particular. Since the right to vote in 1944, following the Liberation, women's emancipation has accelerated thanks to the combined effects of liberal legislation and changes in attitudes and mores. Today, women have gained access to economic and social sectors. In addition, they have become important consumers, and advertisers in all media are eagerly seeking their attention and money (in 1987, 10,376,000 women were employed, i.e., almost 46 percent of the female population aged 15 or older). The feminine press dominates, right after the TV press, the magazine press market.

From Its Birth to the End of the Second Empire

The feminine press goes back to the eighteenth century, although only one title remains of the first feminine periodical, *Le Courrier de la Nouveauté* (1758). A year later *Le Journal des Dames* was founded (1759–78). In the beginning exclusively devoted to literature, it then also discussed fashion. Several characteristics of the feminine press during this period emerged:

—On the one hand, the majority of women's journals were managed by men and had a strong literary, artistic, and fashion element. They printed a few thousand copies for a cultured and leisured elite of bourgeois and aristocratic women. Subjects were treated in a serious, moralizing tone. They conveyed women's traditional image and the sharing of social roles, playing therefore a socially conservative part.

—On the other hand, a feminist press, written and managed by committed women, close to the people, often former factory workers, demanded the emancipation of women and the recognition of their civil rights. It rose during great political upheavals (e.g., the revolutions of 1789, 1830, and 1848). But feminist papers could have a temporary existence only. Ahead of their time, they were suspect to those in power, who stifled them. Thus, *L'Athénée des Dames* and *La Gazette des Femmes* were forbidden to publish. Or, in order not to shock their female readers and to survive, they ended up by abandoning their militant attitude and so lost their raison d'être. This was the case for *Le Journal des Femmes* and *La Voix des Femmes*. Despite their ephemeral existence, however, the themes treated by the feminist periodicals would find their way into the rest of the feminine press. As Évelyne Sullerot has emphasized, there was during this period a progressive shift from the concept of *dame* (lady) to that of *femme* (woman) as the feminine press was developing and diversifying to reach a wider readership who had access to education and work.

The Feminine Press of the Third Republic

Under the Third Republic (1870–1940), the feminine press, like the rest of the press, greatly expanded. We analyzed above the causes for this expansion. In addition, women received then a series of civil rights, and as we saw, there is a direct relation between the feminine press's development and social gains. Directors of nonfeminine papers added feminine supplements to attract a wide female and popular clientele while the feminine press increased. Many women's magazines were created. Some, like *Le Petit Écho de la Mode* or *L'Écho des Françaises*, launched in 1878 and 1903 respectively, enjoyed a long and popular success, with impressive circulation figures. It was a practical press addressed to millions of wives, mothers, homemakers. Two magazines, founded on the eve of World War II, were to be much imitated. *Confidences*, inspired by the American *True Stories*, appeared in 1938 and inaugurated in France *la presse du coeur*. A year later, it reached a million copies. In 1939, Jean Prouvost, owner of the daily *Paris-Soir*, launched *Marie-Claire*, modeled after American women's magazines. It was an immediate success with 800,000 copies. The general lines of modern feminine press were drawn. Sullerot rightly comments in her book *La Presse féminine* that "when the war breaks out, it is interesting to note that the three components of contemporary feminine press already exist: (1) the practical, family-oriented, conservative magazine . . . : *Le Petit Écho de la Mode* and *Femmes d'aujourd'hui*; (2) the modern magazine, wide open to American influences: *Marie-Claire*; (3) the popular magazine of the *Confidences* type." To these three elements should be added a fourth—the feminine press that continues to militate for women's political and social equality. We can cite among these *La Fronde* (founded in 1897) which, besides its feminist demands, contained several columns, such as historical features, municipal council reports, reportages, even a stock market page.

Today's Feminine Press

Like the press in general, the feminine press was severely curtailed by World War II. But the aftermath saw a flowering of new women's magazines. *Marie-France* was founded as early as November 1944 and *Elle* in 1945: *Elle*, by the richness of its presentation and its constant innovation, would remain unequaled for many years. In 1954, *Marie-Claire* reappeared with full splendor. Next to this press, innovative and open to the world, the tradition-bound feminine press speaks first to mothers and housewives. *L'Écho de la Mode* and *Femmes d'au-*

jourd'hui continued to prosper. As for the *presse du coeur*, it knew a phenomenal success. *Confidences* reappeared in 1946 and was followed by numerous rivals. In 1947, Cino del Duca created *Nous Deux*; a year later he bought *Intimité*. It seems that the years following the war were the golden age of the feminine press. All kinds of women's magazines, from the avant-garde to the traditional, coexisted beautifully. However, starting in the late 1960s, the feminine press, like the other press sectors, would experience for a decade a wrenching crisis. Average feminine periodical sales fell by 20 percent, that is, a loss of some 2 million copies. No category, whether luxury or popular appeal magazines, was spared. We would have to wait until the late 1970s to notice an upturn. Luxury titles (*Elle, Marie-Claire*) became fresher and adapted to a new social climate. New titles, specialized according to life-styles, age, or socioprofessional groups, were successfully started and brought a new dynamism to the feminine press. Beginning in the 1970s, to list only a few, were born a French *Cosmopolitan* (1973), *Cent Idées* (1974), *Jacinthe* (1975), *Santé Magazine* (1976), *Vital*, and *Biba* (1980). *Le Figaro* launched in 1980 its supplement *Madame Figaro*, which found favor with the public and advertisers. These magazines, often inspired by American models, are targeted at well-to-do socioprofessional women who constitute, therefore, an attractive group for advertisers. But this dynamism could not prevent the popular press's inexorable erosion. A few statistics will suffice. *Femmes d'aujourd'hui*, despite two successive mergers, went, between 1970 and 1988, from more than 1.4 million copies to less than 450,000. In thirty years (1957–87) *Bonne Soirée* saw its circulation drop by half a million (from 709,000 to 214,000). As for the *presse du coeur*, it could only feel nostalgia for the time of million-plus printed runs. *Nous Deux* sold more than 1.6 million weekly copies in 1957, while thirty years later it had plummeted to 673,000. From 1973 to 1987, *Intimité* fell by more than one-half (from 811,600 to 355,400). *Confidences*, which in 1939 hit a million copies, was selling 250,000 in 1987 and has now gone out of business.

What are the causes of this free fall experienced by the popular feminine press generally and by the *presse du coeur* specifically? From the first, we must note that this fall is typical of the entire French popular press. We have already indicated the decline of great popular dailies like *France Soir* and *Le Parisien Libéré*. It is quite possible, at least in France, as we pointed out for daily newspapers, that a relation exists between educational progress, access to new responsibilities, rise in living standards, and a decline of the popular press. *Presse du coeur* readers, for example, are traditionally found in the most disadvantaged layers of society. We can think, then, that women's social and economic emancipation has brought about women readers' disaffection from popular periodicals. In addition, other factors have been put forth to explain the popular feminine press's decline. First and foremost, the development of several TV channels that telecast popular programs and the existence of new leisure activities have both taken away time needed to read popular magazines. The large increases in popular magazines prices, even if these remain the lowest, have also had an impact. To these external reasons can be added internal ones. While the luxury feminine press could adapt to social and technological changes and hence overcome the crisis, the popular press, especially the *presse du coeur*, had until very recently hardly evolved—in content and format. Finally, a reason that is perhaps paramount, since the press is at once a commercial and cultural product, is that advertisers continue to be uninterested in buying space in popular feminine reviews, and especially the *presse du coeur*. *Presse du coeur* advertising receipts amount to less than 10 percent of its turnover, when they are more than 50 percent for women's monthlies.

Nonetheless, this gloomy report of the popular feminine press could not hide the watershed of the 1980s, which saw the feminine press rebound, successfully start new titles, and even conquer foreign markets. With 10.7 million copies (1987), its market share in the magazine press is 24.2 percent, right behind the TV press (25.5 percent) and far ahead of general information weeklies (12.2 percent). Of magazines with more than 500,000 circulation, half are women's magazines. The feminine press is one of the advertisers' favorite media. In number of ad pages, it is first of the magazine press. What attracts advertisers is not so much a magazine's circulation as the socioprofessional makeup of its readership, hence their marked preference for luxury women's periodicals.

But the phenomenon that has undoubtedly contributed most to energize the feminine press was the creation in the 1980s of new popular feminine magazines which helped to carry it along. In 1982, Axel Ganz, manager of Prisma Presse, a subsidiary of the German company Grüner & Jahr, launched the monthly *Prima*. It met with spectacular success, which surprised the media world. Circulation went from an initial 500,000 to 1.4 million copies in two years. Three years of in-depth research had preceded its publication, which allowed for the systematic coverage of all possible interests of representative women from various socioprofessional groups. *Prima* is for the pragmatic woman who looks for practical information and concrete solutions to daily problems. Every issue presents a variety of subjects, handled seriously, fully, within the reach of all. Thus it offers the greatest chance of interesting a wide range of women readers. Following this success, Ganz started two years later (1984) the weekly *Femme Actuelle* which, with a different publication schedule, adopted the same approach as *Prima*. Its success too was immediate, stunning. In 1987, it published close to 2 million copies. Ganz has overturned the feminine press market. In five years, with only three feminine titles (the third, *Voici*, came out in 1987), his group Prisma Presse controls a third of the feminine press in France and has become its leading publisher. In the wake of *Prima* and *Femme Actuelle*'s extraordinary success, many magazines, imitating their contents, photojournalism, and writing styles, were founded. It is significant to note that these two magazines have attracted women readers who did not read (or no longer read) the popular press. What needs perhaps to be remembered most about Axel Ganz's success is that his titles reconciled the high-circulation popular press with requirements of quality. Moreover, he has waged a merciless quality/price battle.

An issue of *Femme Actuelle* costs 5.50F, just over half the price of *Elle* and even less than *presse du coeur* weeklies (6.50F). He was able to find a formula that could fulfill the tastes and interests of the French feminine public. His new feminine magazines represent a relay of the traditional popular press.

These last few years, the popular press seemed to gain a second wind following Ganz's arrival on the scene. Even the *presse du coeur*, considered the most resistant to change, has reacted. Éditions Mondiales, under the impetus of Monique Pivot, the dynamic managing editor of *Nous Deux* and *Intimité*, has injected new blood into these two titles. The layout has been modernized, four-color printing introduced, the number of pages increased, and contents improved. *Nous Deux*, as well as *Intimité* (*Nouvel Intimité* beginning with No. 2271 of May 18, 1989), publishes photonovels, short stories, and serialized novels, written by well-known authors. Numerous taboos are gone. Whereas the former remains mostly a reading magazine for couples (always pictured on the cover), the latter is both a reading and a women's magazine (reading matter covers about half the editorial space and feminine features the other half), designed essentially for women (always on the cover). The popular feminine press is faced by this dilemma: if it does not evolve, it will perish; if it evolves too rapidly, it may alienate a hard core of women readers displeased by abrupt changes. As Monique Pivot underlines, "Important risks were taken when we modernized our two titles, for our popular readership is more sensitive than any other to changes" (in *Médias*, February 20, 1987). No one, of course, believes any longer that this press can regain its prewar circulation figures, but Madame Pivot's first objective is to brake the sales erosion of the last few years. She still has to convince advertisers, always reticent to invest in the *presse du coeur*.

Despite its diversity, what makes the specificity of the feminine press? Whatever the target, no women's magazines can completely eliminate its traditional features on fashion, beauty, health, knitting/sewing, horoscope, recipes, women's concerns and issues, even if the emphasis can vary greatly from one publication to another. As M.-C. Cosse points out, "The specific function of a women's magazine, compared to radio and television, lies in the practical advice it gives. . . . It is perceived as an entertainment medium but, actually, it is considered above all as a practical guide giving useful information" (quoted in Bonvoisin and Magnien). Studies have shown that, whatever their readership, women's magazines fulfill three main roles: "guide," "companion," or "someone from around here." More than any other, they bring an effective closeness.

The feminine press has come out of the crisis of the seventies. It has shown its capacity to adapt and innovate. It has followed its female readers' evolution and succeeded in attracting a male audience, since 20 percent of its readers are men! It has thwarted the pessimistic previsions regarding its future:

—The fantastic success of a new popular press, which has propelled the entire feminine press, has contradicted those who doomed it to an irreversible decline.

—The nonfeminine periodical press, which, through its many feminine features and columns opened up to women readers, did not bring about their dis-affection for the feminine press.

—In four years (1981–85), forty-one feminine titles were launched. From 1980 to 1987, the feminine press has increased its circulation by 27.4 percent. Since then, the trend continues.

In spite of risky circumstances, the feminine press has proved its deep roots in French society.

RESEARCH AND INFORMATION SOURCES

Press history has in itself become a highly fertile academic field. Press studies centers and research institutes, the considerable publication of monographs, specialized periodicals, congresses, exhibitions devoted to the subject point this out. Among the hundreds of works created by the Bicentennial of the French Revolution, many were devoted to the press, since 1989 also marks the bicentennial of press freedom.

REFERENCE WORKS

Histoire générale de la presse française (Paris: Presses Universitaires de France, 1969–76). This monumental work of historical and bibliographical reference, edited by Claude Bellanger, Jacques Godechot, Pierre Guiral, and Fernand Terrou, covers in five thick volumes the French press from its origins to 1976.

Each volume includes name and title indexes (dailies and periodicals) that are quite complete, plus 24 plates explained and discussed. The 119 pages of bibliography are impressive. (Volume 5 presents a bibliographical supplement to the preceding volumes.) Covering all areas, this bibliography indicates sources of archives and national and departmental newspaper collections; lists books and articles on press legislation, technical evolution, enterprises, the history of the Paris and provincial press, particular newspapers, contemporaneous witness accounts by writers and journalists, political, social, and literary movements, the clandestine press, and the French press abroad. It also gives a list of specialized directories, periodicals, and professional organizations. In addition, Volume 5's appendix provides a list of Ministers of Information from 1944 to 1975 and a table of French dailies with their 1975 circulation figures. In summary, this is an indispensable instrument for any press study.

Nevertheless, this work, however thorough, should not eclipse that by Eugène Hatin, the pioneer of press history. His fundamental work is *Histoire politique et littéraire de la presse en France*, in eight volumes (Paris: Poulet-Malassis, 1859–61; reprinted, Geneva: Slatkine, 1967). Another useful study by Hatin is *Bibliographie historique et critique de la presse française* (Paris: Didot, 1866), which contains an historical essay on the periodical, followed by a catalogue of all periodical writings, from the origins to 1865, with detailed critical and historical notes. It also reprints newspaper excerpts, and at the end there is a table of the Paris press in 1865.

Bibliographie de la presse française politique et d'information générale (Paris: Bibliothèque Nationale, 1964–). A series of departmental pamphlets, each lists periodicals, with an historical preface, in the most exhaustive manner. Periodicals are classified alphabetically with detailed notices on their frequency, place of publication, format, and owning library. Pamphlets, published between 1964 and 1979, do not mention papers before 1865. The collection is being completed, and therefore there are departments missing.

Catalogue collectif des périodiques du début du XVIIe siècle à 1939, conservés dans les Bibliothèques de Paris et dans les Bibliothèques Universitaires des Départements (Bibliothèque Nationale, 1967–81; 5 volumes). Listing alphabetically about 75,000 French and foreign periodical publications stored at the B.N. and seventy other important libraries in France, this catalogue gives very precise descriptions of periodicals, especially their history and their holders. However, it excludes dailies published after 1848. It is to be supplemented as follows:

1. For the prerevolutionary period by the work realized by the Centre de recherches sur les sensibilités (University of Grenoble 3) directed by Jean Sgard, notably:

• *Bibliographie de la presse classique (1600–1789)* (Geneva: Slatkine, 1984). With 1,138 titles, it is to date the most complete inventory of the classical press, and

• *Dictionnaire des journalistes (1600–1789)* (Grenoble: Presses Universitaires de Grenoble, 1976; Suppl., 1980–87). Furthermore, this Centre has been preparing for several years a *Dictionnaire des journaux (1600–1789)*.

2. For the revolutionary period:

• Pierre Retat, *Les Journaux de 1789. Bibliographie critique* (Paris: CNRS, 1988);

• Claude Labrosse and Pierre Retat, *Naissance du journal révolutionnaire* (Lyon: Presses Universitaires de Lyon, 1989); and Jean-Paul Bertaud, *Les Amis du roi. Journaux et journalistes en France de 1789 à 1792* (Paris: Perrin, 1984).

La Bibliographie de la France (Paris: Cercle de la Librairie) devotes its Supplement I (twelve issues a year and an annual microfiche index) to serial publications received by the B.N.'s copyright registration office (*dépôt légal*). Thus, all new titles are itemized. Also, by consulting the subject index (press, mass media, information), one can find all new works published about the press.

Répertoire de la presse et des publications périodiques françaises, 2 vols., 6th ed. (Paris: Bibliothèque Nationale, 1981). This repertory lists, with descriptive notices, 20,400 current periodicals from January 1977 to March 1978. It was realized from Supplement I just mentioned, with the additional advantage of not only being cumulative but of listing periodicals no longer published during the period from October 1, 1965, to December 31, 1976. Besides this *Répertoire, La Presse française. Guide général méthodique et alphabétique* (Paris: Hachette, 1965 and 1967) should also be mentioned.

World List of Social Science Periodicals/Liste mondiale des périodiques spécialisés dans les sciences sociales, 7th ed. (Paris: Presses de l'Unesco, 1986). This list mentions 268 titles of French periodicals (with descriptive notices).

International Bibliography of the Social Sciences. Annual. Prepared on behalf of UNESCO (London: Routledge). It lists, under the Press rubric, important books and articles about the press, many published in France.

Bulletin analytique de documentation politique, économique et sociale contemporaine. Monthly with an annual index (Paris: Presses de la Fondation des sciences sociales). In 1988, it listed 4,932 articles published in 2,431 periodicals (in France and abroad). It peruses the large French dailies and periodicals. Among the latter the following important periodicals dealing with media should be noted: *Médias, Médiaspouvoirs*, and *L'Écho de la Presse et de la Publicité*.

Bibliographie annuelle de l'histoire de France du Ve siècle à 1958 published since 1953 (Paris: CNRS). The 1987 issue contained 13,025 entries from monographs and periodicals of which 1.8 percent (i.e., more than 200) were about printing and the press. A total of 2,105 periodicals (1,350 French and 755 foreign) were perused.

Bulletin signalétique du CNRS. Trimonthly. While it covers several disciplines, the sociology pamphlets are most relevant for the press. At the end of the year, a supplement, titled *Tables annuelles*, recapitulates indexes of authors, concepts, and periodicals analyzed during the year. *Le Bulletin de sociologie* for 1988 had 4,699 entries from books and periodicals, of which 272 concerned the sociology of communication and mass media.

Livres Hebdo (Paris: Éditions professionnelles du livre). This weekly periodical contains bibliographical notices of new publications in France. A section is devoted to works and periodicals about publishing, the press, and audiovisual. As its title indicates, *Livres Hebdo* is the most timely bibliographical guide.

L'Information dans le monde: 206 pays au microscope, edited by Observatoire de l'information (Paris: Seuil, 1989). This is the best and most up-to-date guide to the state of information in the world. In just a few pages (212–19), the section devoted to France offers an excellent overview of French media. Regarding the press, the guide lists general information dailies and periodicals, their circulation, owners, and slants; it examines journalist status and working conditions as well as relations between the press and the state and the juridical system regulating the press.

Guide de la Presse. Annual (Paris: Office Universitaire de la Presse). In the 1989 guide, eighty-five experts (journalists, professors, researchers, writers) chose 1,000 titles from among journals, newspapers, and magazines published in the world and analyzed them.

Ulrich's International Periodicals Directory. A classified guide to current periodicals, foreign and domestic (New York: Bowker, 1932–). Updating between annual editions is provided by *Ulrich's Quarterly*.

Union List of Serials in Libraries of the United States and Canada, ed. Edna Brown Titus, 5 vols. (New York: H. W. Wilson, 1965). Supplemented by *New Serials Titles*, published by the Library of Congress.

French Periodical Index. Annual (but not always on schedule). Comp. Jean-Pierre Ponchie (Westwood, Mass.: Faxon, 1973–date). Each volume draws up the index of some ten French periodicals according to thirty-odd categories arranged alphabetically, from Business and Economy to Travel and Vacation.

Journal des journaux, published monthly by the Press Department of the Centre International d'Études Pédagogiques in Sèvres, edited by Marie-José Leroy and Richard Nahmias. This excellent tool, by far the best of its type, lists hundreds of newspaper and magazine articles, indexed thematically; it tells of new publications, circulations, and suspensions; it reprints short articles, pictures, caricatures, tables, graphs, and even covers. In addition, each issue contains a very good in-depth report on a particular topic (e.g., New Caledonia, 1989 municipal elections, French songs, the press). Finally, copies of articles chosen from the index can be ordered at small cost.

Annuaire de la Presse, de la Publicité et de la Communication (Paris: Écran Publicité). Annual since 1879. The most complete directory of the press currently published in France, it is divided into seven parts, plus an index: (1) Professional organizations and list of journalists; (2) Press agencies; (3) Paris and provincial press; (4) Press by departments; (5) Foreign papers represented in France; (6) Advertising agencies; (7) Suppliers.

Média Sid published by the Prime Minister's Information and Distribution Service (Paris: La Documentation française). Annual. This directory is a reduced version of the one mentioned above, but its pocket-size format and moderate price make it a practical and handy tool.

DATABASES

BIPA (Banque d'Information et d'Actualité) is published by Chadwyck-Healey France. This database of current affairs in France indexes articles in the French press, presidential and ministerial statements, and official communiqués. It also contains a bibliography of French official publications and the full text of communiqués of the Council of Ministers, presidential statements, abstracts of ministerial statements, and chronology of events since 1981. Concerning the press, since 1981, *BIPA* peruses a dozen national dailies and some fifty periodicals. Tens of thousands of references are entered according to 4,000 alphabetical keywords, with four trimestrial updates a year. *BIPA* lists only political information and, therefore, leaves aside the arts and literature, sports and leisure, and so on.

CD-Rom Myriade developed by Jouve-Systèmes d'Information and the French

Ministry for Research and Higher Education, lists references for 425,000 periodical titles (extinct or current), published in the world, of which 185,000 are available in 2,600 French libraries and documentation centers. Moreover, for each title, *Myriade* provides the list of libraries and centers that own it along with the collection's status.

ANTHOLOGIES, SERIES, AND REPRINTS

Les Médias et l'Événement, published by Documentation Française. Each monograph of the series is devoted to an important event of political or cultural history as seen through the press of the time. In two parts, it includes newspaper reproductions in their original format on the day the event was front-page news, and a sizable sample of press texts and illustrations of the time, discussed and explained. A dozen monographs have been published: *Le 8 mai 1945; Le 13 mai 1958; Hiroshima: la bombe; La Bataille de l'avortement; Mai 68*, to name a few. The wealth and availability of materials (difficult to obtain otherwise, except in specialized research centers), plus its low price, make this series an incomparable tool.

Histoire de France à travers les journaux du temps passé (Montreuil: L'Arbre Verdoyant). Nine monographs are out (1976–1989), among which *La Révolution française (1789–1799); De Napoléon III à l'Affaire Dreyfus (1851–1898); La Quatrième République (1945–1958)*. As the series title indicates, the press provides the materials and framework for history.

Journaux du temps passé. Les Grandes Dates de l'histoire à travers 85 journaux d'époque, presented by André Rossel (Paris: Les Yeux ouverts, 1965). Eighty-five great dates are discussed, each through a newspaper issue of the time reproduced in facsimile in the original format. The issues cover three centuries, from Renaudot's *Gazette* (1631) to *Défense de la France* (1941), an underground paper.

Revue des Journaux du Temps Passé, a trimestrial journal founded and edited by André Rossel, published by Histoiremédia. Each number is in two parts: historical articles and columns; and facsimile reproductions of entire old papers. The first number came out in April 1989 and comprised, besides articles, sixteen papers published in 1789, completely reproduced in their actual format.

SPECIALIZED PERIODICALS

La Correspondance de la presse, a daily information bulletin.

L'Écho de la presse (supersedes *L'Écho de la presse et de la publicité*), a weekly.

Médias, a weekly.

Médiaspouvoirs (supersedes *Presse-Actualité*), a trimestrial publication.

Stratégies, a weekly.

These periodicals publish, among other things, a considerable amount of information on the press. They are indispensable for any study of today's press.

BIBLIOGRAPHY

The bibliography of press history is enormous. We saw that *Histoire générale de la presse* contained a 119-page bibliography that stopped in 1976. Below is a list of recent works, mostly published after 1976, that is far from exhaustive. Many of the books cited here have themselves useful bibliographies.

Adler, Laure. *À l'aube du féminisme: les premières journalistes (1830–1850)*. Paris: Payot, 1979.

Agnès, Jean, and Serryn, Dominique. *La Presse des jeunes*. Paris: Syros-Alternatives, 1988.

Agnès, Yves, and Croissandeau, Jean-Michel. *Lire le journal*. Paris: Lobies-Le Monde, 1979.

Albert, Pierre. *La France, les États-Unis et leurs presses*. Paris: Centre Pompidou, 1977.

———. *Histoire de la presse politique nationale (1871–1879)*. 2 vols. Paris: H. Champion, 1980.

———. *La Presse française*. Paris: La Documentation française, 1983.

———. *Journalisme et documentation. les banques de données en France*. Paris: Godefroy, 1984.

———. *La Presse*. 8th ed. Paris: Presses Universitaires de France, 1988.

Albert, Pierre, ed. *Lexique de la presse écrite*. Paris: Dalloz, 1989.

Albert, Pierre, and Terrou, Fernand. *Histoire de la presse*, 5th ed. Paris: Presses Universitaires de France, 1988.

Archambault, François, and Lemoine, Jean-François. *4 milliards de journaux*. Paris: Moreau, 1974.

Assouline, Pierre. *Albert Londres: vie et mort d'un grand reporter*. Paris: Balland, 1988.

Balle, Francis. "Les Formes de la communication. De l'échange confidentiel à la communication de masse." In *Communications* 13 (1987), No. 1.

———. *Et si la presse n'existait pas*. Paris: Lattès, 1987.

———. *Médias et société*. 4th ed. Paris: Montchrétien, 1988.

Balle, Francis, ed. *Le Pouvoir des médias: mélanges offerts à Jean Cazeneuve*. Paris: Presses Universitaires de France, 1987.

Balle, Francis, and Rogers, Everett M., eds. *The Media Revolution in America and in Western Europe*. Norwood, N.J.: Ablex, 1985.

Bailly, Christian. *Théophraste Renaudot*. Paris: Pré-aux-Clercs, 1987.

Bellanger, Claude, et al., eds. *Histoire générale de la presse française*. Paris: Presses Universitaires de France, 1969–76.

Bonvoisin, Samara-Martine, and Maignien, Michèle. *La Presse féminine*. Paris: Presses Universitaires de France, 1986.

Bots, Hans, ed. *La Diffusion et la lecture des journaux de langue française sous l'Ancien Régime*. Amsterdam: Holland University Press, 1988.

Brault, Patrick. *La Presse en Europe*. Paris: DAFSA, 1980.

Brochier, Jean-Christophe. *La Presse écrite*. Paris: Hatier, 1984.

Cavé, Françoise. *L'Espoir et la consolation. Idéologie de la famille dans la presse du coeur*. Paris: Payot, 1987.

Cayrol, Roland. *La Presse écrite et audiovisuelle*. Paris: Presses Universitaires de France, 1973.

Cazeneuve, Jean, ed. *Les Communications de masse: guide alphabétique*. Paris: Denoël-Gonthier, 1976.

Censer, Jack R. *Prelude to Power. The Parisian Radical Press. 1789–1791*. Baltimore: Johns Hopkins University Press, 1976.

Censer, Jack R., and Popkin, Jeremy D. *Press and Politics in Pre-Revolutionary France*. Berkeley: University of California Press, 1987.

Chabrol, Claude. *Le Récit féminin: Contribution à l'analyse du courrier du coeur dans la presse féminine actuelle*. The Hague: Mouton, 1971.

Chollet, Roland. *Balzac journaliste*. Paris: Klincksieck, 1983.

Cluzel, Jean. *Un projet pour la presse*. Paris: Librairie générale de droit et de jurisprudence, 1986.

Cosse, Marie-Claire. *La Presse féminine aux États-Unis et en Europe occidentale*. Paris: La Documentation française, 1969.

Courcelle-Labrousse, Sylvie, and Robinet, Philippe. *Paris et enjeux de la presse de demain*. Grenoble: Presses Universitaires de Grenoble, 1987.

Dardigna, Anne-Marie. *Femmes-femmes sur papier glacé*. Paris: Maspero, 1974.

———. *La Presse féminine: fonction idéologique*. Paris: Maspero, 1978.

Darnton, Robert, and Roche, Daniel, eds. *Revolution in Print: The Press in France*. Berkeley: University of California Press, 1989.

Daudu, Yves. *Les Français à la une*. Paris: La Découverte, 1987.

Delcros, Bertrand, and Vodan, Bianca. *La Liberté de communication. Loi du 30 septembre 1986. Analyse et commentaire*. Paris: La Documentation française, 1987.

Desbarats, Bruno S. *Les Chances de l'écrit face à l'audiovisuel*. Paris: Régie-Presse, 1987.

Dupuis, Micheline. *"Le Petit Parisien": le plus fort tirage des journaux du monde entier*. Paris: Plon, 1989.

Dutourd, Jean. *Ça bouge dans le prêt à porter. Traité du journalisme*. Paris: Flammarion, 1989.

Elyada, Ouzi, ed. *"Lettres bougrement patriotiques de la Mère Duchêne" suivi du "Journal des Femmes."* Paris: Éditions de Paris, 1989. Reprints two feminist newspapers published in 1791.

Faucher, André, and Jacquemard, André. *Le Quatrième Pouvoir, la presse en France de 1830 à 1960*. Paris: Éditions de l'Écho de la Presse et de la Publicité, 1968.

Feyel, Gilles. *La "Gazette" en Province à travers ses réimpressions, 1631–1752*. Amsterdam: Holland University Press, 1982.

Flammant-Paparatti, Danielle. *Bien-pensantes, cocodettes et bas-bleus: la femme bourgeoise à travers la presse féminine et familiale*. Paris: Denoël, 1984.

Fourment, Alain. *Histoire de la presse des jeunes et des journaux d'enfants*. Paris: Éole, 1987.

Gaillard, Philippe. *Technique du journalisme*. Paris: Presses Universitaires de France, 1985.

Gerbner, George, and Siefert, Marsha. *World Communications, A Handbook*. London: Longman, 1984.

Giet, Sylvette. "20 ans d'amour en couverture." In *Actes de la recherche en sciences sociales*, November 1985.

Goldring, Maurice, and Quilès, Yvonne. *Sous le marteau, la plume: la presse communiste en crise*. Paris: Mégrelis, 1982.

Guéry, Louis. *Quotidiens régionaux: les connaître, les utiliser à l'école*. Paris: Centre de formation et de perfectionnnement des journalistes, 1988.

Guéry, Louis; Spirlet, Jean-Pierre; and Vautravers, Constant. *Quotidien régional, mon journal*. Paris: CFPJ-ARPEJ, 1987.

Guide des sources d'information. Paris: CFPJ, 1988.

Guillauma, Yves. *La Presse en France*. Paris: La Découverte, 1988.

Guillou, Bernard. *Les Stratégies multimédias des groupes de communication*. Paris: La Documentation française, 1983.

Jamet, Michel. *La Presse périodique en France*. Paris: Colin, 1983.

Jeanneney, Jean-Noël, and Julliard, Jacques. *"Le Monde" de Beuve-Méry*. Paris: Seuil, 1979.

Jouet, Josiane. *La Communication au quotidien*. Paris: La Documentation française, 1986.

Laisné, Pascal. *La Femme et ses images*. Paris: Stock, 1974.

Lavoinne, Yves. *La Presse*. Paris: Larousse, 1976.

Lepigeon, Jean-Louis, and Wolton, Dominique. *L'Information demain: de la presse écrite aux nouveaux médias*. Paris: La Documentation française, 1979.

Léri, Jean-Marc. *La Presse à Paris (1851–1881)*. Paris: Bibliothèque historique de la Ville de Paris, 1983.

Les 40 ans de "Paris-Match." Paris: Chêne, 1987.

Leteinturier, Christine, and Toussaint, Nadine. *Évolution de la concentration dans l'industrie de la presse en France*. Brussels: Commission des Communautés européennes, 1978.

Leteinturier, Christine, and Tallon, Brigitte. *Communication et médias: guide des sources et ressources*. Paris: Institut Français de Presse et Carrefour International de la Communication, 1985.

Li, Dzeh-Djen. *La Presse féminine en France de 1869 à 1914*. Paris: Rodstein, 1934.

Mabileau, Alain, and Tudesq, André-Jean. *L'Information locale*. Paris: Pedone, 1980.

Mariet, François. "La Presse telle que la connaissent et l'ignorent les étudiants en français aux États-Unis." *The French Review* 59 (December 1985).

Mathien, Michel. *La Presse quotidienne régionale*. Paris: Presses Universitaires de France, 1986.

La Médiaklatura. Paris: Les Documents du *Nouvel Observateur*, 1988.

Mouillaud, Maurice, and Tétu, Jean-François. *Le Journal quotidien*. Lyon: Presses Universitaires de Lyon, 1989.

Noël, Bernard. *Portrait du "Monde."* Paris: POL, 1988.

Palmer, Michael. *Des petits journaux aux grandes agences. Naissance du journalisme moderne*. Paris: Aubier, 1983.

Pinto, Louis. *L'Intelligence en action: "Le Nouvel Observateur."* Paris: Métailié/Presses Universitaires de France, 1984.

La Presse aujourd'hui. Paris: CFPJ, 1988.

Rémond, René, ed. *Cent ans d'histoire de "La Croix."* Paris: Centurion, 1988.

Retat, Pierre, ed. *Le Journalisme d'Ancien Régime*. Lyon: Presses Universitaires de Lyon, 1982.

Retat, Pierre, and Sgard, Jean, eds. *Presse et histoire au XVIIIe siècle: l'année 1734*. Paris: CNRS, 1978.

Retat, Pierre, and Labrosse, Claude, eds. *L'Instrument périodique: la fonction de la presse au XVIIIe siècle*. Lyon: Presses Universitaires de Lyon, 1985.

Rolland, Guy. *Quoi lire*. Paris: Instant, 1988.

Roth, Françoise, and Siritzky, Serge. *Le Roman de "L'Express."* Paris: Julian/Hachette, 1979.

Roux, Bernard. *Chauds les médias! Et la presse écrite?*. Lille: Trimédia, 1985.

Santini, André. *L'Aide de l'État à la presse*. Paris: Presses Universitaires de France, 1966.

Schwoebel, Jean. *La Presse, le pouvoir et l'argent*. Paris: Seuil, 1968.

Seguin, Jean-Pierre. *Nouvelles à sensation, canards du XIXe siècle*. Paris: Colin, 1959.

Servan-Schreiber, Jean-Louis. *Le Pouvoir d'informer*. Paris: Laffont, 1972.

Sgard, Jean, ed. *La Presse provinciale au XVIIIe siècle*. Grenoble: Presses Universitaires de Grenoble, 1983.

———. *Histoire de France à travers les journaux du temps passé. Lumières et lueurs du XVIIIe siècle, 1715–1789*. Paris: Colin, 1987.

Sullerot, Évelyne. *La Presse féminine*. 2d ed. Paris: Colin, 1966.

———. *Histoire de la presse féminine en France, des origines à 1848*. Paris: Colin, 1966.

Terrou, Fernand. *L'Information*. 6th ed. Paris: Presses Universitaires de France, 1983.

Thibault, Danièle. *Explorer le journal*. Paris: Hatier, 1986.

Toussaint-Desmoulins, Nadine. *L'Économie des médias*. Paris: Presses Universitaires de France, 1987.

Tucoo-Chala, Suzanne. *Charles-Joseph Panckoucke & la librairie française*. Pau: Marrimpouey, 1977.

Van Dijk, Suzanna. *Traces de femmes; présence féminine dans le journalisme du XVIIIe siècle*. Amsterdam: Holland University Press, 1988.

Voutley, Maurice. *La Presse clandestine sous l'Occupation hitlérienne, 1940–1944*. Dijon: CRPD, 1986.

Voyenne, Bernard. *Le Droit à l'information*. Paris: Aubier, 1970.

———. *La Presse dans la société contemporaine*. Paris: Colin, 1979.

———. *L'Information aujourd'hui*. Paris: Colin, 1979.

———. *Les Journalistes français*. Paris: CFPJ-Retz, 1985.

Wedell, George, ed. *Mass Communication in Western Europe: An Annotated Bibliography*. Manchester: The European Institute for the Media, 1985.

World Communications: A 200-Country Survey of Press, Radio, Television and Film. Paris: Unesco Press, 1975.

World Press Encyclopedia. New York: Facts on File, 1982. One chapter on France (pp. 341–60) with one-page bibliography.

Translated by Pierre L. Horn

10

Popular Music

ANDRÉ J. M. PRÉVOS

When the French speak of *musique populaire*—a word-for-word translation of the English "popular music"—they do not mean what English-speaking people call "popular music." For the French, *musique populaire* is primarily what is known in English as "folk music"—that is, the music of the people—and it is only recently that, among the younger segments of the French population, the expression *musique populaire* has come to mean what is known as "popular music" in English—that is to say, a music whose "popularity" has become too important to go unnoticed. Consequently, I will use the term *musique populaire* as an equivalent to the English "folk music" and reserve the term *musique pop* as the equivalent for "popular music." The major reason for this remark has to do with the great difficulty found in attempting to separate the histories of the two types of music in contemporary France.

As for folk music and classical music, both types of music have existed in France for a long time and they have often shared themes or rhythms. Such was the case when classical composers took "peasant" dances as their inspiration for their own classical compositions. It is also true that some French folk songs were adaptations or borrowings from the classical repertoire of former times. Consequently, I will mention a few cases when the relations between classical and folk music have been too close to be ignored.

HISTORICAL OUTLINE

It is not the purpose of this brief outline to dwell upon the several theories about the origin of song or its anteriority or posteriority to the advent of instrumental music or dancing. For some specialists (Wiora), instrumental music and dance preceded song; for some others, more religiously minded, song was either the representation of the creator—according to several African mythological tales—or its manifestation; according to Buddhism, the first gods came out of Brahma's mouth. Finally, according to Lucretius, man must have first imitated the sound of birds before producing anything resembling song. These abstract elaborations are of little help here. The only infallible way of dating the beginning of song is the finding of a document including both a text and a musical accompaniment—or at least a suggestion of such an accompaniment. As early as the ninth century A.D., French documents indicate that some passages were to be sung—or at least "vocalized."

The first French songs which originated within the boundaries of present-day France were written in the southern language of the Middle Ages—the *langue d'oc*—and were composed by troubadours (Davenson). The troubadour's task was the composition of new songs. These composers found musical references in religious melodies, while they found their textual inspiration in the world around them: they spoke of crusades (as early as 1137), they wrote satirical songs, they made up songs upon the death of a famous person, they often composed songs about nature—from the rising of the sun to the coming of springtime—but they remain most famous for their songs of courtly love (Boutière and Schutz, Charles-Dominique and Lasseube). By the end of the thirteenth century, the troubadours' influence had reached the Loire River and progressively spread to northern and eastern provinces.

The *trouvères*—the northern equivalents of the troubadours—continued in the same tradition while expanding it. They still sang about the crusades, nature, powerful nobles, but they also innovated. They created *chansons de toile*—narrative songs about love—satirical narrations, or bacchic songs. But they gained fame for inventing fixed-form songs such as the rondeau, where all the songs follow a similar pattern and rhythmic organization. The *trouvères* thus brought back dance songs in the world of the nobility and the bourgeoisie (Rosenberg). The itinerant jugglers and *goliards* represented a much less sophisticated group of musicians; the *goliards* were in fact known primarily for their bawdy songs (Jeanroy and Langfors) which are sometimes seen as predecessors of the Rabelaisian style—as the original *carmina burana* illustrate (Laforte).

Only a few examples of the songs of the troubadours, *trouvères*, jugglers, and *goliards* have survived. They were most often in handwritten collections or in other manuscripts (Raynaud). The tradition of song collecting began early in France, and by the fifteenth century it had become firmly established. Among the significant manuscript collections that have been identified, several give a good understanding of the roles of provincial groups or schools. These not only adapted what they heard coming from Paris or from the courts, but also managed to create styles of their own (Miller). Such was the case with the songs found in the Bayeux manuscript: they have been attributed to the Val-de-Vire school— the name at the origin of the term "vaudeville" (Chardavoine, Gasté, Vernillat and Charpentreau).

Gutenberg's influence was soon felt not only in the literary but also in the musical world. If the manuscripts provide a precious documentation, they did not serve as efficient means of diffusion of the songs they contained. This became possible only after the invention of the printing press. Thus, new anthologies appeared, but unfortunately few melodies were actually printed. Instead, the name of a song or melody was mentioned—"to be sung to the tune of . . ."—as if the reader had been expected to know the tune indicated (Chailley). The technique remained in use for many decades, until the early twentieth century, primarily with popular broadsides. The Renaissance also marked the identification of a truly French tradition with the publication, in 1528, of the famous collection gathered by Pierre Attaignant. One of the consequences of this publication, besides its documentary value, was the emergence of what came to be known as the "Parisian song," as opposed to a large number of other French songs composed by Flemish artists at the court of Burgundy. The Parisian song makes a larger use of popular forms, is simpler than the older fixed forms, and deals more with epicurean topics than its predecessors (Pirro). In addition, the sixteenth century witnessed the "discovery" of the poets by song-makers: until that time, song-makers used anonymous texts. Orlandus Lassus used a poem by Villon, Jeannequin by Marot, Du Bellay, Ronsard. This collaboration between poets and musicians led to a consolidation of the French style. These songs were for sophisticated listeners and members of the court. Unfortunately, their polyphonic arrangements often required a musical background too extensive for most of the royal entourage. Thus was created the *air de cour*—that is, a song where the predominance of the singer becomes evident and where musical accompaniment may be reduced to a single instrument, such as a lute. The advantage of these airs was that they could be performed by small groups.

The Parisian song and the *air de cour* still remained primarily for the upper classes, leaving the lower classes with their own songs. Some of these *chansons populaires* and folk songs found their way into the collections published during the Renaissance. The *musique populaire* of the period included the folk songs and tunes of the different regions of France and also songs issued from the tradition of the itinerant singers. In Paris there was a strong tradition of satirical songs: professional song-makers could invent new words to existing tunes and used their craft to criticize the ongoing political events. These broadsides were then printed or collected in cheap pamphlets and could rapidly be disseminated over a large area beyond the capital by itinerant peddlers. Other popular forms derived from the *goliard* tradition: street singers, men or women, who entertained passers-by on squares, street corners, or at fairs.

By the early eighteenth century the French literary song tradition revived through the creation of the *caveau* movement. The movement originated as a gathering of artists or intellectuals who met to sing their creations (Raunié). The Revolution slowed the *caveau*'s activities, but it continued well into the last century. The *caveau* movement, owing to the publication of its members' compositions, gave a new impetus to the French literary song (Coligny). Later on, in the twentieth century, the *caveau* would be adopted by popular entertainers who sang their compositions in front of audiences in small rooms. The eighteenth century also witnessed the rebirth of the romance, a long-neglected form dating back to the Middle Ages. Composers became specialists in the romance field and a booming business developed thanks to the growing popularity of these songs (Gougelot). The romance further evolved in the nineteenth century, and some classical composers made use of poems by poets of their times. As years went by, the delineation between the popular romance and the *mélodies* composed by classical artists such as Berlioz, Gounod, or Frank became clearer and each style developed within its own environment (Meister).

The Revolutionary years were marked by the emergence of the political song (Brécy), and by a burgeoning of revolutionary hymns—many of minor importance (Coy). With the 1989 celebration of the Bicentennial of the French Revolution came the publication of several works dealing with the songs of the period, whether books on the French national anthem (Luxardo) or on the songs popular between 1787 and 1799 (Marty), including a well-documented collection of Revolutionary songs and melodies (Brécy). As events progressed, songs reflected the hardening of popular attitudes and became symbols sung by each group. This tradition was curtailed under Napoleon, who tolerated popular songs so long as they did not criticize him. The only avenue left to singers of critical political songs was to find refuge among other less evidently political groups. Such a place was the *goguettes*. These were singing groups created early in the nineteenth century, whose members needed to pay only a small fee to be allowed to sing their own works. One of the most famous artists to emerge out of this tradition was Émile Debreaux, who, surprisingly, advocated a curtailing of the *goguettes'* political activities (Cim).

The nineteenth century was also marked by the "discovery" of folk songs and of *musique populaire* by the Romantics. These artists—among them Chateaubriand, Nerval, George Sand—led a movement in favor of the folkloric heritage of the French provinces by featuring folksongs in their works (Guichard). The French public also "discovered" these songs, and they became immensely popular. This renewed interest sparked movements in several directions. In 1852, Fortoul, the Minister of Public Education, decided to launch an official effort to collect as many of these folk songs as could be gathered (Fulcher). Unfortunately, these documents were never published (they may be consulted at the Bibliothèque Nationale). But a great many collections were published by various authors, from true folklorists (Hersart de la Villemarqué, Weckerlin, de Coussemaker) to amateurs, from musicians who transcribed exactly what they heard (Vincent d'Indy) to others who wrote "adaptations for the piano" of some folk tunes (Morpain) or songs with new words to fit the new music (Bourgraud-Ducoudray).

The last decades of the nineteenth century may also be viewed as the beginning of the modern era of popular entertainment in France: the *goguettes* were ordered closed by the government of Napoleon III and were replaced by the café-concert. The tradition of the café-concert was not new; it had started in the 1770s, when café owners decided to invite dancers, singers, and acrobats, who used to perform outside, to perform now inside their establishments. By the mid-nineteenth century, the café-concert had found its definitive style and become one of the most popular forms of popular entertainment. These establishments flourished in Paris and also in large provincial cities. A consequence of their popularity was the creation of what may be termed the first "popular idols"—that is, artists whose fame made them greater than life in the minds of large numbers of French people. Such were Paulus, Thérésa, Félix Mayol, or Béranger. The songs they performed ranged from romances to nonsensical songs and from the sentimental to the pseudo-patriotic—primarily between 1870 and 1914—and to "naturalist" songs in the tradition of Aristide Bruant.

The café-concert was progressively taken over by another tradition adopted from England: the music-hall. The major difference between the café-concert and the music-hall was that, in the first case, patrons were sitting at a table and drinking while watching the acts, and in the second case, patrons were in a hall for the show and could order neither drink nor food. If, at first, both types of entertainment had similar programs, the music-halls became progressively more extravagant in their presentations and more geared toward dazzling the audience (Jacques Charles). The decades between 1870 and 1910 were marked by the continued decline of the café-concert and the corresponding growth of the music-hall (Feschotte). By the early 1920s the music-hall was the only popular form of entertainment left in France. Mistinguett and Maurice Chevalier—two of the most famous stars of the early twentieth century—began their long careers in the café-concert, then moved on to the music-hall, and when the music-hall yielded to the popularity of the movie house, they turned to film and became movie stars. Today only a few music-halls remain in Paris—the Olympia and Bobino are the best-known—and they must compete with records, radio, and television in their quest for spectators.

Parallel to the development of the café-concert and music-hall ran a popular form which perpetuated—in a somewhat different way, to be sure—the tradition of the *goguette* and the *caveau*: the *chansonnier* tradition. The word *chansonnier* meaning "song-maker" used to characterize the members of these older singing groups. It took on an added meaning after the creation of artistic cabarets in the Montmartre district of Paris and came to represent a singer whose acerbic songs were often irreverent or funny, exhibiting a definite lack of respect for hypocritical Establishment leaders and government officials (Fursy, Herbert). The cabarets often catered to a given type of customers: some were known to feature satirists, others featured romantic singers, still others featured entertainers noted for their humor (Ziwes).

The 1920s were characterized by the sudden popularity of the cinema, and the 1930s saw the growth of radio. These means of diffusion greatly helped the development of popular music by allowing most of the population to hear the same popular songs at the same time. They also allowed the widespread diffusion of newer styles both in France and from abroad—America in particular. Afro-American jazz had appeared in France in the last year of World War I and had taken the country by storm. The popularity of Josephine Baker—paralleled by a keen interest in African art among painters and sculptors—reinforced the impact of Afro-American music in France. Jazz suddenly became the latest craze and was found in the productions of French songwriters, like Jean Nohain and Mireille and Charles Trénet, as well as in the works of dance orchestras whose leaders adopted the new rhythms, like Ray Ventura and Jacques Hélian.

This invasion of American rhythms, however, did not signal the end of the more traditional French productions. The French "realist" singers had continued the tradition of Aristide Bruant during the early decades of the twentieth century. If Damia and Fréhel sang about hardships and poverty—often because they had endured both themselves—they were soon replaced by an artist whose fame would endure from the 1930s until today: Édith Piaf (Berteaut, Dureau, Grimault, Lange, Larue, Piaf).

During the Occupation Parisian cabarets and music-halls did not stop their activities; they simply catered to the Germans and to those Frenchmen who collaborated with them. French radio stations were allowed to broadcast French songs—under strict German control, of course. Some performers were forced to flee the country; others decided to quit performing during these years; others decided to continue performing for the German troops. When the country was finally liberated, all the forms of entertainment popular before 1940 took on a new life. The French popular tradition was given a new impetus with the arrival of Yves Montand and Francis Lemarque; jazz continued its evolution—Raymond Legrand's orchestra and Stéphane Grappelli provide a good illustration—and also influenced French artists such as Aznavour and Bécaud, as had been the case earlier. A new breed of French artists emerged during the postwar years. They were composers who sang their own works accompanying themselves on the guitar or the piano—hence their appellation of *auteurs-compositeurs-interprètes*. Most of them would remain at the forefront of the French popular song movement for decades to come, such as Georges Brassens, Jacques Brel, Guy Béart, Léo Ferré. The postwar years also mark the return of the literary song tradition, primarily in the Saint-German district of Paris, where the new intellectuals and artists used to gather in cabarets (Juliette Gréco has become the symbolic figure of this period).

The year 1958 marked the beginning of the French Fifth Republic; it also marked the end of the postwar period and the beginning of a deep change within French society. These changes affected popular music and, in turn, were reflected by its development in France. The first transformation influenced the means of diffusion of the songs. The recording industry gained in importance, and records became a significant means of diffusion, as were radio and, most important, television. New recording techniques gave the artists greater freedom, for they were no longer hampered by the three-minute limit of the old 78 rpm record;

they could use improved recording facilities and splice together parts of their songs to obtain the best version of a recording. These improvements also led to the growing role of technicians, who were removed from the artistic realm and shifted to the technical aspect of recording. The producer was still playing a role, though to a lesser extent. Records became both means of diffusion and elements of mass consumption.

Several consequences emerged. The first was the creation of so-called idols, that is, singers adored by throngs of admirers ready to buy all the records, magazines, and items related to their favorite(s); the growth of merchandizing was a parallel consequence; the development of a specialized press as well as the creation of fan clubs also characterized this new era. Unfortunately for some of these artists, the admiring throngs were fickle and could forget them as rapidly as they had lionized them. The early 1960s in France were also marked by the invasion of American and English artists, primarily rock-and-roll and rock artists. It has been mentioned that jazz had been discovered early in the century in France, and its followers had founded clubs and societies. The postwar years had been marked by a renewed popularity of the newer jazz styles coming from America. But by the early sixties, rock-and-roll gained a foothold in France and its followers were very different from jazz enthusiasts. French artists quickly associated with the rock-and-roll wave and gained great fame. Their wild behavior often attracted criticism from many observers who considered the new music as too "wild" or extravagant. Some of these singers who emerged in the early sixties and reached almost instant stardom have remained at the forefront of the French popular music scene of the past decades. Such is the case for Johnny Hallyday, Sylvie Vartan, Françoise Hardy, or Eddy Mitchell. Claude François, too, was one of them until his untimely death in the early 1980s. Other idols were more clearly within the French singing tradition—France Gall, Mireille Mathieu—while others continued their careers as *auteurs-compositeurs-interprètes*, like Brassens and Brel, groups such as the Compagnons de la Chanson or new artists in the traditional mold such as Pierre Bachelet.

The movement begun in the 1960s continued in the seventies and even in the eighties: the progressive overpowering of the French production by American productions is clear to anyone who listens to French radio or watches French television. More than half the songs played on radio stations are American songs in their original form, while French productions are strongly influenced by American pop music. That was the case with rock-and-roll but also with the folk-song movement issued from the American folk revival of the early 1960s: Hugues Aufray adapted American folksongs and sang them in French; others updated or gave a new life to traditional French ballads or folksongs—Guy Béart, Serge Kerval. Still others used the new popularity of American protest songs to record their own compositions or older French songs—Jean Ferrat, Colette Magny, Graeme Allwright. Some of the "idols" were deeply within the French tradition, like Mireille Mathieu, who continued Édith Piaf's tradition. Other artists may be credited with the creation of a newer tradition in the 1970s: Renaud's songs mix French slang with images drawn from French and American popular culture and have acquired a wide following in France. Other similar performers are Jean-Jacques Goldman, Charlélie Couture, or Jean Guidoni. Some popular performers adapted an Anglo-American style into their own repertoire and gave birth to French pop-rock music: such was the case with Trust or Téléphone. Finally immigrants from Africa are leaving their mark on French popular music: the North African group "Carte de Séjour" or West African artists like the Touré brothers.

During these decades the growth of the recording industry, the merchandising concerns, and the mass media continued to influence the development of popular music in France. Television helped both launch and renew artistic careers; record sales became one of the most common measures of success; a specialized press took on an increasingly noticeable role; publishers did not hesitate to commercialize autobiographies or biographies of the newer artists—the collection "Poésie et Chansons" of Éditions Seghers is just one example. New commercial radio stations, established in the early eighties, allowed for a whole gamut of musical tastes: some of these FM stations are specialized in new pop sounds (for instance, "NRJ"); others pride themselves on playing a majority of French songs from the past decades ("Radio Nostalgie" and "Radio Montmartre").

Today all these diverse traditions coexist: from the older French folksongs to the newest French realist or romantic songs, from the most traditional jazz and blues tradition to the latest free-form jazz styles or even bluegrass, from the old songs of the French provinces to the most recent politically minded songs. This situation is not particular to France and is also found in other West European countries. It is more and more difficult to find a clear-cut way to isolate French popular music from the international—and primarily English-speaking—popular music tradition. The case of French efforts in favor of Ethiopian relief in the mid–1980s (Prévos) shows that French performers may no longer be seen as typically French but, instead, may have just become performers who happen to speak French.

GUIDE TO THE LITERATURE

Background Works

There are studies of French popular music, both of *musique populaire* and *musique pop*. They range from anthologies to regional samplers in the first group and from biographies to sociological studies in the second. Collections of French folksongs such as Decaunes's *Les Riches Heures de la chanson française* and Davenson's *Le Livre des chansons* sample the country's folk production. In their introductions the compilers emphasize the origins and features of *musique populaire*. They contrast theories of folk creation, favored by the Romantics among others, with those giving a significant role to borrowings from classical music and to the diffusion of sophisticated forms into the popular strata of society, because the higher classes did not totally isolate themselves from the lower classes. In addition, the role of priests, who link the upper and lower strata of society and are agents in the diffusion of religious music, should not be neglected by those who see French *musique populaire* as just borrowings and adaptations of tunes and rhythms from classical music. Other works relate the evolution of French popular songs to the historical evolution of the country, for example, Barbier and Vernillat's *Histoire de France par les chansons*, accompanied by a four-record set. For Doncieux, on the other hand, each French folk song may be considered as a variation of an original song whose *ur*-form should be exhumed from all the variants available. Such a theory may lead to oversights owing to the fact that not all the variants may have been collected and, also, that some classical melodies may not be easily identified as originators of some popular songs.

The majority of collections of French popular songs are organized according to their author's preferences and vary in length, focus, and completeness: Jean-Édel Berthier's collection includes 1,000 songs; Botrel's focuses on Breton and Norman songs, Champfleury and Weckerlin offer a regional sampler; S. Charpentreau considers five centuries of songs from Ronsard to Brassens; Decitre's collections include both traditional songs and dances; Dillaz focuses on protest songs between 1871 and 1968; Lagrée deals with songs favored by young adults; Sabatier includes a selection of songs without any defined focus; Saka and Boisseau attempt an historical distribution of their collection, while Sevran's dictionary focuses on contemporary French and francophone artists.

Other collections are more restricted in content or time. Brécy's compilation includes revolutionary songs covering the years between 1789 and 1871; Brunschwig, Calvet, and Klein have songs between the 1870s and the present; Alexandre presents soldier songs of World War I; Blanchard focuses on popular songs and the *naïf* movement; Boukay presents leftist songs; the *Bréviaire du carabin* is a compilation of medical students' bawdy songs; Canteloube-Ferrieu's work deals with poetry and songs from the 1930s to the 1960s with a focus on Trénet, Brassens, Ferré and their relations to the surrealist movement; Carreau and Pinchard's collection is slanted toward songs of social criticism; Charles-Dominique and Lasseube's catalogue focuses on the history of popular music in and around Toulouse over the past centuries.

A significant number of traditional songs from France were gathered by regional specialists during the nineteenth century. This regional movement continues today, and when no new collections were undertaken, older works were reprinted. Here is just a sample of such collections covering most French provinces and regions: Arbaud for Provence; Arnaudin for the Bordeaux region; Barbillat and Touraine for Berry; Garneret and Culot, Buchon, and Beauquier for Franche-Comté; Brachet and Plantadis for Limousin; Morpain, Manot, and Bujeaud for Poitou, Saintonge, and Angoumois; Delzangles and Canteloube for Auvergne; Casse and Chaminade for Périgord; Rouquette, Conte, Caujolle, and Cécile for Occitania; Chepfer for Lorraine; Chevais for the Loire Valley; Sepieter,

Desrousseaux, and de Coussemaker for French Flanders; Delrieux for the Mediterranean coast; Tarbe, Desvignes for Champagne; Emmanuel, Duchon for Burgundy; Durieux and Bruyelles for Cambrésis; Mirat, Gaston-Phébus for Béarn; Vassal, Quellien, Ollivier, Orain, Morand, Malrieu, Luzel, Hamon, and Hersart de la Villemarqué for Brittany; Lambert, Montel for Languedoc; Le Veaux, Piraud, and Redhon for the Mayenne region; Ortoli, Marcaggi for Corsica; Millien for Morvan; Moullé for Normandy; Pelen for the Cévennes; Poplineau and Dehaye for the Ardennes; Poueigh for the French Pyrenees; Puymaigre for the Metz area; Sallaberry for the Basque country; Servettaz for Savoy; Weckerlin, Siffer for Alsace; Stramoy for Nivernais; Tiersot for the French Alps; Trébucq for Vendée.

General studies of more recent developments in French popular songs include studies dealing with the 1960s and the so-called *yéyé* years (Barsamian and Jouffa, Hubel, Torgue, Vincent), articles in specialized magazines introducing the various French groups (the 1977 "Spécial France" issue of *Rock & Folk*, Victor and Régoli), or particular artists, from punk musicians (Birch, Hebdige) to immigrant and métis popular groups (Moreira, Pinguet) to popular music associations (Chapuis).

Theoretical and General Approaches

Specialists have focused on the repertoires of older composers and have attempted analyses of their works following several lines of inquiry. Congleton undertakes a linguistic analysis of thirty-nine texts of Josquin des Prez's *chansons*. Dottin presents the diversity of French songs in the Renaissance period. In his work, Bellugou analyzes the words of songs from 1610 to 1774 found in several manuscripts at the Bibliothèque Nationale and sees them as indexes of the political, social, and personal life of the period. Troubadour works and biographies have been listed in Boutière and Schutz, and the republication of older manuscripts is due to Bordier's efforts.

The diffusion of folk and popular songs had often been hinted at but rarely studied in detail. In his essay, Brech presents the history and reconstructs the text of two songs from the 1870–71 Paris Commune transmitted by oral tradition. In her dissertation, Béraud-Williams offers a semantic and musical analysis of 158 folksongs from the Ardèche *département*. Schenda analyzes the diffusion of folk and popular songs about General Boulanger between 1887 and 1889 in Provence and shows how they participated in the huge upsurge of enthusiasm in his favor. In turn, Chaveau focuses on the use of dialects and its resulting popular image in French folk songs. Debrie details discovery of one unpublished Picard song whose text was found in the Archives Départementales de la Somme, thus giving hope to other researchers who might think that the field of folk music may never again yield useful items. Gergely considers the historical aspects of French folk songs; Friedman analyzes their contents to find what traditional French society thought about love, sex, and marriage. Staub focuses in turn on obscene and bawdy songs. Fribourg considers the role of traditional songs in one area of Brittany. As for Moroz, she focuses on the conscript folk songs, both from the linguistic and sociological standpoints, while Vingtrinier offers an overview of soldiers' songs between the Revolution and the beginning of this century.

A good overall analysis of the history of folk-song collecting in the nineteenth and twentieth centuries is provided by Cheyronnaud. In his work, he details the successive steps of the 1852–57 inquiry ordered by Fortoul and then focuses on the successive steps in folklore collecting and publishing. The latter decades of the nineteenth century saw the creation of the first official bodies responsible for collecting and presenting folklore. During the first decades of the twentieth century, ethnology finally became a university discipline in France and the creation of a Museum of Popular Arts and Traditions finally gave a basis and a popular respectability to the movement. Today the only remaining question, says Cheyronnaud, is whether ethnomusicology can assert itself within a field of study of the anthropology of modern societies. Labelle broaches a similar topic in his article about folklore research and diffusion in France.

In 1989, France celebrated the bicentennial of the Revolution, and it was natural that works about Revolutionary songs would appear for this occasion. But that same year also marked the 150th anniversary of the publication of the *Barzaz-Breiz* by Hersart de la Villemarqué. In his study, Gourvil details the origins, successive editions, sources, various critiques made following its publication, and the influences which marked its author.

There are no easily available works introducing or analyzing the musical developments of the early twentieth century; instead, the new starting point for popular music histories is the post-World War II years. Halimi's study of the music scene—mostly in Paris—during the German occupation indicates that popular entertainment did not completely disappear during those dark years but, instead, led a muffled and closely watched existence.

The book by Leproux, a history of "Golf Drouot," one of the most famous bars and rock-and-roll dance halls of Paris in the late fifties and sixties, is an historical document that offers some sociological insights about these young idols who suddenly gained incredible fame. There are only few works specifically dealing with French rock-and-roll, but it may be assumed that sociological analyses of the phenomenon focusing on sex, drugs, and their associated subcultures apply to France also: Brake's approach and Hebdige's analysis are cases in point.

The evolution of show business is often mentioned in the biographies of individual performers, but few authors have approached the topic in depth. Tenaille's history of show business is an overview, while Bertin offers a description of the deals which may be presented to the aspiring artist. Daeubert describes his own life as an employee of the Barclay Company, while Barclay himself offers the view from the producer's and company owner's side. *L'Officiel du rock 1988* is not so much an historical study as it is a complete guide to all rock-and-roll-related items to be found in France. Demorgon's dissertation introduces the use of the computer in the analysis of contemporary popular hits in terms of the parameters used by students of mass communication. His 1974 study focuses only on the 1946–66 decade but provides the researcher with an interesting methodology.

Ideological studies of French songs have often been vague and general, but Mathis' work on the influence of existentialism in French songs is sharply focused and helps to better understand the interrelations between philosophy and popular songs during the Saint-Germain-des-Près era. Stellberg, on the other hand, examines Georges Brassens' songs and their listeners in order to offer artistic and ideological insights. As for *Le Mouvement pop*, it is an attempt at defining the pop art movement in music and features an interesting interview with Umberto Eco. Torgue's history of pop music also includes a musical and sociological analysis of pop music between 1960 and 1974. Toesca, Conrath, and Kolpa-Kopoul's *Guide du tube* is both historically useful—because it offers a listing of 1,000 hits between 1950 and 1987—and a good indicator of the evolution of popular music during these years. It also vividly illustrates the growing role of Anglo-American popular music in France as one reads the hit titles for each of the successive years.

Sociological studies focus on various aspects of the relationship between popular music, its performers, and the world they live in. Silberman analyzes the changes brought by radio and how the development of radio modified both what was heard and who heard it. Panafieu studies the same phenomenon. As for Vie and Barets, they focus on the image rock performers offer their audience, their "look," without which many would not have gained the popularity they enjoy. For Voyer, rock music is nothing without what surrounds it, at the personal and social level, hence the title of his study which could be translated as "Rock and Role." Hennion offers what he calls an "anti-musicology" of the pop song in his analysis of successful hits. Beaud offers an analysis of the various pop music subcultures in the 1970s. Halimi provides French examples of relationships between show business and politics: from artists singing in favor of their political friends to others singing for noble causes. In his dissertation, Hornig writes on the popular songs of the sixties, their composers, and how they expressed their criticism of the society in which they lived. In his article, Jordania discusses Boris Vian and sees the contemporary *chanson de variétés* as a musical and social phenomenon.

Finally, several studies deal with original or unexpected uses of folk and popular songs in various fields. Popular songs may be used by educators as well as many other professionals for different reasons. Simon offers a collection of anecdotal songs for children. Gudin shows how to use popular songs in speech therapy by having students re-create what they hear or imitate the artists they hear. (She sees this as a more effective technique than simple oral exercises.) Hermelin indicates records that can be used for group discussions on topics like scapegoats, death, the body.

OTHER SOURCES ON THE HISTORY OF FRENCH POPULAR MUSIC

The reader should consider the preceding sections as a component of a source list on the history of French popular music, and this section as a complement to these listings.

Discographies of French popular productions are rare, but there nevertheless exists a discography of French rock-and-roll (Grosse and Gueffier). A listing of movies including rock performances may also help the researcher of French popular music (Lacombe).

In this section I have chosen to focus instead on the works written about the artists themselves, since often, even in the past century, the artists were better known than the composers and writers of the songs they popularized.

One of the earliest "idols" was Thérésa, who sang during the second half of the nineteenth century. She was one of the most popular performers of the time, even though most of her repertoire was made up of ditties. Her biography indicates some of the characteristics found in today's idols: adulation, opposition between public and private sentimental life. It ends on a positive note since she managed to save enough money to live a quiet but happy retirement (Blanche).

Charles Trénet's artistic career spans several eras, from the music-hall to the jazz-influenced popular songs. He is now considered a performer whose contributions to popular music have been remarkable (Beauvallet, Pérez, Trénet). Maurice Chevalier's career also spanned several eras, but, in addition, he came to personalize the cool and self-controlled Frenchman for many Americans (Colin, Sabatès). Édith Piaf's life was as glamorous and, simultaneously, as wretched as the lives of the characters in her songs (Grimault and Mahé) about whom she sang in tormented accents. She was one of the few French artists to enjoy fame and popularity in the United States (Berteaut, Costaz, Dureau, Larue, Vassal). Yves Montand's career spans several decades; he gained fame not only as a singer but as a film actor as well (Cannavo and Quiquère, Lanèque and Gallot, Monserrat, Rouchy, Saiah). Luis Mariano was known as a singer of romantic songs and for the quality of his voice; he was perceived as a seducer and admired by scores of women (Chardan). Tino Rossi, a native of Corsica, first known as a singer of ballads, became extremely famous for his interpretations of traditional French Christmas songs (Plume and Pasquini, Trimbach).

Aznavour's autobiography and his book of remembrances present his private hardships as well as his artistic successes. The life of Jacques Brel is presented in books written by the companion who shared the last decade of his life (Bamy) and by others (Petit, Arban, and Barlatier; Todd). Georges Brassens' artistic songs, renowned both for their poetry and for their underlying bawdiness and trenchant criticism, made him one of the major *auteurs-compositeurs-interprètes* of the postwar years and into the 1970s (Berruer, Charpentreau, Larue, Tillien).

Enrico Macias illustrates an early case of the immigrant singer—from North

Africa—who became popular for the artistry of his songs, while retaining an unmistakable ethnic identity (Macias, Monestier). The 1960s saw the emergence of French rock-inspired artists who soon gained widespread fame. Such was Eddy Mitchell (Bénichou, Mitchell, Page, Pelletier). Johnny Hallyday also became famous as a rock-inspired performer; he still is very popular both among those who listened to him some twenty years ago and among those who could be the children of his original listeners (Chris Long, Rossi, Yonnet). Claude François personalized the so-called *yéyé* artist; he managed to hold on to his popular success until his accidental death (*Claude François . . . , Cloclo . . . ,* Floriant). Petula Clark was an English artist whose French songs—sung with an attractive accent—made her a popular singer during the 1960s (Kon). Serge Lama's career is an example of a performer based in the French tradition (Barthélémy). Duteil's lyrics also belong in the same tradition (Duteil). Mireille Mathieu became famous when she began singing in the style of the great Édith Piaf and became, in the minds of many, her artistic heir (Mathieu, Page). Alain Sardou is a singer in the French tradition, also inspired by contemporary society; moreover, he is known as one of the few to belong to a family where father and son are popular singers—each in his own style (Sardou).

Magma was a group deeply rooted in jazz, whose music was a combination of jazz and other popular forms (De Caunes). Gilbert Montagné, a blind artist, was often nicknamed the ''French Ray Charles'' both because of his fondness for rhythm-and-blues and for his sightlessness—the title of his autobiography is a rather blunt pun (Montagné). Michel Delpech's history and some of his lyrics are also rooted in the French tradition of popular entertainment (Beauvallet). Jean Guidoni's repertoire includes poetic songs associated with a strong mystical element; his stage persona also reflects these preoccupations (Godard). Renaud's career began in the mid–1970s, and since then he has remained among the most popular French singers. His songs, mixing vernacular and slang, present true-to-life situations most likely to be experienced by members of the lower classes; his heroes are in fact antiheroes. He has become accepted by a very large section of the French public at large (Lefèvre, Renaud, Séchan). Jean-Jacques Goldman began singing in English and progressively forged his own style. He is also one of the most appreciated French popular singers, often linked with Renaud in the public's mind as an example of the new French popular singer (Page and Varrod). Hubert-Félix Thiefaine's lyrics, often hermetic and full of puns, represent one aspect of the new popular song (Bigot); he is also associated with Charlélie Couture, who has produced the majority of his records. Couture's style and artistic persona are also hermetic at times (Soulé). Chantal Goya's career took a turn for the better when she decided to devote herself exclusively to children's songs (*Chantal Goya . . .*). Mylène Farmer, a newcomer, has gained popularity for the openly sexual (both heterosexual and homosexual) innuendos found in the lyrics of her songs (Milo).

Jean-Michel Jarre has a style all his own. Known for his musical shows, such as the musical extravaganza he organized in Houston, Texas, in the summer of

1986, he organized a "musical show" for the bicentennial of the French Revolution (Remilleux). So does Claude Nougaro, well known for his dedication and active use of jazz and Afro-American music in his own compositions (Laborde).

RESEARCH COLLECTIONS AND CENTERS

In Paris, there are three major locations to be considered by the researcher of French popular music. The Bibliothèque Nationale offers several types of relevant documents. The book collection may now be consulted through terminals installed in the main building. This greatly helps the reader who may use several key words while searching for a given book. Manuscripts may also be consulted at the Bibliothèque Nationale—for example, the manuscript reports of the 1852 Fortoul effort—but they are more likely to interest the scholar of medieval or older songs found in still unpublished handwritten collections. The Bibliothèque Nationale also houses collections of periodicals. The music section will undoubtedly be even more interesting to the scholar of French popular music, with its collections of books, manuscripts, and musical scores. The music section also includes an almost complete repository of recorded materials—from old cylinders to micro-groove records—since every phonographic recording produced in France must have a copy deposited in the collection. These recordings are easily available. Another collection includes audiovisual documents, and some of these may be of interest as well.

The second location is the Musée des Arts et Traditions Populaires, where a section is devoted to folk songs and to studies about French folk music. The library offers books on French folklore—not only folk music—and the musical section houses field recordings made by folklorists in the various provinces. Owing to the fact that these collections are part of the folklife museum, they include little having to do with French popular music besides folk music, folk songs, and folk instruments. The Musée also houses—temporarily—a collection of tapes donated by radio stations in order to serve as the starting point for a museum of French popular music (mentioned below).

The third location is the public library section of the Musée National d'Art Moderne et Contemporain, better known as the Pompidou Center. American researchers will appreciate the fact that, unlike in the two previous locations, they have direct access to the stacks—books, records, videotapes, and magazines—housed in the library. Here, too, the collections may be searched from a terminal and the use of key words allows for a faster selection and helps determine whether the desired item is available or not. Access to the collections of the Pompidou Center is free and open to anyone, while the Bibliothèque Nationale and the Musée des Arts et Traditions Populaires require proof of the researcher's need to consult the collections.

Temporary exhibition catalogues may also offer interesting materials, such as the one devoted to the 1950s held at the Pompidou Center between June and October 1988.

The archives of radio and television stations may yield specialized data, but access to these may be restricted or forbidden to the researcher. However, some radio programs are available on cassettes, for example, "Radioscopie," a popular talk-show on public radio hosted by Jacques Chancel, who often interviews singers and musicians. These "Radio France Cassettes" may be ordered from Radio France (116 avenue du Président-Kennedy, 75786 Paris Cedex 16).

Future researchers in the field of French popular music will soon have two more locations at their disposal. The Musée Charles Cros will be devoted to the history of sound recording, and its collections may include examples of popular music. The second location will be the Musée de la Chanson Populaire Française, which will be an extension of the collection already housed at the Musée des Arts et Traditions Populaires. The exact location of the museums has not yet been determined, but one hopes that, by the end of 1990, it will be possible to obtain information about collections, operation, and the possibilities offered to researchers. Finally in 1989, Bruno Lion was appointed *chargé de mission* (undersecretary) *pour le rock et les variétés* by Jack Lang, the French Culture Minister. This may be seen as encouraging to French popular music, since it is now recognized to be an important component of both French popular culture and the French economy.

POSSIBILITIES FOR FURTHER RESEARCH

French popular music has been studied for many years and the following bibliography is very brief and incomplete. (Compiling such a bibliography would require several thick volumes.)

There is a need for an easily accessible bibliography or bibliographies of French popular music. There exist already some troubadour biographies, dictionaries of popular performers, numerous collections of French folk songs, and many biographies of individual performers. Unfortunately, it is not easy to discover a particular work or a list of works related to a given topic in the available bibliographical resources such as the RILM (Répertoire International de Littérature Musicale) abstracts database or the Modern Language Association International Bibliography. The need for bibliographical studies is always felt and would be helpful to researchers and students alike.

Historical studies of French popular music abound, but many of these are more anecdotal than historical. Efforts in the direction of historical studies have been noted here, but one hopes that newer and more exhaustive histories will appear. In addition, it should become evident that there is a very uneven historical coverage of French popular music. The early centuries, until 1900, appear to have been well covered, but one is at a loss to find detailed historical studies for the first three decades of the twentieth century, for which there is a glaring absence of works dealing with the history, sociology, and diffusion of French popular music in France.

The world of music publishing, music production, or music distribution is little known in France, and I have not been able to find books or articles similar to those published in the United States, which explain how to earn a living through songwriting or by becoming a studio musician, how to get a composition published, or royalties paid. Such publications would give a better understanding of the French popular music world and its workings.

In addition, I have been able to find only one study (Duverney and d'Horrer) that uses documents of the SACEM (Société des Auteurs, Compositeurs et Éditeurs de Musique). The SACEM centralizes all copyrighted songs and helps redistribute royalties and residuals to lyricists and composers. It remains an excellent though untapped source for the business of French popular music.

Finally, more biographical studies of French performers will undoubtedly come out and will add to our already large store of biographical information.

BIBLIOGRAPHY

Adelman, Anouk. *Chansons à vendre*. Paris: Cujas, 1967.

"Airs de cour, galants et à boire." Disque Calliope, No. CA 18190.

Akai France. *Guide Akai du disque: jazz, blues, pop, rock*. Paris: Editions No. 1, 1985.

Alexandre, André. *Chansons pour les poilus: septembre 1914–octobre 1915*. Paris: Librairie Berger-Levrault, n.d.

"Allons Enfants! Le Jour de Rock Est Arrivé!" *The Washington Post*, April 8, 1990, G1 and G5.

Amade, Louis. *"Et ce sera ta passion de vivre." Amade raconte Bécaud*. Paris: Hachette/ RTL, 1982.

"Amusons–Amusette. Chansons et comptines enfantines." Disque UPCOOP–03.

Antoine. *1965, roman*. Paris: Arthaud-Flammarion, 1987.

Arbaud, Damasse. *Chants populaires de la Provence*. Aix-en-Provence: Makaire, 1862.

Arnaudin, Félix, *Chants populaires de la Grande Lande et des régions voisines. II*. Bordeaux: Groupement des Amis de Félix Arnaudin, 1970.

Association la Sponte. *Chansons de France*. Rosny-sous-Bois: La Sponte, 1979.

Aznavour, Charles. *Aznavour by Aznavour: An Autobiography*. Translated by Ghislaine Boulanger. Chicago: Cowles, 1972.

———. *Yesterday When I Was Young*. London: Allen, 1979.

Bamy, Maddly. *Pour le jour qui revient*. Corcelle-le-Jorat, Switzerland: Yvan Peyret, 1988.

———. *"Tu leur diras" (Propos de Jacques Brel)*. Seyssinet-Parisot: Éditions du Gésivaudant, 1982.

Barbier, Pierre, and Vernillat, France. *Histoire de France par les chansons*. 8 vols. Paris: Gallimard, 1956–61.

———. "L'Histoire de France par la chanson." Four-record set. Chant du Monde, No. CAL 74461–4.

Barbillat, Émile, and Touraine, Laurian. *Chansons populaires du Bas Berry*. 5 vols. Paris: Éditions du Gargaillou, 1930–31.

Barclay, Eddie. *Que la fête continue*. Paris: Laffont, 1988.

Barsamian, Jacques, and Jouffa, François. *L'Âge d'or du yéyé: le rock, le twist et la variété française des années soixante*. Paris: Ramsay, 1983.

———. *L'Âge d'or de la pop music*. Paris: Ramsay, 1982.

Barthélémy, Cécile. *Serge Lama*. Paris: Seghers, 1981.

Beare, W. *Latin Verse and European Song*. London: Methuen, 1958.

Beaud, Paul. "Musical Sub-Cultures in France. Latest Investigations into the Position Held by Sub-Cultures within Cultural Life." 212–218, in *New Patterns of Musician Behavior. Communications presented to the International Symposium, Vienna, 1972. Organized by the International Institute for Music, Dance, and Theatre in the Audio-Visual Media*. Edited by Irmgard Bontinck. Vienna: Universal Edition, 1974.

Beaud, Paul, and Willener, Alfred. *Musique et vie quotidienne. Essai de sociologie d'une nouvelle culture*. Paris: Mame, 1973.

Beauquier, Charles. *Chansons populaires recueillies en Franche-Comté*. 1894. Reprint. Marseilles: Laffitte, 1977.

Beauvallet, Geneviève. *Michel Delpech*. Collection "Poèmes et Chansons." Paris: Seghers, 1988.

———. *Trénet*. Paris: Bréa Editions, 1983.

Beck, Jean. *La Musique des troubadours*. 1910. Reprint. Geneva: Slatkine, 1976.

Bellugou, Henri. *Chansons inédites du temps des trois Louis. La Vie politique, sociale, amoureuse au Grand Siècle et au siècle des Lumières*. Angers: Henri Bellugou, 1974.

Bénichou, Pierre Jean-Baptiste. *Eddy Mitchell*. Paris: P.A.C., 1977.

Béraud-Williams, Sylvette. "La Chanson populaire de tradition orale du Pays des Boutières en Ardèche, région de Saint-Sauveur-de-Montagut." Dissertation, Université d'Aix-Marseille I, 1980.

Berruer, Pierre. *Georges Brassens: la marguerite et le chrysanthème*. Paris: Presses de la Cité, 1981.

Berteaut, Simone. *Piaf*. Translated by Ghislaine Boulanger. Harmondsworth, England: Penguin, 1973.

Berthier, Jean-Édel. *1000 chants: paroles et musique choisis par Jean-Édel Berthier*. 2 vols. Paris: Presses d'Île de France, 1974–75.

Bertin, Jacques. *Chante toujours, tu m'intéresses, ou les combines du show-biz*. Paris: Seuil, 1981.

Bigot, Pascale. *Hubert-Félix Thiefaine*. Collection "Poèmes et Chansons." Paris: Seghers, 1988.

Birch, Ian. "La Vie en Pose. Street Heat: France." *Melody Maker*, May 6, 1978, pp. 20, 22, 29.

Blanchard, Roger. *La Chanson traditionnelle et les naïfs*, Paris: Arts et Industrie/Vilo, 1942.

Blanche, Jacqueline. *Thérésa: 1837–1913, la première idole de la chanson française*. La Fresnaye-sur-Chédant: J. Blanche, 1981.

Blin, Émile. *Chansons du Morvan*. Château-Chinon: E. Boulle, 1925.

Bordier, Henri-Léonard. *Le Chansonnier huguenot du XVIe siècle*. 1870–71. Reprint. Geneva: Slatkine, 1971.

Botrel, Théodore. *Chansons de chez nous*. Paris: G. Oudet, 1898.

————. *Chansons des clochers à jours, suivies de chansons en marge*. Paris: Éditions Fortin, 1946.

Boukay, Maurice. *Chansons rouges*. Paris: Flammarion, 1896.

Bourgraud-Ducoudray, L. A. *Mélodies populaires de Basse Bretagne recueillies et harmonisées, avec une traduction française en vers adaptée à la musique par François Coppée*. Paris: Lemoine et Fils, 1885.

Boutière, Jean, and Schutz, Alexandre-Herman. *Biographie des troubadours*. Paris: Nizet, 1964.

Brachet, Léon, and Plantadis, Johannes. *Chansons populaires du Limousin*. Paris: H. Champion, 1905.

Brake, Mike. *The Sociology of Youth Culture and Youth Subculture: Sex, Drugs, and Rock 'n' Roll?* London: Routledge and Kegan Paul, 1980.

Brech, Robert. "Deux chansons communardes sauvées par le colportage et la transmission orale." *Mouvement Social* 90 (1975): 121–26.

Brécy, Robert, ed. *Florilège de la chanson révolutionnaire: de 1789 au Front Populaire*. Paris: Éditions Hier et Demain, 1978.

————. *La Révolution en chantant*. Paris: Van de Velde-Pirot, 1988.

Breton, Guy. *Le Cabaret de l'histoire*. Paris: Presses de la Cité, 1973.

Bréviaire du carabin. Épinal: Éditions du Sapin d'Or, 1983.

Brochard, Gilles. "Édith Piaf au musée." *France-Amérique* 825 (31 March–6 April, 1988): 32.

Brunschwig, Chantal; Calvet, Louis-Jean; and Klein, Jean-Claude. *Cent ans de chanson française*. Paris: Seuil, 1972.

Buchon, Max. *Noëls et chants populaires de la Franche-Comté*. Paris: Sandoz & Fischbacher, 1878.

Bujeaud, Jérôme. *Chants et chansons populaires des provinces de l'Ouest, Poitou, Saintonge et Angoumois*. 1895. Reprint. Marseilles: Laffitte, 1975.

Calvet, Louis-Jean. *Chanson et société*. Paris: Payot, 1981.

————. *La Chanson française aujourd'hui*. Paris: Hachette, 1980.

Cançon vòla: chants languedociens et gascons. Publiés sous la direction de René Pradère, par Marius Girou, Louis Melet. Toulouse: R.D.P., 1979.

Cannavo, Richard, and Quiquère, Henri. *Le Chant d'un homme: Yves Montand*. Paris: Presses Pocket, 1982.

Canteloube, Joseph. *Anthologie des chants populaires français groupés et présentés par pays ou par provinces*. Paris: Éditions Durand, 1949.

————. *Bourrées d'Auvergne*. Paris: Rivart Larolle & Cie., 1939.

————. *Chants d'Auvergne. Recueillis, traduits et harmonisés*. Paris: Heuguel, 1955.

Canteloube-Ferrieu, Lucienne. *Chanson et poésie des années 30 aux années 60. Trénet, Brassens, Ferré . . . ou les "enfants naturels" du Surréalisme*. Paris: Nizet, 1981.

Carreau, Gérard, and Pinchard, Max. *Chansons d'hier et d'aujourd'hui: 345 chansons du folklore*. Paris: Éditions Ouvrières, 1981.

Casse, Abbé Emmanuel, and Chaminade, Abbé Eugène. *Les Vieilles Chansons patoises du Périgord*. 1902. Reprint. Marseilles: Laffitte, 1981.

Caujolle, Christian. *Cançons popularas d'Occitania per deman*. Paris: Syros, 1979.

Cécile, Marie. *Anthologie de la chanson occitane. Chansons populaires du Pays de langue d'oc*. Paris: Maisonneuve et Larose, 1975.

Centre National d'Action Musicale. *Guide des métiers de la musique*. 2d ed. Paris: Éditions du CENAM, 1989.

————. *Maxi-rock—mini-bruits*. Paris: Éditions du CENAM, 1984.

Chailley, Jacques. *La Chanson populaire française*. Paris: Presses Universitaires de France, 1942.

Champfleury, J.F.F., et Weckerlin, Jean-Baptiste-Théodore. *Chansons populaires des provinces de France*. Paris: Lécrivain et Toubon, 1860.

Chantal Goya: son histoire, ses amis, ses chansons. Paris: C.E.P., 1978.

Chanter made in France. Edited by Brigitte Kernel. Paris: Éditions Michel de Maule, 1987.

Chants folkloriques et danses de nos provinces, Dauphiné, Savoie, Vivarais, recueillis et édités par l'Union des Syndicats agricoles du Sud-Est. Lyon: Union des Syndicats agricoles du Sud-Est, 1939.

Chapuis, Marcel. "Les Sociétés musicales d'amateurs en 1973." *Journal de la Confédération Musicale de France* 278 (1975): 4; 279 (1975): 4; 281 (1975): 8; 283 (1975): 6.

Chardan, Jean-Louis. *Luis Mariano*. Paris: Ramsay, 1980.

Chardavoine, Jean. *Le Recueil des plus belles et excellentes chansons en forme de voix de ville*. (1576). Reprint. Geneva: Minkoff, 1980.

Charles, Jacques. *Cent ans de music-hall*. Geneva: Jeheber, 1956.

————. *Naissance du music-hall*. Paris: Fayard, 1952.

Charles-Dominique, Luc, and Lasseube, Patrick. *Catalogue de l'Exposition 800 ans de musique populaire à Toulouse. Octobre 1984*. Toulouse: Conservatoire Occitan, 1984.

Charpentreau, Jacques. *Georges Brassens et la poésie quotidienne de la chanson*. Paris: Éditions du Cerf, 1960.

Charpentreau, Simone. *Le Livre d'or de la chanson française*. Paris: Éditions Ouvrières, 1976.

————. *Le Livre d'or de la chanson française. I. De Ronsard à Brassens*. Paris: Éditions Ouvrières, 1971.

————. *Le Livre d'or de la chanson française. II. De Marot à Georges Brassens*. Paris: Éditions Ouvrières, 1972.

————. *Veillées en chansons*. 3d ed. Paris: Éditions Ouvrières, 1970.

Charpentreau, Simone and Charpentreau, Jacques. *La Chanson*. Paris: Éditions Ouvrières, 1960.

Chaveau, Jean-Paul. "Le Dialecte dans les chansons et son image d'après les expressions qui les désignent." In Michel Bonneau and Georges Cesbron, eds. *Langue et littératures orales dans l'ouest de la France*. Angers: Presses de l'Université d'Angers, 1983.

Chepfer, Georges. *Textes et chansons*. Présentés par Jean-Marie Bonnet et Jean Lanher. Nancy: Presses Universitaires de Nancy, 1983.

Chevais, Maurice. *Chansons populaires du Val de Loire*. Paris: Heuguel, 1925.

Chevalier, Claude. *Le Roubaisien Léon Delmulle*. N.p.: C. Chevalier, 1982.

Cheyronnaud, Jacques. *Mémoires en recueils. Jalons pour une histoire des collectes musicales en terrain français*. Montpellier: Office Départemental d'Action Culturelle, 1986.

Cim, A. *Émile Debreaux, roi de la goguette*. Paris: Flammarion, 1910.

Claude François. Le livre d'or. Paris: Michel Lafon, 1988.

Cloclo on t'aimait bien. Paris: Éditions Histoire pour tous, 1983.

Cloître, Yves-Marie. *Johnny Hallyday, les idoles et les jeunes*. Paris: Casterman, 1964.

Cocteau, Jean. *Foyer des artistes.* In *Œuvres Complètes*, vol. 11. Paris: Marguerat, 1951.

Coligny, Charles. *La Chanson française: histoire de la chanson et du caveau contenant l'histoire des principales sociétés chantantes et des biographies de chansonniers.* Paris: Lévy, 1876.

Colin, Gerty. *Maurice Chevalier: une route semée d'étoiles.* Paris: Presses de la Cité, 1981.

Coljon, Thierry. "Carte de Séjour au pays de leur enfance." *Le Soir* (Brussels), June 23, 1987, A-9.

Congleton, Jeannie Lou. "The Chansons of Josquin des Prez." Dissertation, Washington University, 1981.

Conte, H. Robert. *Chants d'occitanie et d'ailleurs.* Toulouse: H. R. Conte: 1974.

Costaz, Gilles. *Édith Piaf.* Paris: Seghers, 1983.

Coulomb, Sylvie, and Varrod, Didier. *Histoires de chansons de Maxime Le Forestier à Étienne Daho: 68–88.* Paris: Balland, 1987.

Coulonges, Georges. *La Chanson en son temps.* N.p.: n.p., 1969.

Coussemaker, Edmond de. *Chansons populaires des Flamands de France.* Ghent, Belgium: Guyselynck, 1855.

———. *Chants populaires des Flamands de France.* Ghent: Guyselynck, 1856.

Cowper, Patrick. *Alain Souchon.* Paris: Contrejour, 1981.

Coy, Adelheid. *Die Musik der französischen Revolution. Zur Funktionsbestimmung von Lied und Hymne.* Munich: Katzbichler, 1978.

Daeubert, Raymond. *Vingt ans chez Barclay.* Nice: A. Lefebvre, 1980.

Davenson, Henri. *Le Livre des chansons, ou introduction à la chanson populaire française.* 5th ed. Paris: Seuil, 1982.

———. *Les Troubadours.* Paris: Seuil, 1961.

David, Martine, and Delrieu, Anne-Marie. *Aux sources des chansons françaises.* Paris: Belin, 1986.

Debrie, René. *Une chanson picarde inédite: "Ballade d'ech grand bon Dieu d'bous."* Amiens: Archives Départementales de la Somme, 1973.

De Caunes, Antoine. *Magma.* Paris: Michel, 1978.

Decaunes, Luc., ed. *Les Riches Heures de la chanson française. Complaintes et refrains de la tradition populaire.* Paris: Seghers, 1980.

Decitre, Monique. *Danses et chants traditionnels de la France.* Paris: Éditions de "L'Illustration," 1985.

Delrieux, Georges. *Anthologie de la chanson niçoise.* Nice: G. Delrieux, 1960.

Delzangles, Fernand. *Chants populaires d'Auvergne: folklore cantalien.* Aurillac: Terrise, 1910.

Demorgon, Jacques. "Une communication de masse: la chanson à succès. Essai d'une première systématisation de son étude en France de 1946 à 1966." Dissertation, Université de Paris V, 1974.

Denise, Jean. *Les Enfants de Jean Bart: carnaval, chanson et parler dunkerkois.* Dunkirk: Westhock, 1980.

Desrousseaux, Alexandre Joachim. *Chansons et pasquilles lilloises.* 4th ed. 4 vols. Brionne: Ch. Monfort, 1972.

Desvignes, Geneviève. *Chansons champenoises. Chansons du veilloir.* Paris: Pierre Bossuet, 1929.

Dillaz, Serge. *La Chanson française de contestation. Des barricades de la Commune à celles de Mai 68.* Paris: Seghers, 1973.

Doncieux, Georges. *Chants et chansons, poésie et musique*. Paris: A. Houssiaux, 1852–59.

———. *Le Romancéro populaire de la France*. Paris: E. Bouillon, 1904.

Donnay, Maurice. *Autour du Chat Noir*. Paris: Grasset, 1926.

Dottin, Georges. *La Chanson française de la Renaissance*. Paris: Presses Universitaires de France, 1984.

Duchon, Paul. *Chansons populaires du Bourbonnais*. Paris: B. Roudanez, 1926.

Dumesnil, René. *L'Opéra et l'opéra comique*. Collection "Que sais-je?" Paris: Presses Universitaires de France, 1972.

Dupont, Pierre. *Chants et chansons: poésie et musique*. 4 vols. Paris: A. Houssiaux, 1852–59.

Dureau, Christian. *Édith Piaf vingt ans après*. Paris: Éditions SIPE, 1983.

Durieux, Achille. *Chants et chansons populaires du Cambrésis*. 2d series. Cambrai: A. Durieux, 1868.

Durieux, Achille, and Bruyelles, Adolphe. *Chants populaires du Cambrésis*. Paris: Durieux et Bruyelles, 1864.

Duteil, Yves. *Les Mots qu'on n'a pas dits. 96 chansons*. Paris: Nathan, 1987.

Duverney, Anne-Marie, and d'Horrer, Olivier. *Mémoire de la chanson française depuis 1900*. Neuilly-sur-Seine: Musique et Promotion (SACEM), 1979.

Duviard, Dominique. "Chansons des pêcheurs hauturiers du Golfe de Gascogne vers 1910." In Michel Bonneau and Georges Cesbron, eds., *Langue et littératures orales dans l'Ouest de la France*. Angers: Presses de l'Université d'Angers, 1983.

Emmanuel, Maurice. *30 chansons bourguignonnes du pays de Beaune*. Paris: Durand et Fils, 1917.

Erisman, Guy. *Histoire de la chanson*. Paris: Herman, 1967.

———. *Histoire de la chanson française*. Paris: Waleffe, 1967.

Erwan, Jacques. *Renaud*. Collection "Poésie et Chansons." Paris: Seghers, 1982.

Escallier, Émile. *Le Carnet de chansons de mon père*. Gap: Société d'Études des Hautes-Alpes, 1976.

Feschotte, Jacques. *Histoire du music-hall*. Collection "Que sais-je?" Paris: Presses Universitaires de France, 1971.

Floriant, Guy. *Claude François. Plus vite que la musique*. Paris: Seghers, 1988.

"Français vous chantiez, 1939–1945." Two-record set. Pathé Marconi.

Les Frères Jacques. *36 années de chansons*. Paris: La Source, 1987.

Fribourg, Jeanine. "Vie et rôle de la chanson traditionnelle dans la région de Redon." In Michel Bonneau and Georges Cesbron, eds. *Langue et littératures orales dans l'Ouest de la France*. Angers: Presses de l'Université d'Angers, 1983.

Friedman, Adele C. "Love, Sex, and Marriage in Traditional French Society: The Documentary Evidence of Folksongs." *Proceedings of the Annual Meeting of the Western Society for French History* 5 (1978): 146–54.

Fulcher, Jane F. "The Popular Chanson of the Second Empire: 'Music of the Peasants' in France." *Acta Musicologica* 52 (1980): 27–37.

Fursy, Henry. *Chansons de la boîte*. Paris: Société d'Éditions Littéraires et Artistiques, 1902.

Gagnepain, Bernard. *La Musique du Moyen-Âge à la Renaissance*. Collection "Que sais-je?" Paris: Presses Universitaires de France, 1961.

Gainsbourg, Serge. *Mon propre rôle. Textes 1958–1987*. 2 vols. Paris: Denoël, 1987.

Gardien, Jacques. *La Chanson populaire française*. Paris: Larousse, 1948.

Garneret, Jean, and Culot, Charles. *Chansons populaires comtoises*. Besançon: Folklore Comtois, 1971.

Gasté, Armand. *Jean-le-Houx et le Vau de Vire à la fin du XVIe siècle. Étude critique et historique*. 1874. Reprint. Geneva: Slatkine, 1969.

Gaston-Phébus, D., and de Nesples, Navarrot. *Chants et chansons du Béarn*. Paris: Henri Gauthier, n.d.

Gauthier, André. *Les Chansons de notre histoire*. N.p.: n.p., 1967.

Gauthiers-Villars, Marguerite. *Chansons populaires du Dauphiné*. Paris: Éditions Roudanez, 1929.

Gay, Sabine. *Guide du show-business*. Paris: Société nationale d'Éditions Radio-Phono, 1989.

Gerbod, Paul. "L'Institution orphéonique en France du XIXe siècle au XXe siècle." *Ethnologie française* 10 (1980): 27–44.

Gergely, Jean. "Sur l'aspect historique de la chanson populaire." *Ethnologia Europeae* 2–3 (1968–69): 144–168.

Gérold, T. *Histoire de la musique des origines à la fin du XIVe siècle*. Paris: Laurens, 1936.

Gil, Pierre, et al. *La Danse basque*. Bidart: Association Lauburn, 1981.

Gilson, Alain, and Couture, Charlélie. *Les Chemins parallèles de Charlélie Couture*. Lausanne: Favre, 1988.

Giraudon, Daniel. *Chansons populaires de Basse-Bretagne*. Morlaix: "Skol Vreizh," 1986.

Gobin, Alain. *Le Folklore musical*. Paris: Séguier, 1988.

Godard, Colette. *Jean Guidoni*. Collection "Poèmes et Chansons." Paris: Seghers, 1988.

Gorde, Monique. *Paroles et chansons de France*. Champigny-sur-Marne: Éditions Lito, 1983.

Gougelot, Henri. *La Romance sous la Révolution et l'Empire*. Melun: Librairie d'Argences. 1943.

Gourvil, Francis. *Théodore-Claude-Henri Hersart de la Villemarqué (1815–1895) et le "Barzaz-Breiz" (1839–1845–1867). Origines, éditions, sources, critiques, influences*. Rennes: Oberthur, 1960.

Grassin, Sophie. "Julien Clerc: si on rechantait." *L'Express*, January 15, 1988, p. 47.

Gray, Michael A. *Bibliography of Discographies*. New York: R. R. Bowker, 1977.

Gréco, Juliette. *Jujube*. Paris: Stock, 1982.

Grimault, Dominique, and Mahé, Patrick. *Piaf, Cerdan: un hymne à l'amour*. Paris: Laffont, 1983.

Grosse, Francis, and Gueffier, Bernard. *La Discographie alphabétique du rock français*. Dombasle: Musex, 1988.

Gudin, Jacqueline. *Des chansons pour mieux parler: jeux phonologiques*. Paris: Bordas, 1976.

Guétary, Georges. *Les Hasards fabuleux*. Paris: La Table Ronde, 1981.

Guichard, Léon. *La Musique et les lettres au temps du Romantisme*. Paris: Presses Universitaires de France, 1955.

———. "Notes sur 'Nerval et la chanson folklorique.' " *Revue d'Histoire littéraire de la France* 82–83 (1972): 432–43.

Halimi, André. *On connaît la chanson*. Paris: La Table Ronde, 1959.

———. *Le Show biz et la politique*. Paris: Ramsay, 1987.

———. *Chansons sous l'Occupation*. Paris: Orban, 1976.

Hallyday, Johnny. *Johnny raconte Hallyday*. Paris: Filipacchi, 1979.

Hamon, André-Georges. *Chantres de toutes les Bretagnes: 20 ans de chanson bretonne*. Paris: J. Picollec, 1981.

Hebdige, Dick. *Subculture: The Meaning of Style*. London: Methuen, 1979.

Hennion, Antoine. "The Production of Success: An Anti-Musicology of the Pop Song." *Popular Music* 3 (1983): 159–93.

———. *Les Professionnels du disque. Une sociologie des variétés*. Paris: Métailié, 1981.

Herbert, Michel. *La Chanson à Montmartre*. Paris: La Table Ronde, 1967.

Hermelin, Christian. *Des thèmes et des disques pour débat en groupes: les boucs émissaires, la mort, le corps*. Paris: Centre Documentation et Recherche, 1977.

Hersart de la Villemarqué, Théodore-Claude-Henri. *Barzaz-Breiz. Chants populaires de la Bretagne recueillis, traduits et publiés avec une traduction française*. 2 vols. 1867. Reprint. Paris: Maspero, 1981.

Hornig, Michael. "Die Liedermacher und das zeitkritische Lied der 60er Jahre." Dissertation, University of Bochum, 1974.

Hotier, Hugues. *Vocabulaire du cirque et du music-hall*. Paris: Melvoine, 1981.

Hubel, Alice. *Des Sunset Boulevard par milliers: Sunset sixties*. Paris: Plasma, 1981.

L'Instrument de musique populaire. Usages et symboles. Catalogue de l'Exposition au Musée National des Arts et Traditions Populaires. Paris: Éditions de la Réunion des Musées Nationaux, 1980.

Jasper, Tony, and Oliver, Derek. *The International Encyclopedia of Hard Rock and Heavy Metal*. London: Sidgwick and Jackson, 1984.

Jeanroy, A., and Langfors, A. *Chansons satiriques et bachiques du XIIIe siècle*. Paris: H. Champion, 1974.

Jordania, Redjeb. "Boris Vian et la chanson." *Musique en Jeu*, March 30, 1978, pp. 91–110.

Kastner, Georges. *Les Chants de l'armée française*. Paris: n.p., 1885.

Kirjuhel, "Les Questions." Disque Droug No. D–5101 (French protest songs since 1970).

Kon, Andrea. *This Is My Song: Biography of Petula Clark*. London: Goult, 1984.

Laade, Wolfgang. *Das korsische Volkslied: Ethnografie und Geschichte, Gattungen und Stil*. Wiesbaden: Steiner, 1981.

Labelle, Ronald. "Le Folklore musical en France: Tendances actuelles dans la recherche et la diffusion." *Canadian Folk Music Bulletin* 18 (1984): 9–11.

Laborde, Christian. *Nougaro. La Voix royale*. Paris: Hidalgo, 1989.

Lacombe, Alain. *L'Écran du rock*. Paris: L'Herminier, 1985.

Laforte, Conrad. *La Chanson folklorique et les écrivains du XIXe siècle (en France et au Québec)*. Montreal: Hurtubise, 1973.

———. *Le Catalogue de la chanson folklorique française*. Quebec City: Presses de l'Université Laval, 1977.

———. "Rabelais et la chanson traditionnelle." *Gigue* 2 (1973): 34–44; 3 (1973): 19–29.

Lagrée, Jean-Charles. *Les Jeunes chantent leurs cultures*. Paris: L'Harmattan, 1983.

Lambert, Louis. *Chants et chansons populaires du Languedoc*. 1906. Reprint. Marseilles: Laffitte, 1983.

Lambert, Louis, and Montel, Achille. *Chants populaires du Languedoc*. 1880. Reprint. Marseilles: Laffitte, 1975.

Lancelot, Hubert. *Nous les Compagnons de la Chanson*. Paris: Aubier, 1989.

Lanèque, Michelle, and Gallot, Romain. *Montand: de chanson en image*. Paris: Bréa/ Weber Diffusion, 1981.

Lange, Monique. *Piaf*. London: Allen, 1982.

Lara, Catherine. *L'Aventurière de l'archet perdu*. Paris: Michel Lafon, 1987.

Larue, André. *Brassens: une vie*. Paris: I.G.E., 1982.

————. *Édith Piaf: l'amour toujours*. Paris: Michel Lafon, 1983.

Leduc, Jean-Marie. *Rock Vinyl (Pour une discothèque de rock)*. Paris: Seuil, 1986.

Le Duc, Philibert. *Chansons et lettres patoises bressanes, bugeysiennes et dombistes*. 1881. Reprint. Marseilles: Laffitte, 1978.

Lefèvre, Régis. *Renaud. Dès que le vent soufflera*. Lausanne: Favre, 1985.

Le Mieux, Anne. "Gabriel Yacoub and Malicorne: French Folk Imports." *Sing Out* 30 (1984): 28–31.

Leproux, Henri, with Hubel, Alice. *Le Temple du rock: Golf Drouot*. Paris: Laffont, 1982.

Le Roux de Lincy, Antoine Jean Victor. *Recueil de chants historiques français depuis le XIIe jusqu'au XVIIIe siècle, avec des notices et une introduction*. 1842. Reprint. Geneva: Slatkine, 1971.

Lesure, François. *La Chanson parisienne*. Monaco: Dyer, 1953.

Le Veaux, Denis; Piraud, Anne; and Redhon, Françoise. *Musiques traditionnelles en Mayenne, 1789–1984*. Laval: L'Oribus, 1984.

Linker, Robert White. *A Bibliography of Old French Lyrics*. University, Miss.: Romance Monographs, 1979.

Long, Chris. *Johnny*. Paris: Filipacchi, 1987.

Luxardo, Hervé. *Histoire de la Marseillaise*. Paris: Plon, 1989.

Luzel, François-Marie. *Veillées bretonnes: moeurs, chants, contes et récits populaires des Bretons*. 1879. Reprint. Marseilles: Laffitte, 1979.

Macias, Enrico, and Demarny, Jacques. *Non je n'ai pas oublié*. Paris: Laffont, 1982.

Maillard, Jean H. *Anthologie de chants de troubadours*. Nice: Delrieu, 1967.

Malrieu, Patrick. *Histoire de la chanson populaire bretonne*, Guingamp: Dastum, 1983.

Manoeuvre, Philippe. *L'Enfant du rock*. Paris: Lattès, 1985.

Manot, Suzanne, ed. *Folklore vivant en Aunis, Saintonge et Angoumois (coutumes, chants, danses)*. Niort: Nicolas-Imbert, 1970.

Marc, Edmond. *La Chanson française*. Paris: Hatier, 1972.

Marcaggi, Jean-Baptiste. *Les Chants de la mort et de la vendetta de la Corse*. Paris: Perrin, 1898.

Marty, G. and G. *Dictionnaire des chansons de la Révolution*. Paris: Taillandier, 1988.

Mathieu, Mireille, with Cartier, Jacqueline. *Oui je crois qu'une vie ça commence avec un mot d'amour*. Paris: Laffont, 1987.

Mathis, Ursula. *Existentialismus und französische Chanson*. Vienna: Verlag der österreichischen Akademie der Wissenschaften, 1984.

Meister, Barbara. *Nineteenth-Century French Song: Fauré, Chausson, Duparc and Debussy*. Bloomington: Indiana University Press, 1960.

Micheyl, Mick. *Dieu est-il bien dans ma peau?* Lyon: Rapid Copy, 1984.

Middletown, Richard, and Horn, David, eds. *Popular Music 1. Folk or Popular? Distinctions, influences, continuities*. Cambridge: Cambridge University Press, 1981.

————. *Popular Music 2. Theory and Method*. Cambridge: Cambridge University Press, 1981.

Miller, Lete Ellen Zuckerman. "The Chansons of French Provincial Composers, 1530–1550. A Study of Stylistic Trends." Dissertation, Stanford University, 1978.

Millien, Achille. *Chansons populaires du Nivernais et du Morvan. Édition établie par Georges Delarue.* Grenoble: Centre Alpin et Rhodanien d'Ethnologie, 1977.

———. *Chants et chansons.* 1906. Reprint. Marseilles: Laffitte, 1981.

Mills, Alan, and Silverman, Jerry. *Favorite French Folk Songs. Sixty-Five Traditional Songs of France and Canada.* New York: Oak Publications, 1963.

Milo, Patrick. *Mylène Farmer.* Paris: Michel, 1989.

Mirat, Gaston. *Chants populaires du Béarn. Traduits, annotés et harmonisés.* Pau: École Gastoû Febus, 1969.

Mitchell, Eddy. *Cocktail story.* Monte Carlo: Les Éditions de Monte Carlo, 1986.

Monestier, Martin. *Enrico Macias.* Paris: Encre, 1980.

Monestier, Martin, and Barlatier, Pierre. *Le Livre du souvenir.* Paris: Sand & Tchou, 1982.

Monserrat, Joëlle. *Yves Montand.* Paris: Éditions PAL, 1984.

Montagné, Gilbert. *Tu vois ce que je veux dire.* Paris: Michel Lafon, 1987.

Montel, Achille. *Chants populaires du Languedoc.* 1880. Reprint. Geneva: Slatkine, 1975.

Morand, Simone. *Anthologie de la chanson de Haute Bretagne: Penthièvre, Pays Malouin, Pays de Rennes et d'Outre-Ille, Redon, Brière, Pays de Nantes.* Paris: Maisonneuve et Larose, 1976.

Moreira, Paul. *Rock métis en France.* Paris: Souffles, 1987.

Moroz, Susane. "Analyse des chansons de conscrits de la commune de Saint-Vincent-sur-Oust (Haute Bretagne)." *Cahiers de Littérature orale* 16 (1984): 83–104.

Morpain, Joseph. *50 chansons des Charentes et du Poitou. Avec accompagnement de piano.* Paris: Heuguel, 1924.

Moullé, Édouard. *52 chants anciens recueillis en Normandie.* Paris: Rouart & Lerolle, 1911.

Le Mouvement pop. Paris: Laffont, 1975.

Le Musée de la chanson française (Special Issue) No. 6 (1965). Paris: "Variétés de Paris," 1965.

Naudin, Marie. *Évolution parallèle de la poésie et de la musique en France: rôle unificateur de la chanson.* Paris: Nizet, 1968.

Nick, Christophe. *Téléphone.* Paris: Michel, 1984.

Nicolas, Lucien. *Chanson vivante.* Brezolles: Éditions de l'Auracana, 1984.

Nicoulaud, Gilles. *Aux sources des chansons populaires.* Paris: Belin, 1984.

L'Officiel du rock 88. Paris: Centre d'Information du Rock, 1988.

Ollivier, Joseph. *Catalogue bibliographique de la chanson populaire bretonne sur des feuilles volantes.* Quimper: Ollivier, 1942.

Orain, Adolphe. *Glossaire patois du département d'Ille-et-Vilaine, suivi de chansons populaires avec musique.* 1886. Reprint. Janzé-la-Chauvelière: Y. Salmon, 1980.

Ortoli, J. B. Frédéric. *Les voceri de l'île de Corse.* Paris: Leroux, 1887.

Ouvrard, Jean-Pierre. "Les Jeux du mètre et du sens dans la chanson polyphonique du XVIe siècle." *Revue de Musicologie* 57 (1981): 5–34.

Page, Christian. *Dalida.* Bordeaux: Delmas, 1981.

———. *Eddy Mitchell.* Paris: Bréa Éditions, 1983.

———. *Mireille Mathieu.* Paris: Bréa Éditions, 1983.

———. *Sheila.* Paris: Bréa Éditions, 1983.

Page; Christian, and Varrod, Didier. *Goldman: Portrait non conforme.* Lausanne: Favre, 1987.

Pagnon, Francis. *En évoquant Wagner: la musique comme mensonge et comme vérité.* Paris: Champ Libre, 1981.

Palmer, Tony. *All You Need Is Love. The Story of Popular Music.* New York: Grossman Publishers, 1976.

Panafieu, Jacques de. *Chanson disque radio.* 2 vols. Paris: Blond & Gay, 1966.

Pelen, Jean-Noël. *Le Conte et la chanson populaire de tradition orale en Cévenne rurale.* Nîmes: SEDILAN, 1982.

Pelletier, Chantal. *Eddy Mitchell.* Paris: Seghers, 1981.

Pérez, Michel. *Charles Trénet.* Collection "Poésie et Chansons." 1964. Reprint. Paris: Seghers, 1979.

Petit, Christian; Arban, Dominique; and Barlatier, Pierre. *Jacques Brel: Un homme au large de l'espoir.* Abbeville: Presses Françaises. 1982.

Piaf, Édith. *The Wheel of Fortune: The Autobiography of Édith Piaf.* Translated by Peter Trewartha and André Masvin de Virton. London: Mayflower, 1968.

Pierson, Alain. *Téléphone song-book.* Paris: Import Diffusion Music, 1983.

Pinguet, Francis. *Un monde musical métissé.* Paris: La Revue Musicale, 1984.

Pinton, Abbé Paul. *Chansons bressonnes.* St. Galmier: J. Caudel, 1979.

Pirro, André. *Histoire de la musique du XIVe au XVIe siècle.* Paris: Laurens, 1940.

Plume, Christian, and Pasquini, Xavier. *Tino Rossi.* Paris: Bréa Éditions, 1983.

Poplineau, Bernard, and Dehaye, Pierre. *Histoire et chansons populaires ardennaises.* La Berlière: B. Poplineau, 1979.

Portron, Pierrette, and Dumont-Sorel, Nelly. *Catalogue de l'Exposition de la Collection Legoy Gaston: La Chanson populaire de Béranger à Brassens, du 20 mai au 30 juin 1983.* Le Havre: Bibliothèque Municipale, 1983.

Potel, Jean-Yves, ed. *L'État de la France et de ses habitants.* Paris: Éditions La Découverte, 1985.

Poulaille, Henry. *La Grande et belle bible des Noëls anciens. Noëls régionaux et Noëls contemporains.* Paris: Michel, 1951.

Poueigh, Jean. *Chansons populaires des Pyrénées françaises.* 1926. Reprint. Marseilles: Laffitte, 1977.

Prévos, André. "Singing Against Hunger: French and American Efforts and Their Results." *Popular Music and Society* 11 (1987): 57–74.

———. "The CLARB and Soul Bag." *The Black Perspective in Music* 15 (1987): 243–57.

Privas, Xavier. *Chansons des enfants du peuple: poésie et musique.* Paris: J. Rueff, 1905.

Puymaigre, Théodore-Joseph Boudet, Comte de. *Chants populaires recueillis dans le pays messin.* 1881. Reprint. Marseilles: Laffitte, 1978.

Quellien, Narcisse. *Chansons et danses des Bretons.* 1889. Reprint. Marseilles: Laffitte, 1981.

Qui êtes-vous Yves Montand? Regards neufs sur la chanson. Paris: Seuil, 1954.

Raunié, Émile. *Chansonnier historique du XVIIIe siècle.* 10 vols. Paris: A. Quantin, 1879–84.

Raynaud, Gaston. *Bibliographie des chansonniers français des 13e et 14e siècles.* Paris: Gaston Raynaud, 1971.

Regards neufs sur la chanson. Paris: Seuil, 1954.

Reichardt, Rolf, and Schneider, Herbert. *Chanson et musique populaires devant l'histoire à la fin de l'Ancien Régime*. Paris: Société d'Études du XVIIe siècle, 1986.

Remilleux, Jean-Louis. *Jean-Michel Jarre*. Paris: Orban, 1987.

Renaud. *Mistral gagnant. Chansons et dessins*. Paris: Seuil, 1986.

Renaud, and Armand, Jacques. *Les Aventures de Gérard Lambert*. 2 vols. Paris: Jean-Jacques Martin, 1981–83.

Rioux, Lucien. *Vingt ans de chanson en France*. Paris: Arthaud, 1965.

Rioux, Lucien, and Beauvallet, Geneviève. *Maxime Le Forestier*. Paris: Seghers, 1982.

Robine, Marc. *Le Roman de Julien Clerc*. Paris: Seghers, 1988.

Roland-Manuel, ed. *Histoire de la musique*. 2 vols. Encyclopédie de la Pléiade. Paris: Gallimard, 1960–63.

Rolland, Eugène. *Recueil de chansons populaires*. 1883–86. Reprint. Paris: Maisonneuve et Larose, 1967.

Rosenberg, Samuel N. *Chanter n'estuet: Songs of the Trouvères*. Bloomington: Indiana University Press, 1981.

Rossi, Alain. *Johnny Hallyday*. Paris: Solar, 1981.

Rouchon, Michel, and Rouchon, Catherine. *Souvenir de Joe Dassin*. Paris: La Pensée Universelle, 1984.

Rouchy, Marie-Élizabeth. *Montand*. Paris: Solar, 1980.

Rouquette, Yves. *La Nouvelle chanson occitane*. Toulouse: Privat, 1972.

Roux, Joseph. *L'Épopée limousine: Texte, traduction et notes*. 1889. Reprint. Marseilles: Laffitte, 1980.

Sabatès, Fabien. *Maurice Chevalier*. Paris: Orban, 1981.

Sabatier, Roland. *Le Livre des chansons de France*. Paris: Gallimard, 1984.

Saiah, Isabelle. *Montand, Yves*. Boulogne: Éditions du Sciapode, 1981.

Saka, Pierre, and Boisseau, Jean-Michel. *La Chanson française des origines à nos jours*. Paris: Nathan, 1980.

Sallaberry, Jean-Dominique-Julien. *Chants populaires du Pays Basque*. 1870. Reprint. Marseilles: Laffitte, 1977.

Sardou, Fernand. *Les Sardou de père en fils*. Paris: Julliard, 1981.

Schenda, Rudolf. "Der General Boulanger, Elsass-Lothringen und das politische Strassenlied in der Provence." *Jahrbuch für Volksliedforschung* 23 (1978): 103–23.

Schmidt, Felix. *Das Chanson: Herkfunt, Entwicklung, Interpretation*. Ahrensburg: Damokles, 1968.

Scott, Barbara, ed. *Folk Songs of France*. New York: Oak Publications, 1966.

Scotto, Vincent. *Souvenirs de Paris*. Toulouse: Staël, 1947.

Seca, Jean-Marc. *Vocations rock*. Paris: Klincksieck, 1988.

Séchan, Thierry. *Le Roman de Renaud*. Paris: Seghers, 1988.

Seguret, Christian. "Bluegrass, Old Time and Country Music in France." *Old Time Music* 28 (1978): 4.

Semprun, Jorge. *Montand: la vie continue*. Paris: Denoël, 1983.

Sepieter, Jean-Paul. *La Musique du peuple flamand*. Dunkirk: Westhoeck, 1981.

Sermonte, Jean-Paul. *Georges Brassens*. Paris: Séguier, 1988.

Servettaz, Claudius. *Chants et chansons de la Savoie*. Annecy: J. Aubry, 1910.

———. *Vieilles Chansons savoyardes*. 1910. Reprint. Annecy: Imprimerie Annecienne, 1963.

Sevran, Pascal. *Le Dictionnaire de la chanson française*. Paris: Carrère, 1986.

———. *Le Dictionnaire de la chanson française*. 1988 ed. Paris: Edition 13, 1988.

Sevrette. *Les Vieilles Chansons du pays de France*. Paris: n.p., 1922.

Sicre, Claude. *Vive l'Américke*. Toulouse: PubliSud, n.d.

Siffer, Roger. *Alsace/Elsass, ou à chaque fou sa casquette et à moi mon chapeau*. Paris: Lattès, 1979.

Silberman, Alfons. *La Musique, la radio et l'auditeur: étude sociologique*. Paris: Presses Universitaires de France, 1954.

Simon, François. *50 chansons populaires pour les enfants*. Paris: Imprimerie de la Renaissance, 1928.

Soulé, Béatrice. *Charlélie Couture*. Collection "Poésie et Chansons." Paris: Seghers, 1986.

"Spécial France." A special issue of *Rock & Folk*, No. 127, August 1977.

Stars sans fards (Interviews de chanteurs). Aix-en-Provence: EDISUD, 1981.

Staub, Théo. *L'Enfer érotique de la chanson folklorique française*. Plan de la Tour: Éditions d'Aujourd'hui, 1981.

Stellberg, Rüdiger. *Die Chansons von Georges Brassens und ihr Publikum*. Frankfurt: Peter Lang, 1979.

Stivell, Alan. *Racines interdites*. Paris: Lattès, 1979.

Stramoy, Jean. *Ballades et chansons populaires du Nivernais*. Nevers: Imprimerie de la Tribune, 1902.

Strowsky, S. *Béranger*. Paris: Plon, 1913.

Tarbe, Prosper. *Romancéro de Champagne*. 5 vols. Reims: n.p., 1863–64.

Taylor, Paul. *Popular Music Since 1955. A Critical Guide to the Literature*. Boston: G. K. Hall, 1985.

Téléphone: le livre. Paris: Love Me Tender Éditions, 1983.

Tenaille, Frank. *Showbiz*. Paris: Éditions du CENAM, 1984.

———. *Touré Kounda*. Paris: Seghers, 1989.

Tenaille, Frank, and Delcourt, Thierry. *La Chanson en France*. Paris: Éditions du CENAM, 1986.

Tiersot, Julien. *Chansons populaires recueillies dans les Alpes françaises: Savoie et Dauphiné*. 1903. Reprint. Marseilles: Laffitte, 1979.

———. *La Chanson populaire et les écrivains romantiques*. Paris: Plon, 1931.

Tillien, André. *Auprès de son arbre (George Brassens)*. Paris: Julliard, 1983.

Todd, Olivier. *Jacques Brel: une vie*. Paris: Laffont, 1984.

Toesca, Marc; Conrath, Philippe; and Kolpa-Kopoul, Rémy. *Guide du tube. 1000 tubes de 1950 à 1987*. Paris: Laffont-Seghers, 1987.

Torgue, Henry Skoff. *La Pop musique*. 3d ed. Collection "Que sais-je?" Paris: Presses Universitaires de France, 1984.

Tournier, Jacques. *Barbara ou les parenthèses*. Paris: Seghers, 1981.

Tranchant, Jean. *La Grande Roue*. Paris: La Table Ronde, 1969.

Trébucq, Sylv. *La Chanson populaire des Pyrénées à la Vendée*. Bordeaux: Ferret et Fils, 1912.

———. *La Chanson populaire en Vendée*. Paris: Lechevallier, 1896.

Trénet, Charles. *Boum! Chansons folles*. Paris: Seuil, 1988.

———. *Mes jeunes années*. Paris: Laffont, 1988.

Trimbach, Gérard. *Tino Rossi: cinquante ans d'amour*. Paris: Delville, 1982.

Ullman, Patrick. *Têtes d'affiche*. Paris: Clémence/Plasma, 1980.

Van Parys, Georges. *Les Jours comme ils viennent*. Paris: Plon, 1969.

Vassal, Hugues. *Piaf mon amour*. Villeurbanne: J. L. Lesfargues, 1982.

Vassal, Jacques. *Français si vous chantiez*. Paris: Michel, 1976.

―――. *La Nouvelle Chanson bretonne*. Collection "Rock & Folk." Paris: Michel, 1973.

Vassal, Jacques, and Leduc, Jean-Marie. *Jacques Higelin*. Paris: Michel, 1985.

Verdié, Minelle, ed. *L'État de la France et de ses habitants*. Paris: La Découverte, 1987.

Vernillat, France. *La Chanson française,*. Collection "Que sais-je?" Paris: Presses Universitaires de France, 1971.

―――. *Chansons pour des personnages célèbres par des personnages célèbres*. Paris: Presses d'Île de France, 1977.

Vernillat, France, and Barbier, Pierre. "L'Histoire de France par la chanson." Four-record set. Le Chant du Monde, No. CAL 74461–4.

Vernillat, France, and Charpentreau, Jacques. *Dictionnaire de la chanson française*. Paris: Larousse, 1969.

Vian, Boris. *Derrière la zizique. Textes choisis, préfacés et annotés par Michel Fauré*. Paris: Union Générale d'Éditions, 1981.

―――. *En avant la musique . . . et par ici les gros sous*. Paris: Le Livre Contemporain, 1958.

Victor, Christian, and Régoli, Julien. *Vingt ans de rock français*. Paris: Michel, 1978.

Vie, François, and Barets, Stan. *Look rock. Catalogue publié à l'occasion de l'exposition "Un certain look rock." Angoulême. Xe Salon International de la Bande Dessinée, 1984*. Paris: Temps futurs, 1984.

Vincent, Éric. *Les Idoles des années soixante. Photos de Jean-Marie Périer*. Paris: Filipacchi, 1980.

Vincent d'Indy, Paul. *Chansons populaires recueillies dans le Vivarais et le Vercors*. Paris: Heuguel, 1892.

Vingtrinier, Joseph. *Chants et chansons des soldats de France 1789–1902*. Paris: A. Mezicant, 1902.

Voyer, Pierre. *Le Rock et le rôle*. Montreal: Éditions Leméac, 1981.

Weckerlin, Jean-Baptiste-Théodore. *Chansons populaires d'Alsace*. Bakenbach: J. P. Gyss, 1984.

―――. *Chansons populaires de l'Alsace*. 2 vols. 1883. Reprint. Paris: Maisonneuve et Larose, 1967.

―――. *La Chanson populaire*. Strasbourg: J.-B. Weckerlin, 1886.

Wiora, Walter. *Les Quatre Âges de la musique*. Paris: Payot, 1963.

Yonnet, Paul. *Jeux, modes et masses. La société française et le moderne, 1945–1985*. Paris: Gallimard, 1985.

Zeldin, Theodore. *The French*. New York: Pantheon Books, 1982.

Ziwes, Armand. *À Montmartre le soir. . . .* Paris: Grasset, 1951.

11

Radio and Television

JEAN-PIERRE PIRIOU

Major discoveries and inventions that change forever the way people live have marked the course of history. No one would dispute that the development of printing by Johannes Gutenberg in the fifteenth century had such an impact on civilization, and it is not an exaggeration to say that, in the twentieth century, the development of radio and television has exerted a comparable influence on mankind. Radio and television have played important parts in twentieth-century world history. Very few other inventions have had the same universal appeal and have so profoundly affected cultures and civilizations. Nowadays there is not one inhabited corner on earth that does not have access to radio and television. Everywhere, both media assume the same functions: to inform, to entertain, and to educate.

HISTORICAL BACKGROUND

Radio

Born with the twentieth-century, radio is the oldest of the modern media. It is the one that reaches the largest audience worldwide; and its audience, in spite of the competition of television, is constantly growing, particularly among young people—this against widespread rumors regarding its demise.

At the beginning, radio was primarily conceived as a way to communicate, but some people became leery of the new medium when they realized what a powerful tool it was and when they began to fear that it might get out of control. Its first detractors came from the printed press, when news agencies started using radio to broadcast news. The rapidity with which they could report from anywhere on the globe presented a challenge to the traditional way in which newspapers

were reporting world news. At first, editors were afraid that the foreign correspondents who cabled their stories to their main offices would become obsolete,
since they could not transmit the news instantaneously and almost simultaneously
with the event itself. However, it soon became obvious that the competition to
report the news as rapidly as possible sometimes did not allow reporters time to
verify the authenticity of the news. Pierre Miquel recounts, for instance, in his
history of radio and television that in 1919 one of the major press agencies was
responsible for announcing on the radio that Lenin had died *(Histoire de la radio
et de la télévision,* p. 10). Such an incident shows why, instead of phasing out
their correspondents, press agencies decided to increase their personnel. With
radio, news was transmitted faster, but at a much higher cost.

Aside from witnessing world news, radio began to play a proactive part in
the life of the countries it served. In France, as elsewhere, political leaders
discovered quickly that they could use radio to their advantage. For two centuries,
politicians and statesmen had relied on newspapers to convey their political ideas
and to try to persuade their constituents that they were right. In the thirties, these
people realized that they could discard newspapers and achieve better results by
using radio. Totalitarian regimes began to utilize radio for their propaganda,
whereas more liberal powers also used the medium, but in a more subtle manner.
This was the time when radio started to participate extensively in electoral
campaigns, and as a political weapon it became formidable: statesmen relied on
it to inform their countrymen of events of national importance. Marshall Pétain
announced the armistice of 1940 on the radio, for instance. To this day, however,
the most memorable radio address to the French people is the appeal made by
General de Gaulle to his countrymen from London, asking them to join him in
the fight against the German invaders. If De Gaulle's speech is remembered, it
is undoubtedly because of the message it conveyed, but it is also because of the
way in which it was delivered. Contrary to newspapers, where only the written
text counts, radio can favor certain people and place others at a disadvantage.
A voice, and the personality it reveals, can either charm or alienate listeners.

In the beginning, radio was primarily an instrument of information, but it
rapidly expanded its sphere of influence to entertainment and education. In
France, as in other western countries, radio has become a musical means of
entertainment. Each station, particularly the private local stations, has developed
its own identity with a variety of programs, but for most, music remains the
most popular kind of programming. We mentioned earlier that, contrary to
popular belief, radio had survived well the competition of television, but there
are certain types of programs which attracted large groups of listeners before
television existed and have practically disappeared from radio. Few people still
listen, for instance, to dramatic performances on radio. On the contrary, French
listeners eagerly tune in to games that give them an opportunity to participate
themselves by calling the station. In France, listeners tune in their radios for
two reasons: news and entertainment. Service-oriented programs, where people
can learn about cooking, gardening, or fixing things in the house, are very

popular. The latest musical hits often provide the major part of a station's programming, and they are interrupted by advertising, weather forecasts, traffic conditions for commuters, and news bulletins which often consist of live interviews. The kind of programs people listen to is greatly conditioned by the circumstances during which they listen to the radio. Most of the time, people listen to the radio while doing something else, and this is the main reason radio has been able to withstand the competition of television. The invention of transistor radios has made a significant contribution to this development. People listen while driving, while jogging, while performing household chores, when they wake up in the morning, and when they fall asleep at night.

Radio began as *Télégraphie sans fil, TSF* (wireless telegraph). The first wireless telegraph was invented by Claude Chappe, a French engineer, who established the first link between Lille and Paris in 1794. Signals were transmitted through a series of tall posts and had to be observed with binoculars and relayed to the next post until they reached their destination. Needless to say, the system could not operate when it was dark or at any time the visibility was bad. In 1873 the American Samuel Morse developed the system which bears his name. The transmission was instantaneous, but it required electric lines. What gave radio a major impetus was the building of the first transistor sets in 1955, using a technique invented in 1948 by the Americans Bardeen, Brattain, and Schockley. All of a sudden, radios were everywhere. They were also getting smaller and smaller and they sold for less and less money.

However, before it reached that stage, radio programming had existed in France since 1921. That year, in December, General Ferrié started regular broadcasting from the military station located on the Eiffel Tower. In the beginning, it only broadcast weather bulletins, but they were soon followed by stock exchange and commodity exchange rates. Before long, listeners were treated to a live radio concert. In 1924 the first civilian, Maurice Privat, was able to rent the station for a few hours of programming every day. To finance his enterprise, he formed an organization of listeners called *Association des Amis de la Tour Eiffel*. This event represented the real beginning of modern radio in France. Little by little, Privat added news bulletins, editorials, and finally the first *Journal parlé* (News Show). Radio Tour Eiffel remained in existence until 1940.

On November 6, 1922, the first private radio station was inaugurated by Émile Girardeau. The man sold radio communications equipment, and a business trip to the United States had convinced him that radio broadcasting had a very bright future. He named his station *Radiola*, and his first announcer was nicknamed *Radiolo*. Yet, in France, radio broadcasting was under the authority of the government, and Girardeau, like any of his colleagues, was forbidden to broadcast commercials. To overcome this problem, Girardeau started manufacturing radio sets using *Radiola* as a trademark. That way, the names of the station and of his announcer were being advertised, and this proved to be sufficient to turn the whole operation into a commercial success. Girardeau also became the precursor of sponsoring. For instance, he would find commercial sponsors for a concert, and he would announce their names on the air. He did not have to resort to that gimmick very long, since he received permission to include commercials in his programming in 1925. *Radiola* then became *Radio Paris* and remained for a good ten years the only respectable French radio station. In 1933, *Radio Paris* was incorporated into the national network and became the national radio station, *Radio Paris*.

In 1923, the French government had reaffirmed the state's monopoly on radio stations. Private stations were tolerated, but had to submit to a tight control and pay a tax to the government. In 1945, all private radios were forbidden all over France, and peripheral stations began to appear with their transmitters located on the various French borders. This marked the beginning of *Europe 1, Radio Andorre, RMC* (Radio Monte Carlo), and *RTL* (Radio-Télé Luxembourg), for instance. The same phenomenon occurred again during the sixties when radio stations started transmitting from ships in the North Sea. These stations became known as *radios pirates* (pirate stations). Among them, *Radio Veronica* and *Radio Caroline* transmitted toward England and Holland. In France, a couple of stations appeared in 1968 but soon disappeared. The first true pirate station was *Radio Campus*, which started broadcasting in 1969 for students at the University of Lille. The proliferation of those pirate stations really started in 1977 with *Radio Verte* in Paris. In 1982, however, a new law was passed to legitimize the *radios locales privées*, RLPs, and by 1986, there were about 1,500 of them in France.

Radio has become the most widespread medium in the world. In 1928, the cheapest radio set cost 900 F, or the equivalent of the monthly salary of an elementary school teacher. Sixty years later, the most inexpensive transistor radio is for sale for 50 F ($8) (Ponthieu, p. 73). The affordability of the equipment has turned radio into a true companion for many French people. Constant technological improvements have allowed them to take their radios with them wherever they go, and the multiplication of local FM stations has radically transformed their listening habits. Major peripheral stations and government-run stations are finding it more and more difficult to compete with smaller local and more specialized stations. Listeners have become attached to stations catering to their own interests and allowing them to have an active part in the programming, such as when they call in to express their opinions or to request a particular musical hit.

Today, all French households have at least one radio set, and there are 59 million sets in France compared to 20.5 million in 1971 (*Quid 1989* and Mermet). For the past few years, FM radios, radiocassette players, car radios, and tuners have greatly contributed to the expansion of a market that appeared to be saturated. In 1987 the French purchased 1,450,000 radio sets, 2,220,000 walkmen, and 1,700,000 clock radios. This does not take into account 2,290,000 tape recorders with radios, 2,850,000 car radios, and 270,000 tuners for their stereo systems. According to a poll (*Francoscopie*, 361), in 1987, the French owned 25,505,000 portable radios, 13,740,000 car radios, 10,227,000 clock radios,

7,312,000 stereo systems with a radio, and 1,372,000 radio consoles. The feature that distinguishes the owner of a radio set from another in France is FM, which only 70 percent of the people have. It is not easy to find a pattern among the people who have it and those who do not, but as is often the case, the younger, the wealthier, and the city dwellers tend to be among those with the latest technological developments. Over a fifteen-year period, the number of automobiles equipped with radios has tripled. Now, 70 percent of cars are equipped with a radio as opposed to only 24 percent in 1971. Once again, the younger generations are attracted by the technological improvements which allow them to have in their cars all the equipment they have at home: FM, stereo, equalizers, hi-fi speakers, etc. However, three-fourths of all car radios purchased every year, roughly 2 million, also have a cassette player which, in many instances, is used more often than the radio itself.

In general, French people spend less time listening to the radio than they do watching television. However, both media do not compete for the same time slots during the day. A French person averages 2 hours and 47 minutes of radio during the week; that is 22 minutes less than the individual spends in front of a TV set. Between 7 and 9 in the morning is the time when the greatest number of people listen to the radio. This is also when most of the programs are devoted to news and weather reports. French people who listen the most to the radio are, beginning with the most addicted, women, older people, people with little education, housewives, and people who live in the north of France and in the Paris area. The people who listen the least are men, younger people, well-educated people, farmers, students, and people who live in the western and southwestern areas of the country (*Francoscopie*, 361). Hours of heavy listening are between 7 A.M. and 6 P.M., but the number of listeners decreases as the evening progresses and as people switch to television. Saturdays and Sundays are days when many people tune in their radios, even though these are also days when TV attracts a big audience. For some reason, October and November are months when people listen the most, whereas July and August are times when radio sets stay off, except of course for transistor radios on the beaches and for car radios when people are on vacation (*Francoscopie*, 361).

In spite of its amazing competitiveness, radio is losing ground. The percentage of listeners dropped from 70.4 percent in 1985 to 68.7 percent in 1987. Europe 1 has experienced the sharpest drop (from 18.4 to 13.9 percent); France Inter and RMC dropped a little less, and RTL increased slightly. Since their legalization in 1982, the private local stations have captured almost 25 percent of all listeners. One of them, NRJ, is now in fifth place, immediately after RTL, Europe 1, France Inter, and RMC. The great number of listeners which the private local radios attract is proof that they fill a need in contemporary French society. Initially, 1,400 stations were authorized, and listeners experienced some frustration in trying to find the right frequencies. Half of those stations can advertise individual products, but the other half is limited to generic advertisement. Music still appeals most to listeners. Contrary to the major stations, which must diversify their programs in order to court as broad a segment of the population as possible, the private stations can become very specialized and target groups of listeners who all have something in common: a taste for classical, country, or rock music; an interest in religion or politics; or the same ethnic background.

The future of radio in France is bright, but it is not going to be the same as it has been until now. Instead of selecting their programs on the menus of the major radio stations, French listeners prefer the "à la carte" offerings of the smaller private local stations.

From Radio to Television

By 1939, radio broadcasting had already encountered all the problems that television was going to experience during its infancy, immediately after the war. Television was going to use a much more effective technology than radio, but it would put it at the service of the same triple mission: information, entertainment, and education.

The beginnings of TV occurred in the United States in the forties, but England waited till 1950, and the rest of Western and Eastern Europe experienced the new phenomenon only between 1950 and 1960. In the seventies, television became a worldwide phenomenon and yet, as we have seen, it has never superseded radio. In competing to deliver information, for instance, television requires heavier equipment than radio and has a somewhat limited access to certain events. However, the development of new portable video equipment will give it the advantage which image and sound have over sound alone. As a form of musical entertainment, television is less likely to supplant radio. Any station can play an indefinite number of tunes without ever requiring the services of a singer, something television cannot do when it presents a variety show.

Like radio, television plays an important cultural role in contemporary societies. It is responsible for the propagation of a new form of culture with new characteristics. It is striving to be encyclopedic in its efforts to witness every important happening, everywhere in the world, and at any time. This accounts for the great popularity of medical premieres on television. To read about the first heart transplant would have a much smaller interest than seeing it on TV. The first fifty years of television are thus marked by a series of events which viewers all over the world have shared and which are remembered as the high moments of the medium. The landing of the first man on the moon probably tops the list of such events. The second objective of this new culture is to use world events to engage in a critical appraisal of the great contemporary problems facing humanity. In that role, TV becomes engaged, just as the existentialist writers were engaged. Television can document the scourge of AIDS. No one can remain insensitive in front of pictures that show hunger in the world or the misery of children in certain countries!

Radio has had the same goals, but in many instances it has lost to television because of the tremendous power of suggestion that a picture possesses. In the entertainment area, for example, television now exercises an almost complete monopoly on sports. In France, it is significant that a dramatic increase in the sales of color television sets is always reported just before Olympic Games.

Television, the newer of the two media, is proving to be a serious competitor for its elder sibling, but in no way is it in the process of making radio obsolete or of replacing it completely.

Television

No other twentieth-century invention has been as often criticized and maligned as television. Frequently referred to as the "boob tube," it has been berated for displaying too much sex and violence, for promoting alcohol through ads, for preventing people, and particularly children and teenagers, from reading. . . . There is hardly one evil in modern society that has not been blamed on television. Yet more and more people watch it worldwide and become addicted to its latest developments, such as video cassette players and computers. It is amazing to see the progress television has made over fifty years.

In France, the first TV program was broadcast in 1935. Two years later, the first live report covered the Universal Exposition and regular programming started. It ceased during the war and resumed in 1945 when the RTF (Radio-diffusion Télévision Française) was created as a government agency. In 1946, French television presented its first weather bulletin, and starting in 1948, it offered regular programming again. On June 29, 1949, Pierre Sabbagh, a television pioneer in France, and someone who has been familiar to French viewers for the last fifty years, anchored the first *Journal télévisé* (Evening News). In 1950, French TV started daily programming and on June 2, 1953, French viewers joined other members of the Eurovision system to watch the live coverage of the coronation of Queen Elizabeth II. The second channel started operating in 1964 and featured the first color programs in 1967. In the beginning, color was available only twelve hours a week, and the rest of the time the channel broadcast in black-and-white. From the start, advertising was completely banned on French television; it was introduced in 1968, but gradually and in very small doses. In 1972, France acquired its third channel. The first cable channel, Canal + , became available in 1984, preceded in 1983 by TV5, a francophone channel transmitted by satellite to French-speaking countries across the world. In 1985 and 1986, two more nongovernment channels, channels 5 and 6, joined the others. In 1986 the government decided to privatize TF1. Today, French viewers can choose among two government-run channels, Antenne 2 and FR3; three privately owned channels, TF1, La 5, and M6; and one cable channel, Canal + . Their selection is not as wide as that of American viewers, but with programs seven days a week and access to six channels for most of the country, they have roughly 500 hours of TV programs for their enjoyment.

What do French people like to watch? News reports punctuate the daily programs. On any of the nonspecialized channels, 20 percent of the programs are usually devoted to news (*La Télévision*, p. 25). The *journaux télévisés* are scheduled at times of heavy viewing: between 7 and 8 in the morning, around 1 P.M., at 8 P.M., and when programs cease at the end of the day. Unlike American channels, French television does not schedule its programs on the hour or on the half-hour. A film may start at 9:10 P.M., for instance, and end at 11:20 P.M. The late news begins immediately after, but it is never at the same time, and it is at a different time on each channel. The only punctual programs are the midday and the evening news, *Le Journal télévisé* at 1 P.M. and 8 P.M. They are so important for the channels and for the viewers that the journalists themselves refer to the evening news as "High Mass" (*La Télévision*, p. 11). For many French families, the beginning of the *Journal télévisé* at night signals that it is time to sit down for dinner. People avoid calling each other on the phone during the *Journal* unless it is a true emergency.

In addition to news reports, French people enjoy news magazines that normally appear weekly or monthly. Next come films, both those featured in theaters and those made for TV. Any of the major channels devotes 20 to 30 percent of its programming to films, but specialized channels show as many as three films a day (*La Télévision*, p. 26). Soap operas and sitcoms are also among the favorites. The most popular, many of them American programs dubbed in French, are scheduled during prime time, between 8:30 P.M. and 10:30 P.M. Over the past twenty years, French viewers have been treated to all the American series, from *Mr. Ed* to *Santa Barbara*, but the all-time successes have undoubtedly been *Dallas* and *Dynasty*. French viewers have become so addicted to such programs that channels have doubled the number of hours during which they have programmed them over the last five years. American soaps and sitcoms are also extremely profitable: viewers never have enough of them, and they are cheap to feature. French television can buy foreign, American, Japanese, and Brazilian series or films for five to ten times less than it would cost them to produce new ones in France.

Games and variety shows are also big hits with French audiences. Many people cease all activities every night when it is time for *Les Chiffres et les lettres*, (Numbers and Letters), a combination of Scrabble and a math game. Once again, some popular American TV games have been adapted directly into French. France has its Vanna White who presents *La Roue de la fortune* (The Wheel of Fortune) every evening. Variety shows are the programs for which French channels spend the most money. Scheduled in prime time, they attract the largest viewership. Finally sports occupy more and more time on French TV, particularly live coverage of national and international sports events. Television is responsible for introducing French people to new sports. Ten years ago, for instance, unless they had visited the United States, French people had never seen an American football game. Now, games are regularly scheduled on TV, an American football league exists in France, and the sport is gaining increased popularity.

Television production is expensive. How do French channels finance their programming, apart from government subsidies for the ones that are state-run? There are two main sources of revenues, and a third one which is just beginning to produce income. The oldest source is known as *la redevance*, a tax people pay every year. It started in 1933 with radio, when every owner of a radio set had to pay an annual tax. The *redevance* on radio sets has been abolished, but it has been put into effect for television sets. The income the government gets from this tax is devoted entirely to supporting television. The amount people have to pay depends on whether they have a black-and-white or a color set. In 1987 it was 506 F ($79) for color and 333 F ($52) for black-and-white. This averages to about 1.30 F (20–25 cents) a day, or three times less than a daily newspaper and four to five times less than a pack of cigarettes. In spite of the small amount received from each TV set owner, in 1987 the government collected 6.653 billion francs ($1.40 billion) (*La Télévision*, pp. 28–29).

Advertising is another major source of income. In 1968, when the first commercials appeared on television, they took up only a few minutes every day. Now, they are as popular as any other programs, but they are far from being as intrusive as advertising on American television. The most desirable spot for advertisers is on Sunday evenings, on TF1, immediately before the film. At that time, a one-minute commercial costs around 280,000F ($43,750). Estimates reveal that in 1987 advertising netted 5.7 billion F (around $890 million) (*La Télévision*, p. 29). In the future, cable channels and pay-per-view channels will generate additional revenues, but they are just beginning to become available to French viewers, and it is still too early to know how popular they are likely to be.

The Importance of Television in the Lives of French People

In 1988 a poll indicated that 72 percent of the French people watched TV every day, 14 percent very frequently, and 3 percent never (*Quid*, p. 1126). An estimated 20 million households representing 94 percent of the population had at least one TV set, and the remaining 6 percent were hard-core extremists whose aversion to television was such that they vowed never to allow a set to cross their front doors (*Francoscopie*, p. 354). With such statistics, it is easy to see that, in less than forty years, television has gained a central role in the daily lives of French people. For many, it has become their main source of entertainment; it punctuates their daily schedules, keeps them company during their meals, and occupies their evenings and weekends. Over the past ten years, the number of hours the French spend in front of their sets has increased steadily, from 2 hours 51 minutes per day per person in 1975, to 3 hours 26 minutes in 1988. Part of this increase must be attributed to the fact that the number of hours during which programs are available has grown regularly during the same period of time. People watch more on weekends—3 hours 57 minutes on Sundays and 3 hours 31 minutes on Saturdays—but during the week, they still manage to average 3 hours 19 minutes. Other European countries show very similar statistics, but the United States is far ahead with slightly more than 7 hours a day (*Francoscopie*, p. 355). Before drawing a comparison between Europe and the United States, one must, however, remember, that most Americans have access to at least 40 channels around the clock, and that in American homes it is not unusual for a set to be left on even when nobody is in the room. Such a practice does not exist in France, where, from an early age, people are taught that electricity is expensive and that the last person to leave a room must turn off everything in order to save energy.

Every day of the week, an estimated 34 million French watch television. Of all the channels, Antenne 2 is the most popular. Although it lost some ground to TF1 a couple of years ago, it soon regained its dominance. People think that it offers the greatest diversity of programs, that it is the most entertaining, the most reliable, and the most objective when it comes to news. TF1 remains a close second; FR3 is viewed as a cultural channel, Canal + as an avant-garde channel, and M6 as a channel primarily for young audiences.

The very young, the teenagers, and the young adults constitute a very important constituency, and French TV producers compete to capture it. For the first time, we have generations who have not experienced life without television. It existed when they were born, and contrary to their parents, they were raised with television. It is interesting to note that before TV, when French children misbehaved, a common punishment was to make them go a certain number of days without eating dessert. Today, this has been replaced by the same number of days without television. TV has become an essential part of children's lives. It is a babysitter, a playmate, and a teacher. It has become their favorite medium. However, compared to a young American who watches TV between 900 and 1,800 hours a year, French children only spend 500 to 1,000 hours in front of their sets (*Juniorscopie*, p. 182). On the whole, children aged eight to fourteen years watch an average of two hours a day. They watch less during weekdays, except on Tuesday evenings because they do not have school on Wednesdays, and more on Wednesdays, Saturdays, and Sundays, during the school year. When they have a vacation, their average rises, but mostly during the winter months. In that age bracket, girls watch less than boys, but that changes when they grow older. In general, until children are fourteen, the older they get, the more TV they watch, but as soon as they turn fifteen, the amount of time they devote to it drops sharply. French psychologists have found that teenagers often blame TV for the difficulties they have in communicating with their parents. Because multiple TV sets are still rare in French households, the family set often occupies a central location, the dining room or the family room, and it is turned on at the time the family gathers in those rooms for a meal, or after or before a meal. Teenagers who try to get their parents' attention often find that the latter do not want to miss a part of their favorite game, or the evening news, or the movie.

Under fourteen, French children are easy to satisfy, and 83 percent of them primarily want cartoons. Since, in France, it costs thirty times more to produce one minute of cartoon than it does in Japan, 85 percent of the cartoons shown on French TV are imports (*Juniorscopie*, p. 183). After fourteen, teenagers are especially interested in films. In the fourteen to eighteen group, 60 percent regularly watch five films a week on television, but this does not prevent them from going to a movie frequently. Next to films, that age group favors rock, pop, and folk music. Until 1986 the time devoted to such programs was limited on the major channels, and that is why Maurice Lévy, director of channel 6, announced that his purpose was to create "a musical channel in jeans" (*Juniorscopie*, p. 188). He wanted to attract viewers from twelve to thirty-four, and his channel was going to consist of 50 percent video clips, with concerts, hit parades, films, and a few original shows making up the rest of the time. To sustain a channel with only those kinds of programs proved to be difficult, and from an almost exclusively musical channel M6 has become a channel for the young adding cartoons, sports events, and more films to its programs.

Radio and Television in the Future

The rivalry between radio and television is still alive. There are people who contend that as remarkable as the survival of radio is, it cannot last because of the development of new technologies associated with television. The territory traditionally considered the domain of radio and inaccessible to TV is rapidly shrinking. Television is becoming so portable that it can be found now in places that it could not reach before. Customized vans are outfitted with a TV set and VCR. Portable color TV sets the size of a postcard are available, and their price continues to go down. The television industry has just announced that portable VCRs will be for sale in 1990. Nevertheless, it is not likely that television will ever replace radio completely or even substantially in the twenty-first century. Radio has established its place as the ideal medium for music. Over the past fifty years, we have witnessed a constant improvement in the quality of sound, and the latest technology has demonstrated that it could still be improved. The greater use of satellites in radio broadcasting will also have a dramatic impact.

The competition between radio and television may even become a new partnership. In France, an engineer invented what is known as "radiovision." It is a new medium which combines an FM radio set and a computer monitor. While a program is broadcast on the radio, written information that is not heard appears on the monitor. Someone might be listening to a literary magazine where authors come and discuss their latest works and, at the same time, receive information about the books themselves on their screens (*La Radio*, pp. 62–64). Somewhat paradoxically, French people spend more and more time in front of their television sets, yet complain about the quality of the programs and rely on substitutes to traditional television. One alternative is the VCR (*magnétoscope*). In 1987, 4.5 million French households had a VCR, compared with 7,000 in 1977 (*Francoscopie*, p. 358). With their VCRs, the French not only tape shows which they cannot see when they are broadcast, but they also use them to watch videos made with their camcorders and, even more, to watch video cassettes they rent. In 1987, close to 50 million videos were rented in France (*Francoscopie*, p. 358). Another way to refuse to be a passive viewer is to use television in conjunction with a computer and to reduce the TV monitor to a mere terminal. Until recently, few French families had personal computers. They were very expensive, and they were considered to be part of one's work environment. The moment children began to use them in schools, and when they became more affordable, they found their way into French homes. The introduction of the "Minitel," that small computer which people plug into their telephone line, which allows them to get phone numbers, plane or train schedules, horoscopes, video games, and many other personal services, has also contributed to the popularization of personal computers. There is no doubt that television has a bright future, but it will have to adapt to new circumstances. The time when viewers sit down and flip from one channel to another until they find something they want to watch is fast disappearing. Viewers are changing from passive to very active viewing habits, and television will thus become a more individualized medium.

BIBLIOGRAPHICAL SURVEY

In researching topics such as radio and television, one must consider three types of sources. First, it is essential to acquire a perspective on the evolution of the media. For that, studies dealing with the history of the development of radio and television will provide the necessary background. Then, to understand the impact of the media on their audiences, scholars must turn to sociological studies. Finally, to examine the changes that occur in the way people relate to the media, it is necessary to look at statistical studies.

As far as radio and television in France are concerned, historical studies are the easiest to come across; they are also the ones most predominantly available in book form. Most of them, of course, are written in French. Books such as Pierre Miquel's *Histoire de la radio et de la télévision* and Jacques Mousseau and Christian Brochand's *Aventure de la télévision* constitute excellent starting points. Miquel's volume, however, is not exclusively devoted to France. It provides interesting comparisons with the development of the media in other countries and it contains a detailed bibliography. Mousseau and Brochand's book is abundantly illustrated. Written for a general public, it belongs with volumes usually found on a coffee table. It contains, however, extremely valuable information, and its presentation as a diary of the history of television in France, year by year from 1926 to 1987, is very helpful. As could be expected, the "Que sais-je?" series offers a volume on the *Histoire de la radio-télévision* by Pierre Albert and André-Jean Tudesq. Like Miquel's book, it covers countries other than France.

Among the volumes with a sociological approach, a scholar will find Jean Cazeneuve's *Les Pouvoirs de la télévision*, Enrique Melon-Martinez' *La Télévision dans la famille et la société modernes*, and Michel Souchon's *Petit Écran*, *grand public* particularly useful. More general works, for example, *Mutation de la culture* by Jean Onimus, and *Les Cultures populaires*, a series edited by Geneviève Poujol and Raymond Labourie, provide solid theoretical background.

For statistical information, one may turn to two monographs published in the Hachette "Échos" series: one, *La Télévision*, authored by Édouard Guibert, and the other, *La Radio*, by Gérard Ponthieu. Their usefulness is limited, however, by the fact that they contain several chapters devoted to technical information that is not relevant to a study of media from the point of view of culture. Much more valuable are books like *Quid*, edited by Dominique and Michèle Frémy, and *Francoscopie: Les Français. Qui sont-ils? Où vont-ils?*, edited by Gérard Mermet. Since a new edition appears every year, these volumes offer up-to-date information and reflect changes in public opinion, tastes, and habits.

Media like radio and, especially, television change constantly. Every year, new technological discoveries bring about new opportunities; listeners and viewers assume an increasingly active role in their interaction with these media. Consequently, anyone interested in radio and television as expressions of popular culture will have to rely heavily on newspaper and magazine articles, and also on shows devoted to these issues on radio and television. With books, the danger is that they become dated very quickly, unless they deal with historical aspects of the subject.

BIBLIOGRAPHY

Albert, Pierre, and Tudesq, André-Jean. *Histoire de la radio-télévision.* Paris: Presses Universitaires de France, 1981.

Bertrand, Claude-Jean. "Les Médias en France et aux États-Unis: un parallèle." *Contemporary French Civilization* 13 (1989): 157–69.

Blanckeman, René. *Le Roman vécu de la télévision française.* Paris: Éditions France-Empire, 1961.

Cazeneuve, Jean. *Les Pouvoirs de la télévision.* Paris: Gallimard, 1970.

Daniels, Douglas J. "Television and/in French Politics." *Contemporary French Civilization* 13 (1989): 190–99.

Duforest, Dominique. *NRJ, ma plus belle histoire.* Monaco: Éditions du Rocher, 1988.

Duval, René. *Histoire de la radio en France.* Paris: Moreau, 1979.

Frémy, Dominique and Michèle. *Quid 1989.* Paris: Laffont, 1988.

Guibert, Édouard. *La Télévision.* Paris: Hachette, 1987. Annual.

Lytel, Davis. "The Impact of Minitel upon French Politics." *Contemporary French Civilization* 13 (1989): 236–47.

Melon-Martinez, Enrique. *La Télévision dans la famille et la société modernes.* Paris: Marabout Université, 1970.

Mermet, Gérard. *Francoscopie. Les Français: Qui sont-ils? Où vont-ils?* Paris: Larousse, 1988.

Miquel, Pierre. *Histoire de la radio et de la télévision.* Paris: Perrin, 1984.

Mousseau, Jacques, and Brochand, Christian. *L'Aventure de la télévision des pionniers à aujourd'hui.* Paris: Nathan, 1987.

Onimus, Jean. *Mutation de la culture: émergence d'une aliénation*. Paris: Desclée, De Brouwer, 1973.

Pigeat, Henri. *La Télévision par câble commence demain*. Paris: Plon, 1983.

Ponthieu, Gérard. *La Radio*. Paris: Hachette, 1987.

Poujol, Geneviève, and Labourie, Raymond, eds. *Les Cultures populaires*. Toulouse: Privat, 1979.

Souchon, Michel. *Petit Écran, grand public*. Paris: La Documentation française, 1980.

Sutton, Homer. "The FM Band in Montpellier, France in 1988: Minority Voices and Radio Fric." *Contemporary French Civilization* 13 (1989): 215–26.

Tamisier, Jacques. "Les Nouvelles Technologies de la communication." *Contemporary French Civilization* 13 (1989): 227–35.

Welcomme, Geneviève, and Willerval, Claire. *Juniorscopie: les 10–20 ans, qui sont-ils? . . . Où vont-ils?* Paris: Larousse, 1986.

Wolton, Dominique. *Éloge du grand public. Une théorie critique de la télévision*. Paris: Flammarion, 1990.

12

Science Fiction

ARTHUR B. EVANS

Paralleling socioliterary trends in both America and England, France has witnessed a continual rise in the popularity and the academic study of "SF" during the latter half of the twentieth century. Heavily eclectic during the 1950s and the early 1960s (reflecting the dominance of Anglo-American SF in the French marketplace), SF writers in France have nevertheless succeeded, during the seventies and eighties, in carving out a special niche for *la science-fiction française* in world literary circles. Described by one critic as "a demanding cocktail of Verne, selective American and British genre influences (the paranoia of Dick and Ballard, Herbert's global galactic politics), and French pragmatism and popular romance, with an added zest of structuralism, existentialism, political commentary, and absurdist preoccupations"[1] and by another as "a special combination of acute political awareness, psychological insight, surrealistic whimsy, imaginative fertility, and sheer metaphysical brain power,"[2] contemporary French SF is an intellectually spicy dish that offers a variety of new and unusual tastes to those with a palate for modern speculative fiction.

HISTORICAL OUTLINE

Although the French neologism *science-fiction* has only quite recently gained critical acceptance in France as a generic label for this brand of writing—as opposed to *roman d'anticipation*, for instance—its tradition in the history of French literature is both long and rich. The earliest works of French SF (to the extent that utopian fantasy and imaginary voyages qualify as such) are undoubtedly Rabelais's *Gargantua* and *Pantagruel* along with his *Tiers Livre*, *Quart Livre*, and *L'Isle sonnante* (1532–64). From their creation of the idyllic Abbey of Thélème to their adventure-filled travels to distant lands of wonder, Rabelais's

Renaissance giants exemplify an unabashed nonconformism, a penchant for encyclopedic erudition, and a passion for exploration beyond the limits of the known. These traits will later characterize much of French science fiction.

More identifiably scientific (although just as fantastic) in nature are Cyrano de Bergerac's *Histoire comique des états et empires de la lune* (1657) and *Histoire comique des états et empires du soleil* (1662). In these comically satirical works, the author journeys to the "States and Empires of the Moon and Sun" in order to discuss issues ranging from physics to metaphysics with the indigenous life forms located there. In so doing, Cyrano portrays varying methods of interplanetary travel—bottles of dew attached to the body, spring-and-rocket machines, a lotion of beef marrow (!), lodestones and iron chariots, and even a solar-powered vessel containing an "iconsahedron crystal"—as well as an astonishing number of other wonders like phonograph-books, mobile cities, molecular shape-shifters, and so on. As fast-paced yarns combining cosmic travel, *libertin* philosophizing, and a host of technological marvels, Cyrano's works are perhaps France's first true SF novels.

In a less risqué and more pragmatically didactic mode (a variant followed by a good deal of early French SF), Fontenelle's *Entretiens sur la pluralité des mondes* (1686) sought both to teach the rudiments of astronomy and to rationally speculate on the possibility of human life elsewhere in the universe. The fictional format used—that of a series of instructive dialogues between a learned scientist/ mentor and a curious young noblewoman/acolyte—established a particular SF narrative recipe that would become highly conventional in France from the late seventeenth century through the end of the nineteenth century.

During the *Siècle des Lumières*, French SF generally continues to oscillate between the dual poles of overt didacticism à la Fontenelle (either scientific or moral) and polemical "alien encounters" à la Cyrano. With the growing popularity of the *conte philosophique* and the reports of faraway exotic cultures brought back by explorers like Bougainville and Cook, French writers increasingly chose the "imaginary voyage" narrative to frame their utopian hypothesizing, their pedagogical (and ethical) demonstrations, and their social satires. Such works as Marivaux's *L'Île des esclaves* (1723), Voltaire's *Micromégas* (1752), Diderot's *Rêve de d'Alembert* (1769) and *Supplément au Voyage de Bougainville* (1772)—not to mention the futuristic *L'An 2440* by Louis-Sébastien Mercier (1771), Casanova's subterranean *Isocaméron* (1788), and Restif de la Bretonne's highly imaginative *La Découverte australe* (1781) and *Les Posthumes* (1796, 1802)—all reflect this passionate interest in distant locales and radically different social perspectives.

During the nineteenth century, under the dual impulses of a new freedom of expression in chosen subjects and narrative form (Romanticism) and the revolutionary social—and ideological—impact of unprecedented technological growth (the Industrial Revolution, Positivism), the SF genre flourished in France as never before. During the first half of the century, many new SF variants were born (although most, unfortunately, failed to gain widespread recognition until

late twentieth-century SF scholarship succeeded in resurrecting their memory):
Cousin de Grainville's realistically apocalyptic *Le Dernier Homme* (1805), No-
dier's futuristic short stories *Hurlubleu* and *Léviathan-le-Long* (1833), the first
great uchronia in Louis Geoffroy's *Napoléon apocryphe* (1836), Grandville's
Robida-like illustrations in *Un autre monde* (1844), the first anti-industrial dys-
topia in Émile Souvestre's *Le Monde tel qu'il sera* (1846), the sociology of an
entire alien civilization in Charles Defontenay's *Star, ou psi de Cassiopée* (1854),
and even the first SF literary theoretician in Félix Bodin's *Le Roman de l'avenir*
(1834).

But it was especially during the latter half of the century that French science
fiction was heralded into what might be called its "golden age" by the *Voyages
Extraordinaires* of Jules Verne. Verne's huge influence on the historical evolution
of the genre—not only in France but worldwide—was both pervasive and long-
lasting. Although generally conservative in his speculations (there are no alien
life forms or future societies in his novels) and heavily didactic in his narrative
recipes, Verne's *romans scientifiques* succeeded in firing the Industrial Age
imaginations of several generations of readers. His fictional journeys target very
real but highly exotic and/or then-inaccessible regions of earth, sea, and space;
his heroic protagonists—often via extraordinary travel machines and invariably
armed with encyclopedic scientific knowledge—methodically explore these regions, brave untold numbers of dangers, faithfully recount their observations
and discoveries, and then return (unscathed and triumphant) to their original
place of departure. From his first "scientific fiction" *Cinq semaines en ballon*
(1863), through his early pro-science works *Voyage au centre de la Terre* (1864),
De la Terre à la Lune (1865), *Vingt mille lieues sous les mers* (1870), and *L'Île
mystérieuse* (1874) and his later somewhat antiscience novels *Sans dessus dessous*
(1889), *Face au drapeau* (1896), and *Maître du monde* (1904), to the posthumous
(and much revamped, by his son Michel) *L'Étonnante Aventure de la mission
Barsac* (1919), Jules Verne's 64-volume output of exciting and educational
"armchair voyages" gained him fame, fortune, and the reputation of being (along
with H. G. Wells) one of the "founding fathers of modern SF."

Although this latter attribute is not entirely accurate (narratologically speaking), Verne did accomplish something vital for the SF genre: he was the first to
firmly establish a large readership for this type of writing—that is, the first to
succeed in popularizing the narrative juxtaposition of science with adventure
fiction. Of course, the term "popular" (at least during Verne's lifetime) pre-
cluded recognition of the *Voyages Extraordinaires* as being sufficiently "literary." And it has only been during the last few decades that Verne's oeuvre has
achieved, in the words of one contemporary critic, "a first-rank position in the
history of French literature" (Angenot).

The imprint of Jules Verne's *romans scientifiques* on the developing SF genre
was deep, and during the latter years of the nineteenth century and the beginning
of the twentieth, a host of French novelists imitated his style (some with commercial success, others without). Included in this sudden influx of "Verne

School'' didactic narratives into the French marketplace were Paul d'Ivoi's series of novels (very suggestively titled) *Voyages excentriques* (1894–1914), Louis Boussenard's *Les Secrets de Monsieur Synthèse* (1888) and *Le Tour du monde d'un gamin de Paris* (1890), Henry de Graffigny's *Voyages fantastiques* (1887) and—with Georges Le Faure—his serial *Aventures extraordinaires d'un savant russe* (1889–96), and Maurice Champagne's *Les Reclus de la mer* (1907) and *Les Sondeurs d'abîmes* (1911).

Also inspired by Verne's example during this *fin-de-siècle* period, but refusing to follow in his exact narratological footsteps, were the astronomer Camille Flammarion, the illustrator Albert Robida, the literary *décadent* Villiers de l'Isle-Adam, and two SF authors who would carry the genre well into the twentieth century and leave a permanent mark on its narrative identity: Gustave Le Rouge and J.-H. Rosny Aîné.

Scientific popularizer and enthusiastic zealot of a kind of cosmic spiritualism, Flammarion was an accomplished astronomer who sought both to teach the rudiments of astronomy and to proselytize his own scientifico-religious beliefs through such works as the Académie-recognized series called *Astronomie Populaire* and *La Pluralité des mondes habités* (perhaps an adaptation of Fontenelle's title?) as well as through a number of unusual fictional romances in which his protagonists broach the mysteries of both the physical and the metaphysical universe. This latter group of texts includes *Les Récits de l'infini* (1862), *Rêves étoilés* (1888), *Uranie* (1889), *La Fin du monde* (1893), and *Stella* (1897).

Albert Robida, satirist *par excellence* and the best-known SF illustrator and caricaturist of this era, also penned a considerable number of futuristic novels where technological conjecture was interlaced with (mostly humorous) social commentary. Beginning with a serial parody of Verne's works in *Voyages très extraordinaires de Saturnin Farandoul dans les 5 ou 6 parties du monde et dans tous les pays connus et même inconnus de Monsieur Jules Verne* (1879–82), Robida's most characteristic SF works of futuristic speculation include *Le Vingtième Siècle* (1883), *La Vie électrique* (1893), and the more pessimistic *L'Ingénieur Von Satanas* (1919).

Villiers de l'Isle-Adam, in his very Faustian *L'Ève future* (1886), initiated yet another modern SF variant with his wondrous android named Hadaly: a self-aware Asimovian robot who, invented by Thomas Edison as the ''perfect'' female and the ideal companion, serves to trigger a variety of ontological and aesthetic questions about the fundamental nature of reality and artistic creation in a progressively synthetic world where things are not always what they seem.

It was in the works of Gustave Le Rouge and especially J.-H. Rosny Aîné, however, that ''modern'' French SF was truly born. Partially in the former and more fully in the latter, the SF *novum* reaches a more polysemic configuration and the diagetic structure of the narratives themselves venture well beyond the traditional French patterns of utopian postulation, scientific didacticism, social satire, or pseudo-gothic fantastic. In these two more speculative types of SF, the reader's cognition is increasingly challenged by what Angenot has labeled "absent paradigms" in the reading process itself. And the many "alien encounters" within these fictions tend to be just as often narratological as they are extraterrestrial.

In Gustave Le Rouge's *Le Prisonnier de la planète Mars* (1908) and *La Guerre des vampires* (1909), for example, the functional role of science and technology in the narrative shifts from principal subject to plot accessory—that is, from a means of explaining and "dealienating" the unknown to becoming a verisimilitude-builder of the plot and a purveyor of obscurantist "special effects"—in order to enhance the interplanetary and telepathic adventures of its young scientist-hero. Instead of conveying science via fiction, these texts convey the fiction via science. And the science itself is most often invented, imaginary, and wholly fictional. Written in the "pulp" vein of *Amazing Stories* and Edgar Rice Burroughs' Martian tales, Le Rouge's novels thus exemplify the growing paradigm of *space opera*-cum-*heroic fantasy*—an SF variant very popular in France during the late nineteenth century and early twentieth (predating the era of Hugo Gernsback). Ironically, this popularity made a strong comeback in France in the form of a massive influx of translated Anglo-American SF during the 1950s.

The place of J.-H. Rosny Aîné in the evolution of French SF (and the genre as a whole) is curiously underestimated. In many respects, Rosny could—and should—be considered the true "father" of modern French SF, both chronologically and narratologically. Remembered far more for his exotic prehistoric novels like *Vamireh* (1892), *La Guerre du feu* (1909, Hollywood's version: *Quest for Fire*, 1982), and *Le Félin géant* (1918), Rosny also left an indelible mark on French SF with an astonishing variety of narratives featuring inscrutably alien life forms, parallel worlds, and unexplained natural phenomena—fictions that are highly visionary in nature but, at the same time, firmly anchored in scientific plausibility. Rosny's *Les Xipéhuz* (1887) was the first realistically portrayed tale of humanity's encounter with intelligent (yet totally impenetrable) alien organisms constructed wholly of energy. This basic theme was transposed to an end-of-the-world scenario in *La Mort de la Terre* (1910), where the human species is finally superseded by higher (albeit mineral) life forms called the *ferromagnétaux*. In the same line, *Les Navigateurs de l'infini* (1925) and its posthumous sequel *Les Astronautes* posit a highly evolved Martian race whose physical configuration is based on a ternary symmetry, who reproduce by parthenogenesis, and with a female specimen of whom (for the first time in SF, to my knowledge) a visiting Earthling has a very "alien" love affair. Examples of SF narratives developing the alternate world-parallel dimension motifs range from *Un autre monde* (1895) to *Dans le monde des Variants* (1939) and include *Nymphée* (1893), *Les Profondeurs de Kyamo* (1896), *Le Voyage* (1900), *Le Trésor dans la neige* (1922), and *Les Hommes-sangliers* (1929). In addition, those dealing with strange (though not supernatural) unexplained phenomena include *Le Cataclysme* (1888) and *La Force mystérieuse* (1913), the latter most likely the source for Arthur Conan Doyle's *The Poison Belt* appearing later during the same year. Expanding the frontiers of SF into previously unexplored thematic domains and hermeneutic patterns, Rosny Aîné brought a new level of sophistication and vision to the genre (similar, in some respects, to that of Campbell's *Astounding Stories*) and set the stage for much of what was to follow during the late twentieth century.

Other SF writers and works of this very rich period from 1880 to 1940 include André Laurie's (Paschal Grousset) *Les Exilés de la Terre* (1887), the militaristic Capitaine Danrit's *La Guerre de demain* (1889–1896), Jules Lermina's *À brûler, conte astral* (1889), John-Antoine Nau's unusual but Goncourt-prizewinning *Force ennemie* (1903), the incredibly prolific Jean de la Hire's *La Roue fulgurante* (1908), André Couvreur's *Une invasion des microbes* (1909), Gaston de Pawlowski's highly imaginative *Voyage au pays de la quatrième dimension* (1912, 1923), Claude Farrère's pessimistically Darwinian *Les Condamnés à mort* (1920), Théo Varlet and Octave Joncquel's Martian epic *Les Titans du ciel* (1921) and *L'Agonie de la Terre* (1922), José Moselli's surprisingly prophetic *La Fin d'Illa* (1925), Ernest Pérochon's *Les Hommes frénétiques* (1925), Octave Béliard's *Les Petits Hommes de la pinède* (1927), H.-J. Magog's super-brainy *Trois ombres sur Paris* (1928), André Mad's (Max André Dazergues) *L'Île de Satan* (1931), René Thévenin's tale of mutants *Les Chasseurs d'hommes* (1933), Régis Messac's de-evolutionary *Quinzinzinzili* (1935), Jean d'Aigraives' (Frédéric Causse) *L'Empire des algues* (1935), and René-Marcel de Nizerolles's more conventional Verne-like sagas *Les Voyages aériens d'un petit Parisien* (1933–38). During this ''golden era'' of French SF, even a number of mainstream literary authors successfully dabbled in the genre: Léon Daudet with his *Les Morticoles* (1894) and *Le Napus, fléau de l'an 2227* (1927), Anatole France's *L'Île des pingouins* (1909), Maurice Leblanc's *Les Trois yeux* (1919) and *Le Formidable Événement* (1920), and André Maurois with his *Le Peseur d'âmes* (1931) and *La Machine à lire les pensées* (1937). But two SF authors of this period deserve special attention: Maurice Renard and Jacques Spitz. Maurice Renard succeeded in fusing together a kind of speculative Wellsian SF with Hoffmannesque horror in works such as the very *Moreau*-like *Le Docteur Lerne, sous-dieu* (1908) and his famous *Le Péril bleu* (1911), *Les Mains d'Orlac* (1920, Hollywood's version: *Mad Love*, 1934), and *L'Homme truqué* (1921). Jacques Spitz, writing during the socially turbulent pre–World War II years, perpetuated Renard's hybrid SF/fantastic narrative recipe—but added a pinch of cynical black humor and a dash of political overtones—with such darkly symbolic works as *L'Agonie du globe* (1935), *Les Évadés de l'an 4000* (1936), *La Guerre des mouches* (1938), *L'Homme élastique* (1938), and the very existential *L'Œil du purgatoire* (1945).

This ''golden age'' of French SF, however, came to an abrupt halt with the advent of World War II and, among other factors, the disappearance of an until-then booming ''pulp'' industry of SF journals and magazines like *Lectures pour Tous, Sciences et Voyages, Je sais tout, La Petite Illustration*, and—the flagship of such periodicals—the popular *Journal des Voyages* (which, shortly after the war, was briefly resurrected but soon went the way of its companion publications). A small number of SF veterans from the 1920s and 1930s continued to publish an occasional work—Léon Groc with *Une invasion de Sélénites* (1941) and *La Planète de cristal* (1944), Jacques Spitz with *L'Expérience du docteur Mops* (1939) and *La Parcelle "Z"* (1942), and the Belgian writer Jean Ray with *Malpertuis* (1943)—but the once voluminous flow of SF production in France suddenly dwindled to a mere trickle. The only new SF writers to emerge from the chaos of war-torn France during this period were René Barjavel with *Ravage* (1943) and *Le Voyageur imprudent* (1944) and the playwright Jacques Audiberti with his *Carnage* (1942). Both in tone and narrative subject—pessimistic and antimachinism, escapist time travel, etc.—these few works largely reflect the troubled tenor of their times.

In SF, as in many other aspects of French society, the late 1940s in France was a period of slow rebirth and reevaluation. A few seasoned warhorses of the genre continued to produce: Léon Groc with *Le Maître du soleil* (1946) and *L'Univers vagabond* (1950), Paul Alpérine with *La Citadelle des glaces* (1946) and *Demain dans le soleil* (1950), and Maurice Lionel (Maurice Limat) with *Un drame en astronef* (1947) and *La Comète écarlate* (1948). A few authors who had begun their SF careers during the previous decade persisted in their craft, such as René Barjavel with the apocalyptic *Le Diable l'emporte* (1948) and Jacques Audiberti with *L'Opéra du monde* (1947). And a few younger writers tried their hand at SF for the first time: B. R. Bruss (Roger Blondel) with his antinuclear Hiroshima-inspired *Et la Planète sauta . . .* (1946) and Pierre Devaux (editor of the newly launched SF collection "Science et Aventure," oriented toward adolescents) with his *X.P. 15 en feu!* (1946) and *L'Exilé de l'espace* (1947). But despite these isolated efforts, the SF tradition in France during the immediate post-World War II years could be generally described as weak and weary, sputtering back to life but lacking the vigor of its old prewar self.

Then, between 1950 and 1955, a second (ultimately more salutary, but just as jarring) invasion of France occurred: hordes of translated "golden age" Anglo-American SF novels from the 1930s and 1940s—authors like Asimov, Bradbury, Clarke, Heinlein, Sturgeon, Simak, Van Vogt, et al.—began to find immediate success in the French SF marketplace. Sensitive to their public's desire for more of the same, a number of French publishers quickly responded with imprints: the "Anticipation" series by Fleuve Noir and the "Rayon Fantastique" collection by Gallimard and Hachette in 1951, the French reprints of the American SF magazines *Galaxy* and *Magazine of Fantasy and SF* (called *Galaxie* and *Fiction* respectively) in 1953, and the "Présence du Futur" series by Denoël in 1954—all of which served as major conduits to this growing Anglo-American SF presence on French soil. And, spearheaded by the efforts of a few forward-looking authors and critics like Boris Vian (musician, translator, critic, and writer of a few highly surrealistic SF novels), Raymond Queneau, Stéphane Spriel, Michel Carrouges, and Michel Butor, the SF genre was (once again) very *à la mode* in French popular and literary circles—along with American gadgets, Hollywood films, and jazz.[3]

The effects of this tidal wave of Anglo-American SF into postwar France proved to be both positive and negative. On the one hand, it served to suddenly reawaken French interest in SF and to infuse "new blood" into the French SF genre—new visions of the future, new narrative techniques, and new publishing outlets for aspiring novelists.

On the other hand, it encouraged knee-jerk imitation of these successful foreign authors, temporarily suppressed the development in France of a more identifiably indigenous SF, and created a publishing market strongly prejudiced toward translated imports.

Yet during the fifties and early sixties, a number of French SF authors did manage to rise above the tide. They can generally be divided into two overlapping groups: those who specialized in eclectic space operas (most often publishing in the "Anticipation" collection of Fleuve Noir) and those somewhat more original authors (most often first published in the journal *Fiction* and the "Présence du Futur" series) who would ultimately lead French SF into its sudden renaissance of the 1970s and 1980s.

In the former "space opera" group: the two pulpy but highly prolific writers using the pseudonym F. Richard-Bessière with such works as *Les Conquérants de l'univers* (1951), *Sauvetage sidéral* (1954), *Fléau de l'univers* (1957), and *Les 7 anneaux de Rhéa* (1962); the equally pulpy but no less prolific Jimmy Guieu with *Pionnier de l'atome* (1951), the award-winning *L'Homme de l'espace* (1954), and *L'Ère des Biocybs* (1960); B. R. Bruss with his *S.O.S. Soucoupes* (1954), *Terre . . . siècle 24* (1959), and *La Guerre des robots* (1966); and the sometimes quite innovative J. G. Vandel with *Les Chevaliers de l'espace* (1952), *Naufrage des galaxies* (1954), and *Le Troisième Bocal* (1956).

In the latter more "original" group: Francis Carsac (François Bordes) with his metallic descendants of Rosny Aîné's *ferromagnétaux* in *Ceux de nulle part* (1954), his "Spaceship Earth" voyages in *La Terre en fuite* (1960), and his alien ethnography in *Ce Monde est nôtre* (1962); the incomparable Stefan Wul (Pierre Pairault) with his award-winning *Retour à "O"* (1956), his post–World War III portrait of New York in *Niourk* (1957), the astonishing and evolutionary *Le Temple du passé* (1958), the SF/spy novel *Piège sur Zarkass* (1958), and the apocalyptic *La Mort vivante* (1959); Charles and Nathalie Henneberg with their award-winning mythological epic *La Naissance des dieux* (1954) and their exotic Leiberesque *La Rosée du soleil* (1959); Kurt Steiner (André Ruellan) with his *Menace d'Outre-Terre* (1958) and especially his future-medieval *Aux Armes d'Ortoq* (1960); Gilles d'Argyre (Gérard Klein) with his Stapledon-like galactic voyages in *Le Gambit des étoiles* (1958) and *Les Voiliers du soleil* (1961) as well as *Les Tueurs de temps* (1965); the prolific pharmacist Pierre Barbet (Claude Avice) with his nova-induced mutants in *Babel 3805* (1962); Daniel Drode with his award-winning but controversial SF *nouveau roman*, *Surface de la planète* (1959); Philippe Curval (Philippe Tronche) with his highly imaginative alien life forms in *L'Odeur de la bête* (1957), *Les Fleurs de Vénus* (1960), and his award-winning *Le Ressac de l'espace* (1962); Jacques Sternberg with his absurdist short-story collections like *La Géométrie dans l'impossible* (1953) and *Entre deux mondes incertains* (1957); and, of course, the mainstream writer Pierre Boulle, whose futuristic satire on the human species in *La Planète des singes* (1963) inspired the popular—and loosely adapted—Hollywood movie and seemingly interminable number of cinematic sequels.

Following a brief slump during the early and mid-1960s (and the demise of the "Rayon Fantastique" collection in 1964), French SF truly began to come into its own during the late sixties and especially throughout the seventies and early eighties. No longer imitating the imported "space opera" models prevalent during the postwar decade, new French science fiction surged into the marketplace and increasingly ventured into previously uncharted cognitive and narrative realms. The reasons for this sudden and unexpected renaissance in French SF are very complex and undoubtedly the result of many different factors. But, among them, one must note the following: the social upheaval in France begun by the May 1968 revolutionary protests (and its accompanying anti-Americanism); the pervasive influence of certain antiestablishment Anglo-American "New Wave" SF writers like J. G. Ballard and Philip K. Dick; the advent of structuralism and poststructuralism in university literary studies; the rediscovery and republication of a variety of French SF "ancestors" such as Jules Verne, Rosny Aîné, and Gustave Le Rouge; the rising popularity of adult SF comic magazines like *Métal Hurlant;* and, finally, the sudden proliferation of SF collections among French publishing houses (Gérard Klein's "Ailleurs et Demain" series begun by Laffont in 1969) as well as the establishment of several yearly SF conventions and annual awards (the Prix Apollo in 1972 and the Grand Prix de la Science-Fiction Française in 1974).

A small number of seasoned SF writers—survivors of the difficult 1950s and 1960s—became the recognized standard-bearers of this new boom. In general, their works reflected the new ideological preoccupations of the times—authors whose fictional goals were more political and social in nature and whose narratives foregrounded psychology and experimental hermeneutic structures more often than star cruisers and laser weapons. Riding the crest of this "new golden age" was Philippe Curval, who was awarded the Grand Prix in 1975 for his obsessively Freudian *L'Homme à rebours* and who, two years later, won the coveted Prix Apollo for his prophetic utopia/dystopia *Cette chère humanité*— the first French author to receive the award—and whose popularity has extended into the early 1980s with the erotic *La Face cachée du désir* (1980), *En souvenir du futur* (1983), and *Comment jouer à l'homme invisible en trois leçons* (1986). Michel Jeury, whose first novels (published under the pseudonym of Albert Higon) *La Machine du pouvoir* (1959) and *Aux étoiles du destin* (1960) were successful space operas, expanded and matured his repertoire with a series of imaginative psycho-socio-politico-time-travel tales in *Le Temps incertain* (winner of the Grand Prix of 1974), *Soleil chaud poisson des profondeurs* (1976), *Le Territoire humain* (1979), and other multidimensional and somewhat mystical works like *Les Écumeurs du silence* (1980), *L'Orbe et la roue* (1982, Prix Apollo for 1983), *L'Anaphase du diable* (1984), and *Le Jeu du monde* (1985). Other SF stalwarts enjoying this new prosperity included the prolific Pierre Barbet whose translations of *À quoi songent les psyborgs?* (1971) and *L'Empire de Baphomet* (1973) won him immediate popularity among American SF fans; Michel Demuth with his *Foundation*-like epic cycle of future history titled *Les Galaxiales* (1964–79, Grand Prix in 1977), and Gérard Klein with his "stochasticratic" *Le Sceptre du hasard* (1968) and his narrative mixture of metaphysical musings and space opera techniques in *Les Seigneurs de la guerre* (1971)—both of these writers doubling as editors of SF collections and/or journals during this period; Jean-Pierre Andrevon with his purposely *engagé* political and ecological short-story collections such as *Aujourd'hui, demain et après* (1970, 1982), *Cela se produira bientôt* (1971), *Paysages de mort* (1978), and *Dans les décors truqués* (1979); and finally, the Joycean-cum-Kafkaesque journalist Daniel Walther with his very poetic *Mais l'espace . . . mais le temps* (1972), his SF/fantastic *L'Épouvante* (1979, Grand Prix of 1980), his many Renard-like short stories in *Requiem pour demain* (1976) and *Les Quatre saisons de la nuit* (1980) as well as his intellectually erotic *Sept femmes de mes autres vies* (1985).

An entirely new generation of young SF writers also began to make their presence felt during the late 1970s and early 1980s. This very politicized "New Wave" of writers was led by the militant Bernard Blanc who, both as a writer with his polemical *Pourquoi j'ai tué Jules Verne* (1978) and as an editor with his short-lived but provocative "Ici et Maintenant" collection (Kesselring), proselytized confrontation and social praxis through the SF genre. In 1977 the venerable French SF critic Jacques Goimard characterized this "New Wave SF" phenomenon as follows: "The younger SF has become more radical. . . . The themes remain more or less the same . . . social criticism . . . sexual liberation. . . . But what is really new is this appearance of a militant SF which seeks not only to *analyze* a society but also to actively *transform* it." Despite its ephemeral existence (sinking from view within a few years), this spontaneous movement within the French SF community helped to breed a new generation of young SF writers. Most were only marginally affiliated with the aggressively political "New SF," but all were, in one way or another, affected by it. Some attempted to orient their SF works to the prescribed goals; others reacted violently against them and espoused ideological positions that were diametrically opposite. But out of this ideological civil war within the French SF rank and file would emerge a number of highly imaginative young writers who would carry the genre through the current decade: Serge Brussolo, Jean-Pierre Hubert, Jean-Marc Ligny, Dominique Douay, Pierre Pelot, Philip Goy, Joëlle Wintrebert, Pierre Giuliani, among others.

During the eighties this decade-long boom of French science fiction has (perhaps predictably) begun to slow down. Current production in France is still relatively high and the overall economic health of the genre is not in danger. But, especially in comparison with the market conditions of the late 1970s, SF readership has tended to taper off, new fanzines and journals disappear one after another, and serious critical works on French SF have declined.[4] According to Denis Guiot, a contemporary SF critic:

The "New French SF"—which never really had an audience—was the first victim of the current crisis; an ill-fated movement which has resulted in a certain distrust of SF among publishers, readers, and individual SF writers themselves who, in reaction, have now adopted a more formalist approach . . . avant-garde SF . . . unconcerned with readability, disconnected from socio-techno-political realities, anti-novelistic (don't even ask about characters, plots, or emotions), and who . . . have submerged themselves . . . into the elitist delights of experimental literature.

Nevertheless, despite what some have labeled a "morose atmosphere" (Guiot) in the current SF community, a number of talented young authors have continued to reinvigorate the genre. Foremost among them is the controversial Serge Brussolo, who burst onto the French SF scene with his short story *Funnyway* in 1978 (winning the Grand Prix). Brussolo's wildly imaginative and surrealistic novels throughout the early 1980s—*Vue en coupe d'une ville malade* (1980, Grand Prix of 1981), *Sommeil de sang* (1982), *Carnaval de fer* (1983), and *Les Semeurs d'abîmes* (1983, Prix Apollo, the third French writer after Curval and Jeury to receive this honor)—are a kind of modern SF cross-pollination of the "convulsive beauty" aesthetics of Breton, the hallucinatory dreamscapes of Dali, and the richly obsessive phantasms of Ballard. Alongside Brussolo are the style-conscious and allegorically sociopolitical Jean-Pierre Hubert with his *Mort à l'étouffée* (1978), the somber *Le Champ du rêveur* (1983, Grand Prix of 1984), and *Ombromanies* (1985); the multitalented and highly prolific Pierre Pelot with his *Delirium Circus* (1977, Grand Prix of 1978), *La Guerre olympique* (1980), *Les Îles du vacarme* (1981), *Mourir au hasard* (1982), and a series of evolutionary end-of-the-world novels like *Les Mangeurs d'argile* (1981), *Soleils hurlants* (1983), and *Ce Chasseur-là* (1985); the *nouveau roman*-inspired work of Emmanuel Jouanne with *Damiers imaginaires* (1982) and *Nuage* (1983); the most successful woman SF writer of the 1980s, Joëlle Wintrebert with her *Les Olympiades truquées* (1980), *Les Maîtres-feu* (1983), and *Chromoville* (1984); and a variety of other young authors like Bruno Lecigne, Sylviane Corgiat, Pierre Bilon (Grand Prix of 1983 for his *L'Enfant du cinquième Nord*), Daniel Martinange, Jean-Pierre Vernay, Joël Houssin (Grand Prix of 1986 for his *Les Vautours*), G.-J. Arnaud, Jacques Boireau, Charles Dobzynski, René Sussan, Antoine Volodine (Grand Prix of 1987 for his *Rituel du mépris*), Michel Grimaud, Francis Berthelot, Lorris Murail, Jacques Mondoloni, Jacques Barbéri, Jean-Claude Dunyach, Roland Wagner, and Richard Canal—all of whom constitute the future of the SF genre in France as it approaches the twenty-first century.

REFERENCE WORKS AND CRITICAL SOURCES

English

Aside from the innumerable studies of "mainstream" authors such as Rabelais and Voltaire, the corpus of English-language criticism on French science fiction remains, to date, very meager and—with a few notable exceptions—consists of approximately two dozen articles in scholarly journals and an occasional thumbnail overview in SF encyclopedias. Monographs on individual SF writers of France are rare. Surprisingly, even the legendary Jules Verne himself—by far the most universally recognized French author in this domain and the one whose novels have, during the past 125 years, drawn the bulk of Anglo-American critical attention—has had only a small handful of book-length English-language studies devoted to him. And most of these are either very dated, very shallow and stereotypical, or very recently translated from the French.

The most reliable and up-to-date books on Jules Verne available in English include the bibliography by Edward J. Gallagher et al. titled *Jules Verne: A Primary and Secondary Bibliography* (1980); the translated biography by the author's grandson Jean Jules-Verne titled *Jules Verne: A Biography* (1976); the translated study by Jean Chesneaux, *The Political and Social Ideas of Jules Verne* (1972); Andrew Martin's *The Knowledge of Ignorance from Cervantes to Jules Verne* (1985); William Butcher's *Verne's Journey to the Centre of the Self* (1990); and—in all modesty—my recent study titled *Jules Verne Rediscovered: Didacticism and the Scientific Novel* (1988).

The most valuable English-language articles on Verne include the following: Marc Angenot's "Jules Verne and French Literary Criticism, I, II" (*Science-Fiction Studies*, 1973, 1976) and "Jules Verne: The Last Happy Utopianist" (in Patrick Parrinder's *Science Fiction: A Critical Guide*, 1979); Roland Barthes's translated "The *Nautilus* and the Drunken Boat" (*Mythologies*, trans. 1972); Ray Bradbury's "The Ardent Blasphemers" (preface to Jules Verne's translated *Twenty Thousand Leagues under the Sea*, 1962); Ross Chamber's "Cultural and Ideological Determinations in Narrative: A Note on Jules Verne's *Les Cinq cent millions de la Bégum*" (*L'Esprit créateur*, 1981); Michel Serres's translated "India (the Black and the Archipelago) on Fire" (*Sub-Stance*, 1974) and his "Jules Verne's Strange Journeys" (*Yale French Studies*, 1975); André Winandy's "The Twilight Zone: Image and Reality in Jules Verne's *Strange Journeys*" (*Yale French Studies*, 1969); Peter Aberger's "The Portrayal of Blacks in Jules Verne's *Voyages Extraordinaires*" (*French Review*, 1979); David Ketterer's "Fathoming *20,000 Leagues under the Sea*" (in *The Stellar Gauge: Essays on Science Fiction Writers*, 1980); Andrew Martin's "The Entropy of Balzacian Tropes in the Scientific Fictions of Jules Verne" (*Modern Language Review*, 1982) and his "Chez Jules: Nutrition and Cognition in the Novels of Jules Verne" (*French Studies*, 1983); Marilyn Gaddis Rose's "Two Misogynist Novels: A Feminist Reading of Villiers and Verne" (*Nineteenth-Century French Studies*, 1980–81); Mark Rose's "Filling the Void: Verne, Wells and Lem" (*Science-Fiction Studies*, 1981) and his "Jules Verne: Journey to the Center of Science Fiction" (in George Slusser et al., *Coordinates: Placing Science Fiction and Fantasy*, 1983); Marie-Hélène Huet's "Anticipating the Past" (in George Slusser, *Storm Warnings: Science Fiction Confronts the Future*, 1987); and my own "The Extraordinary Libraries of Jules Verne" (*L'Esprit créateur*, 1988).

Apart from these studies of Jules Verne, examples of English-language books on French SF are fewer and farther between. Standing almost alone in this regard are Paul Alkon's *Origins of Futuristic Fiction* (1987) and Darko Suvin's *Metamorphoses of Science Fiction* (1979)—both of which discuss a number of pre-twentieth-century French SF writers (the latter being more diachronic and theoretical in nature; the former being more synchronic and detailed). Also very useful as historical—albeit necessarily cursory—overviews of the genre in France are Maxim Jakubowski's contribution titled "French SF" in Neil Barron's *Anatomy of Wonder* (2d ed., 1981; 3d ed., 1987, each with a selected and annotated bibliography of French SF); Patrick Parrinder's somewhat pejorative "European SF" in *Science Fiction: A Critical Guide* (1979); John Dean's "French Science Fiction: The Intergalactic European Connection" in the *Stanford French Review* (1979); and those entries (listed under "France") contained in a few SF encyclopedias—the most satisfying being the one in Peter Nicholls' *The Encyclopedia of Science Fiction* (1979).

And finally, those few scholarly articles available in English on non-Vernian French SF include Marc Angenot's "Science Fiction in France before Verne" (*Science-Fiction Studies*, 1978), his "Albert Robida's Twentieth Century" (*Science-Fiction Studies*, 1983), and his "The Emergence of the Anti-Utopia Genre in France" (*Science-Fiction Studies*, 1985); J.-P. Vernier's "The SF of J.-H. Rosny the Elder" (*Science-Fiction Studies*, 1975); Daniel Walther's "Political SF in France" (*Foundation*, 1980); Ceri Crossley's "Émile Souvestre's Anti-Utopia: *Le Monde tel qu'il sera*" (*Nottingham French Studies*, 1985); Anthony Zielonka's "Defontenay's *Star* as Poetic and Philosophical Science Fiction" (*French Forum*, 1986); and my own "Science Fiction vs. Scientific Fiction in France: From Jules Verne to Rosny Aîné" (*Science-Fiction Studies*, 1988).

French

Fortunately for contemporary scholarship in this field, the situation is far less bleak in France and in Quebec. During the French SF boom of the 1970s, and paralleling the substantial rise of home-grown SF narratives published, an increasing number of critical and reference works began to appear on the market as well. They were generally of two types: those devoted specifically to Jules Verne (who, during this period, was enjoying a veritable renaissance of popularity) and those critical studies targeting Anglo-American and French SF writers, both old and new.

Although far too numerous to cite here (consult the Gallagher bibliography mentioned above or the extensive bibliography on Verne included in my book), a few of the more important book-length studies on Verne published in French include the following: Piero Gondolo della Riva's *Bibliographie analytique de toutes les œuvres de Jules Verne* (1977–85), Charles-Noël Martin's *La Vie et l'œuvre de Jules Verne* (1978), Marcel Moré's *Le Très Curieux Jules Verne* (1960) and his *Nouvelles Explorations de Jules Verne* (1963), François Raymond's continuing series titled *Jules Verne* (1976–), Christian Robin's *Un monde connu et inconnu* (1978), Michel Serres's *Jouvences sur Jules Verne* (1974), Simone Vierne's *Jules Verne et le roman initiatique* (1973) and her *Jules Verne* (1986), Olivier Dumas's recent *Jules Verne* (1988), and the several published accounts of Jules Verne colloquia such as *Jules Verne et les sciences humaines* (1979) held at Cérisy-la-Salle in 1978 and *Modernités de Jules Verne* (1988) held at Amiens in 1985.

Among the hundreds of scholarly articles published on Verne during the past two decades, one must mention those few which led the way—Roland Barthes's "Nautilus et Bateau Ivre" (in his *Mythologies*, 1957) and "Par où commencer?" (*Poétique*, 1970), Michel Butor's "Le Point suprême et l'âge d'or à travers quelques œuvres de Jules Verne" (in his *Répertoire I*, 1960), and Michel Foucault's "L'Arrière-fable" (*L'Arc*, 1966), being the most influential—and those many excellent studies by contemporary Vernian scholars like Alain Buisine, Simone Vierne, Daniel Compère, Olivier Dumas, François Raymond, Christian Robin, and others who, throughout the 1970s and 1980s, have succeeded in rehabilitating the myth-worn reputation of Jules Verne and firmly establishing the many novels of the *Voyages Extraordinaires* as "literary" masterpieces. At the forefront of this ongoing effort has been (since 1935) the Société Jules Verne and its quarterly journal the *Bulletin de la Société Jules Verne*.

For French SF writers other than Jules Verne, the most comprehensive (although yet to be translated) compendium on the topic continues to be Pierre Versins's mammoth 1972 (2d ed., 1984—with index) *Encyclopédie de l'Utopie, des Voyages Extraordinaires et de la Science-Fiction*: more that 1,000 pages covering both famous and obscure French and Anglo-American authors and works, facts and figures, themes and publisher collections, and other assorted miscellanea—all arranged alphabetically with extensive (though highly idiosyncratic) commentaries on each.

Supplementing Versins's encyclopedia, and an unsurpassed reference for French SF of the period from 1976 to 1983, is the annual series entitled *L'Année de la science-fiction et du fantastique* edited by one of the publishing deans of French SF, Jacques Goimard (replaced during the final year by Daniel Riche). This 300-page yearly publication features book reviews, club news, critical articles, and detailed summaries of SF from the prior year as it appeared in films, comics, television, music (!), and art. A very rich source of research material for the genre, it sadly was discontinued after the 1982–83 edition.

A variety of bio-bibliographical and historical-thematic works appearing in the 1970s and 1980s (and almost all yet to be translated into English) span both Anglo-American and French SF and offer a broad range of valuable critical perspectives on the genre. In the former (more enumerative) group: Stan Barets' *Catalogue des âmes et cycles de la SF* (1979), the most recent *La Science-fiction* by Denis Guiot, J. P. Andrevon, and G. W. Barlow (1987), Claude Aziza and Jacques Goimard's *Encyclopédie de poche de la science-fiction* (1986), Henri Delmas and Alain Julian's *Le Rayon SF* (1983, 1985), and Alain Villemur's *63 auteurs: bibliographie de la science-fiction* (1976). In the latter (more expository) group: Jean-Jacques Bridenne's *La Littérature française d'imagination scientifique* (1950), Jacques Van Herp's *Panorama de la science-fiction* (1973, 1975), Jacques Sadoul's *Histoire de la science-fiction moderne (1911–1975), Vol. 2, Domaine français* (1973, 1975), Jean Gattégno's "Que sais-je?" publication *La Science-fiction* (1971, 1983), Henri Baudin's *La Science-fiction: un univers en expansion* (1971), and Igor and Grichka Bogdanoff's *Clefs pour la science-fiction* (1976).

Also of special interest are certain issues of periodicals devoted wholly or in part to SF, such as *Europe* 139–40 (1957) and 580–81 (1977), *Opus International* 64 (1977), *Change* 40 (1981), and *Le Français dans le Monde* 193 (1985), which offer a condensed selection of both theoretical and analytical articles on the genre—its evolution, its social and literary significance, and how it is perceived in France.

Finally, one must acknowledge the growing collection of scholarly articles on French SF that have appeared in specialized French journals and fanzines since the 1950s. Foremost among such periodicals is *Fiction* (begun in 1953 as the French equivalent of *The Magazine of Fantasy and Science Fiction*), featuring studies by such veteran SF critics as the late Jean-Jacques Bridenne, Jacques Van Herp, and Pierre Versins as well as contributions by noted contemporary SF writers like Jean-Pierre Andrevon and Gérard Klein (see Bibliography).

As a brief addendum to this overview of French SF criticism available in French, special mention should be made of two Quebec-based SF journals: *Solaris* (begun in 1974 as *Requiem*) and *Imagine*...(begun in 1979, both of which, in addition to their frequent studies of francophone SF published in Canada, occasionally offer very informative essays on their counterparts in France as well.

RESEARCH COLLECTIONS AND SPECIALIZED BOOKSTORES

The most comprehensive (if somewhat museum-like) research collection on French SF and related materials continues to be at the Maison d'Ailleurs located in Yverdon-les-Bains, Switzerland. With over 10,000 items—ranging from original manuscripts and first editions to SF posters, toys, and paintings—and over 5,000 French SF novels and critical works, the Maison d'Ailleurs was originally established by Pierre Versins and Martine Thome to house their private collections. During the past few years, the Maison has experienced financial and legal woes, and (at this printing) has yet to find a permanent home. Its current director is Roger Gaillard. Along with Versins's *Encyclopédie*, the Maison d'Ailleurs should be one of the fundamental touchstones of anyone interested in French SF.

Although geared more to English-language SF, the Spaced Out Library of the

Toronto Public Library (40 St. George Street, Toronto, Ontario M5S 2E4) also contains a good deal of French SF, including an impressive Verne collection.

For the study of Jules Verne, the best collections are in the French cities where the author was born and where he died—Nantes and Amiens. In Nantes, the Centre Jules Verne located at the Médiathèque (15 rue de l'Héronnière, 44041 Nantes cedex) houses not only a complete collection of first editions of the *Voyages Extraordinaires* but also a number of original manuscripts, correspondence, and other valuable research materials relating to this legendary author. Also in Nantes is the Musée Jules Verne (3 rue de l'Hermitage, 44000 Nantes) and the Centre universitaire de recherches verniennes (Université de Nantes, Chemin de la Sensive du Tertre, BP 1025, 44036 Nantes cedex), directed by the noted scholar Christian Robin, which maintains a collection of critical works devoted to Verne. In Amiens, with the help of the city fathers, the Société Jules Verne has converted Jules Verne's residence into a very impressive Centre de documentation directed by Cécile Compère—an essential research collection of both primary and secondary materials. The current president of the Société, Olivier Dumas (himself a respected scholar in the field), maintains a complete collection of first-edition *Voyages Extraordinaires* at his home at 11 bis, rue Pigalle, 75009 Paris and—speaking from personal experience—is most gracious with both his time and resources to all Vernian scholars pursuing research in this field. Finally, on this continent, a sizable collection of Jules Verne materials has been amassed by Andrew Nash (133 Wilton Street, Toronto, Ontario M5A 4A4), including hundreds of novels and critical works, comics, posters, films, postage stamps, and other Vernian miscellanea all collected since 1973.

Although not classifiable as formal collections, a number of bookstores in France specialize in French SF and are often a veritable treasure trove of research possibilities. Generally run by helpful proprietors who are well versed in SF, such bookstores sometimes constitute the researcher's best hope for locating long-out-of-print SF texts, in learning the who's who of contemporary SF circles, and in gleaning some insight into the SF publishing industry in France. Among a few of the more notable in Paris are the following: Temps futurs (8 rue Dante, 75005), Florence de Chastenay (76 rue Gay-Lussac, 75005), Roland Buret (6 passage Verdeau, 75009), Librairie Fantasmak (17 rue de Belzunce, 75010), L'Introuvable (25 rue Juliette Dodu, 75010), and Cosmos 2000 (17 rue de l'Arc de Triomphe, 75017). And, of course, there are the *bouquinistes*.

FUTURE RESEARCH POSSIBILITIES

As a conclusion to this overview of French science fiction, I can only repeat the words of my colleague and friend, Olivier Dumas: "Until now, we have only scratched the surface of this subject matter. There remains so much to discover and to make known." Dumas was speaking of Jules Verne, but the same observation could apply to French SF as a whole. Painfully few French SF novels are being translated into English; fewer still are being discussed in

American universities; and English-language critical studies of French SF, though on the rise during the past decade, still remain far too few in number.

The field is rich. It awaits cultivation. SF is a literary genre which, perhaps more than any other, is the product of the dreams, fears, and creative imagination of an entire culture as it peers into the future and envisions "what if. . . . " The science fiction of France, as one of the world's oldest and most varied, provides unparalleled research opportunities in this regard: both for investigating the historical evolution of such visions and how they were articulated through fiction, and for exploring the various social and epistemological roots from which such visions sprang.

NOTES

1. Maxim Jakubowski, "French SF," in Neil Barron, ed., *Anatomy of Wonder: A Critical Guide to Science Fiction*, 3d ed. (New York: R. R. Bowker, 1987), p. 405. Jakubowski's 36-page study (with an extensive historical outline of the genre's evolution and an alphabetized and annotated listing of authors and works) is by far the best critical English-language overview of French SF to date—at least insofar as the twentieth century is concerned. His treatment of earlier periods is more cursory and occasionally marred by errors in the names of the SF authors and works which remain uncorrected in the third edition: like Fontenelle's 1686 *Entretiens sur la pluralité des mondes*—mistakenly attributed to Fénelon and cited as *Entretiens sur la pluralité des mondes habités* (evidently confused with Camille Flammarion's 1862 *La Pluralité des mondes habités*)—or Cyrano de Bergerac's 1662 *Histoire comique des états et empires du soleil* (cited as, and confused with, Cyrano's previous publication: *Histoire comique des états et empires de la lune*). It should be noted that Jakubowski, in addition to his critical work on French SF, is also responsible for one of the very few English-language anthologies of modern French SF— *Travelling Towards Epsilon* (New York: New English Library, 1976)—along with Damon Knight's earlier collection *Thirteen French Science Fiction Stories* (New York: Bantam, 1965).

2. John Dean, "French Science Fiction: The Intergalactic European Connection," *Stanford French Review* 3 (1979): 404. Dean's brief but interesting five-page synopsis, interspersed with useful quotes from interviews with some of the foremost French writers of today, is intended less as a diachronic study of the genre (he discusses only the post-World War II period and contemporary writers and works) and more as a plea to the anglophone world to become more familiar with French SF. Implicitly addressing the American publishing industry, he contends that "If only more French SF were translated and published in the States, it thus would provide American readers with that kind of intelligent SF which has reached such heights with Huxley, Orwell, and, more recently, with Stanislaw Lem" (p. 409).

3. See "France," in Peter Nicholls, ed., *The Encyclopedia of Science Fiction* (London: Granada, 1979), pp. 230–32. This thumbnail but very lucid discussion of French SF (despite one or two minor errors in titles) is now somewhat dated as far as contemporary developments are concerned. But it does a very credible job of treating pre-1970s French SF and, further, passes on some valuable insights into the social fabric of post–World War II France. For example, "At the end of the War, two factors were to bear heavily on the future of SF in France. The first was the growing separation, at school, in the

universities and in all thinking circles, between *les littéraires* and *les scientifiques*, which made for a lack of curiosity about science and its possible effects on the shapes of our lives on the part of aspiring novelists. . . . Secondly, whatever interest in these matters existed was satisfied from another source, the USA'' (p. 231). See Gérard Klein "Pourquoi y a-t-il une crise de la science-fiction française?" *Fiction* 116 (1967): 122–28.

4. The most important (and illustrative) being the disappearance of the *Année de la science-fiction et du fantastique* yearbook. Edited by Jacques Goimard and published yearly by Julliard from 1977 to 1982 (and by Daniel Riche and Temps futurs for one last time in 1983), this extraordinarily rich annual compendium of French SF information will be sorely missed by scholars and researchers.

SELECTED BIBLIOGRAPHY

The following bibliography is not exhaustive, but it does represent an attempt to compile into one listing a large number of critical studies devoted to French SF (plus a selection of theoretical discussion by French writers and critics) through 1987–88. I have, for the most part, omitted those references which focus exclusively on utopias and/or the fantastic. Further, I have not included those many fine studies targeting French SF produced in Quebec; other SF scholars—like Norbert Spehner, Élisabeth Vonarburg, and Jean-Marc Gouanvic—being far more capable than I in this realm. For purposes of concision, the considerable amount of criticism on Jules Verne has been limited to those sources currently available in English; for more complete bibliographic references on Verne, the reader may wish to consult *Jules Verne: A Primary and Secondary Bibliography* by Edward Gallagher, Judith A. Mistichelli, and John A. Van Eerde (Boston: G. K. Hall, 1980) or my own *Jules Verne Rediscovered* (Westport, Conn.: Greenwood Press, 1988).

General Histories and Bibliographies

Alkon, Paul K. *Origins of Futuristic Fiction*. Athens, Ga.: University of Georgia Press, 1987.

Allard, Yvon. *Écrits sur l'avenir*. Montreal: La Centrale des Bibliothèques, 1981.

———. *Paralittératures*. Montreal: La Centrale des Bibliothèques, 1979.

Amprimoz, Alexandre. "French Language Science-Fiction and Fantasy." In *CDN SF & F* (Bibliography of Canadian Science Fiction and Fantasy). Toronto: Hounslow, 1979.

Angenot, Marc. "Jules Verne and French Literary Criticism." *Science-Fiction Studies* 1 (1973): 33–37, and 3 (1976): 46–49.

———. *Le Roman populaire: recherches en paralittérature*. Montreal: Presses de l'Université de Québec, 1975.

———. "Science Fiction in France before Verne." *Science-Fiction Studies* 5 (1978): 58–65.

———. "The Yearbook of French SF." *Science-Fiction Studies* 8 (1981): 112–3.

Angenot, Marc, and Khouri, Nadia. "An International Bibliography of Prehistoric Fiction." *Science-Fiction Studies* 8 (1981): 38–53.

Atkinson, Geoffrey. *Extraordinary Voyage in French Literature before 1700*. New York: Columbia University Press, 1920.

Aziza, Claude, and Goimard, Jacques. *Encyclopédie de poche de la science-fiction*. Paris: Presses Pocket, 1986.

Barets, Stan. *Catalogue des âmes et cycles de la SF*. Paris: Denoël, 1979.

Barron, Neil, ed. *Anatomy of Wonder: A Critical Guide to Science Fiction*. 2d. ed. New York: Bowker, 1981. 3d ed., 1987.

Barthes, Roland. *Mythologies*. Translated by Annette Lavers. New York: Hill & Wang, 1972.

Baudin, Henri. *La Science-fiction: un univers en expansion*. Paris: Bordas, 1971.

Béguin, Annick. *Les Cent principaux titres de la science-fiction*. Paris: Cosmos 2000, 1981.

Bessière, Jean, ed. *Modernités de Jules Verne*. Paris: Presses Universitaires de France, 1988.

Bisceglia, Jacques, and Buret, Roland. *Trésor du roman policier, de la science-fiction et du fantastique*. Paris: L'Amateur, 1981.

Bogdanoff, Igor and Grichka. *Clefs pour la science-fiction*. Paris: Seghers, 1976.

———. *L'Effet science-fiction: à la recherche d'une définition*. Paris: Laffont, 1979.

Bouyxou, Jean-Pierre. *La Science-Fiction au cinéma*. Paris: "10/18," 1971.

Bouyxou, Jean-Pierre, et al. *65 ans de science-fiction au cinéma*. Brussels: GECF, 1969.

Bridenne, J.-J. *La Littérature française d'imagination scientifique*. Paris: Dassonville, 1950. Reprint. Antarès, 1983.

Carme, Claude. "La Science-fiction française: aperçu historique et critique." *Horizons du fantastique* 11 (1970): 40–46.

Clarke, I. F. *The Pattern of Expectation, 1644–2001*. New York: Basic Books, 1979.

Collins, Robert A., and Pearce, Howard D. *The Scope of the Fantastic: Theory, Technique, Major Authors*. Westport, Conn.: Greenwood Press, 1984.

Dean, John. "French Science Fiction: The Intergalactic European Connection." *Stanford French Review* 3 (1979): 404–14.

Delmas, Henri, and Julian, Alain. *Le Rayon SF: Catalogue bibliographique de science-fiction, utopies et voyages extraordinaires*. Toulouse: Éditions Milan, 1983. 2d ed., 1985.

Diffloth, Gérard. *La Science-fiction*. Paris: Gamma Presse, 1964.

Encyclopédie visuelle de la Science-fiction. Paris: Michel, 1979.

Evans, Arthur B. "Science Fiction in France." *Science-Fiction Studies* 16 (1989): 254–76 and 338–68.

Fitting, Peter. "SF Criticism in France." *Science-Fiction Studies* 1 (1974): 173–81.

Flammarion, Camille. *Les Mondes imaginaires et les mondes réels*. Paris: Didier, 1868.

Gallagher, Edward J., et al. *Jules Verne: A Primary and Secondary Bibliography*. Boston: G. K. Hall, 1980.

Gattégno, Jean. *La Science-fiction*. "Que sais-je?" Paris: Presses Universitaires de France, 1971. 4th ed., 1983.

Georlette, René. *La Science-fiction dans la littérature française*. Brussels: Wemmel, 1965.

Goimard, Jacques, ed. *L'Année 1977–78 de la science-fiction et du fantastique*. Paris: Julliard, 1978.

———. *L'Année 1978–79 de la science-fiction et du fantastique*. Paris: Julliard, 1979.

———. *L'Année 1979–80 de la science-fiction et du fantastique*. Paris: Julliard, 1980.

———. *L'Année 1980–81 de la science-fiction et du fantastique*. Paris: Julliard, 1981.

———. *L'Année 1981–82 de la science-fiction et du fantastique*. Paris: Julliard, 1982.

———. "La Science-fiction au pays de Descartes." *Magazine littéraire* 31 (1969): 22–25.

Goimard, Jacques; Klein, Gérard; et al. *Science-fiction et psychanalyse*. Paris: Dunod, 1986.

Gondolo della Riva, Piero. *Bibliographie analytique de toutes les œuvres de Jules Verne*. 2 vols. Paris: Société Jules Verne, 1977–85.

Goorden, Bernard. *Annuaire bibliographique de la science-fiction et du fantastique 1984*. Brussels: Recto-Verso, 1984.

———. *Annuaire bibliographique de la science-fiction et du fantastique 1985*. Brussels: Recto-Verso, 1985.

———. *Annuaire bibliographique de la science-fiction et du fantastique 1986*. Brussels: Recto-Verso, 1986.

Gouanvic, Jean-Marc. "Rational Speculations in French Canada, 1839–1974." *Science-Fiction Studies* 15 (1988): 71–81.

Gougaud, Henri. *Démons et merveilles de la science-fiction*. Paris: Julliard, 1974.

Guiot, Denis, et al. *La Science-fiction*. Paris: MA Éditions, 1987.

Hall, H. W. *Science Fiction and Fantasy Reference Index, 1878–1985*. 2 vols. Detroit: Gale, 1987.

"History of French Science Fiction." *Fantasy Times* 172 (February 1953): 5–7 and 173 (March 1953): 5–6.

Hottols, Gilbert, ed. *Science-fiction et fiction spéculative*. Brussels: Éditions de l'Université de Bruxelles, 1985.

Jakubowski, Maxim. "Bibliographie de la science-fiction." *La Quinzaine littéraire* 225 (January 16–31, 1976): 8–9.

———. "French SF." In *Anatomy of Wonder: A Critical Guide to Science Fiction*. Edited by Neil Barron. 2d ed. New York: R. R. Bowker, 1981, pp. 399–425. 3d ed. 1987, pp. 405–40.

Knight, David. "Science Fiction in the Seventeenth Century." *The Seventeenth Century* 1 (1986): 69–79.

Lester, Colin, ed. *The International Science Fiction Yearbook, 1979*. New York: Quick Fox, 1978.

Nicholls, Peter, ed. *The Encyclopedia of Science Fiction*. London: Granada, 1979.

Nicholson, Marjorie. *Voyages to the Moon*. New York: Macmillan, 1948.

Parrinder, Patrick, ed. *Science Fiction: A Critical Guide*. New York: Longman, 1979.

———. "SF Studies in France." *Science-Fiction Studies* 7 (1980): 352.

Riche, Daniel. *L'Année 1982–83 de la science-fiction et du fantastique*. Paris: Temps futurs, 1983.

Rochette, Marguerite. *La Science-fiction*. Paris: Larousse, 1975.

Rottensteiner, Franz. *La Science-fiction illustrée*. Paris: Seuil, 1975.

———. *The Science Fiction Book: An Illustrated History*. New York: New American Library, 1975.

Sadoul, Jacques. *Histoire de la science-fiction moderne (1911–1975): Domaine français*. Paris: Michel, 1973. 2d ed., J'ai lu, 1975.

———. "Science Fiction in France." *Algol* 18 (1972): 17–18.

"La Science-fiction en France." *Horizons du fantastique* 11 (1970): 47–60.

Spehner, Norbert. *Écrits sur la science-fiction*. Longueuil, Quebec: Le Préambule, 1988.

Sternberg, Jacques. *Une succursale du fantastique nommée Science-Fiction*. Paris: Terrain Vague, 1958.

Strinati, Pierre. "Bandes dessinées et science-fiction: l'âge d'or en France (1934–1940)." *Fiction* 92 (July 1961): 121–25.

Suvin, Darko. *Metamorphoses of Science Fiction*. New Haven, Conn.: Yale University Press, 1979.

———. *Pour une poétique de la science-fiction*. Montreal: Presses de l'Université du Québec, 1977.

Tewen, San. "Bibliographie de la science-fiction et du fantastique." In Bernard Goorden, ed. *SF, fantastique et ateliers créatifs*. Brussels: Cahiers JEB, 1978.

Tuck, Donald. *The Encyclopedia of Science Fiction and Fantasy*. 2 vols. Chicago: Advent, 1974, 1977.

Tuzet, Hélène. *Le Cosmos et l'imagination*. Paris: Corti, 1965.

Valéry, Francis. "Bibliothèque idéale de livres sur la SF." *Fiction* 315 (1981): 186–92.

———. *Index de la revue "Fiction." Vol. 1: Domaine français*. Cavignac: Ailleurs et Autres, 1980.

Van Herp, Jacques. *Panorama de la science-fiction*. Verviers, Belgium: Marabout, 1973. Reprint. 1975.

———. *Je sais tout*. Brussels: Recto-Verso, 1987.

Versins, Pierre. *Encyclopédie de l'Utopie, des Voyages Extraordinaires et de la Science-Fiction*. Lausanne: L'Âge d'Homme, 1972. 2d ed., 1984.

———. "*Science et Voyages*, éléments bibliographiques." In A. Valérie, "*Sur l'autre face du monde*" *et autres romans scientifiques de "Science et Voyages*." Edited by Gérard Klein and Jacques Van Herp. Paris: Laffont, 1973.

Vian, Boris. *Cinéma/Science-Fiction*. Paris: Bourgois, 1978.

Villemur, Alain. *63 auteurs: bibliographie de science-fiction*. Paris: Temps futurs, 1976.

———. *Lire la SF: bibliographie de la science-fiction publiée en France*. Paris: Temps futurs, 1980.

Vonarburg, Élisabeth. "SF en France." *Solaris* 56, X:2 (1984), 26–28.

Zantovska-Murray, Irena, and Suvin, Darko. "A Bibliography of General Bibliographies of SF Literature." *Science-Fiction Studies* 5 (1978), 271–86.

Monographs, Critical Studies, and Special Issues of Periodicals

Agel, Henri. *Miroirs de l'insolite dans le cinéma français*. Paris: Cerf, 1958.

Arguments 9 (1957). Issue titled "Par-delà la science-fiction. La Pensée anticipatrice."

À Suivre 3 (1978). Issue titled "Science-fiction et politique."

Baudin, Henri. *Les Monstres dans la science-fiction*. Paris: Minard, 1976.

Blanc, Bernard, ed. *Pourquoi j'ai tué Jules Verne*. Paris: Stock, 1978.

Boogaerts, Pierre. *Robot*. Paris: Futuropolis, 1978.

Born, Franz. *The Man Who Invented the Future: Jules Verne*. New York: Scholastic Book Services, 1967.

Brun, Philippe. *Albert Robida, sa vie, son oeuvre*. Paris: Promodis, 1984.

B.T.2 49 (May 1973). Issue titled "La Science-fiction."

Bulletin du Livre 215 (1973). Issue titled "Présence et avenir de la science-fiction."

Bulletin du Livre 351 (1978). Issue titled "La Science-fiction."

Cahier Comique et Communication 2 (1984). Issue titled "Comique et science-fiction."

Cahiers du Sud 37 (March 1953). Issue titled "Nouveaux Aspects d'une mythologie moderne."

Les Cahiers de l'Imaginaire 1 (1980). Issue titled "Gustave Le Rouge."

Les Cahiers de l'Imaginaire 13 (1984). Issue titled "Jean de la Hire."

Caillois, Roger. *Obliques* and *Images, images*. Paris: Stock, 1975.

Caliban 22 (1985). Issue titled "Esthétique de la science-fiction."

Carrouges, Michel. *La Mystique du surhomme*. Paris: Gallimard, 1948.

Casella, Georges. *J.-H. Rosny. Biographie critique*. Paris: Sansot, 1907.

Change 40 (mars 1981). Issue titled "Science-fiction et Histoire."

Chapuis, Alfred. *Les Automates dans les œuvres d'imagination*. Neuchâtel, Switzerland: Le Griffon, 1947.

Chesneaux, Jean. *The Political and Social Ideas of Jules Verne*. London: Thames & Hudson, 1972.

Christinger, Raymond. *Le Voyage dans l'imaginaire*. Geneva: Mont-Blanc, 1971. Reprint. Paris: Stock, 1981.

Cinéma d'aujourd'hui 7 (1976). Issue titled "Demain de la science-fiction."

Cinématographie 12 (1975). Issue titled "Science-fiction."

Cohen, Jean. *Les Robots humains dans le mythe et dans la science*. Paris: Vrin, 1968.

Cosem, Michel. *Découvrir la SF*. Paris: Seghers, 1975.

Costello, Peter. *Jules Verne: Inventor of Science Fiction*. London: Hodder & Stroughton, 1978.

Delcourt, Christian. *Jean Ray, ou les choses dont on fait les histoires*. Paris: Nizet, 1980.

Dispa, Marie-Françoise. *Héros de la science-fiction*. Brussels: A. de Boeck, 1976.

Dumas, Olivier. *Jules Verne*. Lyon: La Manufacture, 1988.

Eisler, Steven. *Images de la science-fiction*. Paris: Grund, 1980.

Eizykman, Boris. *Science-fiction et capitalisme*. Paris: Delarge, 1974.

———. *Inconscience-fiction*. Yverdon, Switzerland: Kesselring, 1979.

Esprit (May 1953). Issue titled "Mensonges et vérités de nos anticipations."

Europe 139–40 (1957). Issue titled "Science-fiction."

Europe 580–81 (1977). Issue titled "La Science-fiction par le menu: problématique d'un genre."

Europe 681–82 (1986). Issue titled "H. G. Wells/Rosny Aîné."

Evans, Arthur B. *Jules Verne Rediscovered: Didacticism and the Scientific Novel*. Westport, Conn.: Greenwood Press, 1988.

Evans, I. O. *Jules Verne and his Works*. London: Arco, 1965.

Fath, Robert. *L'Influence de la science sur la littérature française dans la seconde moitié du 19ème siècle*. Lausanne: Payot, 1901.

Fondanèche, Daniel. *Trois thèmes de la science-fiction*. Limoges: Éditions du CRDP, 1979.

———. *Quatre thèmes de la science-fiction*. Limoges: Éditions du CRDP, 1981.

Le Français dans le Monde 193 (1985). Issue titled "Spécial science-fiction."

Goorden, Bernard, ed. *SF, fantastique et ateliers créatifs*. Brussels: Cahiers JEB, 1978.

Gougaud, Henri. *Démons et merveilles de la science-fiction*. Paris: Julliard, 1974.

Grenier, Christian. *Jeunesse et Science-fiction*. Paris: Magnard, 1972.

Grenier, Christian, and Soulier, Jacky. *La Science-fiction? J'aime!* Paris: La Farandole, 1982.

Guadalupi, Gianni, and Manguel, Alberto. *The Dictionary of Imaginary Places*. New York: Macmillan, 1980.

Le Gué 10/11 (1978). Issue titled "La Science-fiction."

Haining, Peter. *The Jules Verne Companion*. Norwich, England: Souvenir Press, 1978.

Harrison, Harry. *La Queue de la comète (Sexe et S.-F.)*. Paris: Humanoïdes Associés, 1977.

Harth, Erica. *Cyrano de Bergerac and the Polemics of Modernity*. New York: Columbia University Press, 1970.

Horizons du fantastique 11 (1970). Issue titled "La Science-fiction en France."

Imagine . . . 13 (1982). Issue titled "Spécial SF française."

Imagine . . . 14 (1982). Issue titled "Spécial uchronie."

Jaeger, Gérard. *Approche critique et bibliographique des frères Rosny*. Sherbrooke: Naaman, 1986.

Jakubowski, Maxim, ed. *Travelling Towards Epsilon*. London: New English Library, 1976.

Jourda, Pierre. *L'Exotisme dans la littérature française du romantisme à 1939*. Paris: Presses Universitaires de France, 1956.

Jules-Verne, Jean. *Jules Verne: A Biography*. New York: Taplinger, 1976.

Jules Verne et les sciences humaines. Edited by François Raymond and Simone Vierne. Paris: Union générale d'éditions, 1979.

Klein, Gérard. *Malaise dans la science-fiction*. Metz: L'Aube enclavée, 1977.

Klein, Gérard, and Battestini, Monique. *Anthologie de la science-fiction française*. 3 vols. Paris: Seghers, 1975.

Labarthe, André. *Images de la SF*. Paris: Cerf, 1958.

———. *Comment peut-on être Martien?* Paris: Terrain Vague, 1960.

Magazine littéraire 31 (August 1969). Issue titled "La Science-fiction."

Magazine littéraire 88 (May 1974). Issue titled "La Nouvelle Science-fiction."

Magazine littéraire 119 (December 1976). Issue titled "Jules Verne inattendu."

Martin, Andrew. *The Knowledge of Ignorance from Cervantes to Jules Verne*. Cambridge: Cambridge University Press, 1985.

Martin, Charles-Noël. *La Vie et l'œuvre de Jules Verne*. Paris: Michel de l'Ormeraie, 1978.

Mason, Haydn. *Cyrano de Bergerac*. London: Grant & Cutler, 1984.

Matthey, Hubert. *Essai sur le merveilleux dans la littérature française depuis 1800*. Lausanne: Payot, 1915.

Méheust, Bertrand. *Science-fiction et soucoupes volantes*. Paris: Mercure de France, 1978.

Métaphore 9–10 (1984). Issue titled "Images de l'ailleurs, espace intérieur."

Métaphore 11 (1985). Issue titled "Fantastique et science-fiction."

Métaphore 12–13 (1986). Issue titled "La Planète Terre."

Modernités de Jules Verne. Edited by Jean Bessière. Paris: Presses Universitaires de France, 1988.

Moré, Marcel. *Le Très Curieux Jules Verne: Le Problème du père dans les "Voyages Extraordinaires."* Paris: Gallimard, 1960.

———. *Nouvelles Explorations de Jules Verne: Musique, misogamie, machine*. Paris: Gallimard, 1963.

Noiray, Jacques. *Le Romancier et la machine: l'image de la machine dans le roman français, 1850–1900*. 2 vols. Paris: Corti, 1982.

Les Nouvelles littéraires 1565 (August 29, 1957). Issue titled "Faut-il brûler les récits d'anticipation?"

Opus International 64 (1977). Issue titled "Une lecture de la science-fiction."

Parrinder, Patrick, ed. *Science Fiction: A Critical Guide*. New York: Longman, 1979.

Phosphore 6 (1981). Issue titled "Les Mondes de la S.F."

Prévot, Jacques. *Cyrano de Bergerac, romancier*. Paris: Belin, 1977.

Protée 10 (1982). Issues titled "Science-fiction."

Quinzaine littéraire 225 (January 16–31, 1976). Issue titled "De la science-fiction à la fiction spéculative."

Raymond, François, ed. *Jules Verne*. Paris: Les Lettres modernes, 1976–.

La Recherche 49 (1974). Issue titled "Science et Science-fiction."

Reichardt, Jasia. *Les Robots arrivent*. Paris: Chêne, 1978.

Robida. Paris: Pierre Horay, 1980.

Robin, Christian. *Un monde connu et inconnu*. Nantes: Centre universitaire de recherches verniennes, 1978.

Scholes, Robert, and Rabkin, Eric S. *Science Fiction: History, Science, Vision*. New York: Oxford University Press, 1977.

Serres, Michel. *Jouvences sur Jules Verne*. Paris: Minuit, 1974.

Siclier, Jacques. *Images de la SF*. Paris: Cerf, 1958.

Simon, Louis, *À la découverte de Han Ryner*. Paris: Le Prullon, 1970.

Slusser, George E., et al., eds. *Coordinates: Placing Science Fiction*. Carbondale: Southern Illinois University Press, 1983.

———. *Storm Warnings: Science Fiction Confronts the Future*. Carbondale: Southern Illinois University Press, 1987.

Smit Le Bénédicte, J. C. *Guide des soucoupes volantes*. Brussels: Espace, 1976.

La Table Ronde 85 (1955). Issue titled "La Pluralité des mondes et le mythe des soucoupes volantes."

Thomas, Louis-Vincent. *Civilisations et divagations: mort, fantasmes, science-fiction*. Paris: Payot, 1979.

Van Herp, Jacques. *José Moselli et la science-fiction*. Brussels: Recto-Verso, 1984.

Vierne, Simone. *Jules Verne et le roman initiatique*. Paris: Éditions du Sirac, 1973.

———. *Jules Verne*. Paris: Balland, 1986.

———. *Jules Verne, mythe et modernité*. Paris: Presses Universitaires de France, 1989.

Selected Articles, Prefaces, etc.

Aberger, Peter. "The Portrayal of Blacks in Jules Verne's *Voyages Extraordinaires*." *French Review* 53 (1979): 199–206.

Anderson, Paul. "Les 15 grands de la science-fiction." *Magazine littéraire* 31 (1969): 29–32.

Andrevon, Jean-Pierre. "B. R. Bruss avant le Fleuve Noir." *Fiction* 217 (1972): 129–33.

———. "Entretien avec Roger Blondel." *Fiction* 258 (1975): 147–58.

———. "Fantastique et science-fiction dans la bande dessinée française." *Horizons du fantastique* 13 (1970): 67–76.

———. "Jean-Gaston Vandel, écrivain progressiste." *Alerte!* 3 (1978): 113–33.

———. "*Malevil* ou le meilleur des mondes." *Fiction* 230 (1973): 161–67.

———. "Pourquoi la politique fiction?" *Horizons du fantastique* 12 (1970): 15–20.

———. "Régis Messac ou l'humour du désespoir." *Fiction* 236 (1973): 173–78.

———. "Sternberg en deux temps et trois mouvements." *Fiction* 207 (1971): 127–31.

Angenot, Marc. "Albert Robida's Twentieth Century." *Science-Fiction Studies* 10 (1983): 237–40.

———. "The Emergence of the Anti-Utopia Genre in France: Souvestre, Giraudeau, Robida, et al." *Science-Fiction Studies* 12 (1985): 129–35. Reprinted in French.

"Emergence du genre anti-utopique en France: Souvestre, Giraudeau, Robida, et al." In *Imagine* . . . 31 (1985): 18–23.

———. "Jules Verne: The Last Happy Utopianist." In *Science-Fiction: A Critical Guide*. Edited by Patrick Parrinder. New York: Longman, 1979.

Auburtin, Jean. "De Cyrano de Bergerac (Edmond Rostand) et de Jules Verne aux cosmonautes." *Les Annales* 236 (1970): 23–33.

Barjavel, René. "La Science-fiction, c'est le 'vrai' nouveau roman." *Nouvelles littéraires*, October 11, 1962, p. 1.

Baronian, Jean-Baptiste. "Un homme frénétique," in Ernest Pérochon, *Les Hommes frénétiques*. Verviers, Belgium: Marabout, 1971.

———. "J.-H. Rosny Aîné: Les Fins et les manières." In J.-H. Rosny Aîné. *Récits de science-fiction*. Verviers: Marabout, 1973.

———. "Un retour nécessaire." In J.-H. Rosny Aîné. *La Force mystérieuse*. Verviers: Marabout, 1972.

———. "J.-H. Rosny Aîné, visionnaire et précurseur." In J.-H. Rosny Aîné, *Romans préhistoriques*. Paris: Laffont, 1985.

———. "Rosny, le visionnaire." In J.-H. Rosny Aîné. *L'Énigme de Givreuse*. Paris: Oswald, 1982.

———. "La Science-fiction aujourd'hui. Une littérature des limites." In *Aspects du roman français contemporain*. Brussels: Cahiers du groupe du roman, 1978.

———. "La Terre telle qu'elle serait." In J.-H. Rosny Aîné. *L'Étonnant Voyage de Hareton Ironcastle*. Paris: Oswald, 1982.

Battestini, Monique. "Les Origines de la nouvelle française de science-fiction." *La Revue du Pacifique* 3 (1977): 3–23.

———. "Préface." In Gérard Klein and Monique Battestini, eds. *Le Grandiose Avenir: Anthologie de la science-fiction française, les années 50*. Paris: Seghers, 1975.

Baudin, Henri. "Un avatar de l'imaginaire." *Europe* 580–81 (1977): 85–90.

Baudouin, Charles. "Rencontre de Ryner." *Europe* 390 (1961): 21–27.

Baudrillard, Jean. "Simulacres et science-fiction." In his *Simulacres et simulations*. Paris: Galilée, 1981.

Benayoun, Robert. "La Bande à Moebius." *Le Point* 394 (1979): 117–18.

Bergal, Gilles. "Rencontre avec Joël Houssin." *Ère comprimée* 32 (1985): 60–66.

Bergier, Jacques. Preface to J.-H. Rosny Aîné. *Les Navigateurs de l'infini*. Lausanne: Rencontre, 1970.

———. Preface to José Moselli. *La Fin d'Illa*. Lausanne: Rencontre, 1970.

———. "Science-fiction et satellites." *Fiction* 49 (1957): 135–37.

———. "La Science-fiction." In *Histoire des littératures III*. Paris: "Encyclopédie de la Pléiade." Gallimard, 1958.

Berton, C. "Souvenirs de la vie littéraire de J.-H. Rosny." *La Vie des peuples* 4 (1921): 385–95.

Black, Jean-Marie. "Les Paradoxes des univers de Gérard Klein." *Horizons du fantastique* 29 (1974): 7–15.

Blanc, Bernard. "Collections: la qualité conforme." *Le Français dans le monde* 193 (1985): 36–38.

———. "Lexique à l'usage des voyageurs en S.-F." *Le Français dans le monde* 193 (1985): 32–33.

———. "Pierre Pelot." In Pierre Pelot, *Le Sommeil du chien*. Yverdon, Switzerland: Kesselring, 1978.

————. "La Presse d'à côté." *Fiction* 235 (1973): 172–75.

————. "La S.-F. se porte bien, merci, et elle vire à gauche." *Fiction* 245 (1974): 184–87.

Blanchot, Maurice. "Le Bon Usage de la science-fiction." *La Nouvelle Revue Française* (January 1959): 91–100.

Boia, L. "La Conquête imaginaire de l'espace: Jules Verne et Camille Flammarion." *Bulletin de la Société Jules Verne* 67 (1983): 91–95.

Bouquet, Jean-Louis. "Un précurseur: Léon Groc." *Fiction* 34 (1956): 125–27.

Bousquet, Philippe and Paul. "Entretien avec Pierre Pelot/Pierre Suragne." *Tschai* 2 (1974): 4–10.

Bouyxou, Jean-Pierre. "Entretien avec Francis Carsac." *Lunatique* 33 (1967): 20–26.

Bozzetto, Roger. "Le Point sur la SF française." *Requiem* 24 (1978): 34–35.

————. "Les Ambiguïtés du couple SF/Féminisme." *Requiem* 26 (1979): 27–29.

————. "La Science-fiction comme sujet d'une métamorphose: le cas de Serge Brussolo." *Cahiers du CERLI* 13 (1986): 45–60.

————. "Vers une approche esthétique de la science-fiction." *Caliban* 22 (1985): 57–65.

————. "Wells et Rosny devant l'inconnu: la vision de l'Autre." *Europe* 681–82 (1986): 37–43.

Bradbury, Ray. "The Ardent Blasphemers." In Jules Verne. *Twenty Thousand Leagues under the Sea*. New York: Bantam, 1962.

Bridenne, J.-J. "Actualité de Villiers." *Fiction* 34 (1956): 122–24.

————. "André Laurie et la science-fiction d'hier." *Fiction* 18 (1955): 121–23.

————. "Autour du centenaire de Rosny Aîné: du roman archéologique à l'anticipation scientifique." *L'Information littéraire* 8 (1956): 143–48.

————. "Camille Flammarion et la littérature des fins du monde." *Fiction* 42 (1957): 121–24.

————. "Le Capitaine Danrit, l'utopiste de la guerre." *Fiction* 25 (1955): 119–21.

————. "Hommage à Régis Messac." *Fiction* 48 (1957): 133–35.

————. "Le Merveilleux scientifique chez Edmond About." *Fiction* 47 (1957): 131–33.

————. "Nadar ou la science-fiction vécue d'hier." *Fiction* 68 (1959): 121–24.

————. "Robida, le Jules Verne du crayon." *Fiction* 10 (1954): 114–17.

————. "J.-H. Rosny Aîné, romancier des possibles cosmiques." *Fiction* 27 (1956): 108–10.

————. "La Science-fiction est-elle une littérature stéréotypée?" *Fiction* 52 (1958): 123–25.

————. "Théo Varlet, prophète cosmique." *Fiction* 60 (1958): 123–27.

Brouchon, Pierre. "Du surnaturel à la fabrique d'absolu." *Europe* 139–40 (1957): 20–27.

Brussolo, Serge. "Trajets et itinéraires d'un gommeur de frontières." *SFère* 16 (1984): 5–9.

Butor, Michel. "La Crise de croissance de la science-fiction." *Cahiers du Sud* 37 (1953): 31–39. Reprint in *Répertoire*. Paris: Minuit, 1960, pp. 186–94. Also in *Essai sur les modernes*. Paris: Gallimard, 1963, pp. 223–39, and as "Science Fiction: The Crisis of Its Growth." *Partisan Review* 34 (1967): 595–602.

Caillois, Roger. "De la féerie à la science-fiction." Preface to *L'Anthologie du fantastique*. Paris: Gallimard, 1966.

―――. "Science-fiction." *Diogène* 89 (1975): 96–112.

Carrouges, Michel. "Le Spectroscope des anticipations." *Cahiers du Sud* 37 (1953): 6–16.

―――. "Machines pataphysiques pour l'au-delà." *Études philosophiques* 1 (1985): 77–89.

Cartano, Tony. "La Science-fiction française d'aujourd'hui." In *Dictionnaire de la littérature française contemporaine*. Paris: Delarge, 1977.

―――. "La 'Science Fiction' dépassée par la 'Speculative Fiction.' " *La Quinzaine littéraire* 225 (January 16–31, 1976): 13–15.

Chambers, Ross. "Cultural and Ideological Determinations in Narrative: A Note on Jules Verne's *Les Cinq cent millions de la Bégum*." *L'Esprit créateur* 21 (1981): 69–78.

Chambon, Jacques. "Éros au pays des songes." *Fiction* 196 (1970): 141–51.

―――. "Voyages dans le temps ou voyages dans l'espace?" *Change* 40 (1981): 121–31.

Cheinisse, Claude-F. "Pierre Versins, vu à travers les lunettes de Claude-F. Cheinisse." In Jacques Goimard, ed. *L'Année 1981–1982 de la science-fiction et du fantastique*. Paris: Julliard, 1983.

Cioranescu, Alexandre. "*Épigone*, le premier roman de l'avenir." *Revue des sciences humaines* 155 (1974): 441–48.

Colson, M. P. "À propos de *Les Singes du temps* de Michel Jeury." *Nyarlathotep* 10 (1975): 83–86.

Comballot, Richard. "Auteur: Michel Jeury." *Nemo* 1 (1986): 49–51.

―――. "Entretien avec Sylviane Corgiat et Bruno Lecigne." *Fiction* 355 (1984): 142–52.

―――. "Rencontre avec André Ruellan (Kurt Steiner)." *Imagine . . .* 38 (1987): 82–87.

―――. "Rencontre avec Gérard Klein." *Imagine . . .* 31 (1985): 80–84.

―――. "Rencontre avec Jean-Claude Dunyach." *Ère comprimée* 36 (1985): 65–66.

Compère, Daniel. "La Fin des hommes." *Europe* 681–82 (1986): 29–36.

Cossement, Michel. "Entretien avec Philippe Curval." *SFère* 10 (1983): 6–10.

―――."De l'œuvre de Curval." *SFère* 10 (1983): 16–18.

―――. "Interview: Daniel Walther." *Proxima* 6 (1985): 83–88.

―――. "L'Œuvre de Christine Renard." *Proxima* 2 (1984): 45–50, and 3 (1984): 16–33.

Couriol, M. C. B. "À propos de Maurice Renard et Richard Matheson." *Fiction* 30 (1956): 124–25.

Creteux, M. "Science-fiction." *Notes bibliographiques* 3 (1973): 195–99.

―――. "La Science-fiction gagne ses lettres de noblesse." *Notes bibliographiques* 4 (1974): 327–32.

Crossley, Ceri. "Émile Souvestre's Anti-Utopia: *Le Monde tel qu'il sera*." *Nottingham French Studies* 24 (1985): 28–40.

Curval, Philippe. "Existe-t-il une école de science-fiction française?" *Le Monde*, July 27, 1978.

―――. "Habite-t-on réellement quelque part?" *Science-fiction* 4 (1985): 168–80.

―――. "Jusqu'au bout et au-delà avec Michel Jeury." *Futurs* 5 (1978): 39–43.

―――. "Jusqu'au bout et au-delà avec Pierre Versins." *Futurs* 2 (1978): 46–49, 87.

————. "Pourquoi la SF: manifeste pour la science-fiction." *Science-fiction* 1 (1984): 202–10.

Dand, E. "Science Fiction in the Novels of Michel Butor." *Forum for Modern Language Studies* (1982): 47–62.

D'Aubarède, Gabriel. "Une heure avec Pierre Boulle, de planète en planète." *Les Nouvelles littéraires* (February 21, 1963): 1, 7.

D'Ivray, J. "Rosny Aîné." *La Revue des revues* 150 (1922): 394–405.

De Repper, Jean-Claude. "À travers les collections depuis 1950." *Horizons du fantastique* 11 (1970): 64–67.

————. "Entretien avec Gérard Klein." *Horizons du fantastique* 11 (1970): 71–73.

————. "Entretien avec Jacques Bergier." *Horizons du fantastique* 11 (1970): 13–17.

De Repper, Jean-Claude, et al. "Jacques Sternberg." *Horizons du fantastique* 11 (1970), 61–62.

————. "René Barjavel." *Horizons du fantastique* 11 (1970), 37–39.

Dorémieux, Alain. "La Science-fiction dépassée?" *Fiction* 138 (1965): 156–57.

Douay, Dominique. "The Dream and the Reality." *Foundation* 32 (1984): 42–44.

Douay, Dominique, and Giuliani, Pierre. "SF et idéologie: une quête absurde." *Europe* 580–81 (1977): 79–84.

————. "La Science-fiction et la politique." In *Univers 12*. Paris: J'ai lu, 1978.

Douay, Dominique, and Bozzetto, Roger. "Débat à propos de la nouvelle science-fiction française." *Fiction* 287 (1978): 165–78.

Doumic, René. "Les Romans de Rosny." *Revue des Deux Mondes* 129 (1895): 936–47.

Douvres, Michel. "Entretien avec Serge Brussolo." *Fiction* 347 (1984): 173–76.

Duval, R. P. "Dans la jungle littéraire, un labyrinthe: la science-fiction." *Notes bibliographiques* 6 (1973): 564–70.

Duvic, Patrice. "La Mort, le réveil." In *Le Livre d'or de Jean-Pierre Andrevon*. Paris: Presses Pocket, 1983.

Ebstein, J.-P. "La Science-fiction au microscope." *Fiction* 234 (1973): 175–86.

Échassériaux, Bernard. "L'Univers fantastique de Jacques Spitz." In Jacques Spitz. *L'Œil du purgatoire*. Paris: Laffont, 1972.

Ecken, Claude. "Pierre Suragne (Pierre Pelot)." *Altaïr* 9 (1977): 34–43.

Eckerman, Claude, and Martel, Dominique. "Entretien avec Michel Demuth." *Fantascienza* 4–7 (1981): 217–28.

————. "Entretien avec Alain Dorémieux." *Fantascienza* 4–7 (1981): 205–16.

Eco, Umberto. "Science et science-fiction." *Science-fiction* 5 (1985): 210–21.

Ehrwein, Michel. "Lorsque demain s'appelle hier." *Fiction* 90 (1961): 117–26, and 91 (1961): 119–28.

Eizykman, Boris. "Entretien avec Michel Jeury." *Horizons du fantastique* 29 (1974): 23–25.

————. "Entretien collage *Soleil chaud poisson des profondeurs* et l'auteur." *Fiction* 277 (1977): 173–82.

————. "Pseudo-synthèse des penchants science-fictifs de la bande dessinée." *Opus International* 64 (1977): 17–23.

————. "Ronge et dérange le temps incertain . . . À Michel Jeury, prix du meilleur roman français de SF, 1974." *Les Nouvelles littéraires* 2427 (1974): 7.

————. "S-F: Science spéculative, stochastique fiction." *Traverses* 24 (1981): 115–24.

Reprint as "Chance and Science Fiction: SF as Stochastic Fiction." *Science-Fiction Studies* 10 (1983): 24–34.

Elsen, Claude. "Les Romans fantastiques de Jacques Spitz." *Fiction* 113 (1963): 129–31.

"Entretien sur la science-fiction." *Europe* 139–40 (1957): 3–20.

Evans, Arthur B. "Science Fiction vs. Scientific Fiction in France: From Jules Verne to Rosny Aîné." *Science-Fiction Studies* 15 (1988): 1–11.

———. "The Extraordinary Libraries of Jules Verne." *L'Esprit créateur* 28 (1988): 75–86.

Evrard, Lionel. "Entretien avec Michel Jeury." *Opzone* 7 (1980): 17–22.

Favarel, Muriel, and Blanc, Bernard. "Une rencontre avec Jean-Pierre Hubert." *Alerte!* 1 (1977): 156–60.

Favier, Jacques. "Les Jeux de la temporalité en science-fiction." *Littérature* 8 (1972): 53–71.

Faye, Jean-Pierre. "Science (de) fiction?" *Change* 40 (1981): 3–8.

Ferran, Pierre. "Daniel Walther: l'écriture matière de rêve." *Le Français dans le Monde* 193 (1985): 77–80.

Ferrando, Jean-Louis. "Démons et chimères: Philippe Druillet." *Science-fiction magazine* 1 (1976): 14.

Ferreras, Juan Ignacio. "Le Roman de science-fiction: rupture et romantisme." *Fiction* 280 (1977): 163–67, and 281 (1977): 184–89.

Fisson, Pierre. "Barjavel, l'homme qui voyage par tous les temps: une interview." *Le Figaro littéraire* (February 10, 1969): 27.

Gallet, Georges. "J.-H. Rosny Aîné." In J.-H. Rosny Aîné. *Les Navigateurs de l'infini*. Paris: Hachette, 1960.

———. "Vie et mort du *Rayon Fantastique*." In *Univers 3*. Paris: J'ai lu, 1975, pp. 152–63.

Gerould, Daniel. "Villiers de l'Isle-Adam and Science Fiction." *Science-Fiction Studies* 11 (1984): 318–23.

Giraud, Jean. "Jean-Gaston Vandel: une œuvre inachevée." *Horizons du fantastique* 14 (1971): 70–71.

———. "Richard-Bessière ou le panorama d'un genre." *Horizons du fantastique* 13 (1970): 44–45.

Giuliani, Pierre. "Science-fiction et Histoire." *Change* 40 (1981): 20–44.

———. "Le Space Opéra." *Science-fiction magazine* 4 (1977): 39–42.

———. "Science-fiction et politique." *Fiction* 258 (1975): 159–70.

Goimard, Jacques. "Définir l'art de Siudmak." *Futurs* 5 (1978): 57–60.

———. "Modeste Précis d'ortogologie portative." In Kurt Steiner, *Ortog*. Paris: Laffont, 1975.

———. Preface to Gérard Klein and Jacques Goimard, eds. *Ce qui vient des profondeurs: anthologie de la science-fiction française, 1956–1970*. Paris: Seghers, 1977.

———. "Prologue dans le logos." *Europe* 580–81 (1977): 3–13.

———. "Qu'est-ce que la science-fiction?" *Quinzaine littéraire* 123 (1971): 12–13.

———. "Siudmak, l'homme qui fait exister l'impossible, revisité par Jacques Goimard." In Jacques Goimard, ed. *L'Année 1981–1982 de la science-fiction et du fantastique*. Paris: Julliard, 1982.

———. "Le Thème de la fin du monde." In *Histoires de fins du monde*. Paris: Livre de Poche, 1974.

Gouanvic, Jean-Marc. "Boris Vian et la science-fiction." *Fiction* 290 (1978): 175–84.

———. "Enquête sur l'irruption de la SF américaine en Europe dans les années 50." *Imagine* . . . 1 (1979): 95–110.

———. "Étude textuelle de quelques structures de l'imaginaire de science-fiction chez J.-H. Rosny Aîné." *Fiction* 302 (1979): 181–91, and 303 (1979): 214–24.

———. "Positions de l'Histoire dans la science-fiction." *Change* 40 (1981): 85–103.

———. "Rosny Aîné et la science-fiction moderne." *Imagine* . . . 13 (1982): 105–7.

———. "La Science-fiction, une poétique de l'altérité." *Imagine* . . . 14 (1982), 106–11.

———. "L'Uchronie, histoire alternative et science-fiction." *Imagine* . . . 14 (1982), 28–34.

———. "Vers la science-fiction moderne: Rosny, Wells, Verne, Renard." *Europe* 681–82 (1986): 12–17.

Grenier, Christian. "S.-F.: l'aventure des mots." *Le Français dans le Monde* 193 (1985): 70–71.

Grosjean, F., and Schlockoff, A. "Quand le cinéma explore le temps." *Science-fiction magazine* 4 (1977): 30–33.

Goy, Philip. "La Science est à la science-fiction ce que la photo est à la peinture." *Opus International* 64 (1977): 40–43.

Guiot, Denis. "Axes de la perspective curvalienne ou au-delà de la quête de l'identité." *Fiction* 268 (1976): 181–91.

———. "Daniel Walther, questionné par Denis Guiot." In Jacques Goimard, ed. *L'Année 1980–1981 de la science-fiction et du fantastique.* Paris: Julliard, 1981.

———. "Science-fiction et politique." *Opus International* 64 (1977): 33–35.

———. "S.-F. version jeune." *Le Français dans le Monde* (1985): 42–43.

———. "Sur l'œuvre de Pierre Suragne (Pierre Pelot)." *Argon* 6 (1976): 6–11.

———. "Trajets et itinéraires de l'oubli du héros brussolien." *Démons et Merveilles* 1 (1985): 3–6.

Haesslé, Jacques. "*Ravage*, une démarche littéraire, une démarche initiatique." *Altair* 3 (1984): 8–13.

Henry, J. "Interview: Pierre Suragne (Pierre Pelot)." *Nadir* 2 (1974): 6–10.

Hervier, Julien. "Cyrano de Bergerac et le voyage spatial." In Anna Balakian et al., eds. *Actes du Xème congrès de l'Association internationale de littérature comparée.* Vol. 1. New York: Garland, 1985.

Hill, Eugene. "The Place of the Future: Louis Marin and his *Utopiques*." *Science-Fiction Studies* 9 (1982): 167–79.

Houssin, Joël. "S.F. mode d'emploi." In Daniel Riche, ed. *L'Année 1982–1983 de la science-fiction et du fantastique.* Paris: Temps futurs, 1983.

Huet, Marie-Hélène. "Anticipating the Past: The Time Riddle in Science Fiction." In George Slusser et al., eds. *Storm Warnings: Science Fiction Confronts the Future.* Carbondale: Southern Illinois University Press, 1987.

Idels, Ronny. "Stefan Wul, le plus délirant des auteurs de la science-fiction." *Horizons du fantastique* 5 (1969): 87–91.

Ioakimidis, Demètre. "Une idéologie du progrès." *Europe* 580–81 (1977): 22–55.

Issaurat-Delaef, Marie-Louise. "Une épopée cosmique ou l'univers mythique de J.-H. Rosny Aîné." In Jean-Marie Grassin, ed. *Mythes, images, représentations.* Paris: Didier, 1981.

Jeury, Michel. Preface to *Le Livre d'or de la science-fiction: Gérard Klein*. Paris: Presses Pocket, 1979.

———. "Science-fiction, phase 4." *Science-fiction* 3 (1985): 200–15.

Jouanne, Emmanuel. "Mais l'espace . . . mais le temps." *Le Français dans le Monde* 193 (1985): 25–27.

———. "Raison en miettes." *Science-fiction* 1 (1984): 211–20.

Juin, Hubert. "Science-fiction et littérature." *Europe* 139–40 (1957): 53–62.

Kerbow, J. B. "Rosny, romancier maudit." *Revue des Sciences humaines* (1967): 117–24.

Ketterer, David. "Fathoming *20,000 Leagues under the Sea*." In Michael Tolley and Kirpal Singh, eds. *The Stellar Gauge: Essays on Science Fiction Writers*. Carlton, Australia: Norstrilia Press, 1980.

Khouri, Nadia, and Angenot, Marc. "Savoir et autorité: le discours de l'anthropologie préhistorique." *Littérature* 50 (1983): 104–18.

Klein, Gérard. "Contre la notion de paralittérature." *Science-fiction* 3 (1985): 218–50.

———. "La Crise dépassée ou Douze ans après." In *L'Année 1979–80 de la Science-Fiction et du Fantastique*. Edited by Jacques Goimard. Paris: Julliard, 1980.

———. "Jacques Sternberg ou le robot écoeuré." *Fiction* 51 (1958): 122–29.

———. "Exécution et apothéose de Jacques Sternberg." *Fiction* 145 (1965): 135–45.

———. "Mais qu'est-ce que nous avons perdu?" In his *Les Perles du temps*. Paris: Denoël, 1982.

———. "Pourquoi y a-t il une crise de la science-fiction française?" *Fiction* 116 (1967): 122–28.

———. Preface to A. Valérie. *"Sur l'autre face du monde" et autres romans scientifiques de "Sciences et Voyages"*. Edited by Gérard Klein and Jacques Van Herp. Paris: Laffont, 1973.

———. Preface to Gérard Klein, ed. *En un autre pays: anthologie de la science-fiction française, 1960–1964*. Paris: Seghers, 1976.

———. Preface to his *Le Gambit des étoiles*. Paris: NéO, 1980.

———. Preface to Stefan Wul. *Stephan Wul: Œuvres*. Paris: Laffont, 1970.

———. "Le Procès en dissolution de la SF." *Europe* 580–81 (1977): 145–55.

———. "Science-fiction et roman nouveau." In Daniel Drode. *Surface de la planète*. Paris: Laffont, 1976.

———. "Science et science-fiction." *Science-fiction* 6 (1986): 178–93.

———. "Une vue sur l'histoire." In *Le Livre d'or de la science-fiction: Michel Jeury*. Paris: Presses Pocket, 1982.

Klein, Gérard, and Curval, Philippe. "Ici, on réintègre!" *Fiction* 50 (1958): 133–37.

Lacassin, Francis. "Le Communard qui écrivit trois romans de Jules Verne." *Europe* 595–96 (1978): 94–105.

———. "Dans le sillage du *Nautilus*." In Gustave Le Rouge. *Le Sous-marin Jules Verne*. Paris: "10/18," 1978.

———. "Gustave Le Rouge ou le gourou secret de Blaise Cendrars." In his *Passagers clandestins I*. Paris: "10/18," 1979.

———. "Gustave Le Rouge ou le naufragé de la SF." *Fiction* 155 (1966): 137–49.

———. "Gustave Le Rouge, pionnier de la science-fiction ou 'Jules Verne des midi-nettes'?" In Gustave Le Rouge, *Le Prisonnier de la planète Mars*. Paris: "10/18," 1976.

———. "Jacques [Sternberg] le Futuriste." *L'Express* (December 27, 1971): 73.

———. "Le Rouge et Compagnie fabrique de romans . . . et de rêves." In Gustave Le Rouge and Gustave Guitton. *La Princesse des airs.* 2 vols. Paris: "10/18," 1976.

———. "Roman populaire, roman visionnaire." In Gustave Le Rouge and Gustave Guitton. *La Conspiration des milliardaires.* Paris: "10/18," 1977.

Lacassin, Francis, et al. "La Science-fiction." *Magazine littéraire* 31 (1969): 7–33.

Lacarrière, Jacques. Preface to Restif de la Bretonne. *La Découverte australe.* Paris: France Adel, 1977.

Lacaze, Dominique. "Lectures croisées de Jules Verne et de Robida." In *Jules Verne et les sciences humaines.* Paris: "10/18," 1979.

Lamart, Michel. "Nommer le futur: archéologie d'un genre." *Le Français dans le Monde* 193 (1985): 21–24.

———. "S.O.S. science-fiction française." *Fiction* 330 (1982): 184–88.

Laselle, Jean-Paul. "Interview: comme à confesse, Pierre Pelot." *Dimensions 5* 8 (1978): 56–59.

Laugaa, Maurice. "Lune, ou l'autre." *Poétique* 3 (1970): 282–96.

Lavers, Annette. "Anciens et Nouveaux Dédales ou quelques ancêtres français de la science-fiction." *Médecine de France* 129 (1961): 33–39.

Le Bellec, Jean-Luc. "Voyage en Brussoland: entretien." *SFère* 16 (1984): 13–22.

———. "Brussolo au Fleuve." *SFère* 16 (1984): 27–33.

Le Blond. M. A. "L'Épopée évolutionniste de l'énergie humaine (Rosny Aîné)." *Revue des Revues* 46 (1903): 641–55.

Lecaye, Alexis. "SF française: deux romans de Philippe Curval." *Le Monde* (October 18, 1979): 1.

Lecigne, Bruno. "Le Voyage littéraire d'Hareton Ironcastle." *Europe* 681–82 (1986): 90–94.

Leclerc de la Herverie, Jean. "Daniel Walther ou l'apôtre de la New Thing." *Horizons du fantastique* 27 (1974): 16–19.

Leconte, Marianne. "Entretien avec Philip Goy." *Horizons du fantastique* 28 (1974): 47–48.

———. "Les Femmes et la science-fiction." *Opus International* 64 (1977): 31–33.

Lee, Vernon. "Rosny and the Analytical Novel in France." *Cosmopolis* 7 (1897): 280–96.

Lortie, Alain. "B. R. Bruss." *Solaris* 30 (1979): 32–33.

Louit, Robert. "Notes sur la science-fiction au cinéma." *Opus International* 64 (1977): 24–30.

Lyan, Bradford. "Technocratic Anxiety in France: The Fleuve Noir 'Anticipation' Novels, 1951–1960." *Science-Fiction Studies* 16 (1989): 277–97.

Manoeuvre, Philippe. "Moebius questionné par Philippe Manoeuvre." In Jacques Goimard, ed. *L'Année 1979–1980 de la science-fiction et du fantastique.* Paris: Julliard, 1980.

Marchand, Jean José. "Un précurseur: Defontenay." In C. I. Defontenay. *Star, ou psi de Cassiopée.* Paris: Denoël, 1972.

Martin, Andrew. "Chez Jules: Nutrition and Cognition in the Novels of Jules Verne." *French Studies* 37 (1983): 47–58.

———. "The Entropy of Balzacian Tropes in the Scientific Fictions of Jules Verne." *Modern Language Review* 77 (1982): 51–62.

Maurail, Louis. "Les Futurs auxquels vous avez échappé, suivi de *L'Aube du futur* de Rosny Aîné." *Science-fiction* 5 (1985): 50–68.

————. "Nathalie Henneberg." *Fiction* 288 (1978): 173–81.

Maure, Rémi (pseudonym of Jean-Pierre Moumon). "Les Arches stellaires et leur littérature." *Fiction* 291 (1978): 167–90; 292 (1978): 190–222; 293 (1978): 178–90; and 294 (1978): 157–90.

————. "Enquête sur la science-fiction d'expression française." *Espace-Temps* 6 (1978): 9–32.

Messac, Ralph. "Quinzinzinzili." In Régis Messac. *Quinzinzinzili*. Paris: Édition Spéciale, 1972.

————. "La Cité des asphyxiés." In Régis Messac. *La Cité des asphyxiés*. Paris: Édition Spéciale, 1972.

Messac, Régis. "Voyages modernes au centre de la Terre." *Revue de Littérature comparée* (1929): 74–104.

Milési, Raymond. "Les Faux Procès de la science-fiction française." *Fiction* 338 (1983): 160–65.

————. "Science-fiction française. L'Image et la trame." *Fiction* 342 (1983): 190–96, and 345 (1983): 154–61.

Moog, J. "Un disciple de Zola (Rosny Aîné)." *Nouvelle Revue* 82 (1893): 554–71.

Moreau, Charles. "Fantastique et SF: de la grande question des limites." *Le Français dans le Monde* 193 (1985): 54–55.

Morel, J. "Rosny Aîné et le merveilleux scientifique." *Mercure de France* 187 (1926): 82–94.

Mory, Aimé. "Michel Pilotin: 1906–1972." *Galaxie* 113 (1973): 136–47.

Moumon, Jean-Pierre. "Rencontre avec Richard-Bessière." *Antarès* 12 (1984): 123–27.

Moumon, Jean-Pierre, and Blond, Martine. "Rencontre avec Jacques Van Herp." *Antarès* 10 (1983): 119–24.

Mourier, Maurice. "La Science-fiction et l'avenir du roman." *Le Monde* (October 2, 1981): 20–21.

Nahon, Georges. "Kurt Steiner: fascinant magicien des univers fantastiques." *Horizons du fantastique* 12 (1970): 28–32.

Nicot, Stéphane. "Entretien avec Dominique Douay." *Fiction* 326 (1982): 172–77.

————. "Entretien avec Philippe Curval." *Imagine . . .* 31 (1985): 75–78.

————. "Splendeurs et misères de la science-fiction française." In *Univers 1987*. Paris: J'ai lu, 1987.

Oliver-Martin, Y. "Une littérature populaire." *Europe* 580–81 (1977): 127–31.

————. "Science-fiction et roman policier." *Espace-Temps* 11 (1979): 51–59.

Paraf, Pierre. "La Science à travers les cités de bonheur." *Europe* 139–40 (1957): 34–42.

Paucard, Alain. "Pierre Gripari, questionné par Alain Paucard." In Jacques Goimard, ed. *L'Année 1981–1982 de la science-fiction et du fantastique*. Paris: Julliard, 1982.

Pecker, Jean-Claude. "La Science, c'est tout de même autre chose." *La Quinzaine littéraire* (January 16–31, 1976): 11–13.

Perrin, Raymond. "Pierre Pelot: l'étrange symbiose de la violence et de la tendresse." *Les Cahiers de l'imaginaire* 15–16 (1985): 5–31.

Pfeiffer, Philippe and Laurent. "Interview de Daniel Walther." *Option* 4 (1985): 1–8.

Phi, Daniel (Daniel Fondanèche). "Francis Carsac." *Horizons du fantastique* 26 (1974): 27–31.

Philippe, Denis (Jean-Pierre Andrevon). "Stefan Wul ou la grandeur de l'évidence." *Fiction* 229 (1973): 120–30.

Pichon, Jean-Charles. "Science-fiction ou réalisme irrationnel." *Europe* 139–40 (1957): 34–41.

Piroué, Jérôme. "Entretien avec Jean-Pierre Hubert." *Opzone* 4 (1980): 9–11.

Pividal, Rafael. "Une littérature en ut mineur." *Europe* 580–81 (1977), 132–37.

Planque, Jean-Pierre. "Brussolo l'alchimiste." *SFère* 16 (1984): 23–26.

Polette, René. "Rosny Aîné, poète de l'infini?" *Europe* 681–82 (1986): 95–100.

Poinsot, M. C. "J.-H. Rosny." *La Grande Revue* 41 (1907): 449–59 and 595–604.

Pons, Alain. Preface to Louis-Sébastien Mercier. *L'An 2440*. Paris: France Adel, 1977.

Queneau, Raymond. "Un nouveau genre littéraire: les science-fictions." *Critique* 7 (1951): 195–98.

———. "Defontenay." In his *Bâtons, chiffres et lettres*. Paris: Gallimard, 1965.

Raabe, Juliette. "Maurice Renard: un combat contre la folie." *Magazine littéraire* 42 (1970): 35–36.

Raymond, François. "Jules Verne, Albert Robida . . . et les autres. La Fiction prospective au XIXème siècle." *Revue française de l'électricité* 273 (1981): 58–64.

———. "Enquête sur la science-fiction d'expression française." *Espace-Temps* 8 (1978): 9–22.

———. "La Science-fiction française en exil." *Antarès* 11 (1984): 126–32.

Reboussin, Didier. "L'Amertume des temps: interview et étude de l'œuvre de Nathalie Henneberg." *Axolotl* 1 (1974): 3–20.

Renault, Maurice. Preface to Maurice Leblanc. *Le Formidable Événement/Les Trois Yeux*. Paris: Opta, 1968.

Reuillard, Gabriel. "Un précurseur du roman d'anticipation (Gustave Le Rouge)." *Bulletin de la librairie ancienne et moderne* 48 (1968): 11–13.

Riche, Daniel. "Entretien avec Jean-Pierre Andrevon." *Nyarlathotep* 3 (1970): 17–19.

———. "Science-fiction et Histoire: une introduction." *Change* 40 (1981): 9–13.

Rio, Yves. "Science-fiction et refus de l'Histoire." *Change* 40 (1981): 104–12.

Rivière, François. "La Science-fiction à l'heure française." *Les Nouvelles littéraires* 2736 (1980): 26.

———. "Raymond Roussel et la fiction spéculative." In *Univers 9*. Paris: J'ai lu, 1974.

Rodenbach, Georges. "Les Rosny." *Nouvelle Revue* 105 (1897): 289–96.

Roger, G. "Du bon usage de la science-fiction." *Europe* 139–40 (1957): 42–50.

Rose, Marilyn Gaddis. "Two Misogynist Novels: A Feminist Reading of Villiers and Verne." *Nineteenth-Century French Studies* 9 (1980–81): 119–23.

Rose, Mark. "Filling the Void: Verne, Wells and Lem." *Science-Fiction Studies* 8 (1981): 121–42.

———. "Jules Verne: Journey to the Center of Science Fiction." In George Slusser et al., eds. *Coordinates: Placing Science Fiction and Fantasy*. Carbondale: Southern Illinois University Press, 1983.

Rouveyrol, Jacques. "La Mort de l'homme." *Europe* 580–81 (1977): 57–64.

Ruaud, André-François. "Présence du Futur: 30 ans!" *Proxima* 6 (1985): 52–61.

———. "Entretien avec Jean-Pierre Hubert." *Ère comprimée* 34 (1985): 9–10.

Ruellan, André. "Philippe Curval dialogue avec André Ruellan." In Jacques Goimard, ed. *L'Année 1977–1978 de la Science-Fiction et du Fantastique*. Paris: Julliard, 1978.

———. "Un langage perpendiculaire." In *Le Livre d'or de la science-fiction: Philippe Curval*. Paris: Presses Pocket, 1980.

Sadoul, Jacques. "Les Comics de science-fiction." *Fiction* 132 (1964): 154–60.

Sageret, J. "La Sociologie de J.-H. Rosny Aîné." *La Revue du mois* 9 (1910): 270–85.

Saumade, Bernard. "Rencontre avec René Barjavel." *Antarès* 14 (1984): 129–32.

"Science-fiction, 1er avril 2074." *Les Nouvelles littéraires* 2427 (1974): 3–20.

Serres, Michel. "India (the Black and the Archipelago) on Fire." *Sub-Stance* 8 (1974): 49–60.

———. "Jules Verne's Strange Journeys." *Yale French Studies* 52 (1975): 174–88.

Shippey, Tom. "L'Histoire dans la science-fiction." *Change* 40 (1981): 14–19.

Simon, Louis. "Han Ryner: écrivain de l'utopie, de la science-fiction et du fantastique." *Horizons du fantastique* 24 (1973): 18–20.

Slusser, George. "The Beginnings of *Fiction*." *Science-Fiction Studies* 16 (1989): 307–37.

Sormany, Pierre. "La Science au futur (Gérard Klein)." *Québec Science* 16 (1978): 25–29.

Souriau, Jean-Marie. "Science et science-fiction." *La Recherche* 49 (1974): 854–65.

Spriel, Stéphane. "Le Ressac du futur." *Cahiers du Sud* 37 (1953): 21–25.

———. "Sur la science-fiction." *Esprit* 202 (1953): 674–85.

Spriel, Stéphane, and Vian, Boris. "Un nouveau genre littéraire: la science-fiction." *Les Temps Modernes* (1951): 618–27.

Sternberg, Jacques. "La Science-fiction rebute les Français autant que le surréalisme." *Magazine littéraire* 31 (1969): 25–26.

Sternberg, Jacques, and Klein, Gérard. "La Science-fiction est-elle une littérature stéréotypée?" *Fiction* 50 (1958): 119–21.

Suvin, Darko. "Communication in Quantified Space: the Utopian Liberalism of Jules Verne's Science Fiction." *Clio* 4 (1974): 51–71. Reprint in his *Metamorphoses of Science Fiction*. New Haven, Conn.: Yale University Press, 1979.

"Territoires de la science-fiction." *Les Nouvelles littéraires* 2617 (1978): 18–21.

Thaon, Marcel. "Un Klein de pierre." *Fiction* 241 (1974): 185–90.

Thomas, Pascal J. "The Current State of Science Fiction in France." *Science-Fiction Studies* 16 (1989): 292–306.

———. "French SF and the Legacy of Philip K. Dick." *Foundation* 34 (1985): 22–35.

———. "Masters of French SF: Jean-Pierre Andrevon and Michel Jeury." *Fantasy Review* 11 (1986): 15–16, 46.

———. "Some French Science Fiction Trends." *A Foreign Fanzine* 4 (1981): 7–12.

Touttain, Pierre-André. "Les Curieux Romans de Maurice Renard." *Le Figaro littéraire* (March 30, 1970): 15–16.

———. "Le Dossier de la science-fiction." *Les Nouvelles littéraires* 2153 (1968): 6–7.

———. "Les Obsessions de Renard." *Les Nouvelles littéraires* 2225 (1970): 5.

Tronche, Anne. "Une barbarie fondamentale." In Philippe Curval. *La Forteresse de coton*. Paris: Denoël, 1979.

———. "Visionneurs des espaces différents?" *Opus International* 64 (1977): 11–16.

Truchaud, François. "Interview: Gérard Klein." *Le Nouveau Planète* 23 (1971): 142–45.

———. "Interview: Kurt Steiner." *Le Nouveau Planète* 23 (1971): 147–49.

———. "Rencontre avec Stefan Wul." *Galaxie* 80 (1971): 140–52.

Turpin, Pierre. "Denis-Gabriel Guignard: travailleur manuel et romancier." *Cahiers pour la littérature populaire* 3 (1984): 14–34.

Valéry, Francis. "La Série 2000: regard sur la première collection de SF française." In *Univers 19*. Paris: J'ai lu, 1979.

———. "Y a-t-il une nouvelle SF française?" *Solaris* 31 (1980): 16–17.

Van Herp, Jacques. "Avant-propos." In H. J. Magog. *Trois ombres sur Paris*. Verviers, Belgium: Marabout, 1975.

———. "Et la science-fiction naquit. . . ." In J.-H. Rosny Aîné. *Récits de science-fiction*. Verviers: Marabout, 1973.

———. "Il y a plusieurs SF." *Europe* 580–81 (1977): 43–48.

———. "Jean Ray ou le combat avec les fantômes." *Fiction* 38 (1957): 102–7.

———. "Journaliste et magicien." In Léon Groc. *La Planète de Cristal*. Verviers, Belgium: Marabout, 1975.

———. "Un maître du feuilleton: Jean de la Hire." *Fiction* 37 (1956): 112–15.

———. "Maurice Renard, scribe des miracles." *Fiction* 28 (1956): 107–10.

———. "Les Mondes défunts et les mondes cachés." *Fiction* 130 (1964): 139–51.

———. "Le Roman de science-fiction qui eut le prix Goncourt." *Fiction* 57 (1958): 126–27.

———. "Les Romans de *Science et Voyages* et leur temps." In A. Valérie. *"Sur l'autre face du monde" et autres romans scientifiques de "Science et Voyages."* Edited by Gérard Klein and Jacques Van Herp. Paris: Laffont, 1973.

———. "La Science-fiction dans l'œuvre de Maurice Leblanc." *Fiction* 47 (1957): 126–29.

Vernier, J.-P. "The SF of J.-H. Rosny the Elder." *Science-Fiction Studies* 2 (1975): 156–63.

Versins, Pierre. "André Arnyvelde ou le Bacchus mutilé." *Fiction* 89 (1961): 118–21.

———. "Fandom français." *Fiction* 95 (1961): 125–29.

———. "Un mystère littéraire." In Gustave Le Rouge. *La Guerre des vampires*. Paris: "10/18," 1976.

———. Preface to Gérard Klein. *Les Seigneurs de la guerre*. Geneva: Édito-service, 1974.

———. "Une porte peut être ouverte ou fermée." *Fiction* 140 (1965): 126–33; 141 (1965): 130–39; and 142 (1965): 147–59.

———. "Vie et aventures de CORA, suivi d'un entretien sur la science-fiction avec François Le Lionnais et Daniel Drode." In *Entretiens sur la paralittérature*. Paris: Plon, 1970.

Vonarburg, Élisabeth. "Les Femmes et la science-fiction." *Requiem* 15 (1977): 10–15.

Walther, Daniel. "Nouvelles Formes de la SF." *Horizons du fantastique* 22 (1973): 30–35.

———. "Political SF in France, or The Long Night of the Fools." *Foundation* 18 (1980): 37–47.

———. "Pourquoi la science-fiction?" *Science-fiction* 5 (1985): 190–208.

———. "La Science-fiction politique à la française." *Science-fiction* 2 (1984): 180–94.

Wandzioch, Magdelena. "Science-fiction et transposition de la réalité historique." In Jean Bessière, ed. *Récit et histoire*. Paris: Presses Universitaires de France, 1984.

Wennekers, L. "En marge d'un centenaire: un grand méconnu, Rosny Aîné." *Nos Lettres* 20 (1956): 97–98.

Winandy, André. "The Twilight Zone: Image and Reality in Jules Verne's *Strange Journeys.*" *Yale French Studies* 43 (1969): 101–10.

Wintrebert, Joëlle. "SF et normalité." *Europe* 580–81 (1977): 138–44.

Zielonka, Anthony. "Defontenay's *Star* as Poetic and Philosophical Science Fiction." *French Forum* 11 (1986): 317–33.

13

Sports

RICHARD C. WILLIAMSON

> Toute la famille française se réunissait autour de l'enfant qui
> faisait ses premiers pas. Elle l'obligeait à courir, et le rendait
> cagneux en deux jours: sa carrière sportive s'arrêtait là.
>
> Jean Giraudoux, *Le Sport*

While few French people are knock-kneed because their family may have pushed them to run when they were just beginning to walk, Jean Giraudoux's humorous explanation of the relative paucity of athletes in France may not be entirely facetious. If one were to ask an informed American to describe the French, the response might contain these descriptives: "good cooks," "excited talkers," "fast drivers," "interesting lovers." But one does not often hear "excellent athletes." The French are not renowned for their prowess in sports. Even a French scholar of organized sport in France, Christian Pociello, admits that French world champions are usually found in fairly new sports with limited international appeal, and he cites windsurfing, trampoline, team free-flying, and "hotdog" skiing ("La Force," p. 232). Of course, exceptional French athletes do become prominent in major sports: most Americans can correctly identify Jean-Claude Killy, the winner of three gold medals in skiing at the 1976 Olympic Games, or Yannick Noah, a current tennis star, and may recognize the name of Jeannie Longo, the winner of the first Tour de France bicycle race for women. However, three of the most popular sports in France—soccer, bicycle racing, and rugby—are only just beginning to enjoy some popularity in the United States. Americans, therefore, for the most part, remain ignorant of French successes in these activities. (American television coverage of the world's most demanding and prestigious bike race, the Tour de France, was severely limited until an American, Greg LeMond, won it in 1987—and again in 1989 and 1990).

In spite of a dubious reputation on the world scene, the French, both men and women, have been flocking to various sports during the last twenty years, and organized sport, both for participants and viewers, has developed into an important element of modern popular culture. Indeed, sports seem to reflect, like nothing else, a society's myths and beliefs and can be considered the most visible expression of the cultural imagination. Lucien Herr has traced the chronology of the creation of various sporting clubs (*fédérations*) in France; the evolution of the total number of dues-paying, active participants (*licenciés*); and the progression of involvement by women in a certain number of these clubs. His statistics reveal clearly the dramatic rise, even explosion, of participation. For instance, between 1973 and 1978, a mere five years, the number of active club members in sports played in the Olympic Games grew by almost a million. In 1978, ten years ago, a million and a half French were engaged in non-Olympic sports, with the "Fédération française de Pétanque" showing the healthiest increase of 100,000 members (again between 1973 and 1978). Herr's statistics also chart what sports have gained or lost appeal among the French from 1949 until 1978, with soccer the most attractive and boxing the least. Skiing, tennis, gymnastics, and swimming remain the most popular among women, but many females have begun to participate in those sports once considered exclusively male in France, such as soccer and rugby.

According to an article in the weekly news magazine *Le Point* (February 12, 1989), the most popular sports practiced in France during the last decade are cycling, walking excursions (*randonnée pédestre*), tennis, running in road races, skiing, gymnastics, and windsurfing. As Gérard Mermet points out in the chapter of *Francoscopie 1989* devoted to sports, 77 percent of men and 71 percent of women in France regularly practice some form of physical exercise, and the eighties is certainly the decade of individual sports, as attested even by the attraction of solitary sailing races. Sports in France have always been of national importance, however, and a minister in charge of youth and sports (Ministre de la Jeunesse et des Sports) occupies a cabinet-level position in the French government, something lacking in sports-crazed America.

Unfortunately, even with the increasingly important role of sports in the daily lives of the French and the omnipresent impact of the media, especially television, there is little serious, scholarly research about sports in France. As Christian Pociello warns, "Le sport résiste, en France, avec vigueur, à toute forme d'investigation scientifique" ("La Force," p. 232) ("In France, sports vigorously resist any kind of scientific investigation"). Scholars in universities and in the Centre National de la Recherche Scientifique (CNRS), the primary research center in France, disdain working on something so obviously "popular" and "unintellectual" as sports, a prejudice that extends to other domains of popular culture as well. Only a few studies are available, even as general sources; much of the interesting work on the sociocultural aspects of sports is limited to two or three small groups of researchers and to graduate students at the Institut National des Sports et d'Éducation Physique (INSEP), which is the major graduate school for physical education teachers. In addition to master's and doctoral theses, difficult to obtain, these researchers have begun to publish their findings in edited collections and monographs. Thus, while it is easy to complain about the abysmal lack of books and articles dealing with sports from a social or historical perspective, especially those written in English, enough materials do exist to encourage American scholars to study various aspects of the sports phenomenon in France, characterized by its diversity and tradition. Because the number of sports played in the country is overwhelming (some fifty different federations are recognized and financed by the government), I present works of general interest with emphasis, nonetheless, on the most popular sports of soccer, tennis, cycling, rugby, and pétanque.

CLASSIFICATIONS

The first challenge awaiting a researcher of sports in France is how to place them all into meaningful groups. While such categorization may seem a banal, inconsequential matter, it can have critical implications. For example, the facile division into "male" and "female" not only creates problems when dealing with sports played by both sexes, such as tennis, swimming, and skiing, but may also intimate that a particular sport is restricted to one gender. As I mentioned, rugby, long considered a macho sport in the popular imagination, is now played enthusiastically by women in France. Classification does indeed help to reduce the corpus to a manageable level, but it can often reveal hidden biases of a social, cultural, or ideological nature.

Until recently, most general studies of the French sporting scene have followed the categories used by the Ministère de la Jeunesse et des Sports: "Olympic" and "non-Olympic" sports. A list of both groups reveals in what Olympic sports France competes and what other varieties of sports are practiced in the country (see Table 1). One could divide further the Olympic sports into those played at the summer games and those at the winter. Obviously, the ministry's classification can be useful in studies of a socioeconomic nature; certainly, much of a nation's sporting prestige relates to the performance of its athletes in the Olympic Games, and that performance often dictates a country's political priorities toward sports. The classification can also reveal, over time, which sports have remained strong and which may need government subsidies for reinforcement. However, the aura of the Olympic designation relegates the "non-Olympic" sports to something less important, to an inferior status. This is particularly distressing in France, where rugby (dropped from the Games in 1928) and tennis are immensely popular and highly regarded. At the same time, fencing, an Olympic event, is the sport in which France has won the third-greatest number of medals (107); yet its federation, one of the most established in the country (founded in 1852), can boast of only 25,000 active members, much fewer than the ever-

Table 1:
Olympic and Non-Olympic Sports

Olympic	Non-Olympic
athlétisme (track and field)	tennis
ski	rugby
voile (sailing)	parachutisme (parachuting)
natation (swimming)	tennis de table (ping-pong)
football (soccer)	sports automobiles
gymnastique (gymnastics)	course d'orientation (orienteering)
aviron (rowing)	sports sous-marins (underwater sports)
escrime (fencing)	trampoline
basket-ball	vol libre (free-flying)
équitation	ski nautique (water-skiing)
judo	pelote basque (pelota)
canoe-kayak	golf
volley-ball	motocyclisme (motorcycle racing)
sports de glace (figure skating)	jeu à XIII (rugby with 13 players)
haltérophilie (weightlifting)	boxe française (French boxing)
handball (team handball)	patinage à roulettes (roller skating)
tir (shooting)	boules (lawn bowling)
boxe (boxing)	baseball
cyclisme (cycling)	surf et skate (surfing and skateboarding)
hockey	karate et arts martiaux
lutte (wrestling)	pétanque et jeu provençal (a form of lawn bowling)
tir à l'arc (archery)	char à voile (ice and sand sailing)
	billards
	vol à voile (sail gliding)
	longue paume (open-air tennis)
	jeu de paume ("real" or court tennis)
	joute (jousting)
	spéléologie (cave exploring)

Source: Ministry of Youth and Sports, 1984.

popular *pétanque* federation (400,000 plus members). Thus a classification of sports into "Olympic" and "non-Olympic" may be misleading; it does not reflect faithfully the sports scene in France.

In an article which discusses the relationship between sport and politics, "Le sport au pluriel ou les singularités du rugby" (Sport in the Plural or the Singularities of Rugby), Paul Irlinger reviews other possible classifications based on dichotomies, all with advantages and disadvantages. The first is team sports and individual sports. While we may not know where to place bicycle racing or gymnastics, in which an individual victory can aid or be aided by a team victory, such a classification does provide some interesting points of comparison. Irlin-

ger's second classification is socioeconomic: popular and elitist sports, for instance, cycling and golf. A third is directly related to a sport's popularity as
measured by a statistical count of spectators, television viewers, and frequency
of the sport's appearance in newspaper and magazine articles; Irlinger labels
these two groups *sports spectacularisés* and *sports peu spectacularisés*, with the
peu creating a problem of definition and measurement. Another means of clas-
sifying sports is to group those involving contact (*sports de proximité*) and those
with no contact (*sports de distance*). Such a grouping may reveal much about
a people's psyche. For instance, the French adore watching contact sports, but
prefer to practice cycling, tennis, road-running, skiing, gymnastics, and windsurfing. Does this preference validate the myth of the French as individualistic?
Or is the current vogue for these noncontact sports motivated more by the *moi-
je* narcissism of the eighties? Irlinger's final dichotomy is perhaps more useful
in France than in the United States: amateur and professional sports.

Since the advent of structuralism (Lévi-Strauss), semiology (Barthes), and the
"new" sociology (Bourdieu) in France, the attempt to classify sports has become
more imaginative, more creative, and more intriguing for researchers. Although
the dichotomies surveyed by Irlinger remain popular, contemporary scholars
have established other systems of oppositions to aid classification, such as that
between sports requiring some technological thing (skate-boarding, ultra-light
flying, windsurfing) and those played with an instrument (racquet, ball, stick).
Rather than be limited to one identifying element of sports, such as Olympic or
non-Olympic, these researchers are trying to construct a system, based upon a
small number of simple, exclusive, and pertinent criteria, that can function both
to create coherence among the many varieties of sports and to explain their
sociocultural distribution. One example of this effort to arrive at a newer, more
comprehensive classification is Pierre Parlebas's scheme. He groups sports according to their "richness of motor communication" (*richesse de la communication motrice*), thus placing sports together in reference to the following
characteristics: (1) presence or absence of adversaries (A) and/or partners (P);
(2) the uncertainty of the situation (I); (3) the possibility offered by the nature
of the game for socio-motor roles to change. Of eight possible groups, Parlebas
places soccer, sailing, and hockey, for example, into the category *PAI*; judo,
cycling, tennis, and fencing fall into the category *AI*; swimming and weightlifting
into a category *A*; parachuting into *I*; and so on.

The most ambitious and, to date, most satisfying system of sports has been
advanced by Christian Pociello, one of the foremost researchers on sports in
France and one of the few Docteurs d'État in physical education. While too
complex and too detailed to be summarized faithfully, Pociello's system offers
intriguing possibilities for further research. He builds it upon four criteria (*for-
mules génératrices*)—force, energy, form, and reflexes—which he considers
endemic to all sports, but which vary in degree to allow a paradigmatic differ-
entiation between sports and even between different forms of the same sport.
What indeed are the differences between horse racing, cross-country jumping,

dressage, and a vigorous ride in the country on a Sunday afternoon? What might determine socioeconomically who is more apt to participate in one of these forms of equitation? The merits of Pociello's system of sports is to emphasize the intimate relationship between sports and sociocultural factors. The position one occupies in society conditions greatly one's attitude toward the body, which, in turn, determines one's sporting preferences and degree of participation. According to Pociello, the evolution of cultural modalities in France can explain the rapid rise in popularity of "reflex" sports, such as tennis, sailing, windsurfing, and *randonnées*. Because most contemporary researchers refer constantly to Pociello's system, it is vital to any discussion of sports in contemporary France and cannot be overlooked.

BRIEF HISTORICAL OUTLINE

The attempt to create a globalizing system of classification of sports in France leads to an affirmation of the existence of *sport*, in the singular, as a rational, coherent entity, called upon to serve social, cultural, and political functions. However, as soon as one begins to study the phenomenon, its complex and changing nature, in a sociocultural milieu that itself is constantly changing, then it becomes impossible to retain the singular: one must talk of different *sports*. But to sketch a brief history of sports in France is perilous, for in such a survey many sports must inevitably be neglected, rendering the choice of the historian arbitrary and problematical. I must limit my remarks to the sports I consider most popular and refer the reader to specialized studies, in which the histories of other sports are told, mentioned in the section, "Guide to the Literature."

While we need to research more profoundly what forces may have influenced the way in which sports developed in France, we can identify several critical factors. First, people must have time to pursue or watch sports, and they must have some disposable income to spend for leisure activities. The growth of the professional and commerical middle class during this century, the reduction of the work week to forty hours by the Blum government (1936), and the obligatory four-week vacation spurred the growth of organized sports in France. Second, technological innovations not only create new sports, such as the invention of the fiberglass board for windsurfing, but also allow equipment to be mass-produced, thus reducing the cost and making the sport accessible to a wider public. A fine example is the bicycle: until the invention of the modern bike with inflatable tires and chain drive in the late 1880s, cycling was not a popular sport in France, even though races, organized by private clubs, had been held on a regular basis since the early 1870s. Third, a society's attitudes toward its young people and toward the body can determine its support for various kinds of athletic endeavors. In the 1880s and early 1890s, gymnastics became a major, national recreational activity because of the heightened awareness of the need, felt acutely after the humiliating defeat by the Prussians in 1870, to promote physical health, a reinforcement of the ideology of "mens sana in corpore sano."

Likewise, interest in aerobics and in running during the 1980s has been fueled by a desire to maintain physical fitness when eating and sitting seem to preoccupy one's life (the current expression for someone who sits, eats, and watches television all day, a "couch potato," is expressive). Fourth, the rise of literacy, the development of a popular press, and the advent of radio and television have been instrumental in creating the commerical spectator sports. Indeed, the first Tour de France was organized by a magazine publisher, Henri Desgrange, in 1903 to bolster circulation of *L'Auto* over that of a rival publication, *Le Vélo*. Finally, and perhaps more characteristic of the French than other people, politics has pervaded the history of sports. From the growth of gymnastics in the 1880s to the "sports for all" slogan of Léo Lagrange, a junior minister for leisure and sports in the Blum government, to current government subsidies and regulations for various sports, politics and sports have remained inseparably bound together in the web of mass culture.

Chroniclers of the history of sports in France mark the *fin de siècle* as the crucial moment in the transformation of leisure activities from communal games to organized sports. Before the 1880s and 1890s, as summarized in a book on *Le Sport* by Eugène Chapus published in 1854, leisure pastimes included such popular sports as horse racing (*le turf*), hunting, boxing, wrestling, *jeu de paume*, billiards, *boules*, riding, swimming, canoeing, fishing, in addition to dancing, whist, and chess. Chapus devotes much of *Le Sport* to hunting and horse racing, two activities that remain major sport preoccupations in contemporary France and reflect changing patterns of social structure.

Hunting, for instance, was once reserved exclusively for members of the aristocracy: the Château de Chambord testifies eloquently to the social standing of this privilege. By the mid-nineteenth century, however, shooting had become a bourgeois activity; a further "democratization" of the sport to the lower middle class and to workers led to incredible growth from 1900 to the present, with about 2.5 million licensed hunters in 1986. This explosion, in turn, has created a scarcity of game to shoot. Wealthier hunters have thus formed private, co-operative game preserves for their personal enjoyment, thereby re-creating a social distinction that had existed up until the nineteenth century and fostering an outbreak of poaching. The sport of hunting in France continues to be enmeshed in a mild form of class struggle, and the government has stepped in to regulate the sport in an effort to ensure fairness for all.

For most French people horse racing is a purely passive sport: what participation there may be comes from checking the newspaper program, looking over the prognostics by the experts, and betting. Yet village cafés across France fill with racing fans on Sunday afternoons who take part in the weekly PMU (*pari mutuel urbain*), and that activity can be far from passive! Both horse racing and hunting are good examples of traditional French sports that create sex distinctions: hunting gives a good excuse to the male to escape tedious responsibilities in the household, and the weekly gathering of bettors in the café provides an opportunity to foster male bonding. Although women do now participate in these sports, they continue to play an important role in male culture in France, a role that merits further elucidation.

Another traditional sport mentioned by Chapus has developed from a folk, regional, leisure activity to one in which individual, double, and team championships are held on a national level. Its sponsoring organization, the Fédération française de pétanque et de jeu provençal, has some 400,000 members, is presently the third most popular of all sports clubs in France, and is growing rapidly. Indeed, so popular is *pétanque* that one can hear the clicking of metal balls and smell the acrid odor of Gauloise cigarettes in most every town and city in France at any time of the day. On Sunday afternoons, a stroll through any village in southern France would not be complete without encountering a group of *pétanque* players discussing strategy and rubbing their silver balls to a brilliant shine with a special cloth.

The invention of metal balls after World War II propelled a surge in the sport's popularity, for the game of *boules* had been played in France since the Roman conquest. The equipment required to play *pétanque* is minimal: three or four balls, a *cochonnet*, or small wooden target ball, and a cloth to wipe the balls clean. Serious competitors add a *boulomètre à tirette*, a measuring device used to settle arguments about which ball lies closest to the *cochonnet*, and a scoring pad. Another factor contributing to *pétanque*'s popularity is the opportunity to play it anywhere: no special court or terrain is necessary. The rules have also remained the same through the centuries and are fairly basic. What differentiates the traditional game of *boules* and *pétanque* is the approach: in *pétanque* one cannot run up to the throwing line, while in the *jeu provençal*, another form of *boules*, one takes a two- or three-stride run-up. The name supposedly derives from *pieds tanqués*, or pigeon-toed, which describes the position of the feet before a throw. In keeping with the folkloric nature of the sport, the following story accounts for the invention of this particular form of *boules*: Two brothers who lived in Provence were great lovers of *boules* and played all day. After one had lost a leg in a hunting accident, he could no longer run up to the throwing line and found it almost impossible to throw well if he used a wheelchair. So his brother, who was growing bored with winning all the time, proposed a game with no running and with reduced distances. They both loved it so much that they convinced all their friends in the village to play that way: "la pétanque est née" (*pétanque* was born).

Although we lack scholarly studies to explain the different reasons for the sport's popularity among French of all socioeconomic levels, we can attribute its historical growth, in part, to a renewed emphasis in France on regionalization (*pétanque* has always been closely identified with the Midi), to a back-to-the-country movement, to the commercialization of the sport by regional newspapers and by the distillers of pastis, and to the psychological, verbal dimensions of the game. Whatever may be its attractions, *pétanque* has been imported into the United States and is gaining enthusiastic supporters each year.

While hunting, horse racing, and *pétanque* are traditional French sports that have retained their popular appeal into the last decades of the twentieth century, three other major sports—rugby, soccer, and bicycle racing—were imported into France from England during the last decades of the nineteenth century and by the 1930s had become items of mass consumption. Until the arrival of these English sports, gymnastics had been the major recreational activity. Not only was it the cheapest and most convenient form of physical recreation, but it was also considered, by many nationalistic leaders in France, a cornerstone of a general program of moral and social regeneration, which would prepare the country to defeat the Prussians "the next time." (The motto of the Union des sociétés françaises de gymnastique [USFG] was: "Faites-moi des hommes, nous en ferons des soldats" [Make me men, we'll make soldiers out of them].) But when the English sports began to attract the interest of large numbers of young people in the mid 1890s, gymnastics declined in popularity, and it has only recently regained some lost ground through the associated sport of aerobics.

One of these youngsters was Pierre de Coubertin, a Parisian from the wealthy Faubourg Saint-Germain district. He traveled to England in 1883, at the age of twenty, and was profoundly impressed by British team sports. He believed that these new forms of exercise were vigorous, morally uplifting, and competitive, just what was needed to prepare a new ruling elite to succeed in a highly competitive world. In 1886, Coubertin published his first article, calling for the introduction of sports into secondary schools, and he created a committee for the "propagation of physical exercise." He was also instrumental in the creation of the Union des sociétés françaises de sports athlétiques (USFSA) in 1889 from a union of the two existing sports clubs in Paris: the Racing Club de France, founded by students from the Lycée Carnot and the Collège Rollin in 1882, and the Stade Français, begun by several students of the Lycée Saint-Louis in 1883. The USFSA's purpose was to look after the interests of the early French rugby players and organize competition for them, as well as oversee disinterested, "healthy" running and crew races. However, on November 25, 1892, USFSA proposed the renewal of the Olympic Games, for Coubertin was troubled already by the growing commercialism of nineteenth-century sports and visualized the inauguration of an amateur championship for the world's sportsmen. Two years later, seventy-nine delegates from twelve countries met at the Sorbonne to adopt, in principle, the renaissance of the international competition, which was realized on April 6, 1896, at the stadium in Athens, when King George signaled the opening of the first Olympic Games of the modern era.

The first appearance of soccer on French soil was in 1872. A group of Britishers in Le Havre, many of them involved in maritime commerce between their home-land and France, founded an athletic club to sponsor informal rugby and soccer matches. From other French ports, such as Nantes, La Rochelle, and Bordeaux, both rugby and soccer spread inland. By 1879 the USFSA could boast some two hundred clubs, with the great majority involved in rugby and, in its modern form, soccer. As early as 1906, soccer had become *the* dominant sport in France, undoubtedly because of its attraction to a wide spectrum of social types. Both rugby and soccer, first played by the British, then by aristocratic schoolboys attending Paris lycées, gained mass support quickly and developed almost overnight into commercialized sports. What is noteworthy is how rugby became implanted in southwestern France, while soccer, at one time localized in the industrialized belt north of Paris, has had no such geographical limitations and is as important to the life of every commune in France as is the local *boulangerie*. With its complex network of local, regional, and national leagues, soccer is certainly the *sport-roi* (king of sports) of France, and the country manages to produce players of world caliber (Michel Platini) and championship teams (France was runner-up in the 1986 World Cup competition).

The third English import to seduce the French was the bicycle. Although the first city-to-city bike race occurred in 1869 from Toulouse to Caraman, a distance of thirty-four kilometers, and the first Paris-Rouen race the same year, bikes were rather crude affairs and too expensive to own for most people. The development of the English "safety" bike in the 1880s and the invention of the pneumatic tire in 1888 by a Belfast veterinarian, John Boyd Dunlop, infused the sport with an extraordinary following. (The number of bikes in France jumped from 130,000 in 1893 to 3.5 million in 1914.) From the very beginning bicycle racing was seen as a way of attracting buyers and advertisers; in the early 1880s a tournament circuit was set up and a group of semi-pro riders created. The rivalry of two newspapers, *Le Véloce Sport* and *Le Petit Journal*, gave birth to two classic races: the Bordeaux-Paris and the Paris-Brest-Paris in 1891. That between two other competing papers, *Le Vélo* and *L'Auto*, led to the founding of one of the world's great sporting events, the Tour de France, in 1903. In between these dates were held the premieres of other classic races: Paris-Brussels (1893), Liège-Bastogne-Liège (1894), Paris-Roubaix (1896), and Paris-Tours (1896).

The Tour de France, which now includes a race for women (since 1987), is much more than a grueling bicycle race. Run in July and covering hundreds of kilometers around France (and in other countries as well), the Tour is a cultural event, a *fête nationale*, as significant to national pride as Bastille Day. It is also a commercial battleground for major manufacturers who sponsor teams and who use the race to increase product visibility and market share. Winners of the *maillot jaune* (yellow jersey), such as Louison Bobet, Jacques Anquetil, and Bernard Hinault, are guaranteed immortal fame and prosperous retirements.

Although the Tour and other classic road races are favorites of the media and the French public, velodrome racing was much more popular at the end of the nineteenth and beginning of the twentieth century. Types of races included sprints, 1,000-meter time trial, individual and team pursuit, and endurance. While biking on the oval track was somewhat boring in comparison with a road race, it was a lucrative form of public entertainment; because of its popularity, velodrome racing was included in the 1986 Olympics and has remained an important fixture of the summer games.

Tennis has often been associated with English sports, but it almost certainly originated in France, where it was first known as *jeu de paume*, or "real" tennis.

Indeed, many believe that the word in English, "tennis," is a corruption of the French *tenetz*, an Old French form of *tenir*, which may have been used for "play!" (Similarly, "love" may be an Anglicized version of *l'oeuf* ["egg"], signifying a zero.) The *jeu de paume* was first played in monastery cloisters during the eleventh century, then in castle courtyards. Despite attempts to reserve tennis for the nobility, it became popular with the bourgeoisie. The game played without walls, from which modern tennis descends, was known as *longue paume*, as opposed to *courte paume*, the enclosed version, less popular obviously because it required a proper court. In its infancy the game was literally a game of the palm, or handball, which is still played today, but by 1500 the long-handed racket, strung with sheep's intestines, had been invented, the ancestor of all modern rackets.

By 1600, tennis had developed into a national pastime in France: every château had a court and every town courts by the dozens (*longue paume*). According to an English traveler around this time, there were as many tennis players in France as ale drinkers in England. Although we do not know exactly when *jeu de paume* crossed the Channel, it was not later than the fourteenth century: the word *tenetz* is first recorded in 1399. While tennis gained followers in England (and later in Scotland), after 1600 the game declined in France. Unfortunately, the people who owned the enclosed courts found it more profitable to rent them as theaters (Molière acted in tennis courts during his early tour of the provinces). Only after the invention of lawn tennis in England during the latter half of the nineteenth century did the sport regain its popularity in France; as in earlier times, it was primarily played by the elite but soon attracted a more democratic public. Unlike rugby, cycling, and even gymnastics, for a long time tennis was really the only form of exercise permissible to well-bred young women, and many excelled; Suzanne Lenglen won the Wimbledon tournament each year from 1919 to 1925.

In addition to the English sports and the traditional sports, such as hunting and *pétanque*, the history of sports in France has been marked by two other tendencies. First, there continues to be a receptivity to sports played in other countries and imported into France. Both the martial arts and the so-called California sports (windsurfing, skate-boarding, delta planing, etc.) are recent imports which have become fixed in the French sports scene. However, while American basketball has found its niche in France, baseball has not yet enjoyed much popularity, in spite of the existence of a baseball federation since 1924. Second, different modalities of a particular sport have been created. For example, alpine skiing traditionally included only downhill and slalom, but such variations as acrobatic, "hotdog," and mono-skiing now exist.

GUIDE TO THE LITERATURE

General Sources

Several reference works are available to present an overall view of sports played in France. They are quite similar and provide, in greater or lesser detail, the history of the sport, its rules, techniques for playing it skillfully, and note-worthy French exploits, including champions or famous participants. Because many, if not most, sports have been imported and are played in other countries, a useful book for the Anglo-Saxon scholar is the Oxford University *Encyclopedia of World Sports*. It lists not only various sports, but also well-known people who have earned their reputation in the world of sports. Both Jean Dauven's *Encyclopédie des sports* (1961) and the Pléiade encyclopedia, *Jeux et Sports* (1967), resemble the Oxford University volume and have become standard reference works. Each contains a useful history of a sport and a summary of the rules. Although published in the 1960s, their encyclopedic qualities render them indispensable for general information; of course, they have nothing about recent sport importations in France, such as "hotdog" water-skiing.

Dominique and Michelle Frémy's *Quid 1991* is rather schematic, for it is designed as a compendium of facts and figures about all phases of French life during the year preceding its publication. In the section entitled "Sports et jeux," a one-sentence summary of the history of the sport is given, followed by a chronological list of both French and world champions and any records set in the sport. If one wants to discover quickly the winner of the Tour de France in 1976 or the final standings of the professional soccer league in 1984, then *Quid* is a helpful source. Its annual publication ensures its timeliness, but of course it lists only those sports with national, European, or world competitions.

In much the same category of general work is *Sportsguide Solar* published in 1984, and thus quite contemporary. By following an alphabetical presentation (it begins with "aile delta" and ends with "water-polo"), this encyclopedia gives the following information for each entry: a definition, the origin and evolution, the type of competition, the rules, the techniques, the equipment necessary to play the sport, famous participants, award winners (in national, European, and world contests), and the address of the club or other responsible organization. *Sportsguide Solar* thus combines the types of information provided both in *Quid* and in the other encyclopedias on sports, rendering it comprehensive. Of more specialized interest is Jean Dauven's *Technique des sports* which, as its title suggests, presents techniques for playing various sports.

Because sports have a language of their own and confusion can occur between English and French terminology ("handball" is a good example: in French, it refers to a team game, while in English it also means the game played with a small rubber ball that is hit by one's palm toward a wall), Georges Petiot's *Dictionnaire de la langue des sports*, or *Le Robert des Sports*, is indispensable for understanding correct sports terms. For each word Petiot gives its etymology, meaning, and several examples of its use by French authors. "Sport," he tells us, derives from the Old French "de(s)porter" with a sense of "s'ébattre," as used in the late twelfth-century romance, *Énéas*. It is imported into England to become "disport" (1303), then, by apocope, "sport" (1400). Petiot presents a formal definition: "activité de loisir axée sur l'exercice des qualités corporelles" (leisure activity based on the exercise of corporal qualities), followed by seventy-seven nouns, synonyms, slang expressions, metaphors, and technical words that crystallize around *sport*. The volume contains an excellent bibliography with basic reference works, both general and specific, with specialized newspapers and periodicals, and even with the names of authors who have chosen sports themes or who have introduced a sports metaphor into general language use. Finally, for those wishing to know more about a particular sport or to begin playing it, a list of the names, addresses, and telephone numbers of French athletic clubs (*fédérations*) is included.

To learn more about an individual sport, it is possible to consult a number of guides from collections on sports: "Domaine du Sport" (La Table Ronde); "Sports pour tous" (Laffont); "Grands du Sport" (PAC); "Sport + Enseignement" (Vigot); and the titles devoted to sports in the "Que sais-je?" series (Presses Universitaires de France). Now, none of these collections is comprehensive, but all have volumes on the most popular sports in France: soccer, cycling, tennis, basketball, rugby, *pétanque*, skiing, judo, golf, swimming, and so on. The series on French champions, "Grands du Sport," is unique because of its focus. Books in the other collections follow a similar format, with some more sophisticated, more scholarly than others, but we must remark that these titles are designed to inform general readers or, at the most, the student in physical education, and do not attempt to be technical.

For instance, the volume on rugby by Henri Garcia (in the "Domaine du Sport") begins with a history of the sport from its inception, then details its evolution in France. Garcia discusses great teams and exceptional players, and pays much attention to France's involvement in international competition. Almost half of the volume is devoted to the rules of the game, with comments on tactics and techniques. The author, a well-known figure in the world of rugby, writes with an obvious *parti-pris*: he does not want the character of the game to be tainted by professionalism, nor the game to turn solely into a mass spectator sport.

The volume on rugby in the "Que sais- je?" collection contains about the same number of pages as Garcia's, but it is worlds apart. Written by Christian Pociello, perhaps the leading researcher on sports in France, and published in 1988, *Le Rugby* is loaded with fascinating insights into all aspects of the sport: historical, technical, tactical, anthropological, political, and poetical. Pociello first situates rugby in his system of sports; its paradigmatic relationship to other sports informs it with much of its technical and cultural signification. In a discussion of the game's rules, he underlines rugby's kinship to a battle in which tactics involve athletic ability, brute strength, and intelligence. He goes far beyond Garcia's superficial presentation of the history of rugby in France by explaining how and why the game became implanted in southwestern France. A chapter on the sociology and economy of rugby examines the social origin and profession of players, according to the position they play on the field, and the potential "profits" of an amateur sport. Pociello opens up an exciting path of research in the concluding chapter, "La Poétique et la dramatique du rugby"

(The Poetics and Dramatics of Rugby), where he asks these questions: What are the images and metaphors used to describe rugby? How do the media try to portray the game, and, in so doing, do they actually create a myth about the sport? In what ways can we consider a rugby team to be a social microcosm, as Jean Giraudoux first suggested? Why is rugby associated with rural life and violence in the popular imagination? Undoubtedly, as Pociello readily admits, each question deserves much more analysis than he can give in the space limits of his volume. Nevertheless, these questions are important to assess the role of rugby in French society and need to be asked for other sports as well.

In sum, these one-volume guides in different collections devoted to sports can be informative and useful. And, in the case of Pociello's book on rugby, seminal.

Both the encyclopedias and the individual guides contain summaries of a sport's history in France. There is, however, almost a complete lack of books dealing with *sport* in the singular, from an historical perspective. This is unfortunate, for as Pociello has pointed out in his study of rugby and in his system of sport, sports evolve in a paradigmatic relationship to one another (e.g., soccer to rugby, windsurfing to skate-boarding). An historical survey, for instance, that chronicles the commercialism of sports in France, would be most welcome and beneficial (what companies sponsor what sports to what effects). Bernard Gillet's thin volume, *Histoire du Sport* in the "Que sais-je?" series, was published in 1949 and is now in its fifth printing, basically because it is the only such study. Jean Durry only highlights the most significant dates in his short chapter on "Les Origines du sport en France" (The Origins of Sport in France). A special issue of the review *Travaux et Recherches en éducation physique et sportive*, published by INSEP, the Institut national des sports et d'éducation physique, offers different points of view on the history of sports in France, but it is difficult to obtain. Two chapters of Eugen Weber's scintillating description of life in *fin-de-siècle* France recount the increasing popularity of *la petite reine*, the bicycle (Chapter 10), and the rise of the English sports (Chapter 11). The only historical study of sport written in English is Richard Holt's *Sport and Society in Modern France*. The merits of Holt's book are his courage to pose a tough question and his willingness to consult much primary material to attempt to answer it: "What forces influenced the way in which sports developed and in what respects did the emergent forms of amusement themselves reflect wider social change?" Inevitably, he resorts to case studies of individual sports (hunting, gymnastics, soccer, rugby, cycling, and bullfighting) in his search for a response. But he also examines sport in the context of a tradition of violence; sport and sociability; sport and status; and sport and politics. Each of these latter chapters invites a book-length study, and Holt's bibliography can serve as a fine starting point for further investigation.

For the most popular sports in France specialized histories do exist, but they deal rarely with the kinds of questions posed by Holt and Pociello. Fichefet and Corhumel's *Les Jeux Olympiques. Des origines à nos jours* underscores the contribution of Pierre de Coubertin to the renaissance of the games and their occurrence in Paris in 1900; it also lists records, champions, and all medal winners. Henri Garcia expands the historical survey of rugby in his ''Domaine du Sport'' volume by some 900 pages to create *La Fabuleuse Histoire du rugby*. A detailed history, with many photographs, of the Tour de France can be found in Serge Lang's *Le Grand Livre du Tour de France*. For those more interested in the classic bike race from Paris to Roubaix Jean-Marie Leblanc has written an authoritative history. An insider's history of cycling is provided by Bernard Hinault, who has written of his various experiences spanning the decades since World War II in *Moi, Bernard Hinault*. Soccer is so popular that Jacques Thibert publishes yearly *L'Année du football* with final standings, pictures of stars, statistics, and other information to delight historians of the sport and trivia experts alike.

CURRENT RESEARCH

As I mentioned in the opening pa: w scholarly studies of sports, either individual or collective, have been pur!i d in France. Indeed, the bias against such study in the university milieu deserves an analysis itself. Fortunately, what has been written, especially in the 1980s, has benefited from methodological insights gained from the use of structuralism and semiotics in other disciplines. For a researcher new to the field of sports, Higgs's *Sports. A Reference Guide* is a necessary starting point; not only does it include a chapter on the relationship of sports to popular culture, but it also presents an overview of the many dimensions of the subject. Higgs's volume is limited to sports in the United States, but its richness underlines the paucity of materials and studies on sports in France and shows clearly what needs to be done in this area.

The Éditions Vigot (23, rue de l'École de Médecine, 75006 Paris) continues to be the foremost publisher of books on sports. Yearly, under the direction of R. Thomas, it publishes a volume on *Sports et Sciences*, which contains articles on the physiological aspects of sports. Also directed by Thomas is a collection entitled, *Sport + Enseignement*, with ninety-nine titles to 1987, designed for professors and students of physical education. While many of the volumes in this collection are either technical introductions to a sport (No. 13, *Le Ski de fond* [Cross-country Skiing]) or physiological studies (No. 75, *Les Bases scientifiques de la musculation et de la traumatologie musculaire* [Scientific Bases of Muscularity and of Muscular Traumatism]), some titles may appeal to researchers interested in the sociocultural domain of sports. In particular, Christian Pociello's edited collection of articles on *Sports et société. Approche socioculturelle des pratiques* contains valuable information on many aspects, including his innovative attempt to classify sports in ''La Force, l'énergie, la grâce et les réflexes,'' and its publication is considered a turning point in the history of scholarship on sports in France. Another good *mise au point*, though somewhat dated, is *Le Sport en France. Bilan et perspectives*, edited by Enault. Because statistics can inform many different kinds of studies, Lucien Herr's ''Quelques

Indications chiffrées sur les fédérations sportives françaises" is invaluable. He presents the chronology of the creation of sports clubs in France and the evolution of participation during the last thirty years (ending in 1978). Jean-Michel Faure gives more recent statistics in "Les Pratiques sportives" (Sports Participation), published in *Données sociales 1984*. Exemplary for its methodological approach more than for its subject matter is Jean-Paul Clément's "La Force, la souplesse et l'harmonie. Étude comparée de trois sports de combat," in which he discusses the rituals, proxemics, and sociocultural signification of wrestling, judo, and aikido. In a more recent article Clément also examines karate, "L'aïki-do et le karaté."

A few studies have discussed the political aspect of sports in France. A chapter in Holt's *Sport and Society in Modern France* gives an historical outline of the interesting relationship between sports and politics since the rise of the gymnastics movement at the end of the nineteenth century. He highlights the ideology of Coubertin and his followers; the attempts of the Catholic Church to promote a "muscular" Christianity in the early decades of the twentieth century; the encouragement of sports and physical recreation by the Blum government in 1936; and the Vichy government's desire to promote social cohesion and character formation by requiring nine hours a week of physical education and sports in schools. A more detailed survey of the origins of political involvement in sports is provided in Alain Ehrenberg's edited volume, *Aimez-vous les sports? Les origines historiques des politiques sportives en France (1870–1930)*. Augustin and Berger explore the critical role of local government in the development of rugby in "Sports et société locale: le rugby à Bordeaux." Irlinger tries to explain the complex political implications of the "Springbok Affair," the banning from French competition of the South African rugby club in 1979, in his "Le Sport du pluriel ou les singularités du rugby." Jacques Defrance takes a close look at the gymnastics movement to discern how it became ideologically charged and almost paramilitary: "Se fortifier pour se soumettre?" (Fortify Yourself to Surrender?). In "Un olympisme à usages politiques," Xavier Delacroix shows the degree to which the Olympic Games have become politically charged in recent years. A collective denunciation of sports in schools, in the Olympics, or in any other form of competition is offered by a group of militant Marxists in *Quel corps?* Jean-Marie Brohm has gathered together similar critiques in *Critiques du sport*. Two far-ranging studies of sports and politics are Georges Vigarello's "Présences du politique" and Yves Le Pogam's *Démocratisation du sport: mythe ou réalité?*, the latter with important remarks about the economic dimension of sports.

In spite of the longstanding commercialism of sports in France, the most noticeable example being the Tour de France, and in spite of increased leisure time and affluence among the general population, the economics of sports has attracted few studies. The leading researcher in this area is Wladimir Andreff, who has published several items of interest: a book on *Économie du sport* (with Jean-François Nys), an article about inequalities among several sports disciplines

("Les Inégalités entre disciplines sportives: une approche économique"), and two fascinating analyses in collaboration with Nys, *Le Sport et la télé. Analyse économique* and "Le Marché des articles de sport." Andreff and Nys are particularly interested in sports budgets, the relationship between sports and industry, the remuneration and mobility of professional athletes, and national and local government subsidies to sports clubs. Of similar nature are Malenfant-Dauriac's *L'Économie du sport en France* and Katz and Jouanen's *Le Sport et l'argent.*

Di Ruzza and Gerbier have examined the economic factors responsible for a decline in the popularity of alpine skiing in "Un sport en crise: le ski français," while P. Georges studies the destructive power of money through the commercial sponsorship of athletes in *Champions à vendre.* That we indeed have entered the age of commercial sponsorship is made clear by Philippe Simonnot in "L'Âge de la sponsorisation." It is also the age of "Tapisation" in France, so named after the entrepreneur Bernard Tapie, who owns the professional soccer team in Marseilles and who symbolizes a new sports meritocracy, according to Alain Ehrenberg in "Le Show méritocratique: Platini, Stéphanie, Tapie et quelques autres." How much does a particular sport cost to play? The question is important, for from 1959 to 1981 the percentage of the household budget spent on leisure activities in France rose from 5.4 to 6.5 percent, and most of that money is spent on sports. An article on "Le Prix de la consommation sportive" by Michon and Ohl reveals the cost of each sport and details what this may signify about who can play (golf is the most expensive).

Absolutely essential in the popularization of sports are the media and their necessary corollary, advertising. No study yet exists of the role played by the daily newspaper *L'Équipe*, France's fifth-largest daily, which sponsors many athletic events and is a most visible element of the sports scene. We need also an analysis of the various magazines devoted to sports in France. Fortunately, Michèle Metoudi has looked at the role of advertising (who uses what sports to advertise products in which periodicals) in the article "Le Sport, espace de l'immobilité bienséante. Présence du sport dans la publicité." Using an approach informed by semiotics, Metoudi has examined seven widely circulated magazines to discover the impact of sports on publicity and the myths created by sports ads. In a recent update of her study, "Les Leçons de la publicité," she has discovered that contemporary ads show people working out vigorously in their respective sports, whereas the ads from the 1973 periodicals she examined tended to show people relaxing *after* having exercised. Claude-Jean Bertrand has authored one of the few studies to look at sports in other countries, and he focuses on "Sports et médias aux États-Unis."

Except for tennis and horseback riding, most sports in France have been male activities; only recently have women begun to participate in significant numbers, but their participation has dramatically influenced the nature of sports in France. Lucien Herr's statistics in "Quelques Indications chiffrées sur les fédérations sportives françaises" show the dramatic progression of female involvement: a

215 percent increase from 1963 to 1977. Certain sports, such as skiing, tennis, swimming, and gymnastics, continue to attract women. Pierre Chambat explores the change in the ideology of gymnastics from a paramilitary form of recreation at the end of the nineteenth-century to a present-day means of staying in shape, in "La Gymnastique, sport de la République?" Nicole Dechavanne has outlined some of the noticeable differences between men's and women's voluntary gymnastics (*gymnastique volontaire*) in her study "La Division sexuelle du travail gymnique." Catherine Louveau's successful attempt to link the prevailing ideology of female thinness to the participation of women in various sports merits further development, for " 'La forme, pas les formes.' Simulacres et équivoques dans les pratiques physiques féminines" ("Form, not Forms." Images and Ambiguities in Female Physical Activities) explores all too briefly women's motivation to play sports. The economic repercussions of the aerobics craze in France are analyzed by Olivier Bessy in "Les Salles de gymnastique, un marché du corps et de la forme."

The feminization of once-traditional masculine sports, such as soccer and weightlifting, is taking place also in France. It is a phenomenon that has been studied by Catherine Louveau and Michèle Metoudi, two active researchers at the INSEP, in their book, *La Femme d'aujourd'hui et le sport*. Jacques Novak and Bernard Virion demonstrate convincingly how male hegemony can negatively affect women's participation in soccer in *Le Football féminin*. As Laget et al. point out, one of the major reasons for the rise of the number of women in sports is the recent organization of national and international competitions of women, such as a female Tour de France, thus creating appropriate role models for young women to emulate. Their book, *Le Grand Livre du sport féminin*, is comprehensive in its coverage of women's sports in France, but it suffers from a traditional conception of what constitutes a female sport. A worthy synthesis of many issues surrounding women's sports is C. A. Oglesby's *Women and Sport. From Myth to Reality*. However, much remains to be done to understand better women's involvement in and attraction to sports.

Several studies transcend the historical, political, and economic categories by combining elements from them or by focusing in a unique way upon a sport. Pierre Falt's "Les Usages sociaux de la croisière" analyzes the significant elements associated with pleasure-boat cruising, including a sociocultural breakdown of participants. Through an examination of several dynamic dichotomies, the most revealing being "sail/motor," Falt shows how cruising is determined by social standing and how it, in turn, reinforces social distinctions. Philippe Gaboriau compares the Tour de France and the annual Paris-Dakar automobile race to discover a common characteristic: they are modern versions of the epic. Three articles note the increasing competitiveness of individual sports, once practiced in a more leisurely manner: Christian Pociello presents an overview of this phenomenon in "Un nouvel esprit d'aventure, de l'écologie douce à l'écologie dure"; Jean-Michel Faure discusses running and the craze for marathons in France in "L'Éthique puritaine du marathonien"; and Jean-Claude

Ragache examines the evolution of cross-country skiing from 1978 to 1985 in "Du loisir à la compétition de masse, l'exemple du ski nordique."

Jean Giraudoux, the well-known twentieth-century author, played soccer and rugby, was the university champion in the 400-meter race, and began each day with a rigorous set of calisthenics. It is not surprising, then, that he is one of the few French authors to devote a book to sport, *Le Sport*, published in 1928 and reprinted in 1977 by the Association of Friends of Jean Giraudoux. Nicole Priollaud has edited a collection of remarks on sports made by several authors during the Belle Époque: *Le Sport à la une, 1870–1914*. But for someone like Alfred Jarry, literature itself was the primary sport. Jérôme Bruneau and Jules Chancel have assembled essays by writers, journalists, and aficionados of soccer in *L'Amour foot*. However, not many creative writers or filmmakers have included sports as major themes in their works, which may explain the paucity of materials on sports in literature and film.

RESEARCH COLLECTIONS AND CENTERS

We can only wish that a research collection and center for sports existed in France. (A model would be the Center on Sport in Society located at Northeastern University in Boston.) As I have mentioned several times, serious research on sports has only really begun in the last decade and it still involves a limited number of people. The most important research group is directed by Christian Pociello at the Institut National des Sports et d'Éducation Physique in Paris. It has been responsible for much of the material cited here. Since 1980, about twenty university professors throughout France have taught a course related to some aspects of sports, and approximately a hundred theses have been written on sports during the last fifteen years. The universities in Lyons, Strasbourg, Bordeaux, and Grenoble have modest research groups, or UFR (*Unités de formation et de recherche*). The one in Bordeaux has been examining social dimensions of sport, in particular, of rugby. The group in Grenoble is actually located in the Institut de Recherches en économie et en planification and works, as one may surmise, on the economics of sports in France. These are modest efforts, nonetheless, and much needs to be done.

POSSIBILITIES FOR FUTURE RESEARCH

Everything is wide open for research into the role of sports in French culture. First, while recent French studies on the economics, politics, feminization, and evolution of sports are helpful and informative, they are sparse and are not easy to obtain. Contemporary French researchers are producing some exciting work, but it needs to be more accessible, even to the French themselves. Obviously, almost nothing has been written in English on French sports. Holt's book helps to fill this sizable hole, but it deals only with the history of French sports and does not pretend to be comprehensive. What is most lacking in the sports literature surveyed in this chapter is a study of fans: Who are these 25 million French who watch sports, but do not participate actively? What is the impact of sports on their lives? What sports do they prefer, and why? These questions and others deserve reflection, for future research on sports in France may be able to reveal more clearly the myths and beliefs of the French cultural imagination, and a better understanding of that may be crucial to France's future.

BIBLIOGRAPHY

A Selected List of French Popular Magazines and Newspapers

L'Équipe, Quotidien du sport et de l'automobile: 10, rue du Faubourg Montmartre, 75009 Paris.

Loisirs-Jeunes: 36, rue de Ponthieu, 75008 Paris.

Sport-Auto: 43, boulevard Barbès, 75018 Paris.

Basket-ball: Fédération française de basket-ball, 82, rue d'Hauteville, 75010 Paris.

France Football: 10, rue du Faubourg Montmartre, 75009 Paris.

Cyclotouriste: FCyclo 2000, 6, rue Jean-Marie Jégo, 75013 Paris.

Moto Revue: Éditions Larivière, 15–17, quai de l'Oise, 75019 Paris.

Vélo Magazine: 10, rue du Faubourg Montmartre, 75009 Paris.

Neptune Nautisme: 5, rue du Cdt Pilot, 92200 Neuilly.

Voile Magazine: 55, avenue Kléber, 75784 Paris Cedex 16.

Journal du chasseur: 82, quai des Chartrons, 33082 Bordeaux.

Montagne et Alpinisme: 9, rue de la Boétie, 75008 Paris.

Sport et Plein Air: 14–16, rue Scandicci, 93508 Pantin.

Andreff, Wladimir. "Les Inégalités entre disciplines sportives: une approche écono-mique." In *Sports et société*. Edited by Christian Pociello. Pp. 139–51.

Andreff, Wladimir, Ehrenberg, Alain, et al. "L'Économie du sport." *Esprit* 125 (April 1987): 285–95.

Andreff, Wladimir, and Nys, Jean-François. *Économie du sport*. Collection "Que sais-je?" Paris: Presses Universitaires de France, 1986.

Andreff, Wladimir, and Nys, Jean-François. *Le Sport et la télé. Analyse économique*. Paris: Dalloz, 1987.

Arlott, John, ed. *The Oxford Companion of World Sports and Games*. New York: Oxford University Press, 1975.

Arnaud, Pierre, and Camy, Jean, eds. *La Naissance du mouvement sportif associatif en France*. Lyon: Presses Universitaires de Lyon, 1986.

Augustin, J.-P., and Berger, M. "Sports et société locale: le rugby à Bordeaux." In *Sports et société*. Edited by Christian Pociello. Pp. 337–51.

Bertrand, Claude-Jean. "Sports et médias aux États-Unis." *Esprit* 125 (April 1987): 213–29.

Bessy, Olivier. "Les Salles de gymnastique, un marché du corps et de la forme." *Esprit* 125 (April 1987): 79–94.

Blondin, Antoine. *Sur le Tour de France*. Paris: Mazarine, 1979.

Bonhomme, Michel, and Hostal, Philippe. *Premiers Pas vers le basket*. Collection "Sports et loisirs." Paris: Éditions Amphora, 1985.

Bonnery, Louis, and Thomas, Raymond. *Le Jeu à XIII*. Collection "Que sais-je?" Paris: Presses Universitaires de France, 1986.

Bosc, Gérard, and Thomas, Raymond. *Le Basket-Ball*. Collection "Que sais-je?" Paris: Presses Universitaires de France, 1976.

Boulogne, Y. P. *Pierre de Coubertin*. Montreal: Leméac, 1975.

Bourdieu, Pierre. *La Distinction. Critique sociale du jugement*. Paris: Minuit, 1979.

———. *Le Sens pratique*. Paris: Minuit, 1980.

———. "Comment peut-on être sportif?" *Questions de sociologie*. Paris: Minuit, 1980.

Brohm, Jean-Marie. *Critiques du sport*. Paris: Bourgois, 1976.

Bromberger, Christian. "L'Olympique de Marseille, la Juve et le Torino." *Esprit* 125 (April 1987): 174–95.

Bruneau, Jérôme, and Chancel, Jules. *L'Amour foot*. *Revue Autrement* 80 (May 1986).

Chambat, Pierre. "La Gymnastique, sport de la République?" *Esprit* 125 (April 1987): 22–35.

Chapus, Eugène. *Le Sport*. Paris: Hachette, 1854.

Clément, Jean-Paul. "L'aïki-do et le karaté." *Esprit* 125 (April 1987): 110–17.

———. "La Force, la souplesse et l'harmonie. Étude comparée de trois sports de combat: Lutte-Judo-Aikido." In *Sports et société*. Edited by Christian Pociello. Pp. 285–301.

Le Cyclisme. Collection "La Passion de la montagne." Paris: Grund, 1982.

Dauven, Jean. *Encyclopédie des sports*. Paris: Larousse, 1961.

———. *Technique des Sports*. Collection "Que sais-je?" Paris: Presses Universitaires de France, 1948.

Le Débat 19 (February 1982): entire issue devoted to sports.

Dechavanne, Nicole. "La Division sexuelle du travail gymnique. Un regard sur la gymnastique volontaire." In *Sports et société*. Edited by Christian Pociello. Pp. 249–59.

Defrance, Jacques. "Comment interpréter l'évolution des pratiques sportives?" *Esprit* 125 (April 1987): 139–47.

———. "Se fortifier pour se soumettre?" In *Sports et société*. Edited by Christian Pociello. Pp. 75–84.

Dehedin, J., and Thomas, Raymond. *Sports et Sciences*. Paris: Vigot, 1979.

Delacroix, Xavier. "Un olympisme à usages politiques." *Esprit* 125 (April 1987): 231–39.

Di Ruzza, F., and Gerbier, B. "Un sport en crise: le ski français." In *Sports et société*. Edited by Christian Pociello. Pp. 155–68.

Durry, Jean. "Les Origines du sport en France." In *Sports et société*. Edited by Christian Pociello. Pp. 85–91.

Duthen, Georges. *Le Rugby*. Collection "Connaissance et technique." Paris: Denoël. 1976.

Ehrenberg, Alain, ed. *Aimez-vous les sports? Les Origines historiques des politiques sportives en France (1870–1930)*. *Recherches* 43 (April 1980).

Ehrenberg, Alain. "Le Show méritocratique: Platini, Stéphanie, Tapie et quelques autres." *Esprit* 125 (April 1987): 266–83.

Enault, Gérard, et al. *Le Sport en France. Bilan et perspectives.* Paris: Berger-Levrault, 1979.

Falt, Pierre. "Les Usages sociaux de la croisière." In *Sports et société.* Edited by Christian Pociello. Pp. 261–84.

Faure, Jean-Michel. "L'Éthique puritaine du marathonien." *Esprit* 125 (April 1987): 36–41.

———. "Les Pratiques sportives." *Données sociales 1984.* Paris: INSEE, 1985.

Fichefet and Corhumel. *Les Jeux Olympiques. Des origines à nos jours.* Paris: Marabout, 1964.

"Le Foot et la fureur." *Esprit* 104–5 (August-September 1985). Three short articles on violence among soccer fans.

Frémy, Dominique, and Frémy, Michèle. *Quid 1991.* Paris: Laffont, 1990.

Frommer, Harvey. *Sports Lingo. A Dictionary of the Language of Sports.* New York: Atheneum, 1979.

Gaboriau, Philippe. "Les Épopées modernes: le Tour de France et Paris-Dakar." *Esprit* 125 (April 1987): 6–16.

Gallet, P. *La Pratique et l'enseignement du ski de fond.* Paris: Éditions Amphora, 1980.

Garcia, Henri. *La Fabuleuse Histoire du rugby.* Paris: Éditions O.D.I.L, 1973.

———. *Le Rugby.* Collection "Domaire du sport." Paris: La Table Ronde, 1962.

Georges, P. *Champions à vendre.* Paris: Calmann-Lévy, 1974.

Gillet, Bernard. *Histoire du Sport.* 5th ed. Collection "Que sais-je?" Paris: Presses Universitaires de France, 1975.

Giraudoux, Jean. *Le Sport.* Paris: Grasset et Fasquelle, 1928 [1977].

Herbin, Robert, and Rethacker, J.-P. *Football: la technique, la tactique, l'entraînement.* Paris: Laffont, 1976.

Herr, Lucien. "Quelques Indications chiffrées sur les fédérations sportives françaises." In *Sports et société.* Edited by Christian Pociello. Pp. 95–114.

Higgs, Robert J. *Sports. A Reference Guide.* Westport, Conn.: Greenwood Press, 1982.

Hinault, Bernard. *Moi, Bernard Hinault.* Paris: Calmann-Lévy, 1981.

Holt, Richard. *Sport and Society in Modern France.* Hamden, Conn.: Archon Books, 1981.

Huizinga, Johan. *Homo Ludens: A Study of the Play-Element in Culture.* Boston: Beacon Press, 1950.

Irlinger, Paul. "Le Sport au pluriel ou les singularités du rugby." In *Sports et société.* Edited by Christian Pociello. Pp. 361–77.

Jeu, Bernard. *Sport, mort, violence.* Lyon: Presses Universitaires de Lyon, 1975.

Jeux et Sports. Paris: Encyclopédie de la Pléiade, Gallimard, 1967.

Jusserand, Jean-Jules. *Les Sports et jeux d'exercice dans l'ancienne France.* Geneva: Droz, 1986.

Katz, Paul, and Jouanen, Monique. *Le Sport et l'argent.* La Chapelle-sur-Loire: Authier, 1972.

Laget, Françoise; Laget, Serge; and Mazet, Jean-Paul. *Le Grand Livre du sport féminin.* Paris: FMT Édition, 1982.

Lang, Serge. *Le Grand Livre du Tour de France.* Paris: Calmann-Lévy, 1980.

Leblanc, Jean-Marie. *Les Pavés du nord. "Paris-Roubaix."* Paris: La Table Ronde, 1982.

Le Pogam, Yves. *Démocratisation du sport: mythe ou réalité?* Paris: Delarge, 1979.

Louveau, Catherine. " 'La Forme, pas les formes.' Simulacres et équivoques dans les pratiques physiques féminines." In *Sports et société*. Edited by Christian Pociello. Pp. 302–18.

Louveau, Catherine, and Metoudi, Michèle. *La Femme d'aujourd'hui et le sport.* Paris: Amphora, 1981.

Magnane, Georges. *Sociologie du sport.* Paris: Gallimard, 1966.

Malenfant-Dauriac, Chantal. *L'Économie du sport en France. Un compte satellite du sport.* Paris: Éditions Cujas, 1977.

Marty, Christian. *Pétanque, la technique, la tactique.* Paris: Laffont, 1976.

Mermet, Gérard. *Francoscopie 1989.* Paris: Larousse, 1988.

Metoudi, Michèle. "Les Leçons de la publicité." *Esprit* 125 (April 1987): 73–78.

———. "De nouveaux usages pour les sports d'hier." *Esprit* 125 (April 1987): 42–52.

———. "Le Sport, espace de l'immobilité bienséante. Présence du sport dans la publicité." In *Sports et société*. Edited by Christian Pociello. Pp. 327–33.

Michea, A., and Besson, E. *Cent ans de cyclisme.* Paris: Arthaud, 1969.

Michon, Bernard, and Ohl, Fabien. "Le Prix de la consommation sportive." *Esprit* 125 (April 1987): 297–311.

Noret, André, and Thomas, Raymond. *Le Cyclisme.* Collection "Que sais-je?" Paris: Presses Universitaires de France, 1980.

Novak, Jacques, and Virion, Bernard. *Le Football féminin.* Paris: Éditions Chiron, 1981.

Nys, Jean-François, and Andreff, Wladimir. "Le Marché des articles de sport." *Esprit* 125 (April 1987): 312–17.

Oglesby, Carol A., ed. *Women and Sport: From Myth to Reality.* Philadelphia: Lea & Febiger, 1978.

Parlebas, Pierre. "Activités physiques et éducation motrice." *Revue Éducation physique et sports* 139 (May-June 1976): 122–38.

Passevant, Roland. *Et tu seras champion.* Paris: Éditions la Farandole, 1980.

Petiot, Georges. *Dictionnaire de la langue des sports.* Paris: Le Robert, 1982.

Pociello, Christian. *Le Rugby ou la guerre des styles.* Paris: A.-M. Metailié, 1983.

———. *Le Rugby.* Collection "Que sais-je?" Paris: Presses Universitaires de France, 1988.

———. "La Force, l'énergie, la grâce et les réflexes. Le Jeu complexe des dispositions culturelles et sportives." In *Sports et société*. Edited by Christian Pociello. Pp. 171–237.

———. "Un nouvel esprit d'aventure, de l'écologie douce à l'écologie dure." *Esprit* 125 (April 1987): 95–105.

———. "Les Subventions ministérielles aux différents sports." In *Sports et société*. Edited by Christian Pociello. Pp. 131–34.

Pociello, Christian, ed. *Sports et société. Approche socio-culturelle des pratiques.* Paris: Vigot, 1981.

Poulain, Robert. *Le Rugby.* Collection "Que sais-je?" Paris: Presses Universitaires de France, 1961; 3d ed., 1975.

Priollaud, Nicole, ed. *Le Sport à la une, 1870–1914.* Paris: Liana Levi, Sylvie Messinger, 1984.

Quel corps? Paris: Maspero, 1978.

Ragache, Jean-Claude. "Du loisir à la compétition de masse, l'exemple du ski nordique." *Esprit* 125 (April 1987): 123–28.

Rethacker, Jean-Philippe. *Le Football*. Collection "Domaine du sport." Paris: La Table Ronde, 1963.

Simonnot, Philippe. "L'Âge de la sponsorisation." *Esprit* 125 (April 1987): 245–55.

Sportsguide Solar. Paris: Solar, 1984.

Thibert, Jacques. *L'Année du football–1986*. Paris: Calmann-Lévy, 1987.

Travaux et Recherches en éducation physique et sportive 6 (March 1980). Entire issue devoted to history of sports in France.

Verdet, Pierre, and Pastre, Georges. *Les Grands du rugby français*. Collection "Grands du Sport." Paris: Éditions PAC, 1983.

Vigarello, Georges. "Les Deux Violences sportives." *Esprit* 104–5 (August-September 1985): 15–19.

———. "Présences du politique." *Esprit* 125 (April 1987): 240–44.

———. "Un show quasi universel, les métamorphoses du spectacle sportif." *Esprit* 125 (April 1987): 159–67.

Weber, Eugen. *France. Fin de Siècle*. Cambridge, Mass.: Harvard University Press, 1986.

Webster's Sports Dictionary. Springfield, Mass.: Merriam-Webster, 1976.

General Sources

Among the general works dealing with the way the French live, work, and play is the all-encompassing and reasonably recent (1972) *La France et les Français*, edited by Michel François. This collection of essays covers a wide range of topics, many with a popular culture link. Alfred Franklin's twenty-three volume series titled *La Vie privée d'autrefois*, although dated, remains valuable and informative. *The French: Portrait of a People* by Sanche de Gramont, while superficial and marred by errors, offers some interesting insights into the French character and civilization. Better and more perceptive is *The French* by Theodore Zeldin, who also wrote *France 1848–1945*, a superb study not only of its history but also of such topics as ambition, love, taste, and hypocrisy. For a sociocultural approach, Pierre Bourdieu's thought-provoking book on "distinction" is highly recommended.

Van Gennep's monumental *Manuel de folklore français contemporain* discusses in scholarly fashion a fascinating aspect of French culture. In *Village in the Vaucluse* (third edition, 1974) the American observer Lawrence Wylie provides a lively re-creation of village life that is both a psychological study of the inhabitants and a microcosm of French society. *The Horse of Pride: Life in a Breton Village* (1978) by the noted Breton author Pierre-Jakez Hélias presents (appropriately, with an introduction by Wylie) a good French point of view.

Researchers interested in statistics may consult with profit *Pratiques culturelles des Français* (1974), *Les Français tels qu'ils sont* (1975), and many survey results released by the Institut national de la statistique et des études économiques (INSEE) and the Société française d'enquêtes par sondages (SOFRES).

Finally, very useful but unfortunately unpublished bibliographies on myriad subjects, including popular culture, can be found at the Institut national des Techniques de la Documentation of the Conservatoire National des Arts et Métiers (292, rue St-Martin, Paris 3e).

GENERAL BIBLIOGRAPHY

Ariès, Philippe. *L'Enfant et la vie familiale sous l'Ancien Régime*. Paris: Seuil, 1973.
Ariès, Philippe, and Duby, Georges, eds. *Histoire de la vie privée*. 5 vols. Paris: Seuil, 1985–87.

Barthes, Roland. *Mythologies*. Paris: Seuil, 1957.

Beaucarnot, Jean-Louis. *Ainsi vivaient nos ancêtres. De leurs coutumes à nos habitudes*. Paris: Laffont, 1989.

Bercé, Yves-Marie. *Fête et révolte: Des mentalités populaires du 16e au 18e siècle*. Paris: Hachette, 1976.

Bernstein, Richard. *Fragile Glory: A Portrait of France and the French*. New York: Knopf, 1990.

Bloch, Marc. *La Société féodale*. 2 vols. Paris: Michel, 1939–40.

Bourdieu, Pierre. *La Distinction. Critique sociale du jugement*. Paris: Minuit, 1979.

Carroll, Raymonde. *Évidences invisibles: Américains et Français au quotidien*. Paris: Seuil, 1987.

Charpentreau, Jacques, and Kaës, René. *La Culture populaire en France*. Paris: Éditions Ouvrières, 1962.

Curtius, Ernst Robert. *The Civilization of France*. New York: Macmillan, 1932.

Darnton, Robert. *The Great Cat Massacre and Other Episodes in French Cultural History*. New York: Basic Books, 1984.

Dauzat, Albert. *La Vie rurale en France des origines à nos jours*. Paris: Presses Universitaires de France, 1950.

Davis, Natalie Z. *Society and Culture in Early Modern France*. Stanford, Calif.: Stanford University Press, 1975.

Duby, Georges, and Mandrou, Robert. *Histoire de la civilisation française*. 2 vols. Paris: Colin, 1968.

Dupeux, Georges. *La Société française, 1789–1970*. Paris: Colin, 1972.

Esprit. "La France et les Français." December 1957. Special issue.

Farge, Arlette. *Vivre dans la rue à Paris au 18e siècle*. Paris: Gallimard/Julliard, 1979.

François, Michel, ed. *La France et les Français*. Paris: "Encyclopédie de la Pléiade." Gallimard, 1972.

Franklin, Alfred. *La Vie privée d'autrefois*. 23 vols. Paris: Plon-Nourrit, 1887–1901.

Frémontier, Jacques. *La Vie en bleu: Voyage en culture ouvrière*. Paris: Fayard, 1980.

Gramont, Sanche de. *The French: Portrait of a People*. New York: Putnam, 1969.

Hélias, Pierre-Jakez. *The Horse of Pride: Life in a Breton Village*. New Haven, Conn.: Yale University Press, 1978.

Institut Français de l'Opinion Publique. *Les Français tels qu'ils sont*. Edited by P. Miler et al. Paris, 1975.

Menon, Pierre-Louis, and Lecotté, Roger. *Au village de France. La Vie traditionnelle des paysans*. 2 vols. Marseilles: Laffitte, 1978.

Muchembled, Robert. *Culture populaire et culture des élites dans la France moderne*. Paris: Flammarion, 1978.

Nevers, Guy. *Les Français vus par les Français*. Paris: Barrault, 1985.

Reynaud, Jean-Daniel, and Grafmeyer, Yves. *Français, qui êtes-vous?* Paris: La Documentation française, 1981.

Roche, Daniel. *Le Peuple de Paris. Essai sur la culture populaire*. Paris: Aubier Montaigne, 1981.

Roussel, Patrice, ed. *Histoire de la vie française*. 8 vols. Paris: L'Illustration, 1971–73.

Schifres, Alain. *Les Parisiens*. Paris: Lattès, 1990.

Secrétariat d'État à la Culture. *Pratiques culturelles des Français*. Paris, 1974.

Tannenbaum, Edward R. *The New France*. Chicago: University of Chicago Press, 1961.

Van Gennep, Arnold. *Manuel de folklore français contemporain*. 6 vols. Paris: Picard, 1943–58.

Varagnac, André. *Civilisation traditionnelle et genres de vie*. Paris: Michel, 1948.

La Vie populaire en France du Moyen-Âge à nos jours. 4 vols. Paris: Éditions Diderot, 1964–66.

Villadary, Agnès. *Fête et vie quotidienne*. Paris: Éditions Ouvrières, 1968.

Weber, Eugen. *France. Fin de Siècle*. Cambridge, Mass.: Harvard University Press, 1986.

Wylie, Lawrence. *Village in the Vaucluse*, 3d ed. Cambridge, Mass.: Harvard University Press, 1974.

Zeldin, Theodore. *France 1848–1945*. 2 vols. Oxford: Oxford University Press, 1973–77.

———. *The French*. New York: Pantheon, 1982.

PERIODICALS

Arts et Traditions Populaires
Cahiers de civilisation
Contemporary French Civilization
Revue des traditions populaires

COLLECTIONS AND MUSEUMS OF INTEREST

Maison des Sciences de l'Homme, 54 bd. Raspail, Paris 6e. Extensive holdings on the social sciences, with emphasis on France and the French.

Centre Georges Pompidou (Beaubourg), 19, rue Beaubourg, Paris 4e. In addition to a modern art museum, also housed are a self-service library and audiovisual center mostly devoted to popular culture.

Musée des Arts et Traditions Populaires, av. du Mahatma Gandhi, Paris 16e. The finest collection of folk arts and crafts in France.

Musée de Cluny, 6 pl. Paul-Painlevé, Paris 5e. Located in a former abbey, the museum owns, besides *The Lady of the Unicorn* tapestries, many medieval artworks and artifacts.

Musée du Vieux-Marseille, rue de la Prison, Marseilles (Bouches-du-Rhône). An excellent collection of Provençal folklore.

Musée alsacien, 23 quai St-Nicolas, Strasbourg (Bas-Rhin). In this pretty seventeenth-century house are found displays of life and crafts of Alsace.

Musée basque, rue Marengo, Bayonne (Pyrénées-Atlantiques). With its reconstructed furnished interiors and *pelote basque* and dance halls, the museum is a very good introduction to the popular culture of that region.

Musée départemental breton, rue Gradlon, Quimper (Finistère). Interesting collection of artifacts, furnishings, costumes, and ceramic ware of Lower Brittany (Cornouaille).

Index

About the Contributors

EDITH J. BENKOV is Associate Professor of French at San Diego State University. She specializes in Medieval and Renaissance French literature, with an emphasis on women's studies. Her publications include articles on Marie de France, Chrétien de Troyes, and medieval theater. She is completing a monograph on Louise Labé and is currently working on a study of women and religious reform and the relation of propaganda and gender in the Renaissance.

FRANZ G. BLAHA received his doctorate from the University of Graz, Austria. A professor of English and Comparative Literature at the University of Nebraska-Lincoln and present Director of its Institute for International Studies, he has published widely on modern drama and on French, German, and Italian literatures. He is the 1983 winner of the George Whately Award for Popular Literature Scholarship for "Behind the Big Wall: Detective Fiction in the German Democratic Republic."

SYBIL DELGAUDIO teaches film studies at Hofstra University and the New School for Social Research. She has contributed articles to *Jump Cut* and *The American Animated Cartoon*, and is currently at work on a chapter on counter-culture films for a forthcoming anthology on Columbia Pictures.

CLAUDIA DOBKIN is currently employed at Digital Equipment Corporation as a publishing consultant. Her work includes comparative studies of American and French technical communications as well as research in computer-aided translation. Before joining Digital, she taught French language and culture at Harvard University, where she earned her doctorate in 1986.

ARTHUR B. EVANS received his Ph.D. from Columbia University and now teaches French at DePauw University in Greencastle, Indiana. His books include *Jean Cocteau and His Films of Orphic Identity* (1977) and *Jules Verne Rediscovered: Didacticism and the Scientific Novel* (Greenwood Press, 1988). His articles on surrealism and French SF have appeared in numerous scholarly journals here and abroad. He is currently writing a book on the history of French science fiction (from Jules Verne to the present).

JEAN-CLAUDE FAUR is curator at the Bibliothèque Municipale de Marseille, where he established the Comic Strip Department. The founder of the National BD Salon of Toulouse, then of the International Colloquium of La Roque-d'Anthéron, he is also the author of *À la rencontre de la BD* and, since 1976, the managing editor of the specialized review *Bédésup*.

MAURICE HORN is recognized as an international authority on comics. He is editor of the standard reference work on the subject, *The World Encyclopedia of Comics*, and its companion, *The World Encyclopedia of Cartoons*. He has written articles on comics in the United States and abroad and has organized or coorganized exhibitions of comic art, including "Bande Dessinée et Figuration Narrative" at the Louvre and "75 Years of the Comics" at the New York Cultural Center. Among his many books, mention should be made of *A History of the Comic Strip, Women in the Comics, Comics of the American West*, and *Sex in the Comics*. He has lectured on the subject and is a frequent editor and consultant for publishing companies, newspaper organizations, and television producers.

PIERRE L. HORN received his Ph.D. from Columbia University and is Professor of French at Wright State University in Dayton, Ohio. He has written extensively on French literature and culture, including a study of Marguerite Yourcenar and biographies of Louis XIV and La Fayette. He was made a Chevalier dans l'Ordre des Palmes Académiques by the French government in 1978.

JOSEPH MARTHAN is Assistant Professor of French at Stockton State College in Pomona, New Jersey. He has published *Le Vieillard amoureux dans l'œuvre de Corneille* as well as several articles on contemporary French politics and culture, and is presently working on the feminine press in France. He has his Ph.D. from the City University of New York.

JEAN-PIERRE PIRIOU is Professor of French and Head of the Romance Languages Department at the University of Georgia. After graduate work at the Sorbonne he attended the University of Virginia and received his doctorate in 1973. He has published a book on Julien Green, a critical edition of the Julien Green–Jacques Maritain correspondence, and a coauthored study of Jean-Paul Sartre's *Les Mots*. In addition, he has written articles on French culture and twentieth-century francophone literature. He is also the coauthor of a first-year college French textbook now in its second edition.

ANDRÉ J. M. PRÉVOS is Associate Professor of French at Pennsylvania State University (Worthington Scranton Campus). He earned his Ph.D. from the University of Iowa and a doctorate from the University of Paris. He is a student of Afro-American music, French popular culture, and Franco-American cultural relations. He is a contributing editor to *The Black Perspective in Music*, writes articles and reviews for American and European journals, and is American correspondent for *Soul Bag* (Paris) and *Solo Blues* (Madrid).

ROGER SUE holds a Doctorat d'État in Political Science and is Professor of Sociology of Education at the University of Paris V-Sorbonne. He is also a Research Associate at the Centre National de la Recherche Scientifique in Paris and a specialist in the field of leisure. His publications, among others, include *Le Loisir* and *Vivre en l'an 2000*.

RICHARD C. WILLIAMSON received his Ph.D. from Indiana University and is Professor of French and Chair of the Romance Languages and Literatures Department at Bates College in Lewiston, Maine. He has published and maintains research interests in nineteenth-century French literature, Québécois literature and culture, and the methodology of teaching foreign languages.